The Powers of Pure Reason

The Powers of Pure Reason

Kant and the Idea of Cosmic Philosophy

ALFREDO FERRARIN

The University of Chicago Press
Chicago and London

The University of Chicago Press, Chicago 60637
The University of Chicago Press, Ltd., London
© 2015 by The University of Chicago
All rights reserved. Published 2015.
Paperback edition 2016
Printed in the United States of America

24 23 22 21 20 19 18 17 16   2 3 4 5 6

ISBN-13: 978-0-226-24315-3 (cloth)
ISBN-13: 978-0-226-41938-1 (paper)
ISBN-13: 978-0-226-24329-0 (e-book)
DOI: 10.7208/chicago/9780226243290.001.0001

Library of Congress Cataloging-in-Publication Data
Ferrarin, Alfredo, 1960– author.
    The powers of pure reason : Kant and the idea of cosmic
philosophy / Alfredo Ferrarin.
        pages cm
    Includes bibliographical references and index.
    ISBN 978-0-226-24315-3 (cloth : alk. paper)—
ISBN 978-0-226-24329-0 (e-book)   1. Kant, Immanuel, 1724–1804.
Kritik der reinen Vernunft. 2. Kant, Immanuel, 1724–1804. Kritik
der praktischen Vernunft. 3. Kant, Immanuel, 1724–1804. Kritik der
Urteilskraft. 4. Reason. 5. Philosophy.   I. Title.
    B2779.F47 2015
    193—dc23
                                                    2014036406

In memory of my mother, Luciana Marchetti (1933–2008)

Die Arbeit an der Philosophie ist—wie vielfach in der Architektur—eigentlich mehr eine Arbeit an Einem selbst. An der eigenen Auffassung. Daran, wie man die Dinge sieht. (Und was man von ihnen verlangt.)

LUDWIG WITTGENSTEIN, *The Big Typescript*

CONTENTS

ACKNOWLEDGMENTS

This book would have been far less rigorous if I had not received many relevant observations from friends, colleagues, and students. I would like to thank all those who have devoted a great deal of their time and intelligence to comment on the manuscript in its various versions. I take that as an invaluable sign of friendship, respect, and philosophical interest for which I am immensely grateful and consider myself fortunate.

Federico Orsini, Paula Manchester, and Claudio La Rocca have read and responded to what has eventually become chapter 1.

Stefano Bacin, Wolfgang Carl, Nicolas de Warren, Alessandra Fussi, Pierre Kerszberg, Osvaldo Ottaviani, David Roochnik, and Richard Velkley have read the whole work, in many cases more than once and invariably with exceptional care and poignant insight, and offered precious comments and criticisms.

I would like to thank also the two anonymous referees for the University of Chicago Press, as well as David Brent for his support of this project and Susan Tarcov for her editing.

ABBREVIATIONS

Ak   *Akademie-Ausgabe* (*Kants gesammelte Schriften*, ed.
Preussischen Akademie der Wissenschaften zu Berlin, Berlin,
1910–)

Anth   *Anthropologie in pragmatischer Hinsicht* (*Ak* 7)

BDG   *Der einzig mögliche Beweisgrund zu einer Demonstration des Daseins
Gottes* (*Ak* 2)

Bemerkungen   *Bemerkungen in den Beobachtungen über das Gefühl des Schönen
und Erhabenen* (*Ak* 20)

Br   *Briefe* (*Ak* 10–13)

Deutlichkeit   *Untersuchung über die Deutlichkeit der Grundsätze der natürlichen
Theologie und der Moral* (*Ak* 2)

Dissertation   *De mundi sensibilis atque intelligibilis forma et principiis* (*Ak* 2)

Dreams   *Träume eines Geistersehers, erläutert durch die Träume der
Metaphysik* (*Ak* 2)

EAD   *Das Ende aller Dinge* (*Ak* 8)

EE   *Erste Einleitung in die Kritik der Urteilskraft* (*Ak* 20)

Entdeckung   *Über eine Entdeckung, nach der alle neue Kritik der reinen Vernunft
durch eine ältere entbehrlich gemacht werden soll* (*Ak* 8)

Erdmann   *Reflexionen Kants zur kritischen Philosophie. Aus Kants
handschriftlichen Aufzeichnungen*, ed. Benno Erdmann (orig.
1882); new ed., edited and with an introduction by Norbert
Hinske, Stuttgart, 1992

Fortschritte   *Welches sind die wirklichen Fortschritte, die die Metaphysik seit
Leibnitzens und Wolf's Zeiten in Deutschland gemacht hat?* (*Ak* 20)

GMS   *Grundlegung zur Metaphysik der Sitten* (*Ak* 4)

GSE   *Beobachtungen über das Gefühl des Schönen und Erhabenen* (*Ak* 2)

GUGR   *Von dem ersten Grunde des Unterschiedes der Gegenden im Raume* (*Ak* 2)

IaG   *Idee zu einer allgemeinen Geschichte in weltbürgerlicher Absicht* (*Ak* 8)

KpV   *Kritik der praktischen Vernunft* (*Ak* 5)

KrV   *Kritik der reinen Vernunft* (A: 1781/B: 1787)

KU   *Kritik der Urteilskraft* (*Ak* 5)

Log   *Logik Jaesche* (*Ak* 9)

MAM   *Muthmaßlicher Anfang der Menschengeschichte* (*Ak* 8)

MAN   *Metaphysische Anfangsgründe der Naturwissenschaften* (*Ak* 4)

MpVT   *Über das Mißlingen aller philosophischen Versuche in der Theodicee* (*Ak* 8)

MS   *Die Metaphysik der Sitten* (*Ak* 6)

NEV   *Nachricht von der Einrichtung seiner Vorlesungen in dem Winterhalbenjahre von 1765–1766* (*Ak* 2)

NTH   *Allgemeine Naturgeschichte und Theorie des Himmels* (*Ak* 1)

OP   *Opus Postumum* (*Ak* 21–22)

PhilEnz   *Philosophische Enzyklopädie* (*Ak* 29)

Prol   *Prolegomena zu einer jeden künftigen Metaphysik* (*Ak* 4)

Refl   *Reflexionen* (*Ak* 14–19)

RezHerder   *Recensionen von J. G. Herders* Ideen zur Philosophie der Geschichte der Menscheit (*Ak* 8)

RGV   *Die Religion innerhalb der Grenzen der bloßen Vernunft* (*Ak* 6)

SF   *Der Streit der Fakultäten* (*Ak* 7)

TP   *Über den Gemeinspruch: Das mag in der Theorie richtig sein, taugt aber nicht für die Praxis* (*Ak* 8)

ÜGTP   *Über den Gebrauch teleologischer Principien in der Philosophie* (*Ak* 8)

VNAEF   *Verkündigung des nahen Abschlusses eines Tractats zum ewigen Frieden in der Philosophie* (AK 08)

Vorl   Vorlesungen (*Ak* 24ff.)

V-Anth/Busolt   Vorlesungen Wintersemester 1788/1789 Busolt (*Ak* 25)

V-Anth/Collins   Vorlesungen Wintersemester 1772/1773 Collins (*Ak* 25)

V-Anth/Fried   Vorlesungen Wintersemester 1775/1776 Friedländer (*Ak* 25)

V-Anth/Mron   Vorlesungen Wintersemester 1784/1785 Mrongovius (*Ak* 25)

V-Anth/Pillau   Vorlesungen Wintersemester 1777/1778 Pillau (*Ak* 25)

V-Lo/Blomberg	Logik Blomberg (*Ak* 24)
V-Lo/Busolt	Logik Busolt (*Ak* 24)
V-Lo/Dohna	Logik Dohna-Wundlacken (*Ak* 24)
V-Lo/Hechsel Pinder	I. Kant, *Logik-Vorlesungen. Unveröffentlichte Nachschriften II. Logik Hechsel; Warschauer Logik,* ed. T. Pinder, Hamburg, 1998
V-Lo/Herder	Logik Herder (*Ak* 24)
V-Lo/Philippi	Logik Philippi (*Ak* 24)
V-Lo/Pölitz	Logik Pölitz (*Ak* 24)
V-Lo/Wiener	Wiener Logik or Vienna Logic (*Ak* 24)
V-Met/Dohna	Metaphysik Dohna (*Ak* 28)
V-Met/Heinze	Metaphysik L1 (Heinze) (*Ak* 28)
V-Met/Herder	Metaphysik Herder (*Ak* 28)
V-Met-K2 /Heinze	Metaphysik K2 (Heinze, Schlapp) (*Ak* 28)
V-Met-L1/Pölitz	Metaphysik L1 (Pölitz) (*Ak* 28)
V-Met-L2/Pölitz	Metaphysik L2 (Pölitz, Original) (*Ak* 28)
V-Met/Mron	Metaphysik Mrongovius (*Ak* 29)
V-Met/Schön	Metaphysik Schön (*Ak* 28)
V-Met/Volckmann	Metaphysik Volckmann (*Ak* 28)
V-PG	Vorlesungen über Physische Geographie (*Ak* 26)
VRML	*Über ein vermeintes Recht, aus Menschenliebe zu lügen* (*Ak* 8)
VT	*Von einem neuerdings erhobenen vornehmen Ton in der Philosophie* (*Ak* 8)
VvRM	*Von den verschiedenen Racen der Menschen* (*Ak* 2)
WA	*Beantwortung der Frage: Was ist Aufklärung?* (*Ak* 8)
WDO	*Was heißt sich im Denken orientiren?* (*Ak* 8)
ZeF	*Zum ewigen Frieden* (*Ak* 8)

English translations of most of the above-mentioned works are to be found in *The Cambridge Edition of the Works of Immanuel Kant* (Cambridge, UK). English translations are indicated by the abbreviation ENG. Two examples: *KU, Ak* 5: 277, ENG 158 gives the *Ak* pagination of the third *Critique* followed by the page number of the English translation by Paul Guyer and Eric Matthews; by contrast, *Fortschritte, Ak* 20: 261, ENG 363 gives the reference to the *Akademie Ausgabe* followed by that to "What Real Progress" in *Theoretical Philosophy after 1781.*

I have used the following *Cambridge Edition* volumes:

For *BDG, Deutlichkeit, Dreams, GUGR, Dissertation: Theoretical Philosophy, 1755–1770*, ed. David Walford and Ralf Meerbote, 2003

For *KrV: Critique of Pure Reason*, ed. Paul Guyer and Allen W. Wood, 1998

For *GMS, KpV, MS, WA, TP, ZeF, VRML: Practical Philosophy*, ed. Mary J. Gregor and Allen W. Wood, 1999

For *IaG, MAM, ÜGTP, Anth: Anthropology, History, and Education*, ed. G. Zöller and R. B. Louden, 2007

For *Bemerkungen: Notes and Fragments*, ed. Paul Guyer, Curtis Bowman, and Frederick Rauscher, 2010

For *Prol, MAN, Entdeckung, Fortschritte, VT: Theoretical Philosophy after 1781*, ed. Henry Allison, Peter Heath, Gary Hatfield, and Michael Friedman, 2010

For Log and select V-Lo, including V-Lo/Wiener: *Lectures on Logic*, ed. J. Michael Young, 2004

For *EE* and *KU: Critique of the Power of Judgment*, ed. Paul Guyer and Eric Matthews, 2002

For select V-Met: *Lectures on Metaphysics*, ed. Karl Ameriks and Steve Naragon, 2001

For *RGV: Religion and Rational Theology*, ed. Allen W. Wood and George di Giovanni, 2001

Additional English translations used:

Critique of Pure Reason, ed. Norman Kemp Smith, 1929, repr. 1965, New York

Critique of Pure Reason, ed. Werner S. Pluhar, Indianapolis, 1996

Critique of Judgment, ed. Werner S. Pluhar, Indianapolis, 1987

Eine Vernunft die sinnlich bestimt wär wäre nicht Vernunft.

—I. Kant, *Ak* 23: 17

1. Of Kings, Carters, and Palimpsests

"How many beggars one rich man can feed!/When kings build, the carters have their hands full," writes Friedrich Schiller in *Kant und seine Ausleger.*[1]

In this poem carters are separated from the king as conspicuously as light is from darkness, or giants from dwarves. Should this division prove unjust, the king may be overthrown. Schiller's poem, however, has nothing to do with political justice or exploitation. Instead, it is about the sense of awe inspired by an exceptional thinker like Kant, compared with whom writers relying on his philosophy are like laborers. It prophesies that all followers will be forced to refer back to and depend upon him.

There is a harsh edge, verging on contempt, in Schiller's poem, for there is something parasitical and lowly about carters. Post-Kantian philosophy survives on the crumbs dispensed by a great thinker. The king who feeds the *Lumpenproletariat* inevitably engenders a natural resentment and social envy. If so, one wonders whether Schiller takes Kant's writing to contravene the

---

1. "Wie doch ein einziger Reicher so viele/Bettler in Nahrung/Setzt! Wenn die Könige baun, haben die/Kärrner zu tun," in *Sämtliche Werke*, vol. 1, *Gedichte*, 292. (Throughout this book, all translations of which I do not indicate the sources are my own, as in this case.) The German expression *Kärrner* indicates generally hard labor. A multitude of manual workers are set in motion, mostly to clear rubble, by the decision of a king to build. Carters are notable because of their poverty (they are called beggars), not because of the wagon or cart they are supposed to drive. They are fed by the rich man's decision.

maxim Plato teaches in his *Seventh Letter*: "no serious man will ever think of writing about serious matters for the many. Doing so will only make them both perplexed and envious" (644c).

As a carter, I feel enormous gratitude for the wealth of Kant's thought, but I am also torn: not between perplexity and envy, but between perplexity and gratitude. Indeed, this book grew out of precisely this tension. While I have no doubts that Kant's revolution in thinking is utterly pivotal in the history of philosophy, I do not believe that full justice has been done to it. I think the best way to pay a tribute to Kant's depth is to take seriously and address the philosophical problems that threaten its unity. This is what I want to do in this book.

One important debt of gratitude, which is not ambivalent in any way, is toward my students at Boston University and at the University of Pisa. As every teacher knows, we learn more from the unexpected challenges posed by students than from years of research. I have taught the three *Critiques* many times and at different levels. The first *Critique* in particular has been the object of my renewed and repeated study—and ever amazed reading— over many years. Every time I pick it up again, I brace for new surprises. I realize not only that my previous reading missed many nuances or, luck- ily less often as years tick by, something fundamental, but also that once one part is critically reexamined, the whole book, and therefore Kant's en- tire philosophical project, must be subjected to a global reinterpretation. As Kant himself says, changing one minor detail in a building or a system compels us to rethink the whole anew.

In itself this is neither a cause for alarm nor the root of my perplexity. The *Critique of Pure Reason* is so long and complex that it can hardly be mastered in all its details. My perplexity—and it sometimes grows to bewilderment— has to do with Kant's particular kind of obscurity.

It is hard to believe that a genius like Kant, who cared so much about spreading his message, was so careless in revising and often even in editing his works.[2] If the origin of Kant's obscurity were his sometimes awkward and convoluted prose, we could simply rewrite his texts "in a better order, especially in the construction of periods and in regard to their repetitions," as Friedrich Schlegel proposed. "They would thus become as comprehensible

2. Kant's carelessness is all the more surprising if we consider that he could be an exceptional writer, who had an amazing command of language and could occasionally produce brilliant pages of masterful, subtle, and rigorous prose, such as, say, the essay on the regions of space or on Swedenborg, but also many pages of the first *Critique* (say, the two Prefaces), less tormented or difficult than others.

as the work of, say, Lessing."[3] Unfortunately I am less optimistic than Schlegel because what I find problematic, ambiguous, and plurivocal is not Kant's prose but many of his fundamental notions. Nor is my perplexity regarding Kant's obscurity due to the "quite unconcerned narrative" (*unbesorgtestes Erzählen*) that Hegel laments is Kant's style in the first *Critique*.[4] On the contrary, I find that the first *Critique* is a tangled web of elusive concepts whose *superficially precise vocabulary* is actually replete with complicated and *puzzling distinctions* hiding countless ambiguities, oscillations, and occasional contradictions. The hasty writing of a masterpiece (in certain cases put together based on notes from different years during a long decade of gestation) does not help. The often cavalier coexistence in the second edition of important revisions of crucial parts alongside entire chapters dependent on them that have instead remained unaltered helps even less.[5] On some fundamental issues, such as the meaning of transcendental philosophy, reason's ideas, metaphysics, knowledge, even the propaedeutic role of a critique of pure reason, Kant is often confused and shifts position repeatedly. Fortunately it is sometimes possible to save the unitary fundamental sense of his ambiguous concepts. Some inconsistencies can be resolved by appeal to his unpublished work. But other times the tensions prove deep-seated and resist our best efforts to provide a univocal solution.

Finally, let me mention one of the most perplexing experiences the reader of Kant can have. When Kant retrospectively summarizes what he has accomplished in a certain text, he can be maddeningly misleading. He is hardly ever fair to his old intentions, and speaks almost exclusively from the new standpoint that he has reached and the new aims he has set for himself, some of which are incompatible with those inspiring the earlier material. Even when we realize that his shifts can at least in part be clarified and understood by addressing what I would call his hunger for relentless progress, we must recognize and reconstruct rigorously the tensions and problems they leave unsolved. Kant does not merely simplify but utterly recasts his previous positions, a process of which he seems to be unaware.

My reaction, that the more I read the *Critique of Pure Reason*, the more opaque certain distinctions appear, seems to me often quite warranted. Indeed, having gained a closer understanding of the book, as well as the subsequent two *Critiques*, including the reasons for many of their obscurities,

---

3. *Über die Philosophie*, in *Dichtungen und Aufsätze*, 463.

4. *Glauben und Wissen*, in *Werke*, 2: 301.

5. I refer to the different treatment reserved for the Transcendental Deduction and the Schematism, among others.

I am no longer troubled by my reaction; that is, I have stopped blaming myself. Instead, I believe my reaction is justified. Simply put, Kant's work is riddled with problems. The purpose of this book is to share the grounds of my perplexities in order to help others make better sense of both the difficulties in, and also the enormous value of, Kant's philosophy. For what I try to offer is a problematic and systematic investigation that delves deeper into the many questions that remain open in his philosophy while keeping alive its greatness and the keen sense of its ends.

My reaction is not typical, and this is the second aspect of my dissatisfaction. A perusal of the immense secondary literature on Kant shows that some of his most fundamental notions—say, reason's unity, the a priori, the transcendental ideas, pure intuition, even the origin, nature, and status of pure as opposed to empirical concepts—are taken for granted and treated as obvious by most scholars and philosophers. Instead of finding themselves before an embarrassment of riches and a unique display of philosophical intelligence, but also one that threatens to collapse because its key foundations are far from unequivocal or solid, interpreters too often engage in minute discussions of technical distinctions as they debate other scholars' interpretations. Often philosophers resort to wholesale rejections that are based on important but partial truths, or even on biased misapprehensions and perspectives.

It seems, then, that what interpreters and scholars vitally need is some firm and common ground. To recur to one of Kant's famous analogies, after the perils and strain of a seemingly endless navigation, seeing land is nothing less than hoping to live. Being on land makes us feel secure and is, as the poet would have it, sweet (Suave, mari magno turbantibus aequora ventis,/e terra magnum alterius spectare laborem).[6]

The problem in reading Kant, however, is that land is not as firm as it appears; the opposition between an immense and bottomless sea and a solid, if limited, ground is far-fetched. Kant's project of a critique of pure reason takes on so many forms and changes aspect so many times that its land should be studied the way the earth is studied by seismologists. What to the untrained eye seems hard unshakable rock is in fact in constant motion, the progressive sedimentation of layers of meaning that may well be covered over by fresh vegetation, eroded through weathering and fractures, or uprooted and even shattered by a sudden earthquake. Its original configuration

6. "It's sweet, when winds blow wild on open seas, to watch from land your neighbor's vast travail, not that men's miseries bring us dear delight but that to see what ills we are spared is sweet" (Lucretius, *De rerum natura* 2.1–4, trans. F. O. Copley).

may prove very difficult to retrieve. Nonetheless, that is the task of this book. My hope is that by outlining carefully the fault lines in Kant's edifice, readers will be able to traverse it more effectively.

Kant's idea of a unity of reason is comparable to a palimpsest, written upon many times with remnants of earlier, imperfectly erased writing and marks still visible. The assumption of this book is that the unity of reason must be studied comprehensively throughout the three *Critiques*. A truncated reading of the first *Critique* and a compartmentalization of critical philosophy fall short of the interpreter's task. In order to study Kant's philosophy as a whole it must be treated as a work in progress. The scholar must summon all available skills (exegetic, historical, philological, linguistic, etc.) to face and resolve doubts and issues, including minute and technical questions of interest to specialists alone. But every scholarly task must be in service of the project of giving a comprehensive philosophical account of Kant's thought that does not ignore its many ambiguities. In faithfulness to the Greek dialectical inspiration (or, if you will, to the zetetic soul of Kant's thought) I have learned to consider essential to philosophy, this means that the defense of the plausibility of Kant's theses and the unearthing and thematic discussion of their problems must go hand in hand.

Before I proceed, however, I want happily and thankfully to acknowledge another debt of gratitude. Despite the criticisms of Kant scholarship that I have just noted, what I know about him comes from a prolonged study not only of Kant himself, but also of the very rich and immensely instructive literature on his philosophy in the languages I can read. The incredible diversity of approaches and results we find in the Kant scholarship owes its existence to the complexity of Kant's thought, but also to the originality, different perspectives, and intelligence of its many interpreters. This is to say that, whether the works on Kant are intended as commentaries or as forms of appropriation or of critique, they constitute a precious aid, an indispensable assistance, and an invaluable treasure that *nobody* should underestimate, indeed, that nobody interested in Kant can do without. For example, it would be worthwhile to write the history of philosophy after Kant (from German Idealism to Neo-Kantianism, from phenomenology and hermeneutics and deconstruction to analytic philosophy and pragmatism: not exactly carters) from the perspective of their different relations to Kant's thought.

Nevertheless, it is striking that some of the more notable readings of the *Critique of Pure Reason*, and of critical philosophy in general, are one-sided precisely insofar as they are reductive. The first *Critique* is an impressive edifice. Taking it as a whole and trying to do justice to its inner articulation amount to a daunting task, and it is no wonder that many approach it selectively. What is, however, particularly problematic about even some of the more *powerful* readings (from Hermann Cohen's, Martin Heidegger's, and P. F. Strawson's up to many of the contemporary essays on and companions to Kant) is that while they strive to identify the supposed focus of the work (typically found in the common ground of Transcendental Aesthetic and Analytic), they dismiss the Transcendental Dialectic and the Doctrine of Method.[7] As a result, they reduce the whole to one part or section. For such readers independent faculties are seen at best as cooperating under the aegis of this or that function. They are hardly ever understood as originating in an overarching unitary principle shaping the whole book.

All readings that separate, isolate, and privilege one part are guilty of what rhetoric calls the figure of the synecdoche: they take one part as standing for the whole. They misconstrue the inclusion and the interrelation of parts, and their relation to the whole. For example, when he speaks of "reason" Kant sometimes intends reason proper as the faculty of the unconditional, but at other times "reason" is the comprehensive name for sensibility, understanding as well as reason proper. In the latter case, perhaps the synecdoche is typical of Kant's procedure.[8] But this does not mean we must follow it uncritically.

7. I think it goes without saying that I do not mean to claim that those Kant scholars who dismiss the Transcendental Dialectic and the Doctrine of Method are *inattentive*. Nor do I intend to deny that progress has been made since Cohen, Heidegger, or Strawson on the importance of ideas and the architectonic concept of philosophy (Michelle Grier's 2001 book *Transcendental Illusion* is a good example in the Anglophone literature of the general revision of what I call the standard reading). My point is that this undergoing revision is still very timid, and, more importantly, that even the acknowledgment of the value of the Dialectic is insufficient if it does not lead to understanding its connection with the Doctrine of Method and leaves the center of gravity of the first *Critique* untouched. If an interpreter as authoritative, expert, well-versed in the Kant scholarship, and intelligent as Henry Allison confesses he needed Grier's book to be awakened from his dogmatic slumber and revise his book on the first *Critique* to include a new part on the Dialectic (*Kant's Transcendental Idealism*, xvii), what does it take to realize the fundamental unity of Kant's idea of reason as expounded in the Architectonic and the Canon?

Even on the Architectonic I am not claiming there is nothing of value in the literature. In fact, among others the essays by Amoroso, Barale, Böhr, Brandt, Centi, Dörflinger, Garelli, Guyer, Heimsoeth, Hinske, Hohenegger, Höffe, Illetterati, Kleingeld, La Rocca, Lehmann, Manchester, Neiman, O'Neill, Pierobon, Tonelli, Velkley, Yovel, and all contributions but especially those by Ameriks, Baum, König, and Zöller in the collection edited by Fulda and Stolzenberg (see the bibliography for full references) represent important exceptions to the standard reading. Among them allow me to single out Tonelli's book *Kant's Critique of Pure Reason within the Tradition of Modern Logic* as perhaps the most instructive.

8. It is bad enough, i.e., at times it generates confusion, to speak of reason in these terms. But it is perhaps worse when Kant calls the understanding what he typically calls reason, "the higher faculty of cognition." See, among others, the "promiscuity" (lamented as such by Kemp

In the *Critique of Pure Reason* the relation between parts and whole is comparable to a living continuous exchange, a dialectical movement. The whole is active in the parts, and the parts bring vividness and substance to the whole. Therefore it is as if in reading a part we must see it in light of a whole whose lens relentlessly needs refocusing on account of a deepened understanding of the parts. If pure reason is, as Kant says, a living body, the model for reading the *Critique of Pure Reason* cannot be a line (or even a circle). It has to be an organic internal growth, a movement generating its own force, ease, and stability as it is constantly sent back upon its course, not to retrace its steps but to regain itself as it revisits and assimilates its essential moments. The category guiding our reading cannot be the mechanical and transitive causality that rules appearances. Also ruled out is the preliminary dismemberment of the whole for piecemeal analysis, resulting in neat segments to be approached independently of one another.

Hegel writes that the complaint about the unintelligibility of philosophy rests on a mental attitude, the lack of practice in holding onto abstract thoughts due to the impatient wish to have before us familiar representations (*Phänomenologie des Geistes, Werke* 3: 55–56; 1830 *Encyclopaedia* § 3, Remark). To attain the necessary plasticity, philosophy requires that we return to the proposition over and over again and apprehend it in an ever new light by destroying the supposedly fixed and isolated meanings of subject and predicate. It requires that we put in question thought's expectations of comfortable familiarity and force ourselves to face the unexpected.

When it comes to Kant, the first form taken by this invitation to speculative thinking by overcoming the usual attitude regarding a proposition and constantly returning to the text is the imperative to resist hasty sectorialization. All readings that reduce reason to the understanding, and the different forms of comprehension, reflection, and thought to a theory of experience, turn out to be arbitrary. Despite his invitation, even Hegel, who unlike others reads past the Analytic and values the Dialectic and the antinomies more than anything else, does not bring the relation between ideas and understanding to fruition, for he believes that Kant conceives of reason in the shape of representation and presupposes the opposition of

---

Smith, *Commentary*, 2) at *KrV* A 1–2, where Kant uses 'pure understanding' for 'pure reason'; the passage in the V-Met/L1, in which Kant says that the "understanding, and the higher faculty of cognition, is threefold: *understanding, power of judgment and reason*" (*Ak* 28: 241, ENG 59); and the passage from the Introduction to the third *Critique* (*KU, Ak* 5: 174–75), itself more the sign of a changing conception than a real synecdoche as we will see in chapter 3, in which Kant writes that "legislation through concepts of nature takes place through the understanding," as opposed to reason's legislation through freedom.

world and consciousness, sensibility and understanding, passivity and activity.

In this book I will read Kant's philosophy as a developing whole. The architectonic description of reason in the Doctrine of Method and of the ideas as the result of reason's totalizing need in the Dialectic are key to my interpretation, indeed constitute its premise.

2. "Every division presupposes a concept that is to be divided" (*KrV* A 290/B 346). On Kant's Dichotomies

Among the many misguided approaches to reading Kant, I would like to single out two in particular, both forms of the ancient vice of separation. Every *Critique* tends to be read in isolation from the others. On the one hand, the three *Critiques* lend themselves well to this sectorialization (and to the ever-increasing compartmentalized research and teaching in academe). On the other, the results of this approach generate three separate works: one on epistemology or theoretical philosophy, one on morals, and one whose unity is more elusive but that revolves around aesthetics and natural teleology. What is missed here is that in fact the three *Critiques* are actually three different works on one underlying theme, the unity of reason.

The second approach, which is equally misguided, is a linear and piecemeal reading of the first *Critique* that conflates order of exposition and order of constitution. Typically, this approach treats the various dichotomies on which Kant builds his exposition as referring to substantial and real oppositions without ever raising the problem of their overarching and original unity. As Kant writes in the Amphiboly (*KrV* A 290/B 346), if two concepts are opposed, they stand under a superior concept: opposition can arise, and must be understood, only as the disjunction of an original concept. One example among many is the following. In the *Inaugural Dissertation* we find the stark contrast between sensible and intelligible worlds. This enormously important discovery, which marks the beginning of Kant's critical period, is taken by some commentators as a steadfast heritage left virtually unaltered in the pair Aesthetics-Analytic in the Transcendental Doctrine of Elements of the first *Critique*. A quick look at Kant's many famous assertions to the effect that sensibility and understanding are opposed results then in an irreconcilable alternative.

What commentators fail to see is that the opposition is introduced by Kant as the disjunction of an original unity, and as a demonstration of why a mediation is necessary to resolve it. The method of separation (*Absonderung*) of empirical and pure, which Kant claims follows the model of chemistry, is introduced for the sake of clarifying the heterogeneous elements of that unity. This method does at first isolate and advance by progressive dichotomies, but only in order to show how these heterogeneous elements combine in experience.

Unfortunately, Kant himself all too often takes his bearings by such an opposition, even where we may suspect it does not belong. It is Kant who all too often frames questions concerning reason in terms of understanding, and questions concerning thinking in terms of consciousness. Little wonder then that if we do not read the first *Critique* with a panoramic and stereoscopic vision, and a painstaking attention to contexts, we end up charging Kant with the unintelligible attempt at taking back dichotomies he began by supposedly pronouncing as irrevocable—or that we are still debating the extent to which in the Transcendental Deduction receptivity and spontaneity are inextricable.

By and large, those readers who take one part for the whole and thereby reduce reason to understanding want solid philosophical arguments they can test usefully. It could be Kant's philosophy of mathematics, his views on causality in the Second Analogy, his derivation of the role of categories in experience, his presumed response to Hume, his critique of theology, the formulas for the universal law of morality, the real extent of disinterestedness in aesthetics, his possible contribution to current debates in biology, cognitive science, virtue and deontological ethics, cosmopolitanism or a democratic peace.

Unfortunately, this tendency of isolation fails to account for the unity of Kant's philosophy throughout the three *Critiques*. The very idea of a system of pure reason and the first *Critique* as a propaedeutic to metaphysics is brushed aside or even dismissed as obsolete metaphysical baggage. The thesis underlying this book is that even with all its developments and changes, with all its seismic shifts, Kantian philosophy is above all else a whole.

Another decisive problem in contemporary commentary is the view that Kant's pure reason is seamlessly continuous with modern rationality. I would like to show instead that Kant brings the modern notion of reason to a crisis.[9] To put the point simply, in modernity reason becomes a

---

9. Please note that when I speak about "modernity," in this introduction and elsewhere, I do not refer to or rely on a full-fledged theory of modernity. While I try to avoid sweeping generalizations and I definitely admit significant exceptions to what I am claiming, what I have in mind is a relatively homogeneous foil, and thereby a heuristic tool, to highlight Kant's novelty and reversal of dominant positions from Bacon, Galilei, and Descartes to Locke, Leibniz, Baumgarten, and Hume. The same caveat applies to my remarks on cosmic philosophy and artists of reason (below, chapter 1, § 5); on vision, touch, and discursive knowledge (chapter 2, § 2);

logical and calculating tool whose goal is to make possible a scientific and definitive *mathesis universalis* of nature. It is the neutral, internally consistent, and indifferent seat of abstract forms—be they acquired or found in us—that stands opposed to its contents as well as to external drives and forces. Modern reason is a nature opposed to external nature and likewise inert, powerless, and unable to decide and motivate. It is a sort of mechanism,[10] which we must let run its course without encumbering it with metaphysical and teleological concerns and make rigorous by adopting the scientific method that has fueled all our hopes of limitless progress since the scientific revolution.

Even if this sketch is simplistic it is useful as a foil, for it suggests that the continuity between modern reason and Kant's reason is less striking than their differences. Most important is Kant's break with the modern image of reason as timid, heteronomous, instrumental, powerless, prey to passions in practice and in service of the sciences of nature, and thereby experience, in theory. Central to Kant's new image of reason is not a dream of omnipotence but rather, and more fundamentally, a sharp delimitation of its scopes. Its central claim is that reason has legislative powers that give rise to objects that are not actual productions but syntheses of *forms* to which empirical matter will forever remain external and given.

Key to this new notion of reason is its teleology. After all, if reason is an organism, its life as well as the interconnection of its parts must be thought of as purposive and oriented to ends. Kant's conception of system, of science, of the philosopher as legislator, and of reason's *a priori synthesis* is the

---

and on reason and motivation (chapter 2, § 3b). In all these cases, I do not dispute that Kant is a modern. If, for example, modernity means, as in some persuasive systematic interpretations (e.g., Blumenberg's *Legitimacy of the Modern Age*), the Enlightenment's self-affirmation, then Kant is the best champion of modernity. But my point is that the path he chooses to arrive at reason's self-assertion is quite different from, often alternative to, that chosen by most modern philosophers before him. The secondary literature, by stressing Kant's continuity with modernity, misses the extent of Kant's novelty. To realize that Kant is not one philosopher among others in the Enlightenment but a uniquely revolutionary thinker, I think a discussion of Kant's break with the modern tradition is worthwhile, indeed crucial.

10. The widespread complaint about the formality and the "intricate machinery" of Kant's faculties is in truth a complaint about his having gratuitously (i.e., simply and unnecessarily) made Hume's faculties more cumbersome and abstract. I disagree. Not only are Kant's faculties defined quite differently from Hume's; pure reason is everything except a machinery, as Kant's definition of stupidity and the power of judgment shows. 'Machinery' implies the thoughtless functioning of an automaton (expressed psychologically: a chain of reactions), itself dependent on its relation to its producer and master: the opposite of the spontaneity and freedom with which Kant identifies reason.

way he expresses the power reason has to generate its contents and extend itself to the world.

That Kant's idea of reason is continuous with modernity is stressed mostly by those who interpret critical philosophy as a foundational project starting from a Cartesian-like mentalism, whereby the motivation can be a preoccupation with refuting skepticism or overcoming the solipsism of consciousness. As we will see, transcendental philosophy does not primarily intend to provide a foundation for empirical knowledge through the conditions for experience (whereby the question—important, to be sure—boils down to whether its arguments are necessary and/or sufficient). The first *Critique* is of reason as an articulated unity.[11] Reason's laws and principles are a complete system, an organic plan. Therefore reason is its own project. Its medium and element are its ideas, which are usually neglected in that they do not bear directly on any object. Ideas define the goal of reason's inquiry, the guide and the method for all its activities. This is why the first chapter of this book explores the Architectonic, and more specifically Kant's conception of reason and philosophy.

Kant holds what might be termed a cosmic conception of reason. He means that reason has a comprehensive vision, an overarching attitude toward all cognitions, and an awareness of its own interests and ends that inspires all rational activities, in metaphysics as well as in morality. This attitude is grounded in the decision to take pure reason alone as our guide and arbiter, our unconditional judge and only authority. Philosophy consists more in the promotion of reason's ends than in logical self-consistency or in the instrument of mankind's progress.

Philosophy for Kant has extraordinarily ambitious goals, and its function can hardly be compared to familiar forms of philosophical activity. Whatever the merits of contemporary diagnoses of historical situations and crises, of the various kinds of therapy of mental cramps, of linguistic or logical analysis, the hermeneutics of texts or the deconstruction of social institutions and practices, all such forms of intellectual work are neither original nor independent but residual. That is, they are alternative to an autonomous

11. In the Collins Anthropology lectures (*Ak* 25/2: 774), we read a passage that expresses pedagogically, and epitomizes well, this interrelation of some of the faculties of pure reason. In its education, youth first acquires the understanding with its concepts, then the power of judgment with its ability to apply rules pertinently, and finally reason, which looks for causes and ends to what happens ("Wenn die Jugend gebildet wird, so bekommt sie zuerst Verstand, indem man ihr Begriffe beybringt; hernach bekommt sie Urtheilskraft, da man ihr Gelegenheit gewisse Regeln anzuwenden verschafft, endlich erhält sie Vernunft, wenn sie von dem was vorkommt, die Ursachen und Zwecke aufsucht").

project and the *institution of a lawful order*. Like an owl of Minerva, they presuppose a given to whose constitution they have not contributed and on which they invite us to reflect *post festum*: culture, history, language, politics, and so forth. By contrast, for Kant reason is first and foremost autonomous legislation, and thus the originative institution of order. Nothing relevant comes prior to it.

3. Reason's Finitude. Concepts and Ideas

As just mentioned, pure reason's teleology and legislation, as well as its a priori synthesis, are introduced by Kant as gateways to the power reason has to generate its contents and extend itself to the world. But the a priori synthesis is not exclusive to the first *Critique*. It is *the* problem of Kant's critical philosophy in its various scopes of application. Even if in the first *Critique* the question is framed in terms of the exclusive relation between concepts and intuitions and of the discursivity of knowledge, both then and later the problem remains the same: pure reason's ambition to reach beyond itself. This is the thread holding together the three *Critiques* as moments of one and the same project on the unity of reason. The difficulty, as already mentioned, is that this unitary project is a work in progress that shifted and subtly changed countless times. In order to get a comprehensive view of it the interpreter must be equally attuned to both its harmony and its dissonance. We have no choice but to approach Kant's thought architectonically, systematically, but at the same time be alert for the possibility of its problems and ambiguities.

The issues of a priori synthesis, pure intuition and pure concepts, and objective reality are analyzed in chapter 2. It stresses the central role of reason as an activity instituting a world, and addresses a priori synthesis as a production of forms. Obviously, this 'production' cannot produce anything real or give us objects in intuition. Instead, what it gives us are the principles on which all intuitions rest. What acquires objective reality in this production is not an object but the form any object will assume. This is not, therefore, an actual intuition, but the synthesis of possible objects in experience. A legislator, say on matters of right, has nothing to say about an exchange between you and me or about the matter of whatever conventions are established among and agreed upon by citizens. Instead, he or she delimits the space and establishes the rules according to which such conventions are legitimate or not, and gives a code of forms by which you and I must abide in our relations. This space of rules can be considered a world of the legislator's making.

Kant's conception of reason does not intend to replace or surrogate experience, for it is concerned only with what he calls objective reality or real possibility. Nonetheless it produces the forms of experience. Unfortunately, this reading of Kant is not widely accepted, and 'productive reason,' as an a priori synthesis of forms, is hardly ever discussed. The reasons why are several. Some have to do with the historical destiny of Kant's philosophy and/or with one-sided ways of reading him or updating his philosophy such that it can participate in contemporary debates that have little to do with Kant's actual concerns. In particular, there is a prejudiced antimetaphysical reading that risks throwing away the baby with the bathwater.

The fear that naturally comes to mind is shared by Kant himself: the ghost of idealism may haunt all such reading. But idealism may be either subjectivism or a form of absolutism of reason. And here I believe that the fear of the latter typically appears more threatening. Therefore all talk of the powers of reason to extend itself in the world must first clear the ground of a misunderstanding lurking in the widespread preconception of reason's limits. The commonplace that Kant's emphasis on reason's limits points to the inescapable finitude of human reason is so pervasive that the mere mention of the powers of a productive reason looks suspect and overbearing, as if it were an act of *hubris*.

As I suggested, Kant brings modern reason to a crisis; in Kant's conception reason's legislation does not result in a scientific *mathesis universalis*. Even those who see Kant struggling to break free of the conception of his age identify a continuity between modern reason and Kant's. Think, for example, of Heidegger, who has written memorable pages on Kant's unprecedented link between imagination and time. However, when Heidegger takes thought as intrinsically dependent on intuition, he inverts Kant's actual thesis. Thought is in itself unbounded. If anything, it is knowledge that is dependent on intuition, not reason. No *Befindlichkeit*, no thrownness into the world or temporality rooted in an original openness can account for reason's fundamental and defining characteristic. Reason is in all its functions *Handlung*, activity, spontaneity.[12] There is a sharp separation between the fact of our finitude and the *quaestio iuris* regarding reason as law-giving activity, between

---

12. In a very interesting fragment entitled "Answer to the Question: Is It an Experience That We Think?' (to which the answer is negative), Kant points out that while experience is impossible without a connection to the determination of time, the consciousness of experience, as indeed all thinking, can "take no regard of time" (*Ak* 18: 318–19), for otherwise an "infinite regress" would haunt our account of it.

the external conditions of actualization resting on a givenness outside reason and the internal, *transcendental* conditions of that actualization.

The problem with advocates of reason's finitude is not that they remain content with a reasonable defeat before the insurpassable or rest their case before pure reason's insurmountable limits. Instead, the problem is that these limits are taken as sufficient evidence that pure reason's *speculative problems* are insoluble. On the contrary, Kant believes he is giving us the *definitive solution* to them.[13]

This misunderstanding of limits conflates different theses and rests on a purely negative reading of the Transcendental Dialectic, which for Kant does not simply result in the warning that pure reason in its speculative use is irremediably finite and its transcendence must be censored. For in addition, and crucially, the *Critique of Pure Reason* shows that reason is nothing but autonomy: it has no antecedently given standards; it is the government of itself. Autonomy does not at all apply to practical reason alone, as is often said, nor is it pertinent only to morality. Rather, it identifies reason in its purity *before* the division of its realms of application. The autonomy of reason denotes the inner core and destination of reason itself. This implies that speculative reason is moved by imperatives and ends. In turn, morality is moved by the maximum possible consistency and the responsibility to think for oneself. Only critique can test and try the principles of reason: no authority is higher than its tribunal. Nothing is more fundamental to reason than the antinomy of nature and freedom; nothing is more fundamental for reason than the idea of the world it projects before itself as the field of its activity.

Reason, however, discovers it is *divided against itself*. It lives not in one but in two alternative worlds. In the final words of the *Critique of Practical Reason*, it discovers that we are a speck in an unbounded universe we try to grasp as a whole, as we extend our connection to worlds and worlds and to the beginning and end of time in a seemingly infinite regress. And it discovers that my indivisible self is not purely contingent but the universal

13. "Thus *we cannot evade the obligation of giving at least a critical resolution of the questions of reason before us by lamenting the narrow limits of our reason and confessing, with the appearance of a modest self-knowledge, that it lies beyond our reason to settle whether the world has existed from eternity or has a beginning,* whether world-space is filled to infinity with beings or is enclosed within certain boundaries [etc.]. . . . For each of these questions concerns an object that can be given nowhere but in our thoughts, namely the absolutely unconditioned totality of the synthesis of appearances. . . . A clear presentation of the dialectic lying in our concept itself would soon bring us to *complete certainty* about what we have to judge in regard to such a question" (*KrV* A 481/B 509, italics mine).

and necessary citizen of a world that has "true infinity" (*Ak* 5: 162, ENG 269). Neither world is sufficient unto itself; both the causality of nature in the world of sense and the causality of freedom are indispensable to us. What reason discovers is that it is unable to give a unitary *logos* of either world. The causality of freedom exercises itself in legislation over appearances; that is, noumena need phenomena. In turn, a coherent self-enclosed account of a causal order in a spatial-temporal totality is impossible. As the Antinomies teach, we face a dilemma. I must think the whole either as finite or as infinite. In the former case I do not get to the condition of the series of appearances, to the principle of the finite. In the latter, I can think the whole as infinite only as long as I do not realize that space and time, the conditions of sensibility to which I resort to give meaning to my thought and make it determinate, undermine its infinity.

It is not by chance that those who misconstrue limits, by reducing reason to understanding or failing to acknowledge the positive way in which reason proper exceeds the understanding, overlook the difference between *concepts and ideas*. Concepts are rules of which we avail ourselves to judge. Ideas are models (*Urbilder*) and ends. The function of concepts is that of identifying and determining objects according to rules. In particular, mathematical concepts constitute their objects, pure concepts constitute the form of all objects whatever, and empirical concepts denote classes of objects or their predicates. By contrast, the function of ideas is to project a maximum, a totality or perfection to which we hold fast as to a standard.

To use an example from the *Metaphysik L1* (*Ak* 28: 240, ENG 57), in 'Cicero is learned' I use the predicate to judge Cicero's deeds. Therefore it is a rule for my judgment, and the understanding is at once the faculty of rules, of concepts, of judgments. By contrast, in 'Cicero is just' the idea of justice is not related directly to experience, let alone derived from it. Ideas transcend all experience. In and through them we complete concepts, i.e., we "think their objects completely with regard to their species," "without concerning ourselves with whether such a thing is actual or even merely possible" (*Refl* 6206, *Ak* 18: 489–90). What matters is that nothing should be missing from the idea.

Concepts aim at capturing the being of objects; ideas their ought (*Sollen*). Concepts look to objects; ideas look past given objects—or, better, they look to objects in view of their normative standards, which, even though they point to something that does not exist, eventually turn out to be helpful for a better cognition of objects themselves. Ideas seek an encompassing view, a stereoscopic vision that keeps together near and far, presence and its horizon. And, sure enough, the fools who steadily direct their gaze toward *remote ends* and keep their head raised above the ground *looking for something that does not exist* are those at whom the Thracian maid pokes her fun: philosophers. "Philosophy is the true motherland of ideas," says Kant (*Refl* 943, *Ak* 15.1: 419).

Take the idea of world: it is paradigmatic, and often, especially in the *Opus Postumum*, it functions as the mirror image of the idea of God as the totality of all being. The world as such an all-encompassing totality does not exist, for it is our a priori thought. Nothing in reality corresponds to our idea, and we arrive at it not despite but precisely because we know it cannot denote any object. We know we cannot apply an idea for technical or even conceptual ends. The idea of world shows that our gaze is directed toward the whole, to the farthest and most comprehensive horizon. Such an idea can never become the means to something else. Instead, it affirms itself as an ideal we may well never attain. In one sense, from the point of view of the aims of experience, ideas appear as useless. In another, if our perspective is wider than this form of instrumentality, they are the most necessary guide, even for the application of our understanding to experience and the sciences.

Ideas are therefore called regulative, whereas concepts are constitutive. But ideas are regulative of the constitutive use of the understanding. If ideas are necessary and constitutive of our reason's gaze even if not of any reality, then this Kantian characterization of ideas will turn out to need substantial qualification, if not to be quite insufficient. The problem facing Kant in his exposition of ideas will prove to be more poignant, profound, and far-reaching than his proposed solution. We will be compelled to acknowledge Kant's ambivalence and ambiguities with regard to ideas. Once again, Kant brilliantly opens new paths but sometimes unfortunately cannot quite deliver what he has to offer.

Human reason is finite not because all thinking is temporal or constrained to the sensible or relative to its epoch. The thesis of the Transcendental Dialectic is not simply that thought must remain within the bounds of sense. In the terms of the Doctrine of Method of the first *Critique* this would amount to choosing the thrust of the Discipline at the expense of, indeed suppressing altogether, the themes of Architectonic and Canon, as if the first *Critique* were not also an organon and a doctrine. Thought is in itself unbounded. No given order or boundary counts for it until it comes up against the limits posed by its doomed attempt at harmonizing its own several functions.

The finitude of human reason, in sum, is not a form of positivism that cautiously abides by the sciences of nature. The finitude of human reason is not a form of historicism either. Nor does it lie in the corrigibility of its statements, in a supposedly asymptotic approximation to an ideal of complete determination. Kant's finitude is not pragmatism's fallibility. Nor, finally, is finitude the essence of speculation as opposed to morality.

The fundamental and all too common misunderstanding arises from at once reducing the reason of the first *Critique* to theoretical or speculative reason as informed by the rigorous and inescapable bounds of possible experience, and then taking practical reason as opposed to it, as the realm of the noumenon. Unfortunately, and as usual, this reading may be inspired by Kant himself. Consider, for example, the very lines of the second *Critique* just quoted (*Ak* 5: 162, ENG 269), or the presumed result of the Transcendental Deduction of pure concepts, which restricts the use of concepts to appearances. Be that as it may, the common reading pretends to dissolve the antinomy *internal* to pure reason by simply choosing for speculative reason one end of the opposition, namely, finitude. This reading ignores the fact that finite and infinite are equally at home in both the first and the second *Critiques*, and consigns speculative reason to an exclusive employment in the realm of appearances. Thus the common reading "resolves" the contradiction by postponing it and transferring it to the second *Critique*.

The noumenon, however, cannot be expelled from the first *Critique*. The thought of the unconditional is not a mistake of speculative reason that we suddenly realize as we gasp in disbelief at the sight of the ruins of dogmatic metaphysics. Ideas are *necessary* concepts of reason. They are not arbitrarily invented. They are the essential *problems* of reason "imposed by the nature of reason itself," and stand in necessary relation to the whole use of the understanding (*KrV* A 327/B 384).

If ideas are necessary, their tension with concepts and intuitions is a vital relation, not a dead end we must prudently avoid. Although Kant himself sometimes does suggest so, the relegation of ideas to the sphere of morality depends on a sense of finitude that is not Kant's. Kantian finitude is not the situatedness of human nature; it is the finitude of the *powers* of human reason, which are insufficient for a complete self-reliance and mastery of our destiny. Differently stated, that we freely legislate over things does not mean that the effects of our legislation are in our power. Chance, matter, givenness are beyond reason.[14]

14. To borrow an incisive formula from O'Neill, we can say that we "are to construe 'finite rational beings' not as 'beings whose rationality is finite,' but as 'finite beings who are rational'" (*Constructions of Reason*, 74).

But this insufficiency does not affect or alter the autarchy or autonomy of reason, or the monopoly of authority that its tribunal holds. Nor does it make us forget that the solution of speculative reason's questions is both urgently needed and at hand. What it tells us is that questions given in and arising from thought alone must be solved by thought. The speculative solution is that speculative cognition of nature stops at the threshold of the unconditional. And this means not that speculative cognition gives up and sends us beyond reason, but that it grounds the necessity of a rational faith. This is what the restriction of knowledge making room for faith (*KrV* B xxx) finally means. This is Kant's understanding of finitude.

For these reasons, an adequate reading of Kant must focus on a comprehensive view of the powers of pure reason whether or not this defies the taste and tendencies prevalent in our *Zeitgeist* and in many of the most familiar interpretations of Kant. This reading must be pursued even if it defies Kant's own language, which precisely regarding this issue is often misleading or shifts considerably during the 1780s.

Among other things, this makes it necessary to rethink intuition and to distinguish neatly between *passivity* and *receptivity*. When Kant opposes the spontaneity of the understanding to the receptivity of sensibility, the line of demarcation is the givenness of appearances to our senses. The understanding ("the faculty for bringing forth representations itself," *KrV* A 51/B 75) can activate itself regardless of givenness; sensibility cannot, for it must be affected by something independent of itself. But this does not make sensibility's work passive. Passivity denotes sensibility's dependence on givenness, not what it can or cannot do. The sharp distinction between empirical and pure intuition implies a parallel distinction, no less neat and firm, between sensation and a kind of activity already proper to sensibility, and quite different from the understanding's spontaneous acts of unification. The sensibility that belongs to the pure reason we undertake to critique must be understood essentially as the form of receptivity; that is, not as passivity but as the pure intuition of space and time ordering the given sensible manifold for cognition. Although sensibility is the capacity to be affected or modified, affections acquire cognitive status once they are taken up by the mind. That is, no affection makes sense or even exists for us other than through and as an ordered organization of the given manifold in a pure form. And this is the act whereby we shape our receptivity—in Kant's words, a self-affection. All affection is a self-affection in this respect. If we are passive with regard to givenness, in turn we can acquire empirical cognitions only through a synthetic act; and synthesis occurs at two distinct levels: intuitive and conceptual.

If all our cognition begins with experience but not all cognition arises from experience (*KrV* B 1), pure intuition exceeds empirical intuition and must be isolated and studied in itself, as a *forming of intuitive relations*. Generally, reason is what all successive subtractions will not be able to eliminate: the *a priori* that is irreducible to and independent of experience, but that turns out to make it possible.

The gulf between empirical consciousness and reason is as deep as that between inner sense and transcendental apperception. And yet the gulf is not a sheer opposition between two unrelated terms. If temporality does not capture the essence of reason, neither does it fall outside human nature. Thought and reflection are acts; but they also give rise to effects we feel in ourselves. The states of our mind (*Gemüt*) are *felt* as the result of our reason's spontaneity. Thus Kant makes philosophically relevant in many ways (from the *Critique of Judgment* to the *Anthropology*) not only the activity by which we determine ourselves, but also our determinability and our conscious inner states—that is, the relation between faculty of cognition and feeling of pleasure. The worst disservice we could do to Kant is to conflate the two.

In sum, the first *Critique* is not about knowledge or experience, but about reason's a priori legislation: its internal articulation, its two scopes of application (nature and freedom), its limits and powers.

4. Reason and Its Awakening

Kant's conception of reason may appear as an abstract and suprahistorical construction we assume from the outset. How can it not be a metaphysical substance? We may be suspicious of this hypostatization of acts into such an autonomous agent. It must, however, be said that Kant's reason exists only as embodied; and if it essentially transcends experience, it is not as if it were an abstract power we can recognize only because we are already convinced of its force. Simply put, Kant conceives of reason as that which is in but cannot be reduced to experience, as that which is in but cannot be reduced to nature and the body. It is that which is in our finite existence but cannot be reduced to finitude. It is the a priori principle of knowing and acting.

We may still want to bring this reason back to earth and pursue the question of its origin (anthropological or historical), all the while lamenting that Kant shows little interest in such an inquiry. That would be unfair, though. In what I take to be his response to Rousseau's Second Discourse, the *Conjectural Beginning of Human History*,[15] Kant speaks of the awakening of reason (*MAM, Ak* 8: 111, ENG 165). He does not think that behind the ascent from nature to civilization lies the "cunning of reason," or that reason is the secret agent behind our evolution. To be sure, as Kant tells the story, we are neither brutes nor able to give a sensible account of how reason comes to be so that it must be taken as somehow lying dormant in us from the outset. But at some point reason begins to stir, makes connections and comparisons, and eventually rises above nature. In all this, the subject is not reason as we know it but human *needs* and their satisfaction. And the "reason" we become aware of at first is neither Vico's reason nor a logical faculty of thought endowed with its independence or even an upper hand over the other faculties. What Kant means by this awakening of reason is nothing other than the realization that we can be *at variance* with natural impulses, and even invent desires with the help of imagination.

This is how we become conscious of a peculiar infinity in us. We do not entirely depend on nature, but can even work against it; and the first stage of this realization is *refusal* (*Weigerung*), or the suspension of natural impulses (*MAM, Ak* 8: 113, ENG 166). In the prehistory of morality a sense of decency and modesty (*Sittsamkeit*) makes its first appearance as shame and social pressure. Depending on how we react to this pressure, we transform some of the impulses deriving from what originally were natural stimuli dependent on the senses into lasting inclinations. This emancipation from nature, differently stated, is not the triumph of a supposedly transcendental subjectivity or an abstract reason about whose origin and provenance we are bound to remain clueless, but the limited suspension of nature's voice from within nature. In other words, at first "reason" is nothing superior to or other than this *channeling of drives and inhibition of desire* made possible by imagination's anticipation of the future and setting of ends.

Unfortunately, Kant remains reticent on the most intriguing transition, that from prehistory to history, from a quasi-naturalistic reason developing out of needs, desires, imagination, and time to a pure reason above desire, imagination, and time: from a reason that struggles to rise above nature from within nature to a reason that asserts itself as unconditional. Later, in the third *Critique* (*KU* § 83, *Ak* 5: 432–33, ENG 299–300), he claims

---

15. See my "Imagination and Judgment" (the section on the "pre-history of reason"). See also the question of the final end of nature in the third *Critique*, § 83. The importance for Kant of Rousseau's conception of reason as a dynamic force that unfolds historically as it alienates and transforms itself can hardly be overestimated, and yet it is not widely recognized in the literature. For a very valuable exception see Velkley, *Freedom and the End of Reason*.

it is nature that makes us receptive to higher ends and culture generally. Whatever we think of the controversial and prima facie dogmatic notion that nature should be a "moral facilitator" or have a hidden plan for mankind's history,[16] that is, that nature is not a blind mechanism but is intrinsically purposive and thus prepares the way for the development of morality in history, we cannot charge Kant with embracing the abstract idea of a ready-made transcendental subject operating as the cunning of reason from the outset.

It seems necessary to distinguish the ascription of a plan to nature from the justification of the assumption that history responds to a plan. In the former, the reflection on nature's ends leads to the question of whether mankind is a final end and thus to ethico-theology, as in the third *Critique*. In the latter, we limit ourselves to the narrower question of our interpretation of history. If this leads us to raise questions bound to remain tangential in this book, it is yet another way to attest to the importance of ideas. History is a moral task because it is the stage of realization of reason's plan. For Kant the end of history is to produce a political order in which the culture of reason can realize itself and promote self-worth and autonomy.

Strikingly, the same terms used by Kant to describe his concepts of architectonic reason and cosmic philosophy in relation to history in the first edition of the *Critique of Pure Reason* (and later in the *Real Progress*) recur after three years in the "Idea for a Universal History" (1784). Observation of facts or empirical description cannot result in history. Even the bleaker versions of Schiller's slaughter bench need to postulate a continuity and a comprehensive gaze (pointing to either meaning or lack thereof). In order to have something like history we need to choose a particular viewpoint, that is, we need to presuppose a decision on what we deem relevant and a plan. Even merely finding a thread from Greek to Roman states presupposes a regulative idea as a guide, that is, a tendency to find in historical development a direction, a unitary sense, and a purpose. We would get a "planless *aggregate* of human actions" if we did not assume "at least in the large . . . a *system*" (Ninth Proposition, IaG, Ak 8: 29, ENG 118). The function of a regulative idea is that of enabling us to discover regularities, a pattern and a guiding thread to historical development. Only thus can interpretation arise. When, after speaking of reason as a seed growing irrespective of individual will or even awareness in the Architectonic of the first *Critique*, Kant writes that nature has placed in the human species its "germs" (ibid.) and claims that

16. See Allison, "Teleology and History," and Förster, "Hidden Plan."

whatever ends history may have for us are not consciously pursued by individuals, he underscores the strong affinities between the development of history thanks to nature and of reason thanks to its ideas.

5. An Overview of the Book

My interpretation of Kant in this book may appear markedly different from many contemporary readings. Yet it is not fresh and unprecedented, for in many ways it is as old as the debate among post-Kantians on the fate of metaphysics, reason, and transcendental philosophy at the turn of the nineteenth century.

I hope to convince readers that in Kant's case even less than others is it worth appealing to the authority principle. "Kant says that . . ." inevitably has long been the indispensable guide to the scholar, but it turns out to be insufficient to support any position at all and an outdated currency that can hardly be spent without our first establishing a comprehensive interpretation—without, that is, taking Kant's thesis of the authority of reason seriously. For Kant says many things and their opposite, especially about his own work. The third chapter aspires to do precisely this: understand why Kant shifts his views constantly and lends support, despite his best intentions, to the most reductive and partial takes on his philosophy.

In chapter 1 I highlight a tension between two images of reason to be found in the Architectonic: reason is a seed from which an organism grows internally as a systematically articulated unity, and it is an architect who plans the edifice of reason's laws. This tension reflects the two mirror-image sides of ideas. Ideas are both a totalizing drive based on reason's need to project a whole as a unitary scope for its objects and a necessary guide for reason's activities. At the same time, they fall short of the objective reality that pure concepts and intuitions have. It is difficult to deny that in the former case the criterion by which to judge ideas is an internal examination of their function (and of the interrelation of faculties in reason), while in the latter the criterion is objective meaning and the requirement of application to objects of experience. Unfortunately, it seems to me that when he does not favor the latter Kant often blurs the difference between these two criteria. This problem parallels the tension between a reason that finds itself, like an organism, with a life it has not made and a reason that is what it makes of itself. The tension is between life and poietic activity, between an organic and a constructive model.

The problems besetting these respective models are also quite different. The problem with the organic model is that a living body has an internal finality, but that for it to *be* the end of its functions and activities and for it to *set* itself and promote ends are by no means the same thing. The former is what every member of a species does, the latter presupposes individuality as that which distinguishes itself from the species. The problem with the projection of a world, by contrast, is that reason must be able to justify the claim that the world it produces is the same as the world in which it finds and experiences its objects—and not a tidy, neat, orderly dream. This tension proves to be, at best, an open problem for Kant.

The second chapter is an analysis of the concept of a priori synthesis in its different forms (i.e., mathematical, moral, transcendental, and metaphysical). The a priori synthesis involves several theses (such as that of objective reality, of pure reason's a priori legislation, which, as it turns out, means a production of its contents), and compels us to discuss in depth several surprisingly confusing topics (such as the presumed analyticity of philosophy; pure, mathematical, and empirical concepts; the meaning of 'a priori'; and the relative independence of sensibility).

The goal of the third chapter, as I suggested above, is to understand why Kant proves so indecisive about the definition of knowledge, the status of transcendental philosophy, the role of metaphysics, and the propaedeutic function that the critique of pure reason has with regard to metaphysics. I am not interested in determining whether a solution to the tensions that have been highlighted is compatible with the spirit of Kant's philosophy or compels us to move beyond it altogether. In some cases we will be able to do no more than acknowledge a plurality of meanings that cannot be reduced to one. The gain here, however, is that at least we will understand that when Kant does articulate an apparently clear-cut and definite position on certain issues—metaphysics, critical and transcendental philosophy, knowledge—he does so within a specific context that must be considered in a proper interpretation. In other cases, a reconstruction of the many shifts, hesitations, and subtle changes expressed by Kant will help us to understand how, and why, as early as the *Prolegomena* and throughout the 1780s and 1790s, Kant relentlessly modified and indeed began to abandon the standpoint of the first *Critique* on the positive role of ideas, the function of sensibility, the definition and internal articulation of pure reason, and the relation among faculties.

The final chapter is an appendix. It relates to a discussion in chapter 3 of the use of categories relative to noumena. It concerns a question whose importance for the success of the Transcendental Deduction, as well as for reason's causality through freedom, is obvious: does Kant think of categories as already schematized? It is a question that merits an independent and attentive treatment that would not have been pertinent in chapter 3. It is also, however, a question that I leave undecided because I cannot find a convincing or univocal solution to it in Kant's conflicting and ambiguous (when not contradictory) texts. For this reason I discuss it in the form of an antinomy.

CHAPTER ONE

The Architectonic and the Cosmic Concept of Philosophy

Newton saw for the first time order and regularity combined with great simplicity, where before him was found disorder and barely paired multiplicity; and since then comets run in geometrical courses. Rousseau discovered for the first time beneath the multiplicity of forms human beings have taken on their deeply buried nature and the hidden law by the observation of which providence is justified. Before that the objection of Alphonsus and Manes still held. After Newton and Rousseau, God is justified and Pope's theorem is true.

—I. Kant, *Bemerkungen, Ak* 20: 58–59, ENG 9

1. Reason's Needs, Interests, Dissatisfaction

In the first edition of the first *Critique* (1781), long before he realizes the implications of the notion of purposiveness and elaborates the critique of teleological judgment, Kant compares reason to an organism (*KrV* A 832–33).

Generally speaking a living body may be understood as a self-sustaining and internally organized independent being that is an end to itself. Reason has a life, and this implies it is not a neutral spectator, external and indifferent to its objects. In fact, it is inseparable from its interests and what it cares about.[1]

---

1. Kant would agree with Hegel, who takes the first premise of philosophy to consist in care for truth and trust in reason. Kant would therefore also agree with H. G. Frankfurt about care as both a primitive underivable and a self-referential notion (if I care about a course of action, I "care about caring about it," *Importance*, 87).

For an organism, living means turning its passivity into some form of activity. Reason's passivity includes feelings and needs it finds in itself. But needs demand recognition and an activity that fulfills them. This is how passivity begins to be turned into activity. Reason's neediness is not merely its unfortunate predicament of lacking what it desires, for this very condition reveals that it has drives and aspirations it deeply cares to realize. It is involved in its world. It has interests and on that account feels discontent with what it has. It actively pursues them insofar as it sets itself ends and promotes activities that give it satisfaction. Most of all, it values the importance of applying itself to the world in maximally coherent ways.

These are indeed analogies, but not arbitrary or imaginative figures of speech that can be replaced by other metaphors that might prove more adequate or appealing to our literary taste. Kant is describing how reason proceeds, what moves it, why and how, from its needs and desires to its highest and ideal aspirations. The internal necessity of his vocabulary, which borrows its analogies first from the language of the organism and later from that of an architect planning an edifice and of a personality setting itself ends, rests on its underlying theme, namely, reason's purposiveness.

Reason is famously described as allotted a destiny ("to be burdened with questions it cannot dismiss," *KrV* A vii) to which it is subject. It has drives that appear as insuppressible: most notably, it is bound to trespass limits whether it wills or not. Occasionally Kant speaks of reason's instinct.[2] When it comes specifically to reason's needs, he shows how potent they can become. Reason is moved by a fundamental need that guides it: the search for meaning. What "reason seeks and needs" (welches doch die Vernunft sucht und bedarf, *KrV* B xiii, my translation) is the constancy of laws: a sensible nature. In a conception we will have to discuss later, reason seeks itself in the world in the form of a necessary and stable order, for it knows it has insight only into what it has produced according to its own design.[3] This need to find meaning in its experience is a powerful drive for reason. It sets reason into motion, puts it to work, compels it to search for unity, necessity, a tight system of laws.

A need demands satisfaction. When it comes to reason's general needs, as the need for it to orient itself in the field of the supersensible, Kant adds

---

2. For example, the philosophical instinct leads to a systematic extension of knowledge ("Der Instinkt treibt den Philosophen zu systematischen Abhandlungen, und das hat einen grossen Nutzen in der Erweiterung der Erkenntnis": Erdmann 378).

3. Ibid. In the A Deduction Kant says that the understanding is naturally drawn to find regularities in the appearances. It "is always busy poring through the appearances with *the aim of finding some sort of rule* in them" (*KrV* A 126).

that reason has a "right" to see its needs satisfied.[4] And yet if reason seeks lawfulness in its objects, still it cannot find rest or satisfaction in its empirical use. Even a perfectly sensible nature will be insufficient to satisfy reason. Neither the unity of experience in which its pure concepts have a meaningful and legitimate use,[5] nor even mathematics with its shining examples of reason's spontaneous and synthetic advancements,[6] can appease reason and silence its ultimate questions.

If searching for meaning is reason's fundamental need, the most pressing and highest expression of this need is the search for answers, especially to the three questions outlined in the Canon and to the question of man's final destination (What can I know? What should I do? What may I hope?). Not only does this need exert the strongest pull, it is a drive that is at once an end. To put it more sharply: the drive becomes an end, an interest, once we *endorse* it and take it as our motivation.

If in its empirical use reason looks for the unity of appearances under rules, in its pure use reason is the power to go beyond the understanding's manifold cognitions to the minimal number of principles underlying and guiding the use of the understanding. When the series of conditions is given, reason looks for the subordination of the whole series under its maximum unity, its unconditional principle (*KrV* A 302–8/B 359–65). Thus reason produces the highest unity of knowledge. Reason's demand is also reason's maxim: to bring the understanding in its several rules to a complete unity with itself.

Reason rules the cognitions of the understanding, through whose mediation alone it is in contact with appearances. Reason acts on the understanding as the faculty of the unity of its rules under principles. In all this what reason demands is to go beyond experience, to the condition and the

---

4. *WDO, Ak* 8: 136–37; ÜGTP, *Ak* 8: 157. This need is based on the duty to transform the natural world into a moral world (see Nuzzo, *Ideal Embodiment*, 134). Among reason's needs, consider the following: reason has a need to find an absolute first beginning through freedom (*KrV* A 452/B 480); to assume the necessary existence of God (*KrV* A 603/B 631); to assume hypotheses in its speculative use, postulates in its practical use (*KpV, Ak* 5: 142, ENG 254); to find a lawful unity in the contingent (*KU* § V, *Ak* 5: 184, ENG 70), and to find a purposiveness in nature attuned to our cognitive faculties (*KU*, Introduction). On reason's interest, which is ultimately practical, see sections 1–2 of the Canon (*KrV* A 795–819/B 823–47), and the section on the primacy of pure practical reason (*KpV, Ak* 5: 119–21, ENG 236–38). Still, it would be mistaken to think of reason's desires, needs, satisfaction, interests, and so on as only practical. Pure reason has speculative needs, desires, and a satisfaction; it also has its form of interest in the maximum unity of cognitions (*KrV* A 686/B 714), and even in its ends and destination (*Bestimmung, KrV* A 651/B 679).

5. *Ak* 18: 286; *KrV* A 804/B 832; *Prol* § 57, *Ak* 4: 353, ENG 143.

6. *KrV* A 463/B 491; letter to Beck, *Ak* 11: 289–90.

principles that make experience possible as a coherent whole. And what it cares about and seeks is the maximum completeness for all concepts used, because only completeness can satisfy it (Prol § 57, Ak 4: 354, ENG 143; § 44, Ak 4: 332, ENG 123). The ideas are the shape in which reason can think the completeness at which it aims in a determinate way (ibid.).

The distinction between a speculative and a practical interest of reason, and between a metaphysics of pure speculative principles and a metaphysics of morals, follows from this. The complex evolution of the concept of the highest good, from its separate ideal status in another world to its becoming the historical goal of practical reason (from the Canon and the Postulates to the *Critique of Judgment* and *Religion*), must also be understood in this context. And so must, finally, the distinction between a satisfaction unattainable for us in speculative terms and a practical satisfaction we hope for. Strictly speaking, however, a speculative satisfaction does obtain, not in the form of final theoretical answers to questions concerning the supersensible that are bound to remain unanswered, but in that of a solution that finally puts metaphysics on a scientific path, which again has completeness as its key. Except that it is the completeness of a system of cognitions for which the negative determination of limits is constitutive. And this is the full satisfaction Kant refers to in the very last sentence of the *Critique of Pure Reason.*[7] Reason's satisfaction is its full self-possession. The language of satisfaction is the best way to represent the inner dialectic of reason, and expresses Kant's ambition to distance himself from ancient and modern conceptions of reason.

At the end of the Architectonic, Kant speaks of what the essay on Swedenborg first introduced: a sort of unrequited love reason has for metaphysics (*Dreams*, Ak 2: 367, ENG 354; *KrV* A 850/B 878). In the prefaces to the first *Critique* Kant returns to the theme through different analogies, all equally concrete and seemingly naturalizing, or even personifying, an all-too-human pure reason. In the A Preface (x–xi), Kant speaks of what reason must undertake and what it expects. He describes the task, to institute a tribunal, and says it is vain to pretend indifference toward metaphysics for in it lie reason's highest interests. In the B Preface, he announces the promise of a brighter future, when metaphysics finally assumes the secure path of science. Reason's love is unrequited because we are relentlessly sent back to metaphysics as to an estranged lover, who keeps leading us astray. Reason is not Luther's "whore." If anything, it is metaphysics that proves

---

7. "The *critical* path alone is still open . . . to bring human reason to full satisfaction in that which has always, but until now vainly, occupied its lust for knowledge" (*KrV* A 856/B 884).

to be as seductive as it is beyond possession. As in Aristophanes's myth in Plato's *Symposium*, metaphysics (here dogmatic metaphysics) is intrinsically disappointing for reason's love because what reason desires is a completion it cannot achieve, which metaphysics represents as a forever elusive mirage. This desire for completeness accounts for why lower forms of reason are directed outside reason, such as drives and impulses to trespass limits, which make sense only in light of the goal of completeness, of the totality they tend to.[8]

Especially if we are used to a reading of the first *Critique* that privileges the model of the natural sciences (notably, physics and mathematics), we may be surprised by the appearance of this teleological and quasi-psychological vocabulary precisely where we have to deal with what transcends nature and is altogether other than it, i.e., reason, and with science itself, from which teleology has presumably been banned. It might seem as if the model of science were progressively receding into the background as the Architectonic embraces the models of organic nature and of personality to articulate the essence of reason. But it would be quite wrong to conclude thus, for Kant's aim is precisely to turn metaphysics into a science and to understand reason as a system. This is invariably what Kant stresses and is proud of: he has made metaphysics into a science. The organic and practical models are instrumental in this characterization.

If pure reason is compared to an organism, with drives, needs, interests, maxims, and ends, it has a distinct form of teleology we must analyze carefully. And it is in a broad sense *practical* before the specific distinction between knowledge and morality. "It is still one and the same reason which, whether from a theoretical or practical perspective, judges according to a priori principles" (*KpV*, Ak 5: 121, ENG 237). Pure reason is a free power (*KrV* A 738/B 766) that determines its interests (*KpV*, Ak 5: 119–20, ENG 236) and pursues the ends it sets itself. This power is not a power of insight or description. It is a normative power. Whether it is addressed to what is or what ought to be, reason legislates over its domains and prescribes a form of conduct as its end. It commands us to look for the unconditional unity of

8. This love is all the more serious as it is fraught with tensions. It is a mature love, not the infatuation of young thinkers described by Kant in the *Prolegomena* (§ 35, Ak 4: 317, ENG 110) as seduced by a sort of fictional world replete with notions that cannot be refuted or confirmed. The tension between reason and metaphysics is comparable to that between imagination and understanding which the Dohna-Wundlacken Logic describes as "two friends who cannot do without one another but cannot stand one another either, for one always harms the other" (V-Lo/Dohna, Ak 24: 710, ENG 447). Except for the important qualification that reason's love is inherently asymmetrical.

our experience of nature as it extends our cognitions, and commands us to carry out actions according to maxims for categorical imperatives. Its interest is not formal consistency with itself, but the promotion of ends (ibid.).

It is crucial to keep pure reason's need distinct from all need arising from inclination and to distinguish between analogical and literal or descriptive discourse. When Kant speaks about the needs and interests of pure reason, he does mean they dictate its conduct. But they do so in a way that differs from how a need based on inclination makes us pursue objects.[9]

Pure reason needs to objectivize ideas, i.e., to find an object for its problematic concepts of complete and perfect totalities. In other words, a need responds to a problem. The problem arises because reason projects an idea for its consideration and wants to determine it. *Ideas are therefore those ideal totalities in which reason becomes aware of its internal articulation and limits.*

If a rational need is wholly different from a natural need, it is because reason is not a nature at all. Insisting on the interests, needs, love, and ends of reason and comparing reason to an organism do not come down to taking it as natural (if a very peculiar sort of nature). Reason is wholly unlike Hume's nature.[10] Kant's understanding of reason as an organism is a very effective way to highlight the functional and interdependent unity of all members within a whole, but we would misunderstand Kant if we took him to explain or describe human nature the way we describe living beings. Describing nature means for Kant bringing it back to laws, the laws through which we can get an insight into its workings. Nature is given to our investigation as an object of study and a well-defined being. Kant's reason does not purport to identify human nature, and not only because it is a *pure* reason, i.e., it looks for the principles according to which reason *must* think, not what individual minds or a presumed human nature happens to think. More fundamentally, reason is not a given or natural being alongside others

9. According to Kant, the distinction between subjective needs based on inclinations and desires and objective needs rooted in reason is what Thomas Wizenmann did not understand. Wizenmann had objected to Kant that it is illegitimate to infer an existence from a need: a man in love would desire nothing other than to give his fantasy an object. Kant rightly replied that, unlike inclination, pure reason does give rise to something real, in this case pure rational faith. Reason is productive (of a *will* that God exist: *KpV, Ak* 5: 143–46, ENG 255–57; for a discussion, see Beiser, *Fate of Reason*, 108–22). Having said that, I believe Wizenmann has a point when he writes that reason's need justifies a regulative, not a constitutive principle. Realizing morality is a duty, postulating God's existence and seeking the highest good is not.

10. Hume's nature "by an absolute and uncontroulable necessity has determin'd us to judge as well as to breathe and feel" (*Treatise* 1.4.1, p. 183). In Hume it is nature, not reason, that speaks in us. "Reason is nothing but a wonderful and unintelligible instinct in our souls" (*Treatise* 1.3.16, p. 179).

because it has the being of an *activity*. Far from being purely metaphorical, the language adopted by Kant to talk about reason is the most appropriate way to address an activity, not a given. Far from being psychological, this language denotes a pure spontaneity that produces laws.

Reason's proper activity is that of giving rules, laws, and ends to itself. If no laws or rules are given to reason, which is the only possible source and origin of all rules and laws and does not know of any authority outside itself it can pay heed to (*KrV* A xi–xii and n.; *PhilEnz, Ak* 29: 36), then hoping to bring reason back to laws is contradictory. For one thing, the comparison of reason with the organism is no more than an analogy: there is no naturalistic model or biological presupposition. For another, if we need an analogy at all, one with personality seems to fit reason better than that of organism because of reason's most vital concern, its preoccupation with our ultimate destination and final end. This form of teleology definitely has nothing natural. It is qua rational that we have ends, not qua living organisms. Ends are not comparable to bodily urges, drives, or desires we find in ourselves. Ends are such that we must take it upon ourselves to pursue them. We must make them ours for them to be at all.

In fact, reason's teleology is quite unnatural. Typically, an organism feels sorely a certain privation and works to fill the gap by measuring and adapting reality and itself to one another. It desires something and tries to obtain it, whatever struggle it takes. The organism hopes to put an end to its hunger, its poverty, its lack, its want. Here the *ends are given along with the lack*, and it must find the best means. Moreover, an organism is an individual among others in the same species.

This is not the case with Kant's reason. Reason cannot be declined in the plural. It does not pursue its ends in order to overcome its privation, for ends are not given to reason as necessitated.[11] Teleology identifies the mode of reason's activity, not a natural finality we find in ourselves. In other words, that reason is entirely occupied with its ends means that it is directed only to itself. Its unity is a self-enclosed organized unity of interests and ends.[12] Reason cares about and can apply itself only to laws and principles.

---

11. *KrV* A 797–98/B 825–26. "Rational nature is distinguished from all other natures by the fact that it sets itself an end . . . the end must be here conceived not as an end to be effected but as an independent end" (*GMS, Ak* 4: 437, ENG 87).

12. The autarchy of reason, entirely occupied only with itself and its self-knowledge, is a literal refrain disseminated throughout Kant's works. See, e.g., *KrV* A xiv; B xxiii, B 23, A 64–65/B 89–90, A 680/B 708; *Prol* § 40, *Ak* 4: 327–28, ENG 119–20; *GMS, Ak* 4: 391, ENG 47; *KpV*, Ak 5: 120–21, ENG 236–37; V-Met/Mron, *Ak* 29: 756, ENG 116. Among the *Reflexionen*, see 3716 (*Ak* 17: 259), 4284 (*Ak* 17: 495), and 4468 (*Ak* 17: 563), 4849 (*Ak* 18: 5–6). On reason as a

It alone can establish them. In its autarchy reason will not let any restriction stand in its way. It shows its "abhorrence" of limits and of all "principles that are not its own work" (*Ak* 18: 272–75).

Reason's unity as a self-enclosed organized unity is compared to that of an organism because we consider reason as if in it all parts were made in view of the whole, of a design, a project: an idea. Unlike a heap, growing externally by additions and subtractions, the organism grows internally without altering its proportions. In an organism every member "exists for the sake of each other as all others exist for its sake, and no principle can be taken with certainty in *one* relation unless it has at the same time been investigated in its *thoroughgoing* relation to the entire use of pure reason" (*KrV* B xxiii).

In the *Critique of Teleological Judgment* (§ 65), Kant adds important qualifications to this description drawn from the Second Preface to the *Critique of Pure Reason*. An organism is unlike a machine, i.e., the product of an external cause. Not only do the parts of an organism coordinate and exist so as to work together with other parts, but an organism is cause of itself. In it parts are reciprocally cause and effect of their form and reciprocally ends and means. A watch is organized; a living body organizes itself. Parts not only exist through one another and for the sake of the whole. They are to be conceived as organs. The organism then has a formative force (*bildende Kraft*), not just the moving force it receives from its creator, like a watch.

As if apprehensive about the implications of this thought, in the *Critique of Judgment* Kant rushes to add that the idea of the whole is only a ground of our cognition of the form of the object, not its actual cause. In the *Critique of Pure Reason* the system we thus obtain is the system of reason's cognitions, which reason needs for its purposes. In no way can it be confused with a system of reality or reflect an order given in nature, for no order can be given that is not instituted by reason. But it is precisely because reason is directed to itself that it can complete its systematic efforts. If reason is in need of guidance and a principle that hierarchically orders all its pure concepts, it is *subjectively* a system. It is "a system of inquiry in accordance with principles of unity for which experience alone" will provide fulfillment (*KrV* A 738/B

---

self-enclosed unity, see Yovel, *Kant and the Philosophy of History*, 12ff.; Velkley, *Freedom and the End of Reason*, 46ff.; and La Rocca, *Soggetto e mondo*, 218ff. On the life of theoretical reason, see also Dörflinger, *Das Leben*. I believe that speaking of *conatus* for the Kantian conception of reason's needs, as does Kleingeld ("Conative Character," 78ff.), is misleading. The modern doctrine of *conatus*, as it was proposed by such diverse figures as Hobbes, Spinoza, or Leibniz, was introduced precisely in order to reduce all of nature's efforts to the same laws, which is the opposite of what I am claiming is Kant's intention.

766). Reason is so self-contained that when approaching one part we cannot help touching all others. In the *Prolegomena* we read:

> But pure reason is such an isolated domain, within itself so thoroughly connected, that no part of it can be encroached upon without disturbing all the rest, not adjusted without having previously determined for each part its place and its influence upon the others; for, since there is nothing outside of it that could correct our judgment within it, the validity and use of each part depends on the relation in which it stands to the others within reason itself, and, as with the structure of an organized body, the purpose of any member can be derived only from the complete concept of the whole. That is why it can be said of such a critique, that it is never trustworthy unless it is *entirely complete* down to the least elements of pure reason, and that in the domain of this faculty one must determine and settle either *all* or *nothing.* (*Ak* 4: 263, ENG 59–60)

Kant returns to this aim (that metaphysics become science through a critique of pure reason) at the end of the *Prolegomena*, before he compares the critique to chemistry as opposed to alchemy and to astronomy versus astrology. He writes:

> a critique of reason itself must set forth the entire stock of a priori concepts, their division according to the different sources (sensibility, understanding, and reason), further, a complete table of those concepts, and the analysis of all of them along with everything that can be derived from that analysis; and then, especially, such a critique must set forth the possibility of synthetic cognition a priori through a deduction of these concepts, it must set forth the principles of their use, and finally also the boundaries of that use; and all of this in a complete system. Therefore a critique, and that alone, contains within itself the whole well-tested and verified plan by which metaphysics as science can be achieved, and even all the means for carrying it out. (*Ak* 4: 365, ENG 154)

Reason is a plastic and self-contained unity, which plans a systematic order for its two scopes of legislation, nature and freedom. But its gaze here, rather than on reason's products, is on itself, on the criteria of its production, on its need for an order of cognitions and how it satisfies that need.

Reason is "by nature architectonic" (*KrV* A 474/B 502) and plans its edifice independently of determinate cognitions. It is not instructed by the understanding but projects the thoroughgoing form of its cognitions and directs the understanding itself in its use. Reason does not borrow a model from the sciences. On the contrary, the sciences can assume a systematic form only when reason provides "the end and the form of the whole" (den Zweck und die Form des Ganzen, *KrV* A 832/B 860).

Kant's autarchic reason is not Hegel's, for it is not the soul of the world. Nor is it Hume's mind to which the world is inaccessible because the mind cannot step out of itself and is closed in its own sphere. Kant's reason is most essentially a lawgiver and a judge of its own laws. It uses its powers and critiques them. In the tribunal it sets up, its gaze is solely on itself. But it considers itself insofar as it is bound to transcend and extend itself beyond what it is.

Its legislation is directed toward two metaphysical realms, the speculative and the practical orders it constitutes. Unlike logic, reason is not occupied with its internal completeness at the explicit disregard of objects. Completeness for reason is the completeness that includes reason's objects (*KrV* B ix), except that its objects are none other than the laws and rules it formulates as it legislates over nature and morality.

2. Of Edifices and Organisms

I turn now to the Architectonic. I will show how it becomes increasingly complex as Kant employs analogies that shift from an edifice to an organism to personality. The coexistence of these analogies, roughly speaking from the realms of art, living nature, and morality, will turn out to be problematic.

The Doctrine of Method begins by casting a retrospective glance. On the opening page of the Doctrine of Method, Kant writes that in the Doctrine of Elements "we have made an estimate of the building materials and determined for what sort of edifice they would suffice" (*KrV* A 707/B 735). The ambition of erecting "a tower that would reach the heavens" had to fail (ibid.). The image evoked is that of "lack of material" (ibid.), but also of a bunch of unruly workers, dispersed and isolated, as in the story of Babel: poverty, but also disorder.[13] Now that we have made an estimate and seen with clarity the limits of what we can do relative to the means available, we can coordinate the efforts of masons, carpenters, plumbers, and so on who finally have individual specializations and form a team with mutually integrated and functional areas of competence. We can finally plan how to build a "complete system of pure reason" (ibid.).

13. One difference is that here the diverse languages are seen as a cause of disarray, not the effect of God's punishment of men's arrogance (Genesis 11: 9).

When we then turn to the Architectonic we find that the team of artists and construction workers needs more than an estimate and a coordination. The team needs an architect, who, as it turns out, has been planning the design of the edifice and directing the works all along. For no edifice can be built that does not have a plan guiding the workers and an executor of the architect's orders (either the architect or an assistant).

Differently stated, "the government of reason" (KrV A 832/B 860) over cognitions plans their interrelation and provides its operational outline. Notice that there is immediately a problem here (to which we will come back presently), for reason either deliberately and voluntarily erects a system (as seems to be indicated by the definition of the architectonic as the *art* of systems [ibid.]), or operates systematically irrespective of individual designs and projects (as the comparison of reason's idea to a seed two pages below clearly indicates). But notice also that the architect was behind the construction all along because the method is not an external arrangement of independently found contents and elements but the plan of the whole. The plan cannot be borrowed from established sciences, let alone serve as foundations for them. Contrary to the judgment of many, from Arthur Schopenhauer to Erich Adickes to Norman Kemp Smith to Jonathan Bennett, the method is not an external systematic form we must dismiss in order to get to the living contents of Kant's philosophy. The method is the scientific form operating and guiding the several systems of cognitions.[14]

Only a system transforms cognitions into a science. Failing that, cognitions remain an aggregate, whereas they must be conceived as an organism. This distinction runs through Kant's works, lecture notes, and manuscripts. Examples of aggregates include a sand hill (V-Met/Mron, Ak 29: 747, ENG 109; Ak 29: 803, ENG 157) as opposed to a pyramid, and similarly to the tower of Babel and the idea of a disorder born out of individualism and anarchy, a territory divided by settlers over time according to preferences without any respect for a sensible urban planning (EE § xii, Ak 20: 247, ENG 47). As we can see, the good of the whole must be kept in view as the goal. *Caring* about it is itself a criterion distinguishing aggregate from system. In an aggregate there is no internal connection between parts, which are rather

---

14. See Adickes's comments on the "weakest side" of Kant's philosophy, the unfortunate influence of his "äussere systematische Form," no more than "Zierraten" (ornaments) on the philosophical contents (*Kants Systematik*, 1–5, 119). See Lehmann, "System und Geschichte," 15, and Garelli, *La teleologia*, 9–10. The Doctrine of Method shows the plan and design organizing the edifice (KrV A 707/B 736; V-Lo/Dohna, Ak 24: 780, ENG 511: the way cognitions acquire scientific form). As the Pölitz Logic reads, the method is the practical part of logic giving the contents of theoretical logic the form of science (Ak 24: 597; see Capozzi, *Kant e la logica*, 261).

put together arbitrarily and almost by chance. By contrast, in a system every part is understood and known not just in relation to the others, but through that relation. Figuratively speaking, a system is not an external imposition fettering the parts. Instead, as an order made possible by a plan, it guarantees their mutual respect and keeps individual, naturally stronger drives from abusing and overpowering weaker ones.

What is striking about the example of the pyramid, in turn, is the ease with which the plan can be overseen. Gaps are visible. The solidity of the construction is verifiable. "With a sand hill we do not see if a grain is missing, but with a pyramid we do at once" (V-Met/Mron, Ak 29: 750, ENG 113). Gaps reveal deficiencies in construction that threaten to make the whole collapse. If the construction is based on an idea, "the parts, the connection of the parts, and the completeness of the parts is determined" (V-Met/Mron, Ak 29: 747, 803, ENG 109, 157). While an aggregate is a sum of parts, in a system the whole precedes the parts. In an aggregate parts are found and then added together. In a system they are made as parts in light of an idea. Because the plan (the idea) is the touchstone against which we judge the construction, we cannot judge wrongly.

As we can see, the comparison of reason with an organism takes us beyond its simple living unity. Reason's completeness is reached through its autarchy and independence when the relation between means and ends, and between parts and whole, is conceived in light of an idea. The image of the architect supplements that of the organism.

The use in the history of philosophy of terms relating to architecture, from Plato's *Timaeus* to Johann Heinrich Lambert, is well-known.[15] In Aristotle, who begins the *Nicomachean Ethics* with the notion of an architectonic of activities, the architect is not the one who creates or draws a plan to be executed, but rather the politician who arranges the several activities in a relation of means and ends according to a principle. This relation of ends to means seems to me the thought that Kant most forcefully applies in his Architectonic. Certainly it is the thrust behind the relation he sets up between philosophy and the other sciences that pure reason pursues: mathematics, science of nature, and logic. These three disciplines are very important for philosophy, but as means to an end. For the philosopher is the legislator of reason who arranges, controls, and disposes (*ansetzt*, KrV A 839/B 867) the artists of reason in view of reason's ends.

---

15. See Tonelli, *Kant's Critique*, 250–56, and Manchester, "What Kant Means by Architectonic," 624ff., and "Kant's Conception," 135ff.

It may be tempting to criticize the haughty superiority of philosophy as being self-delusional and part of an ideological tradition that we now take to be false. After all, the sciences seem perfectly capable of doing without philosophy. Indeed, philosophy itself is often taken to be subservient to other disciplines. But this temptation should be resisted, and it is important to note the ambivalence of this notion. Philosophy is itself only an idea we can hope to approximate (and through a work we must undertake), not a privilege we share. We will return to this notion shortly. What bears stressing is that if reason's most vital concern is with the ends it sets to itself, a logical or a scientist sense of reason is clearly ruled out.

Kant's opposition of system and aggregate concerns the *principle* through which parts hang together. It is objective, not subjective, i.e., it does not concern how we learn rational contents. We can say that the lack of scientificity of the aggregate of cognitions rests on its empirical source, common knowledge, and is comparable to the limits of historical knowledge, which is itself the lack of spontaneity (*Selbstdenken*). For if the aggregate of cognitions reproduces given materials as they present themselves, our effort at giving them an ordered arrangement is not required. The aggregate thus lacks form. In other words, in an expression borrowed from Hegel (and as Kant himself almost says of Georg Friedrich Meier in the *Wiener Logik, Ak* 24: 831, ENG 287), the problem is not the formality but the lack of form.

If we now come to the opposition between the scholastic and the cosmic or cosmopolitan concept (*Weltbegriff*) of philosophy, the lack of scientificity of the former is of a different sort. The scholastic concept of philosophy does not lack form, because it does aim at "logical completeness" (*KrV* A 838/B 866), at the systematic unity of knowledge. What it lacks is all concern with reason's ends.[16]

Reason is a self-contained unity. Still, nothing would be farther from my intentions than to ascribe to reason the futile desire merely to contemplate itself. It does want to give an ultimate solution to metaphysical questions. Kant is convinced he has offered us nothing less than that. Metaphysics is pure reason's edifice.

We must understand a critique of an edifice in two ways. So far I have talked about its internal articulation and inner limits. An edifice, however, is also limited with respect to what lies outside it, what is not it. But we would again miss the mark if we were to take this spatial analogy literally, for it breaks down at the most important junction, the concept of limit. The

---

16. Kant's position can best be understood in relation to Wolff and Meier. See Hinske, *Zwischen Aufklärung und Vernunftkritik*, 53–59, and Micheli, "L'insegnamento," 147–50.

limit must not be understood as a line that can be drawn at will, an external perimeter that leaves the inner contents it encloses intact. Understanding a building in its totality comes down to understanding it internally but also in relation to the surroundings, that is, to what it is not.

Prohibitions and constraints, which may be perceived as punitive or limiting, are meant to preserve the integrity of the whole. Such limitations have a *positive* function. When Kant compares the negative results of the critique of the three branches of speculative metaphysics to the role of the police (*KrV* B xxv), whose job is to prevent violence and allow for peaceful interaction, his revolution can be compared to that which marks the birth of modern political philosophy: we need limits to set up a new order. The negative is the condition of the positive. Machiavelli and Hobbes denounced classical political thought because it presumed to have identified the political good in an objective and natural order. In truth, at least by their lights, Plato and Aristotle simply wanted to impose one view, the philosopher's, on everybody else. To deflate this pretension Hobbes proposed a new concept of law based on prohibition, on setting precise limits to what we are free to pursue. Far from presuming to know the good and encouraging citizens to internalize laws issued according to such an insight in the shape of customs and a second nature, Hobbes's sovereign is the authority that establishes the bounds of the space wherein activities are allowed. The sovereign punishes all lawbreakers without any pretension of telling them what is objectively good for them. A law is now conceived negatively as the arbitrary tracing of a formal boundary between legitimate and illegitimate, not positively as a direction toward the good into which political philosophy has exclusive insight. Except that this negative line is the very institution of an order out of nothing. *The negative* is in this sense *at once negative and positive*. At the same time, what appears as a lowering of the goals of political philosophy hides a much stronger expectation, for the moderns consider the realization of reason in history necessary.

When reason critiques the ambition to trespass the confines of experience, for Kant it does so not because it gives up on its fundamental questions and wants to censor and suppress all metaphysics, but because it has understood something decisive about its limits and come to know itself in an unprecedented way. In other words, it is not censorship that is valued per se. Since 1766 Kant seeks a critique of reason, and metaphysics as a science of limits, precisely insofar as he is seeking reason's self-knowledge (*KrV* A xi–xii). But reason's self-knowledge can start only by the realization that it alone is the source of its own self-delusion and that it needs to be contained. That is why the passage on the "complete system of pure reason"

(*KrV* A 708/B 736) quoted above is immediately followed by the Discipline. That is why "system" should suggest not a grandiose edifice but an unstinting and rigorous invitation to metaphysical sobriety. As I was saying, the negative is the condition of the positive. At the same time, the theoretical intelligibility of the whole pursued by Plato and Aristotle is replaced by reason's duty to give its design a practical realization.

Kant writes that tracing reason's boundaries and disciplining our ambitions are seen with an unfavorable eye: negative judgments are seen as "jealous enemies" of our desire to expand our knowledge (*KrV* A 709/B 737). It seems to me that those readers of Kant who portray him as a positivist or as the Robespierre of metaphysics (Heine) fail to appreciate the intimate connection between reason's ends and its limits (I will not mention here anything about their preconception of metaphysics). Or, which comes to the same, they take limits in an exclusively negative sense.

Even if this comparison between the Kantian critical project and modern political philosophy proves to be useful, it is also limited. Pressing the political analogy beyond the scope I have outlined—the simultaneously negative and positive aspect of laws and limits—would be misleading, for reason's ends are not immediately political. When Kant understands reason as a lawgiver, he is exploiting a familiar trope in modern philosophy stretching from Machiavelli to Descartes and Rousseau. Reason is the principle of thinking and acting that all can freely make theirs. Neither "*religion* through its *holiness*" nor "*legislation* through *its majesty*" (*KrV* A XI) has a say once we have instituted the tribunal of reason where we publicly examine reason's claims.

This republican thesis,[17] however, finds its paramount application in metaphysics *before* it can be translated in political terms. What it implies is the imposition of an order on nature and freedom, which only through our laws acquire a coherent and reasonable structure. For Kant Kepler is at least as good an example of lawgiver as Rousseau, and probably a better one than Solon or Lycurgus or even Moses or Theseus, to name the examples most often cited in political philosophy in the period from Rousseau to Hegel.[18] Such lawgivers are founders of political orders. As such, they propose an organization meant to promote an idea through a civil religion, mores, and so on. Their decision is a *fiat*; their *will is law*. By contrast, and more like Kepler's laws, Kant's conception of reason's legislation is not directly related to politics or to arbitrary decisions. The focus is on the law a legislator

---

17. Brandt, *Die Bestimmung des Menschen*, 277.
18. Kepler "merits the title of a legislator of the heavens," *Refl* 778, *Ak* 15/1: 393.

issues, whether it brings order to what is given (nature) or to what must be instituted through freedom (right).

In the passage I used as the epigraph for this chapter, Kant says that Newton and Rousseau make us *see* things differently. After the institution of order they made possible, i.e., after they brought to light the order and unity underneath the surface thanks to their boldness, we all are in a position to experience nature and mores as run by laws.[19] And what is most important about a law is that once formulated it can always be subjected to public scrutiny. Just as the architect when planning an edifice verifies its construction as his or her orders are executed, so are lawgiver and judge complementary functions in reason's "negative legislation" (*KrV* A 711/B 739).

The chief object is therefore not politics but metaphysics, in Kant's sense of the word as the science of pure reason's a priori principles. Metaphysics and reason, insofar as they are innerly articulated in an edifice or an organism, are systems. A system is a whole in which all parts not only are dependent on and subordinated to an idea or end but *derive* from it (*KrV* A 833/B 861).

An idea, however, needs a schema for its execution. The idea becomes operative only once it can be translated into clear directions, orders, commands. Kant writes that whoever builds a science has a schema rather than an idea in mind. Often a schema, i.e., the explicit design and directions scientists give to the results of their research, falls short of the idea that must underlie the whole (so that the way the system is put together is technical as opposed to architectonic). This gap between idea and schema means that the idea, which has been there all along because no system can come to be without one, directs the organization more than the schema.

Except that the idea may not even be available to the scientist. It lives in pure reason, as an original seed that can be observed only through a microscope (*KrV* A 834/B 862). If we judge a science based on its author's description, we may fail to glimpse the idea (as we know Kant believes we must understand an author better than he understood himself: *KrV* A 314/B 370). The idea is independent of the individual scientists' intentions and aims. It reaches far beyond them and is their overarching and objective unity because it promotes reason's "essential ends" (*KrV* A 832/B 860) and is based on reason's "universal interest" (*KrV* A 834/B 862). This is why, says Kant,

---

19. In the "Idea for a Universal History" Kepler's audacity consists in subjecting to laws the eccentric paths of the planets "in an *unexpected* way" (italics mine, *IaG, Ak* 8: 18, ENG 109). This kind of talk returns most famously in the B Preface to the first *Critique*. See below, chapter 3, § 5.

systems appear to generate themselves spontaneously like worms whereas in fact they are generated by an idea and develop out of reason itself.

In sum, a system is made. But unlike an artifact or a building produced through a design, it is made by a spontaneity operating over the heads of individuals. If reason develops its system of pure cognitions out of its spontaneity, its making is more comparable to the generation of organisms in epigenesis than to the technical production of artifacts.[20] At the same time, the idea avails itself of deliberate efforts and designs. Without an idea a system is not architectonic. Without a schema and individual plans, the idea risks remaining dormant, forever concealed in reason. Kant needs both the organic unity of reason and the appeal to the architect.

The idea may elude us and remain opaque. Yet it, not the scientist, is the origin of science. The idea does not necessarily attain a complete realization. Yet it must function actively from the outset, however tacitly or unconsciously, if we are to glimpse it once the edifice it has generated is accomplished. In other words, the idea is first in the order of reality and of genesis. But if it lies hidden in reason like a germ still undeveloped and hardly recognizable (*KrV* A 834/B 862), and our best hope is to glimpse it once the system is complete, then it comes last in the order of cognition. As everybody knows, it also comes last in the exposition of the Doctrine of Elements of the *Critique of Pure Reason*.

The scientist's schema is the operative means to make an idea actual. It is properly a tool for a system construction, the outline of a completed whole, but like the arm guided by the mind: by the idea. The schema is a monogram

---

20. The notion of epigenesis is employed by Kant in a number of different ways, not all compatible. There is the analogical use of the biological notion in section 27 of the Transcendental Deduction and in the *Discovery* as the name for Kant's solution to the opposition between innate and acquired notions, between Leibniz and Locke-Hume, i.e., the original acquisition of pure concepts. On this, see Zöller, "From Innate to A Priori"; Oberhausen, *Das neue Apriori*, 86ff. (for remarks on Crusius as preformist and Kant's reaction), 91n (for Kant's astounding wavering on Leibniz's alleged Platonism), 123ff. (for the *acquisitio originaria* in the *Entdeckung*); and Barale, "Forme di soggettività," 253ff. There is also the use in its pertinent context—the reproduction, formation, and development of organisms—from the review of Herder's *Ideen* (and the harsh criticism of the teleology of the organic power in mankind's evolution assumed by Herder and Forster) to the *Critique of Judgment* (and to Kant's admiration of and personal relation with Johann Friedrich Blumenbach). On epigenesis, see Lenoir, "Kant, Blumenbach"; Roe, *Life and Generation*; Beiser, *Fate of Reason*, 150–58; Fabbri Bertoletti, *Impulso*, 19–94; Caimi, *Leçons*, 111–13. So far as I can see, the debate stretching from Caspar Friedrich Wolf to Albrecht von Haller, Charles Bonnet, and Buffon and the opposition of epigenetists to preformists form no more than a historical background. The notion starts acquiring a relevance for Kant, *before* he reads Blumenbach, with Johann Nicolas Tetens, who devotes essay 14 of his *Versuche* (2: 500–555) to a discussion of epigenesis and evolution.

according to the idea and a design used by the formative force (*bildende Kraft*) that the idea is. If the idea is a projected totality, the schema is the way it directs our intellectual drives, the plan for a concrete unification.[21]

Incidentally, the widespread view, based on Kant's standard description, is that imagination is but the mediation between understanding and sensibility. We can notice here that this characterization is unduly narrow. In the Architectonic a schema is the realization of an idea. It is reason that uses imagination's outlines and sketches. Except that these are neither derivative like empirical schemata or images, nor a priori determinations of time like transcendental schemata. Instead they function as pure sketches aiding reason's organization of its contents.

Such schemata are system-schemata, we could say. They do not reach out to objects. They cannot, not only because no idea can be exhibited. More importantly, they point to the mere form of a system, to reason's subjective organization of its pure cognitions, not to a classification of reality.

In sum: a system is an ordered arrangement of cognitions under one idea.

3a. Ideas. Reason's Internal Articulation

The analogy with the organism fits reason better than anything suggesting a voluntary design or a deliberate project, and living nature is a better model than art, insofar as the idea is a superindividual motive and force. The trouble with it, however, is that it downplays the active role scientists and philosophers have in conceiving and promoting the idea of a system. If the idea is like a seed, it seems to precede thinkers, who are reduced to the unwitting instruments of an impersonal reason. The suggestion of an involuntary or unconscious power of the idea can hardly be applied to reason's autonomous pursuit, the activity of philosophizing. The seed needs the architect indeed.

But if we turn to the analogy with the architect, we notice Kant's ambiguity. However strongly we may insist that an architect is not an artist because he/she directs artists, the architect nonetheless is an individual who plans, designs, and willfully produces on the basis of knowledge, intentions, and purposes. What is not as clear, as we are going to see presently, is if by architect Kant means the person who designs a building or the very plan

---

21. As an organizing tool, it is more than a symbol, which for Kant is the way in which we interpret reason's idea of system and reflect on it. For a contrary interpretation, see Lehmann, "System und Geschichte," 28ff.

behind the construction: either the schema or the idea.[22] And that points us to another problem. How distinguishable are plan and execution, idea and schema? If the idea of cosmic philosophy (philosophy's relation to reason's ends, to which we will turn presently) lives in and through its several historical manifestations, should we not say, conversely, that schemata are constitutive of the idea?

Let us take a closer look at ideas. We have seen that an idea of system is first in the order of genesis. It has formative power. Its spontaneity, unlike a natural one, is directed to one comprehensive end. All ideas are reason's concepts of the form of the whole. As such, they do not amount to the sum total of the parts, but precede and determine the parts. Each part refers to the end and the form of the whole (whereby 'form' and 'end' mean the same principle that shapes the unity among parts).

If we study the genesis of the term 'idea' in Kant's thought in the 1770s, we realize that it does not refer first and foremost to a supersensible being or to a system of reason's pure cognitions, but denotes a certain arrangement of parts. Since the whole informs the parts, in every part the whole is present and no member can be understood apart from its reference to all other members and to the whole: "wholly in the whole and wholly in every part."[23] In poetry an idea precedes the sentiments and images whose play it unifies. Ideas are essential for genius and art.[24]

In these *Reflexionen* of the 1770s Kant already establishes a connection of 'idea' to philosophy, system, art, genius, and organism.[25] Strikingly it is living nature and art, not the supersensible, that first provide the ground for ideas. These are generative processes presupposing a totality to its parts. *An idea is at once an end and a principle of organization of parts.* 'Idea' means a comprehensive design to be realized, in nature or art. A concept—whether an empirical concept as a class and function or a pure concept as an a priori rule for experience—is substantially different, for *a concept has no similar connotation of plan or project.*

This is the original core of the notion of idea, but in the Transcendental Dialectic Kant's stress is on the ideas' transcendence. Ideas are at once ends

22. Notice that a seed (*Keim*) is first an idea (*KrV* A 834/B 862) and later a schema (A 835/B 863). I return to this problem in section 5.

23. *Ganz im Gantzen und Ganz in iedem Theil*, Reflexion 945, Ak 15/1: 419.

24. Among other sciences, mathematics does not have ideas, unless it introduces a completely new method (a Kuhnean paradigm shift, we could say), as did Thales according to the B Preface of the first *Critique*. See *Refl* 943 (*Ak* 15: 418).

25. See *Reflexionen* 918, 921, 932, 933, 942, 943, 945, 961 (*Ak* 15: 403–29), and Tonelli, "Kant's Early Theory of Genius," 117ff.

and organizing principles insofar as they transcend the concepts to which they nonetheless comprehensively refer. They are essentially different and lie on a different level. The difference can be compared to that between a system and an aggregate, a whole and the sum of its parts, the universality of a concept and the generality arrived at through induction, duty, and even the best inclinations. If ideas are reason's ordering principle for cognitions, there is *nothing descriptive* about them. They cannot be drawn from experience, for their source is a paradigm or model (*Urbild*) that reason forges for its own use. It falls short to say simply that they are a priori. More than that, they are reason's autonomous pursuit and production (*KrV* A 313/B 370, A 548/B 576).

An obvious problem, however, arises at this point. If an idea can in no way be put together out of previous elements but governs the whole, i.e., if an idea is first, then is it not a given? Is it an original being we discover has been operative all along? If the origin is a cause, must it not be presupposed? Or must the origin and the cause be understood differently? What keeps us from calling this account a form of Platonism?

Simply this: even if reason's ideas for Kant are paradigmatic as concepts of a maximum or an unconditional perfection, they have no being. They are neither substances in the order of being nor substances for thought, i.e., fixed poles to be presupposed, for they are themselves a *result*. An idea does not come ready-made in reason. An idea is a concept of reason as it strives to bring to maximum coherence the use of the understanding (*KrV* A 305/B 362). On the one hand, this suggests that the maximum unity is not an acquired concept or a datum we can take for granted. It has to be produced. On the other, without reason's ideas the understanding is incoherent, like an aggregate without unity. It is like a series of distinct pictures that may each make sense internally but cannot be apprehended together in a coherent whole.[26] This is why reason is an activity of inquiry guided by ends, not a *theōria* of what is. The ends that orient and guide us are focal points. They are comprehensive outlooks to which we aspire, not givens we must discover.

An idea is never an abstraction or an assemblage of given materials. Unlike the understanding, the idea generates a unity that is not a synthesis of intuitions, a unification of the manifold in a concept, or the unity of

---

26. Reinhard Brandt has recalled for other purposes an image that would illuminate this point perfectly, Escher's paintings (see "Deductions", 183). My suggestion is that the understanding's cognitions without ideas are like Escher's paintings.

several concepts and cognitions in genera and species. The unity is purposive.[27] I mean that reason, which is here a full-blown activity that knows no boundary, projects a unity as a focal point. It is the idea of a maximum, i.e., a totalizing effort whose job is to indicate a direction we must pursue, not denote an actual object. If the understanding looks for an *identification* of the given, for a concept unifying the manifold, reason seeks to *comprehend* the given. It seeks to find for the given synthesized by the understanding its ultimate condition, which by definition is not given in and with the concept. The understanding's gaze is focused on its object. Reason's gaze is comprehensive and tries to include, along with the object, its other: its first and last, its condition and its consequences.

A look at reason's internal articulation helps us to shed light on this. *Reason as a whole* is divided into three faculties that direct themselves to different objects and function according to different rules. Still, they are not *disiecta membra*, isolated faculties to be treated each as a separate substantial agent. They are the different modalities of a unitary power.

A faculty generally can be distinguished from a power (V-Met Volckmann, *Ak* 28: 434) and a power from its substance.[28] Faculties can be taken as the faculties of the soul (of knowledge, desire, and feeling of pleasure) or as lower and higher cognitive faculties (sensibility, or understanding, power of judgment, and reason: *KU* Introduction, § 3). Finally, faculties can be shown to overlap with, substitute for, even become other faculties as their definition progressively changes in the course of a deduction.[29]

---

27. *Refl* 961 (Ak 15: 429). In the Collins Anthropology lectures, ideas are formed (*gebildet*), not inborn; they are shaped (*erdichtet*) through the inclination to give completeness to the wise man, the heaven, etc. (*Ak* 25/1: 98–99). There are thus rules for the formation (*dichten*) of an idea that belong in reason, and rules for the formation of images that belong in sensibility (ibid.).

28. Baumgarten did not adequately distinguish them, so that his definition of the *vis repraesentativa universi* was false (V-Met Dohna, *Ak* 28: 671, ENG 372–73).

29. I am thinking of the middle pages of the A Deduction. At A 106–9 understanding, synthetic unity, transcendental apperception, and original self-consciousness often complement or replace one another. At A 119 understanding, apperception, and imagination are inextricable, and the understanding is a product of the unity of apperception in relation to imagination. Here we bear witness to a fluidity, if not dialectical shift in meaning, role, and function, that has always troubled Kant scholars. I mention this conundrum only as an example of such fluidity of faculties. I am not interested here in offering yet another solution to it. See also this passage in the B Deduction (which in many readings has clarified matters once and for all by discarding the imagination): "It is one and the same spontaneity that, there under the name of imagination and here under the name of understanding, brings combination into the manifold of intuition" (*KrV* B 162 n).

But whatever the context and the aims of his talk of faculties, Kant is always adamant on two points: their orders are internally articulated, and they cannot be derived from a common principle. He would therefore agree with Descartes and Leibniz who insist that faculties are not isolated and abstract agents but names for the different modes of a unitary activity of the mind.[30]

Faculties are thus coordinated in a unitary effort and have mutual relations that constitute them. Sensibility is directed to the singularity of intuition. The understanding has an indirect relation to objects, through sensibility. *Reason proper* is not directed to objects at all or to a domain of its own. Instead, it is directed to the understanding, whose object is nature (the scope of appearances). If the understanding is the unity of appearances according to rules, reason is the unity of the understanding's rules under principles (*KrV* A 302/B 359). The ideas of reason therefore unify and direct all use of our faculties.

Some of the consequences we must draw from this are of the utmost importance. The understanding is like a good soldier under reason's command.[31] It is reason, it now turns out, that has needs, interests, drives, ends, not the understanding.[32] If reason legislates and the understanding is the arm realizing and executing reason's project, it is because the understanding's rules are means, while reason's laws determine the ends according to plans.[33]

30. Cf. Descartes's rule 12 of the *Regulae ad directionem ingenii* (*Oeuvres*, 10: 416) and Leibniz's *Nouveaux essais sur l'entendement humain* 2.21.6.

31. Speaking of this relation between reason and understanding in the Friedländer Anthropology, Kant says that subjects, soldiers, must listen, not reason ("So sollen die Unterthanen, die Soldaten, gehorchen, aber nicht vernünfteln," V-Anth/Fried, *Ak* 25/1: 546).

32. The only aim the understanding has is, as we have seen, that of finding a rule in appearances (*KrV* A 126).

33. On this contrast between rules and laws, see the Pillau Anthropology lectures (*Ak* 25/2: 777). On the understanding as obeying the commands of reason, which in turn cannot be ordered around, see the Collins Anthropology lectures (*Ak* 25/1: 158). On reason's intolerance of despotism in the sciences, and the Greeks as an example thereof until they subjected themselves to the "yoke" of Aristotle's philosophy, see the Friedländer Anthropology (*Ak* 25/1: 542). On the judgment largely shared in German thought before Kant, from Leibniz to Jakob Brucker, of Aristotle's philosophy as a 'yoke' implying servitude, see my *Hegel and Aristotle*, 402–3; on Kant's judgment of Aristotle as an artist of reason rather than a philosopher, see *PhilEnz*, *Ak* 29: 9, and *VT*, *Ak* 8: 393, ENG 434. Here is adumbrated the later distinction between the notions of technical and architectonical and between reason's legislation and cognitions. In the Friedländer Anthropology we read: "A minister needs only understanding in order to execute the king's commands, but he needs reason to make plans. Reason is as creative in the higher faculties as the *facultas fingendi* in the lower" ("So braucht ein Minister um die Befehle des Königes auszuführen, nur Verstand, aber um selbst Plane zu machen Vernunft. Die Vernunft ist eben so schöpferisch

Ideas order the cognitions of the understanding in a thoroughgoing purposive unity. We would misunderstand Kant's thought, however, if we reduced this prerogative of reason to a traditional sense of teleology. Reason is organized purposively because it is first and foremost a logical faculty. Unlike the understanding, a faculty of rules and judgment, reason is the faculty of inferences (*schliessen*), i.e., of ordering in syllogisms the understanding's cognitions for maximal coherence. The understanding treats particulars as instances of rules, while reason derives particulars from universals. Whether reason's inferences are logical conclusions or illegitimate leaps, reason is the faculty of passing from the series of conditions to its principle. Instead of producing its concepts through a unitary *reflection* on appearances, reason obtains its ideas through an *inference* from concepts to their condition and consequences (*KrV* A 310/B 366–67).

In its *logical* use, reason abstracts from all content, while in its *real* use it is the *source* of ideas. This is why it is called the faculty of principles, which strictly speaking the understanding cannot have because it cannot produce cognitions through concepts alone but always needs intuition (*KrV* A 301/B 358). This is how Kant reconciles the two senses of reason he has isolated and discovered as reason's divergent poles: the production of inferences and the production of noumena, that is, positive ideas of the unconditional such as freedom.

This makes ideas indispensable for all use of our faculties, including for the understanding's knowledge of nature. Without ideas the concepts of objects afforded by the understanding would at best give us an aggregate of many cognitions. Indeed, they could not even be formed in a unitary and thoroughgoing way (*KrV* A 651/B 679). The form of the whole or idea "precedes the determinate cognition of the parts" (*KrV* A 645/B 673). Such "concepts of reason are not created by nature, rather we question nature according to these ideas, and take our cognition to be defective as long as it is not adequate to them" (ibid.). The scientist's idea of pure air (and of pure elements generally) is not derived from observation of nature. It is rather an idea that makes possible the progressive abstraction in the investigation of nature.

---

in den Oberkräften, als die Facultas fingendi in den Unterkräften," *Ak* 25/1: 545). Later, in the *Critique of Judgment*, once Kant has contrasted determinant judgment to reflection, he will lean decidedly toward a purely mechanical sense of the understanding's operations: "the understanding proceeds necessarily unintentionally, in accordance with its nature" (*KU*, *Ak* 5: 187, ENG 74; Guyer and Matthews's translation skips *nothwendig*).

Ideas define the goal of all inquiry. They are methodological guides. Ideas do not constitute objects or make possible knowledge of objects. They are themselves no more than maxims, subjective guides regulating the understanding. They are also the expression of a *need* felt by reason that cannot find satisfaction in the understanding's knowledge of appearances: the need to project a coherent whole before its gaze.[34]

The brilliant discovery that Kant makes here is that, far from being irrelevant for objective purposes, reason's subjective need to project a whole gives rise to ideas, which in turn give rise to a system of cognitions, a world. As the *Prolegomena* says (*Ak* 4: 359, ENG 148), ideas bringing the understanding to the highest possible coherence with itself grant "the greatest possible use of reason within the world." The confusion of maxims of reason for objects, or of ideas for a natural or cosmological order, is inevitable and we must watch out for it. But *this* is the satisfaction reason was looking for. Representing the world as if it were a totality accessible to us on which reason can get a grip and in which reason can be relatively at home (even if eventually it turns out that ideas have only a practical or regulative use) is the satisfaction reason was looking for.

Ideas are not on the one hand the source of the illusions of metaphysics and on the other guides for our research. They are the origin of illusion just because they are at once a totalizing drive. They are heuristic means for our knowledge of nature, directing induction and research in the empirical sciences, precisely insofar as they tend beyond nature to its ideal and maximum unity and are not abstracted from cognition of nature. Reason's speculative interest lies in what transcends the cognitions it has: in what is beyond the crumbs of experience. However fertile its lowlands may be,[35] reason is bound to look farther.

Kant, however, seems to do his best to obscure this discovery. Of the Dialectic he emphasizes time and again the negative results and the critique of special metaphysics. As in an afterthought, he then relegates the positive and indispensable function of the ideas to an Appendix. This is the amazingly unfortunate choice of a terribly misleading title. It suggests that the Appendix is a corollary, if not a virtually superfluous addition, to the destructive function of the Dialectic.

Further evidence of this tendency to obscure emerges if we consider these two conflicting passages. The former reads: "*transcendental illusion*

---

34. The *desire* or predilection for unity (*favor unitatis*) was the name for this *need* in the *Dissertation* (§ 30, *Ak* 2: 418).

35. "Mein Platz ist das fruchtbare Bathos der Erfahrung" (*Prol*, *Ak* 4: 374n, ENG 161n).

[*Schein*] . . . influences principles whose use is not meant for experience [and] carries us away beyond the empirical use of the categories" (*KrV* A 295/B 352). Now contrast it with this: "transcendental ideas . . . have an indispensable necessary . . . [use] . . . if besides the objects before our eyes we want to see those that lie far in the background, i.e., when, in our case, the understanding wants to go beyond every given experience" (*KrV* A 644–45/B 672–73).[36] Why does the former passage conclude that unless checked by critical philosophy this misuse leads to transcendent (illegitimate) principles, while the latter takes deception (*Täuschung*) and illusion (*Illusion*) as not simply necessary, but indeed quite useful? (In fact, they are so useful as to be compared to the principle of perspective in mirrors, thanks to which we can see the objects behind our back.) Why is every Kant scholar thoroughly familiar with the former and only some immediately recognize the latter? I am afraid the answer is plain enough. This time it is Kant who architectonically separates negative and positive and gives the impression we can feed our preference for what we like better. After 1781 his preference goes more and more decidedly and exclusively to the negative results of the Dialectic.

3b. Ideas. Regulative Ideas and Empirical Cognition

An unfortunate pattern in the way Kant gives misleading indications or inadequate reformulations of some fundamental themes in his work begins to emerge. We will return to this point especially in chapter 3. The basic problem here, it seems to me, is the supposed opposition between 'regulative' and 'constitutive.' A few distinctions are in order to summarize how this opposition arises and allow us a more insightful grasp of the problem this gives rise to.

When he introduces the distinction between mathematical and dynamical *principles of the understanding* in the Analogies of Experience (*KrV* A 178/B 221ff.),[37] Kant explains that the former (Axioms of Intuition and Anticipations of Experience) are *constitutive of objects* of intuition with regard to their possibility, while the latter instead are regulative for them, with regard to their existence. Still, the *regulative* principles of the understanding are "constitutive in regard to experience" (*KrV* A 664/B 692): they are not required for our intuition of objects, but they are required for our experience

---

36. David Lachterman notes this contrast, but unfortunately only in passing ("Kant," 196).

37. The understanding's principles are *Grundsätze*. In the passage (*KrV* A 301/B 358) mentioned above where Kant claimed that only reason has principles, the term was *Prinzipien*.

as an interconnected synthetic unity of cognitions of appearances. The difference is between *objects* we can intuit and *events*, i.e., relations among given intuitable objects. The regulative principles of the understanding, Kant writes, make possible a priori the concepts without which experience would not be (ibid.). As a result, the constitutive and regulative principles of the understanding are not two different kinds of principles with different claims to necessity and validity. Let me rephrase this point for the sake of clarity through the admittedly inelegant repetition of 'constitution': the regulative principles of the understanding constitute relations among the objects constituted by the mathematical principles of the understanding.

In this case we are speaking of the constitution of the understanding's concepts of objects and events respectively. In the case of the *principles of reason*, by contrast, we have in view a unity and order of the concepts of the understanding, not of objects or events. The unity that ideas of reason provide cannot be shown to be in any way given, i.e., it cannot aspire to reality. It is no more than a guide for the understanding. Regulative ideas of reason, however, project for the understanding ends that extend its use in experience. This use can aim at a greater empirical unity than what the simple constitutive and regulative principles of the understanding could afford. The regulative ideas of reason extend the cognitions of the understanding with regard to experience. They are indispensable to promote empirical cognition.

Kant's example of chemistry provides a good illustration of this epistemological principle. I said earlier that the chemist's idea of pure air is not derived from observation of nature through progressive abstraction. It is rather the progressive abstraction in the investigation of nature that is made possible by an idea that comes first. Kant writes that it is admittedly hard to find pure earth or pure air or pure water (*KrV* A 646/B 674). Why, we may want to ask, would we need such ideas in our natural investigation? Kant would reply that they are required in order to reduce all materials to earth (weight), salts and combustibles (force), and finally to air and water as vehicles, and this reduction in turn explains the chemical effects of materials in accordance with the idea of a mechanism. Accordingly, concludes Kant, it is easy to discover the influence of reason on most classifications of natural scientists (*KrV* A 646/B 674).

It is interesting to notice how in Kant's epistemology empirical sciences are not content with observing or registering general regularities about their objects. Without the guidance of ideas, hypotheses, and experiments, that is, without the hypothetical use of reason, observation is sterile, and empirical sciences would not go far. It is even more interesting, however, to raise the question of which sciences adopt, or are bound to be led by, this epistemological principle, and quite instructive to realize why Kant's example should be chemistry. As I pointed out above, mathematics does not have ideas. What explains this contrast? In mathematics we "do not proceed from the whole to the parts but from the universal to the particular" (*Refl* 943, *Ak* 15: 418). In chemistry instead we have a hypothetical use of reason, not an apodictic proof structure as in mathematics. Ideas are not necessary if all we need to do is follow rigorously the steps of an intuitive construction. Unlike chemistry, then, mathematics does not need reason proper, even if, as we will see in the next chapter, it does need the imagination perhaps even more than the hypothetical use of reason in chemistry does. In a 1789 letter to Marcus Herz, Kant criticizes Salomon Maimon's introduction of "ideas of the understanding" in mathematics (for example, the infinite divisibility of a line). The fact that a property can be predicated of the *totality* of lines requires a Kantian idea, thinks Maimon. Kant rebuts that the mathematician does not make use of the *idea* of whole, for it is a logical function of the universality of judgment that a property applies to "each" line (not to the "totality of lines," *Ak* 11: 52–55).

But there is another reason that Kant does not mention (here or elsewhere I am aware of) but that can be reconstructed from his arguments. Unlike the mathematician, whose only object is pure intuition, i.e., an idealization, the chemist is working with sensible matter. In fact, the chemist's job is to a good degree that of finding ways to reduce empirical intuition to simple and pure elements. The mathematician must not be guided by the idea of a pure triangle the way the chemist must be guided by the idea of pure water, for an impure triangle does not exist. As we will see in chapter 2, a triangle can be empirically instantiated as the side of a pyramid, but that does not make the triangle less pure a figure than it is for the geometer who studies its properties in isolation. The chemist is busy with sensible elements, not pure intuitions. And here *approximation to an ideal* is pertinent; in fact, it is key. A drop of water will always contain residues of several elements in nature (traces of calcium, sodium, magnesium, etc.), but the chemist will allow only reason's idea of pure water to guide his or her research. It alone makes possible the empirical concept and definition we use in chemistry: hydrogen and oxygen.

The term 'regulative' in the principles of the understanding and in the ideas of reason has thus two different meanings. But this does not make the regulative ideas dispensable or optional for the understanding. The heuristic value of the ideas of reason is not a methodological expedient. Ideas are not simply economic—a useful tool that the understanding would be well-advised to adopt. For the understanding ideas are *necessary*. Kant puts it thus: "the law of reason to seek unity is necessary, since without it we would have no reason, and without that *no coherent use of the understanding, and, lacking that, no sufficient mark of empirical truth*" (*KrV* A 651/B 679, italics mine). In particular, without reason's principle of genera and species "no empirical concepts and hence no experience would be possible" (*KrV* A 654/B 682).

Among the countless deficiencies of the standard reading, which finds the heart of the first *Critique* in the Aesthetic and Analytic, this incapacity to see experience as ultimately rooted in reason's ideas is one of the more egregious. The idea of a systematic unity of the understanding's knowledge helps us discover a principle for the use of the understanding by directing it to cases that are not given so as to make it coherently connected (*KrV* A 656/B 684). Through the assumption of systematic unity (homogeneity, specification, and continuity of forms), reason both arranges the understanding's concepts and gives rise to new concepts as it fills in the gaps the unassisted understanding is bound to leave. Indeed, if the understanding is guided by the law of specification, it seeks always further differences and suspects their existence even when the senses are unable to disclose them (*KrV* A 657/B 685). Without ideas—without the assumption of nature as a system—no empirical discoveries are possible.

There is more, however. As we can see, empirical truth depends on the *use* of the understanding, but that use itself depends not on the understanding but on reason. The law of reason is "to *seek* unity" (that is, not to *discover* a supposedly given unity it has only to *inspect*). But in this search reason presupposes "that this unity of reason conforms to nature itself; and here reason does not beg but commands" (*KrV* A 653/B 681). Reason's need to project a whole is subjective, but this search demands the evidence of objective and empirical results. For the purposes of knowledge of nature, regulative ideas *in themselves* are heuristic fictions, as Kant reminds us again in the Discipline ("*heuristische Fiktionen*," *KrV* A 771/B 799), but the *use* of regulative ideas is not a heuristic fiction, for it helps the understanding to attain an *actual* system of empirical cognitions.

In light of this, the contradiction regarding the objectivity of the maxims of reason that seems to mar these pages turns out to be only apparent. At A 648/B 676 Kant distinguishes the logical principle by which reason helps the understanding to make progress in its empirical cognitions from the transcendental principle according to which the constitution of objects is a systematic unity. Since it is a *maxim* of reason to *seek* unity (i.e., unity is not available to simple observation), Kant seems to suggest that the latter principle is illegitimate. At A 651/B 679 instead he writes that we must presuppose the systematic unity of nature as objectively valid and necessary.[38] In truth, the contrast is resolved when Kant claims that the logical principle presupposes the transcendental principle, which extends itself to the principle of systematic unity articulated in the three transcendental laws of homogeneity, specification, and continuity of forms.[39]

So far so good. Kant would have every reason to lament he has been misunderstood if we conflated the meanings of 'regulative' in the principles (*Grundsätze*) of the understanding and the principles (*Prinzipien*) of reason and if we took a 'regulative idea' as a sheer heuristic fiction or logical principle. Ideas are regulative, but what they regulate is the experience they make possible. Reason's subjective needs make possible induction and investigation of nature through the homogeneity of nature's empirical laws. Ideas are constitutive of reason's legislating activity and thereby of the search for a system of cognitions and thereby, finally and however indirectly, of a system of objective laws. If the homogeneity of nature is "a necessary law" and a "transcendental presupposition" (*KrV* A 651/B 679), reason's ideas stand or fall with their making possible a unitary experience of nature. The proof to which reason's ideas can aspire can be none other than the systematic connection of a unitary experience. The unity of experience as the product of reason's principles is the source of legitimacy for reason. Only thus can subjective principles ultimately contribute to grounding objective laws. Only thus can ideas be necessary for knowledge.[40]

Unfortunately, however, this is not what Kant stresses more often. Why does Kant insist rather on the exclusively regulative function of ideas? Occasionally he does give us precious indications otherwise, as when he writes that ideas are not dialectical but become dialectical once we are inattentive and misunderstand them (*KrV* A 680/B 708). In themselves maxims to promote indefinitely the empirical use of reason in view of reason's end, which is to lend systematic unity to its cognitions, ideas are understood

---

38. The passage in question is the continuation of the one on empirical truth mentioned a few lines above: "the law of reason to seek unity is necessary, since without it we would have . . . no sufficient mark of empirical truth; thus in regard to the latter we simply have to presuppose the systematic unity of nature as objectively valid and necessary" (*KrV* A 651/B 679).

39. *KrV* A 650/B 678, A 657/B 685ff. In the *Dissertation* (see § 30 regarding the principles of harmony, *convenientia*) what are here called *regulative* ideas were a *method of inquiry*. For an interesting attempt at finding in the Canon and in the practical ideas of God and immortality the other side of reason's systematization for the demands of morality, like the foil to the idea of systematic unity in empirical knowledge of appearances, see Rauscher, "Appendix."

40. Because ideas are the thought of what transcends what is experienced, Kemp Smith aptly writes that "the metaphysical is immanent in our knowledge" (*Commentary*, liv).

instead as representations of objects. In order to represent to itself this un-conditional as determinate, reason misunderstands the completeness at which it aims.

This precious point is itself both telling and problematic. It is (1) telling in that it shows that the question to which Kant regularly returns is ever the same: whether or not an object corresponds to ideas.[41] This is the question of the Transcendental Deduction of the pure Concepts of the Understanding: the need for a foundation that he rehearses here in the Dialectic (as shown by his several inconsistent references in these pages to a "deduction" of ideas). This foundational question is a concern with *objective reality*. Ideas have no corresponding object or reality.

But this foundational question is (2) problematic because it tends to obscure what I have called the constitutive role ideas have for reason's leg-islative activity, and is thus bound to *undermine the positive function of ideas*. It is no wonder that ideas as reason's indispensable guides progressively disappear from Kant's horizon after 1781.

It is a pity that Kant did not consistently recognize and value the im-portance of ideas he introduced. If his concerns had been less biased (i.e., if he had not imposed the problems of the understanding's pure concepts from the Transcendental Analytic onto reason), he could have asserted more forcefully what he otherwise discovers and teaches: that is, ideas are not a failed correspondence with what can never approximate them, but the way reason guides, projects, and produces itself. Ideas are thought's inner life and activity. They do not serve to ground an impossible possibility of ob-jects. They are the unconditional and autonomous element in which reason produces its inner unity and pursues its ends.[42]

We saw that reason is both defendant and judge in its courtroom. In a trial no mistrial can be suspected if the judge remains impartial and calls all relevant witnesses to testify; otherwise he or she could be recused. Now it is as if in this trial reason stopped being the prosecutor of itself, and the understanding, from the instrumental role of good soldier under reason's command, suddenly became the accuser that presses its charge against rea-son proper. The problem is that by itself the understanding cannot have this ambition, for it has no ends, will, or desire, as we saw. It is therefore reason that has let it rise to this new position of power, in fact lent it its power. We may speculate that this is possibly because, in the typical insecurity or

---

41. This point is repeatedly stressed by Hegel (see for example the 1830 *Encyclopaedia*, §§ 46–47).

42. This criticism is indebted to Barale, *Kant*, 208, 223.

guilt of philosophers, reason either has a bad conscience about governing a subordinate whose concrete results in the sciences far exceed its own or is envious of its soldier. But this does not change the fact that it is reason that has let one of its own parts take over. It is reason that has appointed it judge.

It is Kant who undermines the positive function of ideas and runs the risk of misrepresenting if not misunderstanding the comprehensive import of his own project.

3c. Ideas. The Idea of System

Kant can stress the negative result of ideas over their inner dialectic and their positive unifying function and can, more fundamentally, separate positive and negative because he thinks that reason can be separated from its employment. By separating reason from ideas and blaming dogmatism on the *misuse* of reason, he wants at once to destroy the pretensions of special metaphysics that lead us astray and, through his *cathartikon*, rescue reason from being dragged to its eventual collapse in this downfall.

Let me propose a different angle from which to view the same ambivalence regarding ideas as respectively an independent object of investigation and the result of a self-defeating thought combining in itself intuitions and concepts: Ideas appear at once as a *first* and as a *last*.

I have been emphasizing the unifying role of ideas. But the division internal to and the dialectic of ideas should never be lost sight of. Kant has introduced both, but emphasized neither as strongly as the negative result of the dialectic. In the antinomies, reason is divided against itself. Intuitions are necessary to interpret concepts referring to the world: say, spatiotemporal finitude vs. infinity. But this implies that when reason thinks its ideas (as it tries to determine them and give them a content), it is bound to contradict itself. For example, all spatial or temporal attributes predicated of infinity finitize it.

Ideas are the highest unity. But theirs is always a unity run through by a tension. If the understanding is a good soldier, it is never a docile or submissive instrument in the hands of reason. When unwatched, or confidently invited to join reason in its activity, it wreaks havoc in reason's unity.

This is reflected in Kant's notion of idea as at once an original totality owing nothing to its conceptual elements and a result: that is, a first and a last. Kant is asking us to think together two seemingly incompatible theses:

1   the thought of the whole precedes the knowledge of its parts;
2   ideas are the result of an inference.

According to (1), ideas are principles and reason's original totalities. According to (2), ideas are the understanding's schematized concepts freed from the limitation of possible experience.[43]

Whatever the lesson we must draw from all this, e.g.—ideas always and intrinsically refer to the intuitions and concepts that threaten to mar their consistency—all ideas qua totalizing efforts are systematic. We cannot separate an idea of system from the several metaphysical ideas. Still, one difference is that systematicity is the main if not the sole business of the *architectonic* idea. The idea of a system is the highest idea. At the same time, it is a purely methodological one. It represents the world as if it were a totality accessible to us (*KrV* A 672–73/B 700–701). This formula, as-if, will later be the constitutive dynamic of reflective judgment and the principle of analogy.

In these pages of the first *Critique,* viewing nature as if it were ordered according to reason is a principle of systematic unity regulating the use of the understanding, which itself achieves at most synthetic unity. The purposive unity of things regards the order in the world as if it had originated in the purpose of a supreme reason (*KrV* A 686–87/B 714–15).

In the *Critique of Judgment,* which is not, as is often thought, a book on art and organic nature, Kant inverts this perspective and offers his most mature form of critical reflection on the architectonic of reason. The First Introduction calls the third *Critique* "the system of critique of pure reason" (*EE* § 11). It is the pursuit of the problems originating in the sections discussed so far and stretching through the second *Critique.* In the third *Critique* purposiveness becomes the a priori principle of reflection, itself guiding the search for systematic unity. Here, too, the concept of a system of nature is "entirely alien to the understanding" (*EE* § 2, *Ak* 20: 203, ENG 9), except it is no longer reason's idea but the transcendental principle of the power of judgment (*EE* § 4, *Ak* 20: 209, ENG 14). Systematicity is subordinated to formal purposiveness as one of its aspects. Reason's idea of totality is now subordinated to a principle of reflective judgment. The whole conception of *ars inveniendi,* thinking and investigating nature heuristically, changes. Pure reason's ideas, which in the second *Critique* are actualized practically through freedom's causality but simultaneously deprived of positive speculative function, are brought back to our attention in the *Critique of Judgment* in the notions of a technique of nature and aesthetic ideas. Now beauty and

---

43. A good example of (2) is this passage: "reason cannot really generate any concept at all, but at most can *free a concept of the understanding* from the unavoidable limitations of a possible experience" (*KrV* A 409/B 435). On this ambiguity, indeed this dilemma, see the appendix below on schematized categories.

organic nature are exemplary realizations of a more basic purposiveness for reflective judgment. At the same time, the final end finds a new access to Kant's philosophy in its connection with ethico-theology.

Unfortunately, we cannot follow this line or the many consequences of this shift. We are now, however, in a position to grasp why 'end' and 'form' are used as synonyms in the Architectonic and thus to answer the questions raised earlier. An idea, far from being presupposed, is a projected unity, a focal point we tend toward. It is an end and a principle of organization. As such, it guides our construction of the whole. This amounts to saying that it is a cause of the whole insofar as it is an end. In this narrow and precise sense, we can say that the end is at the beginning.

4. A Comprehensive Gaze: The Cyclops and the Cosmic Philosopher

Historically, the notion of a system and that of a systematic plan for investigation have separate roots. In Greek philosophy completion is expected, if at all, of a system as an ordered arrangement. But this order belongs to the cosmos as a *taxis*, and not to our cognitions. Indeed, the starry heaven is the exemplary case. Once the metaphor of a tree or of an encyclopedia of sciences (*arbor scientiarum*) is formulated at the dawn of modernity by Bacon and Descartes down to D'Alembert, and the idea of organism replaces that of an objective structure in nature, a system in development becomes a given and self-sufficient order. As a consequence, it will be more and more difficult to separate nature's order from reason's system.[44]

Here, too, Kant brings this tradition to a halt. The world reclaims its rights. But it does so because it is reason's thought of an unconditional totality, not in virtue of its having a natural or cosmological order.[45] The world, qua universal connection of all things according to a principle in a *universitas* and *totum* (as the *Dissertation* characterizes it, § 13), is itself paradigmatic for Kant's conception of idea.[46] Kant drives a wedge between nature and

44. For Plato and Aristotle philosophy is more about *diairein* than about an independent construction deriving from an idea. They do use the word 'system,' but meaning a union (an aggregate, in Kant's words). It is with the Stoics that the word 'system' acquires the meaning of a self-enclosed whole we still attach to it. See my *Hegel and Aristotle*, 56–65 and 82–91.

45. See Brague, *Sagesse du monde*, especially chapter 14.

46. The idea of the world is presented as the correlate of the transcendental ideal. Both totalities, as such, are unique (this comes up regularly in the *Opus Postumum*: e.g., "Es ist ein Gott und eine Welt," *Ak* 21: 24). Still, the totality of the world is less comprehensive than the *omnitudo realitatis* or whole of all conditions that God is. As Heidegger notes, the world is beyond all

what becomes the world as an object of thought. Nature is the thoroughgoing unity of appearances under the understanding's rules. The world, like all totality, is in principle on a different level from nature. It cannot be known, nor is it an ontological presupposition or a metaphysical warrant. For it has to be made, and again it is made as a *totum*, not a *compositum*: as a system, not an aggregate. Only thought can give rise to a world because the world is itself an idea. Conversely, ideas form a world, a system—*an organism*—unto itself. System and ideas are divorced from nature in order that a nonnatural world can emerge. Actually from the perspective of cognition, this systematicity is a detour through which we eventually come back to nature; but more important is the fact that the intelligible order is unconditional and does not derive from observation of nature in any way. In it, reason's speculative and practical interests are unified. All of reason's employments stem from the same original unity in thought.

From now on in Kant's thought the connection between world, ideas, and ends becomes constitutive. Indeed, this connection turns out to be immanent in all of reason's activities. If the whole is *prior* to the parts, no question is intelligible in isolation, in and of itself. No rational activity can be pursued independently of the larger picture—the guiding ideas—it has to fit into. If the whole is *immanent* in all parts, internally present to them, then reason's ends cannot be bracketed. That is, the rational ends we ignore are those we simply have forgotten.

I believe that when Kant introduces the cosmic concept of philosophy, this connection between ideas and ends is fundamental. To be sure, the cosmic concept of philosophy generates the cosmopolitan idea of rights. But all 'world' first originates in reason's ideas as a totality and a system of ends. Because Kant's emphasis is largely on the negative results of the Dialectic, it seems as if he is reinstating in the Canon and the Architectonic, from different points of view, those ideas he has denied could contribute to knowledge. In truth, it now turns out that ideas form a *system*, i.e., an interrelated whole in which all rational activities are subordinated to the ends from which they at once derive. All of reason's questions are connected to one another and to the ultimate question of our final destination and the highest good: a world in which morality and happiness can coincide. This is the idea underlying

---

appearances, but nonetheless, qua their totality, refers to them. Here the idea oversteps experience from within experience. The transcendental ideal instead oversteps the level of appearances altogether in a supreme substrate ("Vom Wesen des Grundes," 32–33). In the third *Critique* the world will be a whole in accordance with ends and a system of final causes (*KU* § 86, *Ak* 5: 444, ENG 310).

all other ideas that satisfies reason's highest need and the idea behind a system of philosophy.

The world indeed does not exist in itself. It is an idea, a maximum. It is first encountered on a speculative ground in the empirical regress in the series of appearances. But this encounter awakens our attention to the moral world, which the Canon represents as a systematic and teleological unity in conformity with moral laws (*KrV* A 808/B 836). This idea acquires an "objective reality" and thus an influence on the sensible world, which we want to make congruent with the intelligible world (ibid.). The world becomes the world of which I hope to be a satisfied citizen (*KrV* B 426).

This means that the idea of the world unites in itself reason's basic questions (what can I know, what ought I to do, what can I hope for?) because it represents the highest good; because, that is, reason sees the sensible world and the moral world under the star of a final end and of a possible, however remote, conciliation. In the idea of the world human reason is not estranged from itself. On the contrary, it sees its highest interests satisfied. In fact, this end is the ultimate source of meaning for pure reason.

I have been extensively exploiting Kant's analogies so far. In agreement with § 59 of the third *Critique*, I believe it is vain to purge language of analogies. All dreams of a *characteristica universalis*, of a technical language free of all that is natural and in which we can focus on arguments alone, are over. Analogies are no more than instruments and do not determine anything. As they introduce movement into thought's expression, however, they are helpful in propelling thought to far-reaching conclusions. Kant's analogies are clearly pertinent, intelligent, and useful in allowing us a better grasp of his arguments and intents. They do help our judgment to perform its double task, as Kant puts it: applying its concept to the object of an intuition, and "applying the mere rule of reflection on that intuition to an entirely different object of which the first is only a symbol" (*KU* § 59, *Ak* 5: 352, ENG 226). In other words, analogies are a form of reflection resting not on likeness but on proportion. As such, they are partial perspectives that, if chosen attentively, illuminate fundamental philosophical points.

Still, sometimes Kant does not push his analogies to all their philosophical consequences. Doing so is as important as seeing where and why they break down or are one-sided, because of the light this sheds on some problems internal to Kant's thought. If, for example, the idea of a philosophical system is compared to a seed, then to an architect's design, the ambiguity, if not incompatibility, of the analogies should give us pause. In this case, the only way to ease the tension between seed and architect, between an analogy from the organic and one from the technical realm, between a potentiality or force and a design, rests on the conception of idea. And yet an idea, though at once a force and a plan, exceeds what is implicit in the images of both seed and architect insofar as it gives voice to reason's comprehensive awareness and its unitary gaze on its horizon.

This analogy with the gaze calls for a more precise discussion. Ideas direct the understanding to a goal, where all "lines of direction of its rules converge at one point" (*KrV* A 644/B 672). Kant calls it *focus imaginarius* to stress that it is a requisite optical focus, a point of orientation, which moves along with the observer. It has no reality of its own and is rather a fiction giving all cognitions a systematic unity, giving experience an order. Again, neither the imagination nor reason alone suffices: reason uses a sensible image but only insofar as it is driven to a totality that is entirely beyond the sensible.

An idea is the analogue of a schema because it specifies the conditions of applicability of the understanding as it tries to seek and to know the uniformity and specificity of nature, its highest unity and differentiation (*KrV* A 665/B 693). As with the experience of the moon appearing bigger at the horizon when it rises, the illusion we fall prey to when we give this projected unity an object is inevitable and cannot be corrected. Unlike logical illusion due to simple inattentiveness, and like optical illusion in which our judgment is led astray by the imagination, transcendental illusion leads reason to false hopes and needs to be removed over and over again (*KrV* A 295/B 352). Here, too, reason uses the imagination but must keep it in check.

There is one image used by Kant that illustrates the architectonic idea wonderfully. *Reflexion* 903 is about the worth of a science and the need for scholars to reclaim their humanity, lest they trust their forces too much. Modesty is wished for, but that is not all. In this passage the scholar is identified simply by the exclusive focus on his or her subject matter.

> I call such a scholar a cyclops. He is an egoist of science, and he needs still another eye which would enable him to look at his object also from the point of view of others. The humanity of the sciences is based on this, i.e., giving the sociability of judgment through which we subject ourselves to the judgment of others. It is properly in the overly reasoning [*vernünftelnde*] sciences, those one can properly learn . . . , that we find cyclopes. The cyclops of literature is the most arrogant; but there are cyclopes in theology, law, medicine. Also cyclopes in geometry. A special custom-made eye must accompany each one of them: the physician needs the critique of our natural knowledge, the jurist our juridical and moral knowledge, the theologian our metaphysics; and the geometer, the critique of our rational knowledge in general. *The second eye then is the self-knowledge of our human reason*, without which we have no good

eye to gauge the extent of our knowledge. . . . It is not his strength, but his being monocular, that makes a cyclops a cyclops. It is also not enough to know many other sciences. Rather, [we must seek] self-knowledge of understanding and reason. *Anthropologia transcendentalis*.[47]

The words 'cyclops' and 'encyclopedia' share the same root: the Greek *kuklos*, roundness. A cyclops has one round eye but does not learn in a cycle, in a well-rounded way, as the etymology of the word 'encyclopedia' suggests.

Little over ten years earlier (1764–66), Kant had proposed a very different analogy. In one of the *Bemerkungen*, he had called for a comprehensive gaze that would coordinate the philosopher's eyes (which "are microscopic . . . [and] see with precision but little," *Ak* 20: 19) and sensibility's gaze in the imagination. Imagination sees much farther and can for this very reason move us to fanaticism. We need both forms of vision. One compensates for and corrects the other. The philosopher's eyes have a narrow focus. The microscopic view is absorbed by the object whose larger context and significance might escape it. Imagination wanders too much. Nonetheless, by helping us put the microscopic vision in perspective and thereby leading us away from it, it keeps us from losing sight of the unitary picture.

In the image of the cyclops, by contrast, there is no appeal to imagination. The challenge is not that of coordinating two pairs of eyes that seem to look in different directions and function differently, but that of getting back the second eye. Furthermore, the two passages both issue an invitation to a double seeing. Kant's fresh enthusiasm for Rousseau and the critique of reason's abstractions may partially explain the remarks from the *Bemerkungen*. But the new reflection on ends that occurs in the passage on the cyclopes bears stressing.

---

47. "Ich nenne einen solchen Gelehrten einen Cyclopen. Er ist ein Egoist der Wissenschaft, und es ist ihm noch ein Auge nötig, welches macht, dass er seinen Gegenstand noch aus dem Gesichtspunkte anderer Menschen ansieht. Hierauf gründet sich die humanität der Wissenschaften, d.i. die Leutseeligkeit des Urtheils, dadurch man es andrer Urtheil mit unterwirft, zu geben. Die (vernünftelnde) Wissenschaften, die man eigentlich lernen kan . . . sind es eigentlich, darin es Cyclopen giebt. Der Cyclop von Litteratur ist der trozigste; aber es giebt Cyclopen von Theologen, iuristen, medicis. Auch Cyclopen von Geometern. Einem ieden muss ein Auge aus besonderer fabrike beygesellet werden. Dem Medicus Critik unserer Naturerkentnis, dem iuristen unsrer (Rechts und) Moralkentnis, dem Theologen unsrer Metaphysik. Dem geometra Critik der VernunftErkentnis überhaupt. *Das zweyte Auge ist also das der Selbsterkentnis der menschlichen Vernunft*, ohne welches wir kein Augenmaas der Grösse unserer Erkentnis haben. . . . Nicht die Stärke, sondern das einäugigte macht hier den Cyclop. Es ist auch nicht gnug, viel andre Wissenschaften zu wissen, sondern die Selbsterkentnis des Verstandes und der Vernunft. *Anthropologia transcendentalis*" (*Ak* 15: 395, dated between 1776 and 1778).

Whenever Kant makes use of analogies we must be careful in our interpretation. His attention is always on the few details he focuses on rather than on the broader implications one would quickly think of. In this case, no mention is made of the deformity and monstrosity, or the violence, typical of a cyclops.[48] Instead, Kant concentrates on the cyclops's vision alone in very abstract terms.[49] Consider the following.

1. The idea that we must get back one eye implies that at some point someone decided to see with one eye alone. As in *What Is Enlightenment?*, the minority is a state some have put themselves into, not a historical destiny or the misfortune of chance or of a stepmotherly nature.

2. It is Kant's philosophy that takes on the task of giving scholars back their second eye. More importantly, if in the passage from the *Bemerkungen* neither vision was sufficient and philosophy had to integrate its microscopic vision with the wings of a passionate imagination, here in the cyclops *Reflexion* a philosophical vision is all it takes. Philosophy is itself the remedy to monocular vision.

3. Philosophy does not thereby promise a 360 degree vision, a view from nowhere. Whatever I see I see from one point of view. In the unpublished manuscript of the Preface to the *Confessions*, Rousseau denounced Montaigne because in his autobiography he painted himself in profile. Who can tell if he was hiding a scar or a wounded eye on the unseen side? Rousseau's remark is understandable when it comes to the hypocritical mask he detects in Montaigne's flaunted frankness. Literally, however, he demands the impossible. For even a frontal view might hide major flaws on the unseen side. We need not be familiar with Husserl's stress on adumbrations to know that all vision leaves something unseen. Now, in Kant's *Reflexion* philosophy is not a perfect vision but one that contextualizes and reminds the scholar of reason's ends.

4. It is not the sociability of judgment per se that is missing in this monocular vision. In fact, sociability is missing because it is itself the symptom of a more glaring absence, that of a relation to ends and to humanity.

48. If we follow Ricoeur's theory of metaphor, we can hardly blame Kant for being selective in his analogy. Ricoeur argues that unlike conceptual abstraction, which does not eliminate secondary attributes, metaphorical denomination "does not consist in perceiving the order of a structure, but in 'forgetting,' in eliminating—really, in making us abstract from—several attributes that the metaphorized term evokes in us in its normal usage" (*Rule of Metaphor*, 106–7).

49. In all languages I know there are terms for peripheral and frontal vision, for being near- or far-sighted, etc., but only in German do we find a word for 'seeing stupidly' (*Blödsichtigkeit*). I wish to thank Wolfgang Carl for teaching it to me and pointing me to its occurrence in the *Prolegomena* (Ak 4: 264).

Philosophy can make cyclopes realize that their monocular vision is so-lipsistic and has fixed boundaries because its reflexivity puts things in the perspective of the whole. (It is serendipitous here but not a mere accident that reflection has originally an optical meaning.)

5. The examples of law and medicine will be used in the Introduction to the transcendental power of judgment in the first *Critique*. We may know many important rules, but unless we know how and when to apply them we are like idiot savants: we are stupid (*KrV* A 133/B 172). On the other hand, in the *Conflict of the Faculties*, theology, law, and medicine, the university's three higher faculties, appear together again. In contrast to its use in philosophy, the use of reason in those faculties cannot be public but must undergo censorship.[50]

6. When Nietzsche, mocking Wagner in *Zarathustra* ("On redemption"), says that some people are like one big ear, he underscores the deformity of the sense organ. By contrast, Kant is stressing that a binocular vision is impaired, but adds that it can be restored because there was no permanent physiological damage to a sense organ to begin with. The problem is not that the vision is too acute and oversensitive, but that it is partial. Not subtlety but the overview of the whole (*die Übersehung des Gantzen*, *PhilEnz*, Ak 29: 6) is missing in monocular vision.

7. Kant writes that cyclopes are found in reasoning sciences, which can be learned. But it is not clear exactly what learnable reasoning sciences are, or how geometry and literature can be in the same lot.

8. More importantly, it remains obscure what Kant is arguing against here. In the terms of the later Architectonic, what is wrongheaded, the historical way of learning rational disciplines or the vision typical of an artist of reason? Certainly the mention of the scholar in literature seems to indicate the former, but the 'egoist of science' the latter.

9. This image of the cyclops shows Kant's preoccupation with a correct use of reason, which we must discipline and remind of the whole. Thinking on our own, the supreme maxim of an enlightened reason's struggle against prejudice, is not so much an emancipation from the darkness of ignorance or the call to acquire new cognitions useful for whatever progress is hoped for. It is rather a negative principle directed against all self-absorbed *misuse* of knowledge blind to its larger, especially practical, consequences.[51] The

---

50. This was duly noted by Hohenegger, *Kant*, 49ff.

51. As *Was heisst sich im Denken orientieren* will have it (*Ak* 8: 146n). It is noteworthy that Meier, in his *Auszug* (§§ 218–19), stresses the insufficiency of speculation. The erudite does not, or does not want to, understand the connection of cognition with man's behavior, and thus

self-important solipsism of the scholar is more dangerous than prejudice and ignorance.

10. The transcendental anthropology has obviously nothing to do with the later pragmatic anthropology—but much with critical philosophy and metaphysics.[52]

This analogy with the cyclops returns in the logic lecture courses when Kant speaks of the logical perfection of knowledge. 'Polyhistory' is historical knowledge, and 'polymathy' knowledge of reason. They are both unbounded. Together they are called 'pansophy.' Here, too, Kant wavers on whether the second eye granted by philosophy cures only polyhistory or also polymathy.[53]

Either way, a cyclops is someone who holds philosophy dispensable (*Log*, *Ak* 9: 45, ENG 554, and *Refl* 2020–23, *Ak* 16: 198–99) because he or she presumes to know a great deal without caring about "how all the cognitions of the one eye agree with reference to a common end" (V-Lo/Wiener, *Ak* 24: 819, ENG 277). In this passage sociability and humanity reappear together in philosophy (ibid.). In the science that philosophy is, we understand how "all these cognitions can be drawn together into a main science and are regarded as means to that science" (ibid.). The second eye is driven by reason's teleology and is concerned with the ends of humanity. We need not tarry over many books and be learned once we have taken the maxim to think for ourselves as our guide.

Philosophy, despite its lofty-sounding architectonic role of arranging the sciences it subordinates to itself, is about simplicity and modesty. Simplicity is an economic criterion. Erudition requires prolonged study of books. Memorizing books becomes superfluous once we grasp the principles on which they are based. This grasp gives us self-reliance and significantly reduces our toil. Modesty, in turn, is more important than simplicity because it is a philosophical criterion. Erudites and scholars are puffed-up minds, inflated by their learnedness (V-Lo/Wiener, *Ak* 24: 818, ENG 276; *Log*, *Ak* 9: 45, ENG 554). The second eye of philosophy tears down their pride. But this is not merely a matter of countenancing self-righteousness or the salutary bursting of gasbags. What Kant wants us to keep steady before our gaze is a

---

offends him/herself ("welcher ihren Zusammenhang mit dem Verhalten des Menschen nicht einsehen kann, oder nicht einsehen will. In dem letzten Falle beschimpft sich der Gelehrte selbst," *Ak* 16: 520n).

52. See *Log*, *Ak* 9: 25, ENG 538.

53. See the different examples at V-Lo/Wiener, *Ak* 24: 818, ENG 276, and *Log*, *Ak* 9: 45, ENG 554. See also the *Reflexionen* 2020–22 (*Ak* 16: 198–99) and 5081 (*Ak* 18: 81–82). Here Baumgarten is a metaphysical cyclops: he had a sharp sight in small things but could not see far.

question of *meaning* and *worth*. In his view this is the question of *ends*, which in turn implies *limits* (*Log, Ak* 9: 25, ENG 538).

Neither erudites nor artists of reason, who employ a method they take for granted in their sciences and are solely focused on their object, which they presuppose as given, care about the final end of their science or about the limits of the scope they are investigating. They need not raise their heads. After all, this is why their reason's gaze remains so focused and they are so good at extending their cognitions.

In fact, we could argue that Kant is not very generous with artists of reason. What would reason be without them? If an idea is the organization of its parts and we show only contempt for the parts, is the idea not affected by this value judgment? In this analogy Kant fails to say that there is something inherently good about a cyclopic vision. Consider aiming at a target. It is necessary to use one eye only both generally and in the particular case of using a weapon, where the eye is in line with the arm being used. The focus works when we *exclude* everything else from the aim, i.e., at the expense of the context. A binocular vision would hamper the precision needed; it would blur vision, put it out of focus. The reason is clear: one eye aims at one object at a time, whereas binocular vision gives the object back its context. We could therefore say that a cyclopic vision guarantees precision, but in a narrow segment of space. By contrast, a binocular vision naturally connects the object with its surroundings. But it would be wrong to infer that a contextual vision *puts* the object in a context. It is not our arbitrary imposition. In fact, it is rather cyclopic vision that is abstract: things come not in isolation but always in relation to their surroundings. To account for such *relation*—for the limits of our visual field—we need more than one eye.

To artists of reason, limits are mere boundaries that are relentlessly pushed back at every new scientific discovery. Because the field they are concentrated on is homogeneous and allows for indefinite progress, boundaries for them are contingent and fluid. They are found as such in each determinate epoch. Artists of reason have no interest in or patience for reason's needs, drives, aspirations, concern with ends, satisfaction, or self-consciousness, that is, with reason's desire to see what it is doing and what it is heading toward in its progress. Their science fulfills their questions and keeps them busy. To them the rest smacks of psychology.

A limit (*Grenze, terminus*) gives determinacy to what it encloses and keeps it apart from its other. A boundary (*Schranke, limes*) refers to an indeterminate magnitude that can change size. It is perceived as a *provisional obstacle* to be overcome. By contrast, a limit can be understood only in relation to *the totality within which* we are moving—which means with a consciousness of its apparent horizon moving along with it and of what lies beyond it.[54] When artists of reason pursue their science, the boundary is not the explicit object of their thought but what they strive to overcome and push further away. By contrast, philosophers make limits the thematic object of their thought. The consciousness of a horizon and of the totality of cognitions makes limits visible and thematic per se.

Even if it cannot experience, let alone modify, the limits of experience, philosophy (i.e., metaphysics and a critique of reason) aims to determine limits; that is, to know them as definite and capable of genuinely separating. Unlike a boundary, a limit does not change over time and thanks to historical progress. It is not negative and provisional. It is instead a *positive and constitutive division* of two heterogeneous domains, the sensible and the supersensible (*Prol* § 57). The limit is not only necessary. It also reflects the realization of a sore lack and dissatisfaction that the artists of reason, who don't know what they are missing, are spared.

In *De anima* (3.2, 427a 10ff.), Aristotle says that the unity of consciousness in perception is comparable to the point. As convergence and division of two segments that originate in it, the point unites and separates at once. It is a limit, the one and many of what finds its origin in its divisions. In the *Physics* (4.10–13), the 'now' is both the contact and the separation of anterior and posterior. Likewise with Kant's limit: it connects what it separates because it is their source and common origin. Kant's limit implies the insufficiency of appearances and their reference to the supersensible. As actual connection of nature and freedom, it is their necessary mutual reference. In critical philosophy reason treads on a borderline as on a wall that separates two regions. It looks both ways, i.e., to the sensible and the supersensible. We gain "a view into the realm of the supersensible, though only with weak glances" (*KpV, Ak* 5: 147, ENG 258), as we are compelled "to look beyond the sensible" (*KU* § 57, *Ak* 5: 341, ENG 217). This gaze is denied to the sciences and the understanding, as was the feeling of dissatisfaction.

If sciences enjoy the advantage of a boundless advancement, this also implies they are structurally incomplete. By contrast, philosophy, aware of its definitive limit, has the privilege of completeness. Philosophy can come to final results because the division of scopes is internal to reason itself and carried out by it. As we saw, if reason is examining not being but itself as the source and origin of all rules and principles allowing us to approach being, nothing outside of it is left to investigate.

54. See *KrV* A 759/B 787: "all questions of our pure reason pertain to that which might lie outside this horizon or in any case at least on its borderline [*Grenzlinie*]."

If the limit is constitutive, then merely saying that we cannot know the supersensible is utterly reductive and simplistic. The supersensible is accessible to us in practical ways, but also in speculative ways, through the metaphysics of analogy. I cannot develop this theme here.[55] What I want to highlight, however, is that the knowledge of limits does not compel reason to stay away from what it cannot presume to know. The result is rather that eventually *reason knows why it cannot know.* The result is not a negative prohibition of venturing into alien lands, but a positive cognition that only reason's self-knowledge can afford. And reason's self-knowledge shows it has ends that go beyond knowledge. Knowledge is a means toward reason's ultimate questions. This is metaphysics as science.

5. Philosophy as an Idea. Reason's History

Philosophy's invitation to modesty is evidenced by yet another paradox we have come across briefly before. Philosophy is no more than an idea we can at best hope to approximate, but not instantiate. At the same time, there is no downplaying the thesis that philosophy is the only lawgiver of pure reason.

Before we take a closer look at this paradox, let me recapitulate the main results of our reading of the Architectonic. We have seen that reason is compared to an organism because all parts are organized according to a principle from which they derive. Unlike an organism, however, reason is the faculty of ends that are not natural. Reason projects an architectonic unity of its cognitions in an idea. Reason's object is the understanding, but in this relation it maintains precedence, for it is prior to the understanding's several cognitions as it is prior to the sciences. In fact, only reason's system counts as a science because it is the only systematic ordering of parts. Sciences do not enjoy the comprehensive gaze that philosophy has. If the artists of reason must be harmonized by philosophy, then scientific cognitions are the means to reason's self-knowledge. No redemptive power of knowledge nor the emancipatory ambition of science to make this a more comfortable world will satisfy reason. No scientistic, logical, or instrumental sense of reason can hold. Reason does not import a method, mathematical or scientific or otherwise, from without. Its only method is the form of the whole it devises as the principle organizing its cognitions. Even if it seeks knowledge of itself and is a self-enclosed unity, reason aims beyond itself

---

55. See chapter 3, §1 below.

as a lawgiver of nature and morals. Through its ideas, reason generates not only a world but also a schema we can work with in our constructions. It is crucial to remember, however, that unlike schemata, ideas are superpersonal, i.e., they exceed individual minds and intentions.

With Galilei and Descartes, science and philosophy had to join forces to build explanatory models that would enable us to understand nature methodically as a lawful mechanism amenable to causes rather than grant us insight into its inner workings. As causes were reduced to the efficient and external, they produced physical processes. Concepts were no longer meant to depict or reproduce given essences. Instead, their job was to help us solve problems. Technique and art were no longer opposed to science, which in its all-encompassing ambition not only overlapped with philosophy but eventually sought to replace it.[56]

This trend is reversed by Kant.[57] Philosophy, not science, is the highest lawgiver. Scientists are artists whose gaze is absorbed by their object and thus are far too narrow for thought, which aims at the whole. As a result, science should be directed by philosophy. This move beyond modern reason, however, is not a return to the premodern or classical thesis of the superior dignity of philosophy over sciences, because it does not rest on a notion of *theōria* as an unhampered vision of the way things truly are or on philosophers basking in their disinterested haughty nobility. In fact, it is only because philosophy is the most comprehensive science and the philosopher proposes the ultimate paradox, that of a *successful experiment in metaphysics* that brings about a revolution in thinking analogous to the revolution in astronomy and physics, that philosophy can subordinate the artists of reason to itself.[58]

In the words of the *Philosophical Encyclopaedia*, philosophy's legislation produces norms or maxims. Logical norms give us the rules for the employment of the understanding. But maxims concern ends and use those norms

---

56. See my *Galilei*.

57. Cf. Kerszberg, *Critique and Totality*, 35.

58. Kant's Architectonic reverses also the relation between science and philosophy put forth by Locke, the first philosopher who elevates the study of the limits of our faculties to paramount importance, in the Epistle to the reader of the *Essay*. "The commonwealth of learning is not at this time without master-builders, whose mighty designs, in advancing the sciences, will leave lasting monuments to the admiration of posterity." We cannot hope to be a Boyle, a Sydenham, a Huygens, let alone a Newton. "[I]t is ambition enough to be employed as an under-labourer in clearing the ground a little, and removing some of the rubbish that lies in the way to knowledge" (*Essay concerning Human Understanding*, 1: 14). For Kant, philosophy does not make such a profession of modesty but invites to modesty precisely because it gives us the awareness of totality that sciences lack.

as means (*Ak* 29: 7). A cosmic concept of philosophy has absolute worth, or dignity. Its dignity reverberates in all cognitions (*Log, Ak* 9: 23–24, ENG 537). "All philosophy has as its object reason: maxims, limits and the end. The rest is art of reason" (*Refl* 4987, *Ak* 18: 52). In philosophy we must acquire not cognitions but a method to philosophize (*PhilEnz, Ak* 29: 6).[59]

In the *Critique of Pure Reason*, as we saw, two contrasts are made. One is between historical and rational learning, the other between the scholastic and the cosmic concept of philosophy. The former contrast has to do with a subjective way of learning (*KrV* A 836/B 863). Learning historically arises according to facts, not principles, and the knowledge that results is the work of an "alien" reason dependent on external material that is given. Such learning, then, is not real thinking. It is no more than repetition and the aping of reason.

This distinction is based not on the subject matter we are talking about but on the way we learn it. Here Kant does not draw conclusions concerning, among other things, the status of history, because strictly speaking the connection of this 'historical learning' to history is loose.

The second contrast (scholastic versus cosmic) is internal to rational cognition, i.e., a distinct kind of knowledge. But this second contrast does not bring us directly to the subject matter itself, because it also is introduced with an eye to learning. Kant notices how we can learn mathematics (by following steps using our power of inference and of criticism) but cannot learn philosophy. Philosophy presents a distinction that mathematics lacks: that between subjective learning and an objective point of view. Seen in this objective perspective, philosophy is no more than a model (*Urbild*), the idea of a science that can never be given *in concreto*.

This Kantian line of thought is well-known but puzzling nonetheless. After all, Kant is convinced that he has turned a page for good and that the change he has wrought is irreversible. Metaphysics from now on is like chemistry where before we had nothing but alchemy. The certainty, truth, and definitive status of mankind's self-knowledge after 1781 are not a matter of opinion. No room is left for tentative conclusions or provisional half-truths once we have finally put metaphysics on a scientific path. It took

---

59. In *Reflexion* 1651 (*Ak* 16: 65–66), the emphasis on method explains the contrast between learning a determinate philosophy and learning to philosophize. Simply put, learning a determinate philosophy comes down to learning to philosophize subjectively, i.e., going through the steps of a determinate philosophy without being able to judge it or take a stand on it. Learning to philosophize objectively, instead, means to learn how we *must think*. The former is the spirit of a philosopher, while the latter is the philosophical spirit. It is original and contains genius because it is the method of reason.

a revolution, but we cannot pretend it never occurred. Yet a fundamental question remains: does not Kant's confidence here conflict with his repeated insistence that all attempts to actualize the idea of philosophy will forever fall short? True, with the *Critique of Pure Reason* Kant has given us the critique and not the actual system.[60] But the first *Critique* is doubtless a scientific propaedeutic to a system that, deriving from the principles of pure reason alone, is announced as no less definitive. How then should we understand Kant's profession of modesty? How can he reconcile the fact that the idea is never given *in concreto* with his description of transcendental philosophy as a definitive science? Does not transcendental philosophy realize an idea?

Learning a determinate philosophy is learning historically. The only alternative, writes Kant, is learning to philosophize. This is tantamount to exercising the talent of reason in "prosecuting its principles," "always with the reservation of the right of reason to investigate the sources of these principles themselves and to confirm or reject them" (*KrV* A 838/B 866). This shows why nobody can claim the high-sounding name of philosopher. Considering oneself the personification of the model is vainglorious, for it flatly contradicts the modesty the philosopher teaches as he/she comes to know reason's powers in their limits. The reason why Kant claims philosophy is an archetype, however, is not his realization of this contradiction. Philosophy is an archetype because it is pure reason's activity and not a determinate historical product. This is not a comment on the futility of our efforts, as if they were forever doomed to fail, but on the irreducible essence of the activity that presides over them. All determinate products have to be themselves assessed and judged, and not in the name and spirit of one determinate philosophy, but of pure reason.

If I were to consider Kant's philosophy the last word on pure reason, assuming I learned it *ex principiis*, how would I teach it? If the answer is 'rationally,' then I would treat it as one way to delve deeper into rational questions. I would treat it as an example, not as a given: as a regulative idea from which to take my bearings as I assess and judge, not as a historical product. There will always be a gap between philosophy and a determinate philosophy. Once the activity has objectified itself in a product, philosophy has lost the power to assess and judge. But if I want to appropriate a method to evaluate rationally, then the historical data do not matter. The idea of

---

60. Tonelli (*Kant's Critique*, 269–70) aptly points this out, but he does so because he intends to minimize the problem. Capozzi suggests that the idea is complete but the systematic science is not (*Kant e la logica*, 614). It seems to me that the idea works like a seed as it guides our efforts. It is the execution in a system that must claim completeness, not the guide.

philosophy is a spontaneity of thought. Reason is irreducible to its products; its activity demands of itself to work through every step of its science on its own and recreate from scratch the high road that leads to our conclusions. All acquired cognitions are at loggerheads with this idea of the autonomous pursuit that *Selbstdenken* is. But more generally the activity of philosophizing is on a different plane than all knowledge. A maxim, a method, and a principle are higher than all cognitions they may generate.[61]

To be sure, it is in the essence of an activity to result in products. In the Preface to the *Metaphysics of Morals*, sixteen years after the Architectonic, Kant will write that the ambition to have the last word is not only natural but necessary for every philosophy. From an objective point of view that has only principles of pure reason as its object and for which there cannot be more than one system of philosophy, each philosopher pretends to understand what must be the only truth. From this perspective, even if this sounds arrogant and belittling toward predecessors, it is again inevitable to present one's philosophy as a fresh start, as if the past did not exist or consisted merely of experiments meant to prepare the way for us (*Ak* 6: 207, ENG 366).

Even so, an activity is intrinsically elusive, always one step ahead of its products. The problem is not one of a final realization, as if all accomplishment were vain and all completeness were impossible, precisely because we are talking not about the cognitions philosophers have but about the method of philosophy. Mastering a method and being able to use it on our own substantially differ from appropriating cognitions, because a method helps us find a criterion to exercise judgment. In themselves cognitions are dumb, like writing for Socrates in Plato's *Phaedrus*. It is always our judgment that brings them to life.

Notice that here the idea of philosophy, like the architectonic idea it uses, is prior to all historically determinate schemata. As an *Urbild* it precedes its several *Nachbilder*. Also, as a method and a maxim, the idea of philosophy is a guide for our judgment (after all, if it were more than regulative, it would make the whole system dogmatic). At the same time, the idea is beyond individuality. This is the other aspect of this priority. Earlier we saw that the idea is like a seed growing whether or not we know or will. Every schema presupposes it. Here this presupposition takes the following form:

---

61. Besides *Reflexion* 1651, see the Philippi Logic (*Ak* 24: 85–86). In his comments on Kretzfeld (*Ak* 15/2: 912), Kant writes that we do not call a treatise philosophical only because it deals with the history of philosophy. "*Predicatum enim ab arte vel scientia sumtum non* obiectum *notat, sed* modum *quo illud exponimus.*"

the model of philosophy is presupposed by all determinate philosophies because the cosmic sense of philosophy "has always grounded" philosophy (*KrV* A 838/B 866). That is, the idea has always been the guide, regardless of its realization in schemata and despite the fact that before Kant nobody called it that or even knew about it. The idea is again superpersonal—even as it personifies its archetype in the ideal of the philosopher. The ideal, mind you, is an idea *in individuo*. But this ideal cannot exist, for it is an unreachable model.

The model is at once unreachable and yet somehow given. If it were not given, I could not assess and judge determinate philosophies, nor could Kant say that the philosopher "is still found nowhere, although the idea of his legislation is found in every human reason" (*KrV* A 839/B 867). To explain why the model is also unreachable, I believe it is instructive to draw a comparison with the idea of the Saint of the Gospels to be found in the *Groundwork*. In fact, Kant himself, in the lectures on the *Philosophical Encyclopaedia*, prompted us to draw a similar comparison (the argument will return later in the Dialectic, *KrV* A 305/B 371–72, and is, all truth be told, as old as Plato's *Euthyphro*). In reality we never find a true Christian or a true philosopher (*PhilEnz*, *Ak* 29: 7–8). The reason is straightforward. In order to do so I would need to take them as examples respectively of sanctity and of wisdom. That is, I would need to relate them to the idea I am using to evaluate how good they are as examples.[62] But that means that it is the idea that counts and allows me to evaluate examples. The idea is there, and I either follow its lead or do not. If I do not, I cannot recognize someone as an example of wisdom or of sanctity (or of anything else). If I do, the original I have is the standard I use to judge whether the existing occurrences are good copies or not. As we read in the Transcendental Dialectic, the Stoic sage is an ideal or archetype granting the perfect determination of the copy (*KrV* A 569/B 597). I cannot arrive at an idea through examples. On the contrary, examples are such because when I judge a determinate philosophy I see it in comparison with the idea grounded in reason.[63]

---

62. *Groundwork*, *Ak* 4: 408–9, ENG 63. See also the letter to Jacobi (August 30, 1789, *Ak* 11: 76).

63. In the third *Regula* Descartes writes: "even though we know other people's demonstrations by heart, we shall never become mathematicians if we lack the intellectual aptitude to solve any given problem. And even though we have read all the arguments of Plato and Aristotle, we shall never become philosophers if we are unable to make a sound judgment on matters which come up for discussion; in this case what we seem to have learnt would not be science but history" (*Oeuvres*, 4: 367).

If the archetype is at once unreachable and given, thought measures the distance between any existing occurrence and the rule. Like all thinking and all cognitions, philosophy thus inevitably results in judgments that are to be used in their application to instances. Possessing them without being able to apply them is, as we know from the Introduction to the Analytic of Principles, stupidity. To *philosophize* is this activity of thought, nothing but the power to judge in philosophy. To *know* in turn can be considered the fixation or objectification of the cognitive activity on determinate products. To philosophize is in this sense an end unto itself and has an intrinsic dignity, which cannot be said of cognitions.

These distinctions between scholastic and cosmic, and between historical and rational, are, however, more problematic than they appear. A key theme of this book is that often Kant uses sharp distinctions he cannot hold fast to because they are based on ambiguous or generic concepts or, finally, because he shifts his views on one of the elements of the distinction at stake while presuming to maintain the distinction itself intact. In this case I believe Kant has inadvertently shifted ground as he introduces this idea of philosophy as judging activity. Perhaps part of the problem is that it is misleading to call the idea of philosophy an archetype and a model as if the idea were itself given as an object—as a touchstone we could look to in order to size up copies against it—and were not a simple guide for thought. Perhaps it is misleading to use the language of archetype and copies to begin with, as if the relation between idea and example were identical to the *casus datae legis*, the relation between concept and intuition in the subsumption of determinant judgment. Perhaps, finally, despite Kant's insistence on the critique as a propaedeutic to metaphysics, we should note the striking result that critical philosophy seems superior to metaphysics. Alert, watchful thinking for oneself seems higher than knowing.

What is beyond all doubt, however, is that philosophy as a judgment of determinate philosophies and as a legislation resulting in a system are by no means identical notions. Likewise there is a twofold sense to the idea of philosophy. It is either productive and systematic or called upon to judge systems. Granted, in both cases what counts, in the lexicon of the Second Preface to the *Critique of Pure Reason* (B xiv), is the secure path of science. I cannot think systematically without at once judging what I am producing. A judgment evaluates actual, already formed systems no less than possible articulations of thoughts in a consistent whole. It evaluates historical systems no less than the one I am shaping as I philosophize: the foreign and the own, the possible and the actual. But thinking systematically is the *projected form* of a whole of cognitions, while judging is a *test* of the relation between idea and example based on the result that each particular system offers. The former idea is the form of totality. The latter is still a guiding maximum, but as it is bent on evaluating and verifying the former. The former results in an actual organic construction. The latter rejects in principle all objectification, even if its very possibility rests on the former, which it has to presuppose as given. The former proposes, the latter examines.

The two sides must belong together as do defendant and judge in reason's tribunal. Still, when Kant says that the idea is invoked to judge determinate products to evaluate their congruence with the model, he assumes an external standpoint and shifts from identifying reason with the defendant to identifying it with the perspective of the judge. Much as in the radical difference between original apperception and empirical consciousness, here Kant holds fast to the alternative between activity and results. But by emphasizing only the difference and not also the identity between the two perspectives, he divides the idea of philosophy respectively into a force philosophers are driven by and into our privileged and free spontaneity.

At this point the following question can no longer be evaded: if we judge the Christian based on the idea, what moves the Christian if not the idea? What directs the philosophers' efforts and keeps their gaze steady and focused on the goal if not the idea? The idea is both the motivation for the philosopher and the standard for our judgment of the congruence of the copy to the model. What we now get instead is that Kant stresses the super-individual and external perspective according to which philosophers operate under an idea. They schematize a model that was operative from the outset. They are and always remain the *unwitting* executors of philosophy's idea. And yet they *willfully* pursue nothing but that idea as they set themselves the imperative to realize the maxim to think for themselves. Unless we want to take philosophers as passive executors and the idea as external to them, this is another way to realize that philosophy cannot be compared to the microscopic seed in epigenesis. The idea of philosophy in a cosmic sense seems rather to form the deliberate and conscious object of philosophers' efforts. Philosophers are in this sense more than the simple instruments of pure reason. They actively realize pure reason, which without them would not be. Idea and schema seem intertwined, almost indistinguishable. If the idea of cosmic philosophy lives in and through its schemata, why are schemata not constitutive of the idea?[64]

---

64. The duality of perspectives (the *Selbstdenker* and the judge) owes its existence to the difference between learning to philosophize and learning mathematics. But if we look closer, the duality does not hold in mathematics (learning mathematics and doing it do not differ).

If earlier the notion of idea as awareness of ends and totalizing drive integrated and subordinated in itself the complementary functions of seed and architect, here, as Kant insists on the opposition between activity and results, the problem of the ambiguity between judgment and its results seems more acute. To be sure, clearly a judgment is always addressed to contents and contents do not make up the judgment. But Kant is not simply distinguishing the power of judgment from its contents. He is isolating the activity from its realization and defining the activity negatively as separate from and opposed to the contents it makes. What is not clear is what the proper activity of philosophizing and thinking for oneself consists in, whether judgment or legislation.

The passage on criticism and dogmatism in the B Preface to the first *Critique* (*KrV* B xxxv) would seem to suggest that the idea of cosmic philosophy as activity and judging is inevitably bound to objectify every system it examines and thus automatically reduce it to a scholastic one, regardless of its origin in the cosmic idea.[65] As we have seen, Kant actually claims that the cosmic idea generates and grounds all philosophy. Every system owes its coming to be and its inspiration to cosmic philosophy. But it does seem that when philosophy judges historically determinate philosophies, it effaces what is most characteristic of cosmic philosophy, its relation to ends. Actually, as we will see in the next section, there is a deep truth to this Kantian thesis and an important reason for it that also helps us at least to mitigate the problem: the reference to wisdom.

The other connected problem has to do with the relation between philosophy and history. It is easy to misunderstand Kant and ascribe to him

---

In philosophy it is assumed, but only to be dismissed. In fact, it cannot hold for long because without a commitment to the idea, the judgment based on the idea would not even be possible. I do believe that this duality is a problem for Kant.

65. The suggestion is definitely reinforced by the cryptic remark in the Architectonic that "until now [*Bis dahin*] . . . the concept of philosophy has been only a *scholastic concept*" (*KrV* A 838/B 866, trans. Guyer–Wood). This remark is cryptic because it is not clear how we must interpret the *bis dahin*. Kemp Smith (like Guyer–Wood) disambiguates this notion ("Hitherto the concept of philosophy has been a merely scholastic concept"), but in both translations the cost of arbitrariness is a dear one. They interpret the *bis dahin* as if it were a temporal adverb referring to a historical situation (Kant's new standpoint). They are therefore forced to turn the verb, which in German is in the present tense (*Bis dahin ist aber der Begriff von Philosophie nur ein Schulbegriff*), to a present perfect tense (*has been*). As a result, the remark is understood as pertaining to Kant's own philosophy as opposed to previous philosophies. Instead the remark should be read in light of the previous paragraph, i.e., as a description of the standpoint we have reached once we have learned to philosophize. If read thus, the *bis dahin* is the repetition of the same expression we had seven lines before ("Bis dahin kann man keine Philosophie lernen").

an outright ahistorical conception of reason. Kant's conception of reason, however, is not radically opposed to history. In the writings on history and religion and in the Critique of Teleological Judgment, history will be the necessary stage of reason's progressive deployment in the world. But already in the notion of the history of reason sketched at the end of the first *Critique,* and in that of the two prefaces (the battlefield of metaphysics of 1781 and the Copernican revolution in metaphysics of 1787), reason must be understood historically in the context of a progressive development.

It is by realizing itself in the speculative and practical realms that reason attains itself fully, i.e., it understands its principles and the progressive acquisition of its autonomy. Through its retrospective gaze reason now understands its progress as governed by a purpose, which is its full rule over itself. If the idea of a system of philosophy is a seed at work since the most ancient of times and reason must be made the guide for everyone's thought and action, the conclusion is inescapable. Not only is every system realized in history. Also, because the system is fully realized once reason legislates over itself and freedom rules over nature, the enlightenment of reason in both speculative and practical terms is not a readymade given to be presupposed but takes place progressively as a conquest to be made in history. Reason has directed our efforts since the beginnings, but we must discover it and assert it in order to reach maturity.

If approaching rational cognitions historically boils down to a betrayal of reason, it now emerges that it is in turn possible, indeed necessary, to understand history rationally, *ex principiis.* Here, in terms that should remind us of the definition of synthesis (with its *durchgehen, aufnehmen und verbinden* of the manifold, *KrV* A 77/B 102), reproduction is active. The synthesis of the historical manifold runs through the steps of reason's progressive affirmation of itself. These steps—dogmatic, skeptical, critical philosophy— reflect the ideal laws of reason that become visible only at the end of a historical progress, once reason is enlightened.

History is then reason's history, for an idea rules its stages. We must study history in reason; that is, in its a priori form. This, however, implies that reason grounds history, which itself is suspended. What counts is not what happened, but what should have happened according to reason's inner laws.

After the advent of critical philosophy it is possible to start a philosophical history of philosophy, in other words, an a priori history. In the "History of Pure Reason" in the first *Critique,* the past offers to critical philosophy, i.e., to the enlightened reason's retrospective gaze, a poor show, a wasteland littered with edifices in ruin.[66] Philosophy was living in its childhood until it became critical (*KrV* A 852/B 880). Later, in the *Fortschritte der Metaphysik*, we find a sketch of this "philosophizing history of philosophy" in which we do not borrow "the facts of reason" from historical narration but draw "them from the nature of human reason, as a philosophical archaeology" (*Ak* 20: 341, ENG 417). Three consequences follow.

1. The first has to do with philosophy as judgment. If, once more, I can judge empirical historical stages only because I am clear about the idea, only the *critical* philosopher's pure gaze can decipher empirical history in its a priori laws.

2. The second consequence is that even in its most empirical form, the history of philosophy cannot tolerate any talk of either a mechanistic or a chance succession. History has its own teleology because whatever progress reason makes owes its being to reason's own ends. In the *Fortschritte* this teleology is clearly asserted as integral to the new notion of a philosophizing history of philosophy. The notion of seed returns in this form: the idea of metaphysics is an "embryo" that has an urge to develop. It is, differently stated, inevitable for reason to develop historically insofar as it has a need to transcend nature and rise to first principles, which explains its interest in the supersensible (*Ak* 20: 342). The history of philosophy is a peculiar genre in which nothing can be told "without knowing beforehand what should have happened, and also what can happen" (*Ak* 20: 343, ENG 419). This is tantamount to saying that nothing new can happen. But strictly speaking it means that what happens is irrelevant because we know the a priori grounds internal to reason why everything in philosophy happens. This history is possible because once again reason has only itself as its object and its end is implicit before it is realized in history, which in turn is but the making explicit of both reason's end and its beginning, which are one and the same.

3. The third consequence is that even if Kant's reason is historical, it does remain abstract. It must not study the historical unfolding of systems. In fact, it *must ignore* the historical and empirical data because its gaze remains pure insofar as it affirms its independence from history's contingency. For the cosmic philosopher, in the words of the *Jaesche Logic*, "all systems of

66. The enlightened reason's retrospective gaze and Benjamin's angel of history have this petrified look on rubble in common: "Wo eine Kette von Begebenheiten vor uns erscheint, da sieht er eine einzige Katastrophe, die unablässig Trümmer auf Trümmer häuft und sie ihm vor die Füße schleudert" (Benjamin, *Über den Begriff der Geschichte*, thesis 9, *Gesammelte Schriften*, 1: 2, 697).

philosophy [are] only as *history of the use of reason* and as objects for the exercise of his philosophical talent" (*Ak* 9: 26, ENG 539; V-Met/L1/Pölitz, *Ak* 28: 533–34, ENG 301).

I find it odd that the history of philosophy should be compared to a gym in which past philosophers are at best examples or instruments for exercising our skill, and not moments of our own essence that constitute who we are. More importantly from a Kantian standpoint, the idea of philosophy as sheer activity in opposition to all of its products amounts to the sovereignty of a *spontaneity without receptivity*. Even if Kant would not go so far as Saint Paul in claiming that the letter kills the spirit, there is nonetheless a fear that the spirit may lose part of its life once it mingles with the letter, as if Kant feared reason's alienation. If we agree that without the letter spirit cannot reign and that we cannot think in a void, then in the history of philosophy interpretation and study—and that means learning *ex datis*—are an essential part of our philosophizing. Interpretation does not get started until we learn to cultivate our receptivity, our sensitivity to texts, the empathy and patience that allow us to follow the steps of another mind without imposing our views on it. It requires care for what matters and the recognition of the value of inheritance. It begins in the shape of a familiarity, an interested and eager attentiveness, a raising to focus and relief, an isolation of what deeply matters, to become a reshaping of connections, an imaginative appropriation and a meditation on our past. This is not an invitation to passivity, to some form of *Gelassenheit*, scholarly piety, or historicist indifference. On the contrary, treating texts from our tradition as relics, unalterable givens for antiquarians, even models, is the flip side of the coin Kant is forging in opposing active thought and passive reception. Mine is the plain consideration that if you are reading these pages it is because Kant's opposition between rational and historical was wrong. Not only was it wrong—we know it is, too.

Gratitude toward the ancients who benefited us with their teachings is not a duty we must be reminded of by section 33 of the Doctrine of Virtue (in the *Metaphysics of Morals*). It is a vivid and strong feeling, surely one many share about Kant, which in some of us can become a powerful motivation. A history of philosophy, unlike Kant's, does not have to be a second-best option, falling short of self-appointed so-called systematic philosophy or reflecting the discomforting realization that this is what many of us are good at. It can be philosophizing at its best once we take to heart the possibility, if not the promise or hope, that in the study of our tradition we can discover who we are: that the texts of classics like Plato and Aristotle, like the works of Kant, disclose our highest interests to us—and deserve better than Brucker's abridgment. Of course this is true only provided we learn to interrogate them. To use Kant's words, that means that we do not wait to be instructed by them as pupils, but compel them, like an appointed judge, to answer questions of our own asking (*KrV* B xiii).

If to philosophize is to think for oneself, obviously one cannot learn philosophy because it is not yet given and one philosophizes as one thinks (*Log, Ak* 9: 25–26, ENG 538–39). Kant's argument seems in its terse simplicity to defy all criticism. But it is a negative simplicity. That is, it works at the cost of *suppressing* all reference to contents. If to philosophize is first of all a judgment of determinate philosophical contents, then it simply does not work. I think that valuing the first maxim of an enlightened reason—to think for oneself, *Selbstdenken*—has everything to gain from the integration of the other two maxims of the third *Critique* (§ 40), the enlarged mentality and the consistent thought.[67] Tuning into the wavelength of predecessors, the second maxim, is key to that. It requires the receptivity and imagination I was mentioning and the dissatisfaction with the dichotomy of principles and givens, grounds and facts.

In a confidential report to Friedrich Niethammer, the chancellor of higher education in Bavaria, Hegel, commenting not on Kant but on some Bavarian pedagogues, writes that the invitation to learn to think for oneself has become a fad of the times. What is thinking that is not for oneself?, asks Hegel. Simply raising this question implies that thinking cannot be repeating or imitating. The idea of a servant of reason, passively obeying its commands, is contradictory.[68] But it also implies that to think is to think through contents. Hegel mocks the idea of a philosophizing that does not result in knowledge of contents. He compares this to an invitation to a relentless travel, during which I do not learn about cities, rivers, countries, people, but . . . travel. Getting to know such things, objects Hegel, *is* to travel. Likewise, when we learn the content of philosophy we are not simply learning to philosophize but actually practicing philosophy. Hegel goes on

---

67. In the *Anthropology* (§§ 43 and 59), the three maxims of the power of judgment are connected with, and may lead to, wisdom, but only insofar as they relate to conduct among other people.

68. For Hegel's report, see *Werke*, 4: 410–12. See also the 1830 *Encyclopaedia*, § 23 on *Selbstdenken*: "nobody can think for someone else, just as little as they can eat and drink for them. That expression is thus a pleonasm." In the Jaesche Logic Kant actually says: "the true philosopher as one who thinks for himself" must not make a "slavishly imitative use" of reason (*Ak* 9: 26, ENG 539: notice that Kant is speaking of thinking for oneself as opposed to prejudice, so Hegel's question should not remind us of the characterization of the understanding sketched above as the good soldier realizing the commands of reason). Here my question is: What is a false philosopher? What is imitation when it comes to reason? These are not questions raised by Kant but possibilities he takes for granted and leaves up in the air.

by stressing that philosophy must be learnt like every other science. He adds an example, the theorem of Pythagoras, that is striking in light of Kant's opposition between learning mathematics and philosophy. It makes no difference whether I am learning one or the other, writes Hegel, for in both learning comes down to apprehending an existing patrimony of acquired and already constituted contents.

As we can see, the target of Hegel's irony is partly different from Kant's idea. Rather than the attitudes reason may assume towards its object, by learning Hegel has in mind the relation between teacher and pupil, whereby the former offers a constituted body of cognitions that the pupil must take apart, reconstruct, and assimilate. More importantly, the distinction between philosophical and historical knowledge, which is to Kant the most pressing maxim of an enlightened reason striving to assert itself in its fight against prejudice, can be taken for granted by Hegel only thirty years later. Still, this passage does highlight that when it comes to philosophizing, thinking through contents means *making ours* thoughts first thought by others.

To sum up so far: in philosophy as a cognition from principles there is a difference between the a priori legislation over nature and freedom and the judgment of determinate philosophies, which is reflected in the tension between the productive and systematic use of the idea of philosophy and its function as judge of systems. But systems are historically given. And Kant's opposition between rational and historical not only rests on a false opposition between active thought and passive reception, but also works at the cost of suppressing the internal connection between the activity of thinking and its thoughts.

6. Cosmic Philosophy

Kant stresses reason's projective gaze, rather than the retrospective comprehension and use of the past. After all, he is a revolutionary who looks confidently ahead and wants to shrug the past off himself. The discontinuity between the time of ruins and the time of science inaugurated by critical philosophy is sharp.[69] The title 'History of Pure Reason' designates a place

---

69. It is also a problem, on which others (e.g., Yovel, *Kant and the Philosophy of History*, 282–83) have written important pages. In Kant time applies only to appearances, but the time that will measure the future, as well as all time regarding the manifestation of reason, needs a different understanding. Another problem is that Kant can claim that history is reason's history only if he speaks of a reason that is at once practical and speculative. In the History of Pure Reason and in the *Fortschritte*, however, he focuses only on moments in the history of speculative metaphysics as opposed to practical reason (see Höffe, "Architektonik und Geschichte," 639).

left vacant in the system which "must be filled in the future" (*KrV* A 852/B 880). The future is what really drives Kant and, so he thinks, human reason in the question of what we can hope for.

To add the last piece to the puzzle of reason's teleology, let us finally consider the definition of cosmic philosophy. It is "the science of the relation of all cognitions to the essential ends of human reason (*teleologia rationis humanae*), and the philosopher is not an artist of reason but the legislator of human reason" (*KrV* A 839/B 867). The philosopher is a "teacher in the ideal" who arranges and uses the artists of reason (mathematician, naturalist, logician) as means to promote our essential ends.

We saw, however, that the philosopher is an idea that cannot be personified and that an idea needs a schema as an execution of its project. The scholastic concept of philosophy also requires a systematic unity of knowledge, but only in terms of the logical completeness of cognitions. Cosmic philosophy differs because it aims at a relation between means and ends that must always remain in view. The cosmic concept is executed by an architectonical schema, the scholastic by a schema that is neither technical (it is not empirical or ad hoc) nor architectonical (it is not organic and teleological).[70]

The ends in cosmic philosophy are not an aggregate. Nor, given that they are guides, are they objects among other objects. The ends present themselves as a plurality that must be coordinated architectonically in an organic unitary system. That is, they have to be harmonized and reciprocally connected (*Refl* 1668, *Ak* 16: 71). In addition, they must also be subordinated to one final end, which cannot in any way be conflated with the essential ends, because the latter are themselves means to it. This final end is the ultimate destination of human beings and is the object of moral philosophy. Rational cognitions are means to reason's essential ends, and these are means to reason's final end.

As we can see, there are, over and above two kinds of ends, two different perspectives from which to consider cognitions: their *origin* and the *use* they are put to. The latter rests on the restriction to rational knowledge established by the former. The use rests on the origin, but it alone counts in the cosmic concept. Except that the use cognitions are put to is by definition not the object of a special competence, nor can it become a cognition. It involves a comprehensive and hierarchical horizon, a unitary perspective on the whole, and a special insight.

---

70. I thereby disagree with both Tonelli and La Rocca. Tonelli thinks that the schema of scholastic philosophy is technical (*Kant's Critique*, 272), and La Rocca implies that it is architectonical because it is organic (*Soggetto e mondo*, 221).

Reason is an organic unity addressed to its own ends. But unlike an organism, it does not have ends that are prescribed to it or presupposed as external and prior to it. For reason sets itself ends. If ancient philosophy discussed whether or not we should pay heed to ends we can draw only from nature, and modern philosophy has suppressed all ends from nature and from the questions it can concretely get hold of, Kant's teleology of reason crucially reinstates ends. The ends, however, are now entirely beyond all givenness. They neither are given to reason nor form a fixed ideal structure we must discover. Instead, reason's ends are projected as a goal we must take as a point of orientation.

If ends are not given, neither is their unity something we can grasp. It has to be made. This is another way to see how reason is driven toward the future, not the past, and by the hope of a unity we can shape. This unity, in turn, has nothing objective and cannot be objectified. In the words of the Vienna Logic, it is the unity of a horizon in which we judge the congruence between our cognitions and our essential ends (*Ak* 24: 814, ENG 272–73). In sum, the hierarchy of ends we let ourselves be guided by is the product of our philosophical activity.

In *Reflexion* 1652 (1769–75, *Ak* 16: 66), Kant writes: "wisdom is the reference [of a cognition] to the essential ends of humanity." The connection between ends and wisdom is prominent in all the lecture courses on logic and metaphysics where Kant speaks about ends and the cosmic concept of philosophy. In the passage from the Architectonic we are considering there is no mention of wisdom. It will appear only at the close of the chapter (*KrV* A 850/B 878). There is a notable rigor, however, when it comes to the inner distinction among ends throughout the *Critique of Pure Reason* and in the Architectonic in particular.[71]

Before we focus on that let me explain the terminological choices that face us here. Kant writes: "es gibt aber noch einen Weltbegriff," and for "Weltbegriff" he adds in parentheses the Latin equivalent, *conceptus cosmicus* (*KrV* A 839/B 867). I have been using the phrase 'cosmic concept,' but my choice is not self-evident or shared. Paul Guyer and Allen Wood use 'cosmopolitan concept' here; Norman Kemp Smith simply evades the problem

---

71. In the order of appearance: *KrV* A 832–33/B 860–61 (*wesentliche Zwecke; Hauptzweck; allerlei beliebige äussere Zwecke* versus *oberste und innere Zwecke*); *KrV* A 839–40/B 867–68 (*wesentliche; wesentliche, nicht die höchsten Zwecke; subalterne Zwecke vs Endzweck*); *KrV* A 850/B 878 (*wesentliche Zwecke; notwendige und wesentliche Zwecke*); see also the *Endabsicht* in the Canon, *KrV* A 798/B 826.

by omitting the translation;[72] Werner Pluhar uses 'world concept'; Michael Young 'worldly concept.'

Kant inherits from the logical tradition of the German Enlightenment, along with many other notions such as Meier's critique of erudition and prejudices, the distinction between philosophy 'for the schools' and philosophy 'for the world,' which is cognate with that between scholastic and popular philosophy. Philosophy addressed to the world educates to become a *Weltbürger*, a citizen of the world.

There is a connection between cosmic and cosmopolitan, clearly. Kant is remarkably indecisive regarding it, though. When he writes in the footnote that the *Weltbegriff* necessarily interests everyone (*KrV* A 840/B 868n), his is a *husteron proteron*. By making it sound as if this universal preoccupation exhausts the question, he inverts cause and effect. I think that what follows from his premises is instead that it is only because reason stands or falls with its relation to ends that for everyone the concern with cosmic philosophy is vital and primary. Then Kant blurs the picture even further when he translates *Weltbegriff* by the Latin *cosmicus* in the Vienna Logic (*Ak* 24: 798–99, ENG 258–59), by *cosmopoliticus* in the Pölitz Metaphysics (*Ak* 28: 3–4), and by either in turn in the *Jaesche Logic* (*Ak* 9: 23–25, ENG 537–38). This is another terminological vacillation that perhaps threatens, certainly obscures the consistency of his thought.

If Kant draws from Christian Wolff the distinction between historical and rational, he more or less leaves it as it stands.[73] By contrast, as Kant appropriates the established distinction between scholastic and cosmic, he subverts it and is profoundly innovative. It is thus reductive to understand Kant's concept of cosmic philosophy in light of his predecessors', for it misses its novelty and originality. Most important, it misses the connection between idea of the world and the ends underpinning it.

When Kant speaks of the use of our cognitions for the world instead of for schools, he has in mind a difference in exposition and the theme of popularity.[74] But, as readers of the *Prolegomena* know, there are dry and com-

---

72. "There is another concept of philosophy, a *conceptus cosmicus,*" is his rendering. In his *Commentary* (581n), he writes: "By *conceptus cosmicus* Kant means 'concept shared by the whole world.'"

73. See Hinske, *Zwischen Aufklärung und Vernunftkritik*, 22–23.

74. In the Vienna Logic, for example, a cognition "for the world" is popularity. It is the "accommodation of a science to the power of comprehension and taste" of common people, which may lose "in thoroughness" (*Ak* 24: 820–21, ENG 278). Popularity "requires familiarity with the world and intercourse with men" (ibid.). The very notions with which the Preface to the *Anthropology from a Pragmatic Point of View* opens (application of cognitions for the world's use,

plex notions that can never be made popular. The *Critique of Pure Reason* as a whole is one, and the idea of cosmic philosophy in particular another.[75] My suggestion is that cosmic philosophy and popularity are by no means kindred notions. The cosmos of the *Weltbegriff* of philosophy, as it were, is not mundane at all.

In turn, translating *Weltbegriff* by 'cosmopolitan' is an arbitrary choice that not only ignores Kant's distinction between cosmic and cosmopolitan contexts, but also suggests that Kant has in mind a broadly political application of philosophy, as if he were thinking of rights, the cultivation of our original dispositions, and institutions—which he doubtless also is—instead of the world. This leads to the same defect as the reduction of cosmic to popular. What gets lost here is the connection between ends and the architectonic idea, between philosophy and the world.

To shed further light on the connection between cosmic and cosmopolitan let us recall briefly two points regarding the world and the shortcomings of monocular vision. We have seen how Kant distinguishes nature and world; now let us add the third encompassing totality, the pragmatic anthropological perspective as the geographical stage for the civilization process. Regarding the cyclops, we have seen why the motif of vision is central. Philosophy's vision is not the all-knowing view from nowhere; its virtue is contextualization. It is a negative principle directed against all self-absorbed misuse of knowledge blind to its larger, especially practical, consequences, and can for this reason remind the scholar of reason's ends and the cyclops of the solipsism of monocular vision.

The problem of solipsism can be rephrased in terms of the opposition between public and private use of reason and between *sensus communis* and *sensus privatus*. The public use of reason is the presentation of our ideas "to the world," as we read in *What Is Enlightenment?* (*WA, Ak* 8: 37–40). The egoist of reason, instead, is "a world unto himself" or herself (*Refl* 1505, *Ak* 15/2: 811). The egoist lives in a dream, a bubble, in that he or she has lost

---

coming after school knowledge—*die Schule*—and dealing with the human being as a citizen of the world, and the distinction between *Weltkennen* and *Welthaben*) clearly belong in the knowledge of the world of anthropology and physical geography. They bear at best an indirect connection to the *Weltbegriff* in the Architectonic. On Locke and Rousseau as antecedents to the distinction between school and world, see the Introduction written by Brandt and Stark, the editors of the lectures on anthropology (in *Ak* 25/1: xx).

75. In the Preface to the *Metaphysics of Morals* Kant replies to Christian Garve's demand that "every philosophic teaching be capable of being made *popular* (that is, sufficiently clear to the senses to be communicated to everyone)," as follows: "I gladly admit that with the exception only of the systematic critique of the faculty of reason itself, along with all that can be established only by means of it" (*Ak* 6: 206, ENG 366).

the *sensus communis* and only sticks to a "logical private sense" (*Anth, Ak* 7: 219, ENG 324). "The opposite of egoism can only be *pluralism*, the way of thinking in which one is not concerned with oneself as the whole world, but rather regards and conducts oneself as a mere citizen of the world.—This much belongs to anthropology" (*Anth, Ak* 7: 130, ENG 241–42).

What defines our vision are its vantage point and its horizon. The enlarged mentality (the second maxim of the power of judgment in the third *Critique*) consists in setting oneself "apart from the subjective private conditions of the judgment" (*KU* § 40, ENG 175). The "man of a *broad-minded way of thinking* . . . reflects on his own judgment from a *universal standpoint* (which he can only determine by putting himself into the standpoint of others)" (ibid.). As is clear, the "universal standpoint" means different things when it comes to power of judgment and reflection, knowledge, science, the supersensible, the practical, and the pragmatic cosmopolitan dealings with others.

In all such cases vision appreciates the *whole* because prior to that it values *distance*, especially distance from what is one's own. There is thus a clear connection among all meanings insofar as we must not regard the world as alien and limit ourselves to being world spectators, but must be actively involved in what we see and do and become world citizens, as a striking *Reflexion* says ("Nicht Weltbeschauer, sondern Weltbürger seyn").[76] Some people are limited with respect to their heart, as in this *Reflexion*, and live in the judgment of others, as Rousseau said (courtesans are one of Kant's examples here); or they are limited with respect to their way of thinking (not to their intelligence but to the purposive use of it), as in the second maxim of the third *Critique*. Likewise in the *Anthropology* the egoist can be logical, aesthetic, or practical (*Anth, Ak* 7: 129–30, ENG 240–41). The imperative is

76. The full text of this note is as follows: "Man kan in Ansehung des interesse, was man an dem, was in Welt vorgeht, hat, zwey Standpunkte nehmen: den Standpunkt des Erdensohnes und den des Weltbürgers. In dem ersten interessirt nichts als geschäfte, und was sich auf Dinge bezieht, so fern sie einflus auf unser wohlbefinden haben. im zweyten interessirt die Menschheit, das Weltganze, der Ursprung der Dinge, ihr innerer Werth, die letzten Zweke, wenigstens gnug, um darüber mit Neigung zu urtheilen. Der Standpunkt des Erdensohnes führt uns zu unsrer nächsten Pflicht, nur muß man daran nicht geheftet seyn. Es macht einen thatigen, wakeren [aber] Mann, aber doch von engem Herzen und Aussichten. Im Umgange, vornemlich der Freundschaft, muß man seine Gesinnungen erweitern. Der Erdensohn hat nicht gnugsam stoff in sich selbst; er hängt an den Menschen und Dingen, von denen er befangen ist. Juristen lieben auch selten einmal geographie und politic. Hofleute sind Erdensohne. Weltbuerger muß die Welt als Einsaße und nicht als Fremdling betrachten. Nicht Weltbeschauer, sondern Weltbürger seyn. Oft ist man ein Erdensohn, weil die Begriffe, oft: weil das Herz sehr eingeschränkt ist. Die Unterredungen haben nichts, was das Herz und das Gemüth interessirt, und sind der Materie nach sehr eingeschränkt" (*Refl* 1170, *Ak* 15/2: 517–18).

to widen our vision: that is, see far as well as consider our particular things from afar.

Distance is key. In the *Opus Postumum* Kant writes that the sense of touch is essential for technical-practical reason, the sense of vision for moral-practical reason (*Ak* 21: 31). Before practical philosophy, however, we have the speculative perspective studied by the "architectonic of pure reason" (ibid.). The standpoint of the Architectonic is that of speculation. Kant explains the etymology of speculation by reference to the view from a height over the plain of experience allowing us to see far,[77] to gaze at the horizon. But if seeing far is key, the distance with which we live detachedly from our properties or drives, for example, differs from the distance of philosophy's vision. It is for this reason that I insist on the gap between cosmopolitan and cosmic vision as strongly as on their continuity.

Cosmic philosophy is philosophy according to its *Weltbegriff*. A *Weltbegriff* is the idea of an absolute and unconditional totality, an intelligible order. The architectonic idea organizes the totality of cognitions purposively. If, as in an organic system, this whole is immanent in and prior to the parts, no question or rational activity can be pursued in isolation. We should not lose sight of reason's ends. When we do, we have lost what is most important to us. Cosmic philosophy, therefore, is neither contemplation nor a therapy. Instead, it is a reminder.[78]

---

77. "Specula—Aussicht von einer Höhe über den flachen Boden der Erfahrung nicht betastend oder durch Stecken prüfend sondern um sich in der Ferne beschauend zu seyn" (ibid.). A remark on a different etymology that might interest those who are curious about the historical background of the notion of world is this. A few lines below, Kant writes that a *Cosmotheoros* is one who creates a priori the elements of a world knowledge from which one builds a worldview in the Idea qua world-citizen at the same time ("Cosmotheoros der die Elemente der Welterkentnis a priori selbst schafft aus welchen er die Weltbeschauung als zugleich Weltbewohner zimmert in der Idee," ibid.). The strange word 'Cosmotheoros' calls for historical references, and Adickes appropriately points out that Christiaan Huygens had written *Cosmotheoros, sive de Terris coelestibus earumque ornatu conjecturae*, which was published posthumously in 1698 in The Hague and translated into German in 1743. Huygens's title shows he knew that in Greek *kosmos* does mean world or universe, but it also means 'jewel,' 'ornament' (on *kosmos* as ornament, see Brague, *Sagesse du monde*, 31–32). For example, when Aristotle writes that magnanimity (*megalopsuchia*) is the "*kosmos . . . tōn aretōn*" (*Nicomachean Ethics* 4.7, 1124a 1), he means not that it is the universe of all virtues but their crown. It presupposes all other virtues while remaining distinct from them. We could perhaps say that Kant's methodological and architectonic idea as the idea of a systematic totality arranging all sciences and cognitions is not the addition of another material science to the parts but rather their crown.

78. I am aware that 'cosmic' is hardly a good word for this characterization of philosophy. But I prefer it because, unlike 'cosmopolitan' with its natural associations, it compels us to pause and think through its meaning.

What is the connection between essential ends and the final end? What are essential ends to begin with? For all the care they show in avoiding all conflation between essential ends and the one final end, these pages are surprisingly reticent. What seems clear, however, is that essential ends pertain to metaphysics and morals. They are the correlate of reason's legislation in its two realms. The gist of this thought is unequivocal and very strong. If artists of reason are means to reason's essential ends, cognitions should not be pursued for their own sake but instead be used for ends that transcend specialistic-scholastic knowledge. Philosophy cannot be dispensed with, not because it pretends to superiority over the sciences, but because it gives us back the second eye. In cosmic philosophy, theory and practice, irreconcilable and divided with respect to their realms of application, are unified. In fact, reason's speculative and practical employments and interests stem from the same original unity in thought.

A hasty and careless reading that does not pay close attention to the distinction between essential and final ends in these pages results in what is unfortunately a common misreading of the architectonic idea of philosophy. The invitation to wisdom should not be mistaken for a leap beyond knowledge.

For Kant morals are brought back to reason, to principles, which means to metaphysics.[79] Ethics in a strict sense (i.e., the investigation of the principles of action and the foundation of duty) and speculative metaphysics in a strict sense are unified in that they equally originate in reason's laws.[80] Whether these concern what is or what should be, they stem from pure reason.

At the same time, pure reason's laws are broadly moral insofar as the interest motivating them lies in the question of our ultimate destination.[81] It is not therefore in the shape of a metaphysics of morals grounding our autonomous actions that cosmic philosophy points beyond itself to moral philosophy and to the question about our ultimate destination, but rather in that of a broad metaphysics that includes speculation within itself. This is why Kant writes here that "the metaphysics of speculative reason is that which has customarily been called metaphysics *in the narrower sense;* but insofar as the pure doctrine of morals nevertheless belongs to the special

79. See Tonelli, "Kant's Ethics as a Part of Metaphysics," 236–63.

80. "Now the legislation of human reason (philosophy) has two objects, nature and freedom, and thus contains the natural law as well as the moral law, initially in two separate systems but ultimately in a single philosophical system" (*KrV* A 840/B 868).

81. "The philosophy of the entire vocation of human beings . . . is called moral philosophy" (*KrV* A 840/B 868).

stem of human and indeed philosophical cognition from pure reason, we will retain this term [metaphysics] for it" (*KrV* A 842/B 870).

As the Vienna Logic has it, understanding the connection of all cognitions of reason with ends includes the determination of the sources of human knowledge, the scope of its use, and its limits (*Ak* 24: 799, ENG 259). We have returned to the connection between ends and limits and to philosophy's invitation to modesty. And yet, once again philosophy does not seem very modest. It cultivates its ambition, which is the highest possible aspiration: teaching wisdom. When, in these very years, Papageno is asked if he is not ready to fight for wisdom, he squirms: "Kämpfen ist meine Sache nicht, ich verlang' auch gar keine Weisheit. Ich bin ein Naturmensch." Wisdom is philosophy's categorical imperative. Its maxim requires a resolute will, a sustained effort, and the use of reason's cognitions. It is not, however, the extension of our knowledge, but a form of anamnesis: the reawakening of an acute sense of limits through reason's self-knowledge.

If we saved ourselves the trouble of going through our cognitions and the sciences in the hope of getting to wisdom directly, maybe we would still attain the frugality we are being invited to pursue, but at the cost of losing the world, of retiring into our inner citadel.

Kant, who opposes *Arbeit* to *Schwärmerei*, calls this attitude misology, the hatred of reason. When he takes Epicurus and Rousseau as examples of forsaking science in favor of wisdom, and when he claims that the ancients rightly privileged in their idea of philosophy the model of the sage over artists of reason such as Wolff (*PhilEnz, Ak* 29: 8–9; see *GMS, Ak* 4: 405, ENG 59; *KpV, Ak* 5: 108–9, ENG 227), he is not advocating a revitalization of a Hellenistic moral philosophy leading to "the choice of a way of life," as "a concrete and practical" existence, as Pierre Hadot thinks.[82] Rather, what he values is the question of our final destination and the highest good seen through the lenses of reason's actual legislation.[83] We cannot choose wisdom over science. It would be like seeing through the second eye alone: we would be no less a cyclops than are artists of reason. Only the drive to wisdom resting on science can give us a comprehensive vision, which alone is sobering.

One philosopher Kant invariably recurs to in this context is Socrates, who, as far as I can tell, is never mentioned in the first *Critique*.[84] In the

---

82. *Qu'est-ce que la philosophie antique?*, 257–59.

83. In the *Opus Postumum* we read that philosophy as a doctrine of wisdom, even though it is the practical cornerstone (*Schlussstein*) of the edifice, will always have to deal with the principles and the question of human reason, even in its scholastic aspects aimed at sheer knowledge (*Ak* 22: 489–90).

84. The "Socratic method" is mentioned once (*KrV* B xxxi).

Dreams, Kant writes that if erudition indulges in boundless curiosity, wisdom instead can choose what it cares about. Socrates is the example of a thinker who puts things in perspective (*Ak* 2: 369, ENG 355). According to Kant he was the first to drive a wedge between speculation and wisdom, to show that the former is of no use for our ultimate destination, and to practice what he preaches, offering himself as a model of conduct (*PhilEnz*, *Ak* 29: 9).

That Socrates teaches by his own example returns in the Blomberg Logic. Here we also read that Socrates not only values his ignorance, but philosophizes about it, too (*Ak* 24: 35, 72, ENG 23, 54). Ignorance is not a destiny, but the judgment that there are many things "we do not need to know." Here Kant takes Socrates as the original skeptic, driven by the motto "quod supra nos, nihil ad nos" (What is above us is nothing for us, *Ak* 24: 212, ENG 168). In the Vienna Logic, Socrates is he who denounces artists of reason as philodox, i.e., lovers of opinion, because they provide means for any end we wish to pursue. This instrumental sense of reason is opposed by Kant to true philosophy as the legislation of reason (*Ak* 24: 798, ENG 259). In the *Jaesche Logic* (Ak 9: 29, ENG 541–42), Socrates diverted speculative minds to a practical direction. He is "almost the only one whose behavior comes closest to the idea of a wise man."[85]

As we can see, philosophy is first of all an *attitude with regard to cognitions and an awareness of ends* based on a keen sense of reason's interests. Modesty is tantamount to the awareness of the insufficiency of our cognitive efforts with respect to our destination. Speculation cannot decide conclusively on our ultimate questions. What we must keep in view at all times is the highest good. The window to our final destination is opened up for us by reason's self-knowledge.[86]

---

85. The last time Socrates is mentioned in this logic is when Kant says that his "*nichtwissen* was a laudable ignorance, really a knowledge of non-knowledge" (*Ak* 9: 44–45, ENG 553). This is "representing ignorance through science." It "presupposes science" (ibid.). In this sense Socrates, who is often paired with Epicurus, cannot be considered a misologist (in spite of his stress on the uselessness of speculation). Maybe it is fair to say that Socrates questioned the limits of speculation, not the limits of reason. *Reflexion* 4849 says that philosophy of ignorance is very useful but also difficult, because it leads us straight to the sources of knowledge (*Ak* 18: 36). On the first *Critique*'s Socratic inspiration, let this passage from the Discipline suffice: the "cognition of ignorance, which is possible only by means of the critique of reason itself, is thus *science*" (*KrV* A 758/B 786).

86. See *Ak* 21: 121: "The highest point of view of human practical reason is a drive of knowledge to wisdom (philosophy). The *nosce te ipsum*. The system of cognitions insofar as it contains the guide to wisdom is transcendental philosophy" (see also *Ak* 21: 104, 127–28, 156, and La Rocca, *Soggetto e mondo*, 217–42). See *Reflexion* 4849 (*Ak* 18: 5–6): "The goal of metaphysics. . . . Reason is the faculty of the absolute unity of our cognitions. The principles of the completion of

If that is true, then we may wonder if the criticism I formulated earlier, that philosophy rejects all objectification, misses the mark. Not only are philosophers are judged not for the cognitions they have but for the use they put them to. Even more important is the fact that cosmic philosophy must be thought of as a living engagement and a practice inspired by the idea of the world.

7. A Final Look at Ends and Wisdom

In the Dohna-Wundlacken Logic Kant remarks that "Socrates never purported to be a philosopher" (*Ak* 24: 699, ENG 437). In the *Jaesche Logic* Socrates teaches wisdom "through doctrine and example" (*Ak* 9: 24, ENG 537). That Socrates *teaches wisdom but is not a philosopher* is a very curious inversion. In the *Philosophical Encyclopaedia*, Kant, who is well aware of the etymology of 'philo-sophy' (desire to be wise), divorces wisdom from desire (*Ak* 29: 7). In fact, unlike Socrates, he ignores the eros or love of wisdom, and equates wisdom with the admonition to turn our gaze beyond science.

Despite these subtleties and apparent lapses in coherence, the general thread of Kant's thinking is clear and intelligible. That Socrates teaches wisdom means not that he provides wisdom but that he sets an example meant to show its importance for us all and an ideal toward which we can only strive. If we manage to approximate wisdom at all, it is because our conduct shows our awareness of reason's ends. Since nothing is good in itself, the sciences need reason's guidance because otherwise they are instrumental to any goal whatsoever. Means are neutral, for it is the use that qualifies and gives them the dignity they acquire. To borrow another distinction from the *Nicomachean Ethics*, some activities are means to ends but some are such that their own exercise has a sufficient value and meaning. They are not the final end, yet they are pursued for their own sake. Pursuing them is reason's excellence, dignity, and worth.

It seems to me that artists of reason are means to our essential ends, which in turn are but the exercise of pure reason. The "necessary and essential ends" (*KrV* A 850/B 878) are but the use of our cognitions and reason's legislation in speculative and practical metaphysics.

---

our knowledge . . . contain the conditions of wisdom, i.e., of the congruence to the sum-total of all our ends." This is called reason's practical unity. In the *Fortschritte*, the "doctrine of wisdom [is] the transition to the final end of metaphysics" (*Ak* 20: 273, ENG 364), which consists in a practical-dogmatic faith (*Ak* 20: 297, ENG 386).

Reason's activity then is not only divorced from and prior to its products. It is *an end* for them. Reason's teleology therefore is a genitive in both senses: reason aims at ends, and reason (the practice of rational activity) is the end of its own strivings. And yet, if the unity and hierarchy of ends are established by philosophy, reason's activity is not an absolute or *final* end. In the many aspects of its activity, in its questions and its legislation, reason is subordinated to the question of our destination. It is addressed to a world in which the highest good is a definite possibility.

In the *Critique of Pure Reason*, cosmic philosophy is concerned with essential ends. It "relates everything to wisdom, but through the path of science" (*KrV* A 850/B 878). Wisdom is here the end of philosophy, and philosophy is reason's legislation. The gap between wisdom and philosophy is as sharp as that between essential ends and final end.[87]

The solution seems adroit. Reason is the end of its activities but is itself subordinated to the final end, mankind's destination. Even so, however, the ambiguities of wisdom loom large. The problem is that often outside the *Critique of Pure Reason* and invariably after 1787 Kant takes back the distinction between essential and final ends (and sometimes the gap between philosophy and wisdom). He seems to recast the notion of cosmic philosophy accordingly. In fact, to be more precise, it is possible to argue that the distinction between essential and final ends is key only in the 1781 Architectonic (and reappears in B because Kant has neglected to suppress it).

As we will see in chapter 3, after 1781 Kant tends to recast the internal structure of the critique of pure reason from several perspectives. If the relation between metaphysics and moral philosophy is one of the first and main targets of this profound reconsideration, then the very distinction between essential and final ends, and between philosophy and wisdom, should also

---

87. The subordination of philosophy to wisdom is a thread uniting Kant's scattered *Reflexionen* long before the Architectonic. The use of metaphysics is to serve as a propaedeutic to wisdom (*Refl* 4459, Ak 17: 559). Again using Socrates, Kant writes that metaphysics is the organon of wisdom in that it teaches to "do without" (*Refl* 4457, Ak 17: 558: "Kritik der Wissenschaft und Organon der Weisheit (welche mehr aufs entbehren als erwerben ankommt. Socrates)"). In the *Inaugural Dissertation*, metaphysics is first the organon of intellectual knowledge (§ 3) and then the organon of wisdom as moral philosophy (§ 11; see Tonelli, *Kant's Critique*, 105–6). Philosophy is the organon of wisdom in that it shows the limits and ends of our faculties in *Reflexion* 5100 (*Ak* 18: 87; see also *Fortschritte*, *Ak* 20: 261, ENG 354, and the *Proclamation*, *Ak* 8: 421). In the *Opus Postumum*, transcendental philosophy is "the doctrine and exercise of wisdom" (*Ak* 21: 141) or leads to it (*Ak* 21: 121). "Sophus (der Weise) ist blos ein Ideal und nur einzig. Philosophus Homo est" (the wise man is an ideal, while the philosopher is a man, *Ak* 21: 157).

be redefined. This interpretation is made plausible by ample supporting evidence.

The *Jaesche Logic* says that "the cosmic concept of philosophy is the science of the *final ends* of human reason" (*Ak* 9: 24, ENG 537, italics mine). This is taken word for word from a passage in the Pölitz Metaphysics (*Ak* 28: 3) and is in line with passages from later essays.[88] Here wisdom is exclusively connected with the final end(s). Strikingly there is no trace of essential ends. And Kant almost lapses into misology himself when he writes that, for philosophy as "the doctrine of wisdom," "science is not required. The doctrine of the highest end (command) everyone knows" (*Ak* 21: 117). Perhaps, in contrast to what he wrote in the Architectonic, that cognitions should not be pursued for their own sake but are used for ends that transcend scholastic knowledge, Kant should then claim simply that all speculation is without further ado subordinated to moral philosophy. Wisdom would then be about morality, not about philosophy's relation to our end (*Ak* 8: 417–18). The three questions of the Canon would be basically reduced to the last two (what should I do? what may I hope for?). The final end would not depend on the preliminary pursuit of essential ends orienting reason in its direction, but would be the object of will and rational faith.[89]

The contrast can also be summarized along these lines. In the Architectonic philosophy is an organic and concrete endeavor. Later, philosophy seems to point beyond itself to morality. In these later writings the idea of a rational world, which we consider as if nature were designed by a wise maker, is a unity in the idea of the highest good as a world in which morality and happiness can coincide.[90] If all ideas form an interconnected system pointing to the highest good in the first *Critique*, later the cosmic concept of philosophy leans more and more exclusively toward the question about our ultimate destination.

Here, too, we can say that whether cosmic philosophy is about essential or final ends, the whole of philosophy is moral in its inspiration even if not in its objects. The question about our final destination uses as means all questions on metaphysics and morality, which in turn presuppose the critique.

---

88. See the *Philosophical Trials in Theodicy* (*Ak* 8: 256n, 263, ENG 25, 30–31), *The End of All Things* (*Ak* 8: 336, ENG 228), *Proclamation* (*Ak* 8: 417–18, ENG 456) and the *Opus Postumum* (*Ak* 21: 149). In the *Opus Postumum*, philosophy is the love we feel for human reason's final ends (*Ak* 21: 121).

89. For a similar conclusion see Yovel, *Kant and the Philosophy of History*, 232.

90. *Ak* 8: 263. We saw above (note 46) how the ideas of God and the world are mutual correlates in the dialectic of pure reason. Consider now *Ak* 21: 16–24 and 140 on this correlation in light of the highest good.

That, however, risks downplaying the undeniable difference between these two versions of cosmic philosophy. More importantly, what is left undecided is the very *reality* of philosophy. What matters to me is not denouncing Kant's ambivalence on wisdom or even voicing the legitimate suspicion that Kant may be confused on essential and final ends when he bends the first *Critique* to an instrument for the safeguard of morality and religion.[91] My primary interest here is discussing the problem concerning cosmic philosophy this incoherence highlights. (Unless, that is, it should turn out that Kant is not incoherent but consistently executes his program, a conjecture

91. The critique determines "the possibility, the scope, and the boundaries of our speculative faculty of cognition *so that* Epicurean philosophy will not take over the entire field of reason and drive morality and religion into the ground" (*Ak* 18: 626, italics mine). Likewise, in all conflicts of reason with itself Kant is never impartial between thesis and antithesis. That his heart goes to the thesis because dogmatism satisfies reason's architectonic and practical interest in its conflict (*KrV* A 475/B 503) and reinforces the hope to avert the dangers of fatalism, naturalism, and materialism (*Prol, Ak* 4: 363, ENG 152) is quite clear. That this should lead to an ethico-theology, as it does eventually in the *Critique of Judgment*, seems to me more the desideratum of a philosophical agenda than the fruit of a rigorous argument. In the third *Critique*, reason's access to the supersensible is not through the postulates. The supersensible, through the connection of freedom, teleology, and a moral order, is felt by reflective judgment in the world of nature. Among the many perplexities I have about ethico-theology and the highest good, let me limit myself to a concise note on Kant's notion of hope for a happiness guaranteed by God to the righteous. To Jacobi, who wrote that on this earth inclinations would debase man while in a future better world our reward is full satisfaction and man has repressed inclinations before the grave only to see them reawaken much more vividly afterward (*Über das Unternehmen*, in *Werke*, 3: 191), Kant could retort that Jacobi does not recognize the difference in forms of happiness (*Vergnügen, Zufriedenheit, Seligkeit*). Still, as L. W. Beck puts it, it is hard "to frame a conception of the happiness or bliss of a being no longer affected by desire" (*Commentary*, 271). Beck therefore thinks that the highest good is not a practical concept but a dialectical ideal of reason conceived as a system of ends. It is "important for the architectonic purpose of reason in uniting under one idea the two legislations of reason . . . in a practical-dogmatic metaphysics wholly distinct from the metaphysics of morals" (*Commentary*, 245). Either the highest good is a postulate for a future life, and then no happiness *as we know it* can accrue to the virtue of an immortal soul; or the highest good is exhibited in mankind's moral history, and then happiness consists simply in the satisfaction of culture, not in a future life (see Orsini, *Il metodo della critica di Hegel*, 196ff.). As I already pointed out, reason commands duty but cannot command hope. Yet Kant claims exactly that when he faults Spinoza, the atheist, "the righteous man . . . who would merely unselfishly establish the good to which that holy law directs all his powers," for not being able to count on a lawlike agreement of nature with ends such as only a moral author of the world could design. Because his efforts are limited, Spinoza is therefore forever "subject to nature" and "all the evils of poverty, illness, and untimely death" (*KU* § 87, *Ak* 5: 452–53, ENG 317–18). All of that makes his morality unreliable until he assumes the existence of God. In the Mrongovius Metaphysics we read: "If we assume moral principles without presupposing God and another world . . . then I am a virtuous dreamer, because I expect no consequences which are worthy of my conduct" (*Ak* 29: 777). Pure virtue for a nonbeliever "is wholly impossible" (*Ak* 29: 778). I confess I am as unable to grasp this as Descartes's cognate argument at the end of the Fifth Meditation (as long as I do not understand God's existence, my geometry cannot be a true and certain science).

we will examine in the concluding pages of this chapter.) Indeed, we can no longer postpone a question: what exactly is philosophy? Is it real or ideal? Is cosmic philosophy, the only genuinely architectonic science, reason's essential end or a mere dispensable step to our final end? What is the relation between philosophy and wisdom?

Often philosophy and wisdom are not subordinated to one another at all but are indistinguishable insofar as they are equally unattainable for us: philosophy, because it is an idea, and wisdom, because strictly speaking only God is wise.[92]

This introduces a serious dilemma regarding the reality and ideality of philosophy as well as the extent to which Kant thought that his philosophy was an example of cosmic philosophy.

Thinking on our own is definitely available to us and defines the activity of philosophizing. As we saw, the critique is a point of no return. The Architectonic is an organic unity of the totality of pure reason's cognitions (KrV A 835/B 863), and the philosopher is the legislator of human reason. Therefore, it is impossible to see why Kant's philosophy should differ from cosmic philosophy.[93] In that case, however, the problem is that philosophy is quite real for us, so real that it appears as the execution of a determinate

92. In *The End of All Things* only God is wise (*Ak* 8: 336). This becomes a refrain in the *Opus Postumum* (*Ak* 21: 120, 124, 130, 134, 157). Kant asks himself if the term *Weltweisheit* is fit to denote philosophy and replies in the negative (*Ak* 21: 120, 130, 149). The term is good "for the school" (*Ak* 21: 120: for scholastic, not cosmic, philosophy). It implies a contrast between world and God, which in cosmic philosophy are thought together (*Ak* 21: 140). Elsewhere in the same pages we find a different understanding of *Weltweisheit*, as "an analogue" to actual wisdom and therefore as a possible equivalent of philosophy (*Ak* 21: 120). In this analogical sense alone (not in the merely defective sense where *Weltweisheit* falls short of philosophy) is *Weltweisheit* a good term for our love for wisdom (ibid.). Because of this analogical sense, Kant can say that, since only God is wise, it is a mockery (*Spott*) to call a being of this world wise ("Denn es wäre ein Weltwesen der Weise aber ist niemand anders als Gott," *Ak* 21: 157). Naturally, it would not be a mockery and nobody would feel mocked if the definition of *Weltweisheit* had nothing to do with our efforts at cosmic philosophy. The figure of the philosopher (as an archetype it would be vainglorious to compare oneself with and as "a teacher in the ideal" in the Architectonic: *KrV* A 839/B 867) is called a "teacher of wisdom" in the Dohna-Wundlacken Logic (*Ak* 24: 698, ENG 436) and *Jaesche Logic* (*Ak* 9: 24, ENG 537). (The philosopher is called even a "knower of wisdom" in the Pölitz Metaphysics, *Ak* 28: 354, ENG 301, which raises new problems of its own on wisdom as the actual object of knowledge rather than what inspires conduct.) In the Dohna-Wundlacken Logic (*Ak* 24: 699 and 704, ENG 437 and 443) we find the sheer opposition between "wise man or legislator" and artist of reason, suggesting an opposition between an ideal (philosophy *and* wisdom) and what is available to us humans.

93. "[P]hilosophy in a *genuine* sense" is "metaphysics of nature as well as of morals" and "critique of reason" (*KrV* A 850/B 878, italics mine). If Kant thought he was doing scholastic philosophy, he would deprive the Architectonic of all sense and use. Besides, how would he know there is a cosmic philosophy beyond what he practices?

plan. The essential ends to which we subordinate cognitions stop being guides to become reason's self-sufficient objectives. Whether we have already acquired them or not, whether they form a doctrine or not, they are not unattainable for us.

Consider the alternative interpretation, the ideality thesis. If philosophy qua idea were as unattainable as wisdom and not only teaching philosophy but also practicing it were reduced to an ideal, then all talk of science and legislation would lose meaning, including the critique of pure reason's negative legislation and reason striving to rule over itself, without which no enlightenment is possible. The Architectonic, the highest point in reason's self-understanding, is not a dry classification, an uninteresting taxonomy, as Neo-Kantians thought. It is a philosophical organization of rational sciences. But if philosophy is not real, what remains of that? If philosophy claims to give us back the second eye, what is left of its promise? Replying that philosophy is real as an attempted approximation to the ideal risks becoming a play on words that settles nothing. In fact, it delays or reduplicates the problem.

This dilemma of cosmic philosophy reverberates in another opposition. As we know, the highest good (Kant's private obsession, judging from the number of *Reflexionen* devoted to it) is at first projected into an indefinite beyond to be later translated, in the third *Critique* and the writings on religion and history, into the goal of history. Likewise, there are two senses of future in what I have been saying about cosmic philosophy: the not-yet (a goal we are moving toward in a process of realization) and what lies ahead of the present and is pushed to an indefinite *focus imaginarius* beyond any reach. These are respectively a temporal future in historical time and an indefinite eschatological 'beyond' lying outside time, at the end of time, as it were.

Kant's conflicting statements reflect these alternatives. As he sets himself the problem of the relation between his philosophy and history, Kant says that the idea of cosmic philosophy has always grounded philosophers' efforts (*KrV* A 838/B 866). Then (regardless of how we construe the cryptic *bis dahin* discussed in note 65), he writes as if we are moving closer and closer to the archetype and realizing the idea.[94] At A 838/B 866 Kant speaks quite

---

94. This famously sparks Reinhold's enthusiasm. Reinhold is justified in drawing a distinction between progress toward science and progress in science. The former is complete and achieved once science, which means Kant's critical philosophy, is discovered. Here the movement finds its point of arrival in a change of state, from the different ways of groping among concepts to the one science (*Briefe*, 2: 177–78). Reinhold's enthusiasm is no less famously

paradoxically of the possibility that the copy approximates and even "equals the archetype."[95]

The notorious problem that an indefinite progress is contradictory because it affirms for us humans what it at once declares impossible is nowhere nearly as strong in the Architectonic as Kant's oscillation between the drive to approximate the model and the insistence on the ideal status of the philosopher. Maybe Kant fears that the conceptual pair 'idea and example' suggests the impression that we might realize an end and that this pair might be equivalent to something like 'plan and execution *in concreto*,' which would deny the excess of the cosmic idea and its irreducibility to examples. Or he is afraid of sounding boastful.

Certainly, it seems to me, his hesitations on the identity and difference between critique and metaphysics, on whether or not transcendental philosophy is a science and can be equated with the system of pure reason, on canon and organon and on discipline and doctrine, and his equivocal and shifting use of the concept of metaphysics (general and special, immanent and transcendent, positive and negative, speculative and practical), are the basic problems behind his indecisiveness.[96]

One last question concerning the reality of philosophy involving the public use of reason is how we recognize a philosopher. This is a problem Kant finds ostensibly less urgent than Plato does in the *Sophist*. We know it is impossible to teach philosophy. And yet Kant opens the *Prolegomena* by addressing himself to the "future teachers" of a science whose completion he has proudly affirmed all along and made possible in the first place. The only solution to this apparent tension, as we saw, is to state unequivocally that philosophy can be taught as a method, an awareness of the horizon or a comprehensive view, and a maxim. As a result, philosophers do not distinguish themselves on the basis of the contents they have acquired. It is

---

dampened as he acknowledges that the ideal of science as a complete system derived from one idea is never realized or deduced a priori by Kant (*Über das Fundament*, 72–75).

95. In the *Philosophical Encyclopaedia* Kant says that philosophy is reason's legislation, a doctrine of wisdom, but this archetype cannot be reached ("if an archetype could be reached, it would no longer be an archetype," *Ak* 29: 8). If this can be considered the *ideality* of philosophy, contrast this passage with the following passages in favor of the *reality* of philosophy (respectively from the Pölitz Metaphysics and the Vienna Logic). The cosmic "philosopher is he who has maxims of the use of our reason for certain ends" (*Ak* 28: 354, ENG 301: clearly, this is within everybody's reach). "The philodox is related to the philosopher as the businessman is to the legislator in the state. . . . This is one of the hardest, but also most sublime things in philosophy, which presently only a few have attained" (*Ak* 24: 799, ENG 260). A legislator in a state is as real as Kepler, the legislator of the heavens.

96. See below, chapter 3, § 3.

not *what* they teach, but *the spirit* with which they do so that sets their science apart from other rational cognitions. It follows that philosophers are not merely clever and quick minds, excellent at solving puzzles, or endowed with an outstanding intelligence. What identifies them is a maxim. They are driven by an imperative and sustained by a method, as well as reminded not to lose the second eye.

As we know, however, we can never be sure about the maxims of our conscience. *Gewissen* is opaque to itself, and our heart is impenetrable. When Kant asks how the philosopher is to be recognized (*KrV* A 838/B 866), he throws himself into an impasse from which there would seem to be no viable escape. How can the public use of reason claim to identify certain philosophers as examples of the cosmic idea? The requirement that only the idea in us makes it possible to judge examples does not seem to help us solve this problem. Nor can the concrete effects made possible by a maxim decide who is to count as a philosopher, for success in the realization can hardly be taken as a criterion to judge maxims for Kant. Unlike the two eyes on our face, a comprehensive vision cannot be seen by others. Nor can a maxim.

Whatever our solution to this problem, the spirit of Kant's concept makes it impossible to keep separate wisdom, an enlightened reason, and the command to autonomy. There is a note in the *Opus Postumum* that eliminates all hesitation and unites them. Kant writes: "self-knowledge (*nosce te ipsum*) is a command of reason containing everything: *sapere aude*, be wise."[97]

But we must realize that if we take this invitation as Kant's last word on the connection between philosophy and wisdom, we do not solve but rather downplay the problem of the relation between theory and practice. Do I reach my destination and realize myself as a world citizen or as cosmic philosopher? Are we allowed to claim there is no real gap between the two without having to efface their difference?

If we take the note from the *Opus Postumum* as definitive, we must conclude that we also turn the aspiration to wisdom into a *concrete program*. In Schiller's interpretation of *sapere aude* in the eighth letter on the education of mankind inspired by Kant's essay on the Enlightenment, this was the choice, if not the solution. But this choice, like all applications of a maxim, reduces the richness and complexity of cosmic philosophy to one of its aspects.

97. "Selbsterkenntnis (*nosce te ipsum*) ein Gebot der Vernunft welches Alles enthält: *sapere aude* sey weise," *Ak* 21: 134.

What can we say to untangle this intricate web? Can we rescue this point from the numerous contradictions and oscillations that seem to mar its consistency and ultimately undermine its importance?

8. An Attempt at Interpretation

It is worth returning to the theme of misology to see if we can pull diverse threads together into a unified reply to the several questions and doubts raised so far: the exclusive stress on the negative result of ideas and the Dialectic, the practical interest underlying metaphysics, the relation between science and philosophy, between reason and understanding, between reason's legislation and our final destination, between essential and final ends.

Readers of the Canon will hardly be surprised by the occasionally more explicit statements on these issues to be found in Kant's lecture notes on metaphysics. Consider the following quotes:

"The *practical* philosopher is the *genuine* philosopher" (*Ak* 28: 533). Once again, what characterizes the philosopher is a concern, a care, an interest that inspires a conduct. To reiterate a crucial point, the practical or moral philosopher is not the virtuous person, for 'moral' is used in two different senses. Philosophy is moral in its spirit and destination. It points to wisdom and the hope for a rational and just world. But this morality is not the sphere of duty and what we can issue laws about, for philosophy does not legislate over our final end. We can legislate on a metaphysics of morals and do concretely legislate every time we decide on a moral course of action. But we do not legislate over the result, the highest good, we hope a virtuous life can bring us. That is given to us, as an expectation human beings share.

"Were there no hope for a future life then the vicious . . . would be the happiest. Therefore one sees that metaphysics first arose from this practical interest of our reason" (*Ak* 29: 937). Metaphysics arises to address this 'moral' interest. Metaphysics and critical philosophy share this task. "The dialectic is the greatest end of transcendental philosophy," as it shows "how illusion can be discovered."[98] As we can see, *for Kant the Dialectic is central.* But this is not so much because Kant is intent on destroying the old world as because he thinks that if speculation proves unable to accomplish anything, then room is left open for a different, nondogmatic concern with the

---

98. V-Met/Mron, *Ak* 29: 805, ENG 159. "The negative use of metaphysics is the greater because it consists in the prevention of imperfection." The main use of metaphysics "is to purify our cognition from errors and to guard it from them. The main ends of metaphysics are the cognition of God and the hope of a future life" (*Ak* 29: 938, ENG 284).

same two questions about God and another world that could not be settled by special, speculative metaphysics (or philosophy in a scholastic sense, we could also say). It is not just that Kant wants to limit knowledge to make room for faith. After all, his faith is a pure rational faith, not a mystical leap.

Besides, faith itself, presupposing from a practical point of view a wise world ruler, makes the negative results of the Dialectic appear in a different light. "If I have a ground to suspect there is another world and a world author, then an entirely other interest opens up. What must I thus do? In the practical respect these two propositions are thus of the highest importance and more important than all other ends" (*Ak* 29: 774). "Metaphysics is not the foundation of religion . . . but rather the bulwark against the attacks of speculative reason" (*Ak* 29: 776). "Because [metaphysics] is thus built upon critique and guards us from errors, it is a bulwark of religion against all speculative doubt" (*Ak* 29: 939).

The Canon was no different in this respect. The only two questions of practical interest for pure reason are "Is there a God? Is there a future life?" (*KrV* A 803/B 831). All that "pure reason accomplishes in opening up prospects beyond the bounds of experience" are these two articles of faith, as Kant famously concludes at the end of the Canon (*KrV* A 830/B 859). In the *Fortschritte*, the final end of metaphysics is a "*practical-dogmatic* doctrine" leading us to take to be true (*fürwahrhalten*) a *theoretical* proposition (such as "there is a God") through *practical* reason (*Ak* 20: 297, ENG 386). Kant goes so far as to write that "the new astronomy has in this way done a great benefit to theology" because we are no longer under the illusion that our earth is the entire stage for divine wisdom.[99]

We may cherish this result if we are concerned with religious or moral issues of consummate justice and the realization of a rational order on earth. Or, if we are suspicious of ontotheology and admire Kant's rigor in excluding from the motives of morality all principles that are not tested by pure reason and all language of reward and expectations, we may find it disappointing because it reintroduces a practical ethicotheology we thought had been banned. But whatever our reaction, ignoring that this is what Kant thought—as do all readers who take Kant as a positivist or want him rid of all metaphysical ballast—is simply a mistake.

The *Critique of Practical Reason* closes with these words:

99. *Refl* 6091, *Ak* 18: 447. See also the passage from the *Bemerkungen* quoted as the epigraph for this chapter.

> Science (critically sought and methodically directed) is the narrow gate that
> leads to the *doctrine of wisdom*, if by this is understood not merely what one
> ought *to do* but what ought to serve *teachers* as a guide to prepare well and
> clearly the path to wisdom which everyone should travel . . . ; philosophy
> must always remain the guardian of this science. (*Ak* 5: 163, ENG 270–71)

Science is here supervised by philosophy, and so there is a strong connection between them. What they jointly produce is a disciplined investigation, a systematic method, and an active involvement. These are opposed to the passive awe of reason in its infancy before the starry heaven, which resulted in astrology, and before morals, which resulted in fanaticism and superstition. What science and philosophy jointly produce is a secure path in which we can no longer lose our direction. The path to wisdom through this narrow gate can be traveled by everyone. It is within everyone's reach to be concerned about his or her ultimate destination: It is everyone's interest to hope for the highest good. Philosophy's essential ends, by contrast, are not necessarily to be pursued by everyone. Still, I might add, the realization of the highest good is not in our control.

This argument is worth unpacking. Every idea, precisely by being a standard for what is to be realized, has intrinsic worth and dignity. The idea of philosophy is, like the idea of wisdom, to be asserted as a goal in its purity and perfection with the awareness that any realization falls short of it. Ideas have at best examples, not intuitive occurrences. Their ideal character, scorned by the consideration 'it is only an idea, you cannot find an adequate object for it,' is their value (*KrV* A 328/B 385). This implies that realization is not the right word for ideas, for they are not embodied in concrete manifestations the way, say, a triangle is *exhausted* in its intuitive exhibition. They retain their excess and are at best, and rarely, exemplified in history. Philosophy denotes the activity of *Selbstdenken*. On the other hand, this opens up the participation in the idea to all who are educated to think for themselves.

Now, philosophy through its knowledge—which means pure reason's self-knowledge—makes pure reason aware of its limitations (Proclamation, *Ak* 8: 421, ENG 459). We can see then that science *disciplines* philosophy and establishes the model of a secure path. Philosophy adds not only a consciousness that appearances point beyond themselves but also the fundamental awareness of reason's *finitude* by pointing beyond itself to the highest good and our final destination.

Differently stated, knowledge through experience points toward what is beyond nature. But this turns out now to be a simple premise, however necessary, before we acknowledge that reason points toward what is *beyond the forces in our control*. We would misunderstand Kant's emphasis on reason's legislation if we thought of reason only in terms of self-reliance and self-sufficiency. No less important is the recognition that human reason, for all its metaphysics and all laws of which it is the exclusive source, for all its autarchy, is not in possession of the highest good. This does not depend on us. The consideration of reason as an organism must then be supplemented by the consideration of the environment this organism lives in and is in constant relation to. Metaphors and analogies aside, Kant has focused on reason in itself and left us precious intimations of reason's otherness: givenness, chance, luck. If in its autarchy reason had no authority outside itself, in this wider perspective reason is not a master of its own destiny. Completeness in pure reason's self-knowledge is what critical philosophy accomplishes. But this completeness returns us to our structural incompleteness.

There is another way to justify this interpretation. The pages from which the passage just quoted comes employ the familiar image of chemistry, which to Kant is tantamount to a model of scientific separation of empirical from rational. Recall that in the *Prolegomena* chemistry replaces alchemy much as astronomy is the mature substitution for astrology. While in its infancy reason is prey to diverse forms of *Schwärmerei* and cannot orient itself and emancipate itself from its minority, in its maturity, in critical philosophy, reason has reached the status of science. This stage is a clear, methodical inquiry leading to certainty and establishing truths that can be subjected to public scrutiny.

But there is something else in this passage. The 'narrow gate' is a quote from the Gospels.[100] Kant himself now cashes in on his repeated connection between wisdom and his idea of Christianity.

In the second *Critique*, Kant contrasts Stoic and Christian virtue. The former, the "heroism of the *sage*," "made consciousness of strength of soul the pivot" (*Ak* 5: 127–28n, ENG 242–43n). Greek schools, whether they thought common human understanding (Cynics) or the path of science (Stoics and Epicureans) was sufficient to achieve prudence and wisdom, relied on "the mere *use of natural powers*" (ibid.). By contrast, Christian morals (reduced to its "philosophic side," ibid.) represents the law in its purity and strictness. Thus Christianity "deprives the human being of confidence that he can be fully adequate to it, at least in this life, but again sets it up by enabling us to hope that if we act as well as is within our *power*, then what

---

100. Matthew 7: 13–14, Luke 13: 24. Philosophy is, if you will, the angel guarding it.

is not within our power will come to our aid from another source, whether or not we know in what way" (ibid.).

This then is the verdict. Unlike the Greeks, we cannot rely on our powers alone. The compensation for the deprivation of self-confidence is hope in a benevolent supreme judge rewarding us in another life.

The autonomy of reason and the will rests on the heteronomy—or, better, the insufficiency—of our forces. Again the powers of pure reason in its *unnatural* autarchy rest on the finite powers of our human nature. The finitude of human reason is connected to the finitude of our powers and of the forces affecting our self-reliance; it is not an intrinsic finitude of reason originally dependent on sensibility and time as in Heidegger's interpretation.

Consider further the connection between the Christian idea of wisdom and the relation established by Kant between ends, science and philosophy, morals and rational faith, wisdom, and the highest good and eternal life.[101] In the Book of Wisdom (Solomon's Book), we read that virtue does not bring happiness on this earth, where the virtuous cannot be recognized. Thanks to God's plan, human beings received an immortal life that is the reward for our moral efforts (1:13–15, 4:1–2, 4:10–15).

Saint Paul opposes knowledge to faith, which he calls human and divine wisdom respectively. The former is acquired, even though with the help of God. For God not only created the world but also gave us two distinct languages. Human wisdom uses the language of science, but basking in this knowledge is folly. Conversely, divine wisdom appears as a scandal to Jews and sheer foolishness to Gentiles,[102] for God made human or mundane wisdom ("the wisdom of the world," *tēn sophian tou kosmou*, 1 Cor. 1:21) foolishness.

We must forsake human knowledge if we want to have an insight into divine wisdom's design and be saved (1 Cor. 1: 18–31). We must "become foolish to become wise" (1 Cor. 3: 19). Becoming wise amounts to following in Christ's footsteps, willing the unity of our community and liberating ourselves from all diversions from the path chosen after the revelation of the cross. The revelation through Christ is the spiritual insight into God's intervention in history (Col.).

101. In what follows I have profited from the reading of the several entries on *Sagesse* (by M. Gilbert, J. Cazeaux, J. N. Aletti, A. Solignac, C. Béné, B. Schultze, and F. Marty) in the *Dictionnaire de spiritualité*, the first two chapters of Wolfson's *Philosophy of the Church Fathers*, and Scribano, *Angeli*.

102. *Mōria*, 1 Corinthians 1: 18. "Jews demand signs, Greeks desire wisdom, for us the message is Christ crucified," 1 Corinthians 1: 22–25.

Another opposition set up by Paul is that between science and love (*agapē*, 1 Cor. 8: 2). Science puffs up, while love edifies. But what is interesting here is that while science knows but does not know *how* it must know, love is both love and knowledge at the same time.

In book 12 of *De Trinitate*, Augustine rephrases Paul's opposition between science and wisdom. Now science is concerned with the order of action and knowledge with that of temporal things, while wisdom is the intellectual contemplation of eternal truths. This is an inversion of Aristotle's concepts of wisdom (*phronēsis*) and science (*epistēmē*) in book 6 of the *Nicomachean Ethics*.[103]

In the *Opus Postumum* (*Ak* 21: 129–30), Kant writes that wisdom can be predicated only of a perfect reason (i.e., God's). Modesty compels us to describe philosophy as the aspiration to such wisdom or love of wisdom. Then he adds that "you cannot know wisdom without loving it" (ibid.). In a sense, therefore, when pure reason awakens us through its essential ends to the thought of a final destination and philosophy prepares the path to wisdom, it must desire it because it knows it.

For all its differences from the Christian idea, this is the gist that Kant wants us to pay heed to. Through the indispensable mediation of science and philosophy, through awareness of its own limits and insufficiency, pure reason is driven to reach its destination. It is driven to work to do what it can in order legitimately to desire and hope to deserve what is beyond its reach.

Wisdom then is reason's categorical imperative not despite its unreachability, but because it is the perfect design of a consummately rational world that we can never know.

103. Augustine's contrast is one of the remote sources of many medieval and early modern oppositions up to Kant's dichotomy of an *intellectus archetypus/intuitus originarius* and the empirical employment of reason through the understanding's concepts in experience.

CHAPTER TWO

A Priori Synthesis

In every experience there is something through which an object is given to us and something through which it is thought. If we take the conditions that lie in the activities of our mind through which alone an object can be given, we can know something a priori about objects. If we take the conditions through which alone an object can be thought, we can also know something a priori of all possible objects.

—I. Kant, *Reflexion* 4634, *Ak* 17: 618

1. A Productive Reason

As we have seen, reason is an articulated unity. Its laws and principles form a complete system, an organic plan. Therefore reason is its own project. The medium and element of this project are its ideas, which define the goal of reason's inquiry by directing all its activities. At the same time ideas, by representing unreachable standards, make us aware of our limits. And they form a purposive and self-contained unity prior to all subsequent division and application to the distinct spheres of theory and practice.

Cosmic philosophy as the epitome of reason's essence and vocation gives us a comprehensive vision that, as an attitude toward cognitions and an awareness of reason's interests and ends, sustains all rational activities. As reason's highest legislator and spokesman for *Selbstdenken*, philosophy arranges all the cognitions of sciences in view of its own ends. If philosophy is so ambitious, it is not comparable to familiar contemporary postideological forms of philosophical activity. Nor is it reducible to textual or conceptual explanation. Accordingly, metaphysics is not an analytic enterprise.

This, however, should give us pause. For does Kant not explicitly call philosophy explanation (*Erklärung*)? Does he not claim to denounce the pretensions of dogmatic metaphysics as empty and illusory? Does he not seem to say that reason cannot presume to do more than synthesize given materials and unify external contents, which it finds and certainly cannot produce? We surely need to draw some urgent distinctions. Before we do, however, let us dwell on a further consequence to be drawn from chapter 1.

I have been speaking about philosophy's ambitions and about reason as a "productive" power. This also seems to jar with the stress laid by both Kant and most interpreters on its limits.[1] It is not that I intend to encourage forsaking the melancholy and meek attitude of those resigned to censure reason for its false pretensions and instead embrace enthusiastically the audacity of a daringly fresh look at the first *Critique* (or for that matter at the three *Critiques*). My point is that limits and power are mirror terms and mutually define one another. The limits are the limits of a power that has the ambition of extending beyond itself. My point, differently stated, is that reason is a power to exercise its causality in the world (from a system of cognitions to laws and principles and ideas without a corresponding object, from a moral order to motivation, feelings, judgment, and reflection). But it can easily misunderstand the extent of its causality. Kant calls this power "a priori synthesis."

Of course, from the point of view of general logic, which looks only to consistency and conceptual relations, we must acknowledge that reason has no power to get a purchase on things at all. From a transcendental point of view reason instead produces its contents as a response to its needs and interests. Such contents are quite limited in number and scope. And, paradoxically, they are forms. As such *forms-contents*, as I propose to call them, they differ from logical formal requirements, which have to respect only the principle of noncontradiction. Forms-contents must not be confused at all with the indefinitely rich and diverse matter we experience to which our pure concepts refer, for this can be given only empirically. If matter is inevitably given, the pair form-content is a rule, a law, a principle we constitute.

Consider the following two examples. The logical concept of a self-identical subject can be used indifferently for any object whatever (a heptagon, a chimera, a table, a novel, justice). It denotes no more than a formal requirement, empty of content and reference. When I turn this concept into that of substance, I get a quite different result (according to Kant traditional

1. Kant mentions a *Macht der Vernunft* exemplified by mathematics as the intoxicating thrust that misleads the light dove to imagine a flight without the resistance of air (*KrV* A 5/B 8).

metaphysics had no inkling of this major difference). The logical concept becomes a pure principle organizing my *experience of objects*. It is now a principle that allows me not to sort out abstractly subject and predicate but to distinguish between change and permanence in experience. I have a rule under which I can subsume the particulars I experience and to which I can bring back all perception of alteration and becoming. I cannot anticipate anything of what I will each time experience, except that it will have to conform to this rule in order to be objective. In fact, all experience will have the form of an object in general that only my pure concepts and intuitions jointly have constituted. What allows me to turn subject into substance and, more broadly with other categories and pure intuitions, to generate rules for experience out of pure concepts is the addition of a supplementary condition to the logical concept: the schema of time as permanence.

This is an *a priori synthesis*, a production issuing from reason. The pure concept of substance has *objective reality* (i.e., the possibility of being applied to experience as a rule that makes it amenable to universal and necessary knowledge) and the possibility of *reference* (to whatever appearance I will each time experience). Last but not least, it also gives rise to a universal law in the general science of nature whose principles precede and make possible physics: substance remains and persists (*Prol* § 15).

Another example is this. When I promise my son to play with him, I have instituted something that previously did not exist. What interests Kant is not that the performative utterance makes an intention real, as in John Austin, but that once I make a promise I am bound by it. My reason has freely issued an imperative that I can break or make good on, but that determines my conduct. My afternoon changes accordingly, and, by extension, so do my time, my world, my history: who I am. The conduct to which I am bound once I have made a promise and thereby instituted something real is the product of my autonomous choice. Here too we have an a priori synthesis.

Through these forms of a priori synthesis I produce new objects. A merely logical reason, which can operate only with its concepts and has no criterion for or even possibility of transcending them, is not in a position to give rise to anything similar to this. If this is true and a priori synthesis and objective reality are connected, we must also recognize that the question raised in chapter 1—the question of the objective reality of reason's pure concepts—offers a different perspective on the same issue as that of a priori synthesis: pure reason's power to go out of itself and determine something real that was not implicit or given in its starting position.

The *Critique of Pure Reason* famously turns on the problem of synthetic a priori *judgments*. I want to suggest that this is one, not the only and not necessarily the best or most comprehensive, way to address this power. Furthermore, I want to suggest that the a priori synthesis is not a problem exclusively pertaining to the first *Critique*. Pure reason's ambition to reach out of itself is *the* problem of Kant's critical philosophy in its various scopes of application. In chapter 1 I have examined the problem of ideas and of reason proper. In this chapter I want to show how reason's a priori synthesis is the effect of an innerly articulated reason, that is, a reason that is inclusive of pure intuition, understanding, and reason proper.

In the introduction I have already called attention to the limits of the reading of Kant that segments his unitary critique of reason into three separate *Critiques* and to the linear and piecemeal reading of the first *Critique* that is supported by its many dichotomies and oppositions. If now I were to put it facetiously, I would say that reading the first *Critique* backward has merits and advantages worth exploring. Beginning with the Doctrine of Method, turning to the Transcendental Dialectic, thereby preparing for the rest of the work, is an instructive alternative to the unit-by-unit progression so common in the standard reading described in the introduction. In Pascal's words, this strategy has reasons that reason does not know. But obviously this is no more than a provocation intended to call into question a linear reading that breaks the book apart into independent segments. Even if proceeding backward like Nietzsche's crab had been my intention in chapter 1, there are serious reasons why this approach would not work.[2]

For one, the Doctrine of Method is not a long-forgotten gem whose rediscovery would suffice to make sense of the whole. It is not a unitary and homogeneous tract to begin with, because the themes that run through it not only refer to different layers of Kant's thought, but also are in deep conflict with one another.[3] It is therefore quite confusing to take it, to name but one example, as a guide to understanding the essence of philosophy. The cosmic idea in the Architectonic and the opposition of philosophy to mathematics in the Discipline result in quite different descriptions. We also saw that what the Dialectic teaches and what Kant says it does do not overlap. For Kant emphasizes only one of the aspects of the Dialectic, the negative result of a divided reason.

---

2. *Goetzendaemmerung*, in *Sämtliche Werke*, 2: 1018–19, § 43: "No one is free to be a crab. There is no avoiding it: one *must* go forward."

3. Also, it is probably the oldest part of the first *Critique*. Judging from the letter to Herz of November 24, 1776, it was ready at least in its conception five years before the book was finished (*Ak* 10: 200).

It is not so much a cyclopic vision that cannot see comprehensively the scope of the critique of pure reason that is a stumbling block for a comprehensive reading. True, the problem is the lack of a stereoscopic vision. However, it is due not to the one eye but rather to the separation and selective reading of Kant's texts. And yet, this is but one obstacle. It is no less necessary to clarify some specific theses and understand several ambiguities, beginning with the notion of a priori synthesis; the presumed analyticity of philosophy, especially in comparison with mathematics; and the comparative examination of pure, mathematical, and empirical concepts. The correct understanding of what '*a priori*' means constitutes another surprisingly troublesome point.

Another difficulty here facing the interpreter is this. As we will see, describing reason's internal articulation in the form of *faculties* and *transcendental conditions of possibility* can result in as misleading an interpretation as approaching Kant with a presupposed ready-made opposition between sensibility and understanding. These conceptions need to be unpacked.

I mentioned Kant's indecisiveness on the relation between critical and transcendental philosophy and metaphysics. These are not the only ambiguous or plurivocal concepts, for *knowledge, science,* and *objectivity* also turn out to cover a wide spectrum of meanings, wider probably than a desire for univocity and clarity would care to consider.

Addressing such ambiguities is necessary in order to interpret the first *Critique*. Recall a point made in the introduction. Frequently when Kant seems to summarize or recall his earlier conclusions he actually betrays or oversimplifies and distorts them. At times he introduces a quite new perspective on an earlier point, depending on the task he wants it to perform. At the very least, when Kant gives us his retrospective judgments on his previous work he is not faithful to it and can hardly be counted as an authority. If he cannot be trusted, the only hermeneutical guide left to the reader is a painstaking reconstruction of Kant's intentions in the several different contexts in which he comments on his philosophy.

This sort of understanding of Kant's thought in its progressive unfolding will dictate the organization and aims of this and the third chapter. We will examine each of these questions in the order announced. But first a clarification of the notions of synthesis and intuition is in order.

2. Form, Synthesis, and Intuition. On Blindness

The indispensable premise for any treatment of a priori synthesis is the acknowledgment of what for Kant is a basic thesis: that is, thought is a synthesis. If to unify is to unify a multiplicity, it follows that all thought needs a preliminarily given manifold. The question of how the manifold is given is quite important, but to Kant the emphasis on the 'manner of given-ness' is less discriminating than it is, say, to Husserl. To him the different forms of synthesis and unification are more worthy of our attention. Here, too, we find an inversion of both a classical and a modern thesis. Let me illustrate it once again in terms of the analogy with vision—or, to be more precise, with blindness.

The cyclops, recall from chapter 1, had chosen to see with one eye only. Philosophy gave us the second eye. However, the binocular vision was made possible not by pure reason's legislation but by a reference to reason's ends and to the pure rational hope for the highest good. Hope is by definition not certainty. It may be rational, but it remains other than knowledge. When Aeschylus says that Prometheus gave humans "blind hope," this blindness is the pious gift allowing us to turn our gaze away. The hope that does not see is a *pharmakon* that spares mortals the sight of death.[4] The blindness I have referred to when I mentioned Kant's inversion has little to do with either piety or hope. It is a reversal of the notion of intuition and a "purification" of both sensibility and understanding, each assigned mutually independent functions.

A noble and well-known tradition links knowledge with vision. "I see what you mean" is a well-justified phrase. Vision means perceiving something evident, seeing directly a given we take to be true or real. Typically, this is an instantaneous grasp. Such vision can culminate long efforts at understanding and result from the trials of experience or be the premise for an investigation or a debate on whose terms we agree before beginning. It can even be the absolute first and indispensable origin of all understanding, as in the Platonic dialogues. In classical Greek thinking, intuition had a noetic connotation. In and through a thing you see an *eidos* (itself a term, like *theōria*, from the realm of vision), an essence or form. An analogue of "I see what you mean," equivalent to 'I know', is the Greek *oida* (I have seen) in the perfect tense. *Eidein* and *noein* have a similar sense, superior, in Plato and Aristotle among others, to discursive thought and knowledge of the sensible world (predication, the world of becoming and appearance). The Latin equivalent to those verbs is *in-tueri*, which, just like the German *an-schauen*,

---

4. *Prometheus Bound*, l. 250. Goethe's Prometheus is a tragic hero who liberates humans from the superstitions the gods have used to subjugate them and make them beggars. In an enlightened move that had a tremendous impact on Lessing and the *Spinozismusstreit*, his Prometheus frees mortals from "*stolid hope*" (*Werke*, 3: 124–25; see my "Homo Faber").

means literally "to see in": *in-sight*. (These are the words for "intuiting" used by Kant respectively in the *Dissertatio de mundi sensibilis atque intelligibilis forma et principiis* and in the *Critique of Pure Reason*.)

In Plato and Aristotle this vision is an original identification. Aristotle sets up this proportion: touching is to manipulating as saying to predicating (*Metaphysics* Θ 10; see *De anima* 3.6). The virtue of touching and saying (*thigein kai phanai*) and the reason for their superiority is the simplicity of a direct and unimpeded contact with an undivided essence. This is deemed superior to the gradual and laborious approximation to it: identity over difference, unity over multiplicity. As a consequence, discursivity is usually instrumental to *noēsis*, which some translate as 'intellectual intuition.' The highest moment in knowledge, even where the *nous* is at its most active, always presupposes an original passivity. Not that there is anything passive to thought; what I mean is rather that the mind's genuinely speculative goal is to attest to—to *see*—the way things truly are, and they *are* independently of us. This passivity is the mimetic rendering of an intelligible structure, not the empiricist thesis of a sensible affection. In sum, intuition is understanding.

In turn, understanding is fundamentally modeled after vision. In Plato this is clear from many famous analogies found in the dialogues. In Aristotle we have a puzzling image. After writing that the intellect has the same relation to intelligibles as sense to sensibles (*De anima* 3.4, 429a 15), he compares the soul to a hand (3.8, 431b 21). We might take him to claim that, like the hand, the soul allows us to grasp, control, and appropriate things. What he means instead is that the hand is a model because it is plastic and, like the *nous*, can assume all forms whatever. Touch can be either the grasp that seeks a grip on things and can manipulate them materially, or the sheer contact that leaves the thing, as it were, 'untouched,' i.e., unaffected, unaltered. It tries to let it appear at its truest and is respectful of its distance from the thing (our meaning of *tact* is the survival of this form of contact). Contact then is understood as an immaterial contact, grasp in terms of material modification. This is to say that contact is understood in terms of vision, attestation.

Touch is the most fundamental sense because it is shared by all animals, but sight discriminates most differences and is cognitively more refined. Sight has a superiority deriving from a basic teleological anthropology: it is a sense working at distance through the medium of light. Because humans stand erect naturally (*De partibus animalium* 4.10, 687a 5ff.) and can move their head up and their "upper part is upper in relation to the whole [*tou pantos*] while in other animals it is midway" (*De juventute* 468a 5–8; cf. Plato's *Timaeus* 44d–45b), humans' gaze is not absorbed by the earth.

They can thus fulfill their divine nature as thinking beings. That is, they can live at a distance, in abstraction from sensible presence, and have a purely theoretical relation to things as well as an estrangement from the needs and concerns of life. Contemplation of the unchanging cosmos, the encompassing whole, is the paradigmatic example of what theory amounts to. In sum, sight is privileged and becomes paradigmatic because of its mediation and removal.[5]

Even thinking seems dependent on this model both in the intellection of indivisibles and in its several other forms (especially when forms are meant as proxies for sensible presence). The well-known Aristotelian thesis that we think in images[6] follows from the necessity that thinking have a present object of thought. Thinking needs an intuition filling its thematic consideration just as sensation needs a sensible thing in order to be activated (*De anima* 3.7, 431a 14–15; 3.8, 432a 4–11). I need to place the thing "before my eyes" (*pro ommatōn, De memoria* 450a 4) and consider the absent thing in its image "as if I saw it" (*hōsper horōn, De anima* 3.7, 431b 7).

This is at the root of the theory of knowledge as transmission of forms. There is a continuity between the world of perception and the intelligible world, however distinct these may be. Things have an intelligible form, an essence. The crux is translating the sensible form we are acquainted with in perception into the intelligible form that we can then use as a species form or, later, a concept and a word. Aristotle famously bequeaths to posterity a very influential theory that we find in most subsequent philosophers, who adopt it virtually unmodified, from the early Stoics to Plotinus to Hume.[7] The percept has an inertial force needing no more impulse. It lives in us (in imagination and memory) as an image before the inverse movement (whether initiated by the active intellect or by another agent) thematizes it

5. That from a cognitive point of view touch is thought in terms of vision and not vice versa is also apparent in Aristotle's strange theory of the heart as the organ of touch, following from the necessity of a medium for touch analogous to what light is for vision (*De anima* 2.7–11).

6. *De memoria* 450a1; *De anima* 1.1, 403a 8; 3.7, 431a 16–17, 431b 2; 3.8, 432a 10.

7. Even the examples we find as late as in Hobbes, Descartes, Spinoza, Berkeley, and Hume are variations on the Aristotelian theme of the projectile or the javelin. When the examples are not the same, such as the concentric circles in water after a stone has been dropped (Hobbes) or after oars have set a galley in motion (Hume), they mean the same. That is, the image survives in us without the need for further impulse from perception. The definition of imagination given by Wolff and Baumgarten repeated by Kant (*KrV* B 151) as the faculty for representing an object even without its presence in intuition is thus quite traditional, whereas in many other ways Kant's imagination breaks with all its antecedents. See my "Kant's Productive Imagination," "Aristotle on *Phantasia*," and *Kant on Imagination*.

and turns it into a form in discourse, a name, a concept, a representation, and so on.

It is with Stoicism that touch begins to be transformed materially.[8] It is with modernity (Bacon, Descartes, Hobbes, Locke) that perception begins to be understood in terms of impressions, immediacy, and material affection: in terms of touch. Modern philosophy inverts the priority of touch and vision.

But modern philosophy, for all its huge differences from and determination to break with classical thought and for all its inversion of vision and touch, does not differ from Plato and Aristotle *as to the subordination of discursive reason to an intuitive grasp*. Descartes's criterion of truth is evidence, a clear and distinct vision. In Descartes the *intuitus* is opposed to the step-by-step *deductio*.[9] In his theory of *scientia intuitiva* and *amor dei intellectualis*, Spinoza makes the third and highest degree of knowledge superior to discursive thought.[10] For Leibniz *cognitio caeca seu symbolica* is only preparatory and preliminary to the intuitive vision.[11] These are some notable examples of the intuitive core of the *lumen naturale* (natural light of reason) that Kant will deliberately reverse and against which he will construct his theory of intuition, judgment, and knowledge.

By ascribing intuition to a sensibility that cannot comprehend what it sees unless a concept sheds light on it, Kant effectively deprives intuition of its noetic aspect. All analogies with vision are replaced by analogies with blindness. If the cyclops has only one eye, intuition has none. Sensibility is blinded. It is the immediate relation to an appearance that modifies us. We cannot grasp this affection unless we think it through the understanding's concepts.

This, however, does not mean—contrary to what most readers think— that intuition is now unable to stand on its own feet.[12] It implies that there is no simple and undivided intelligibility to be attested in what is given to us. If there are no essences to things, a fortiori there is no grasp of essences, so that there is no passivity attesting to what things are. Synthesis and unification are a pure spontaneity. The mind's activity is a synthesis resulting in the logical connection of conceptual terms in a judgment.

8. See my *Hegel and Aristotle*, 165 and n.

9. See the *Regulae ad directionem ingenii*, rule 3 (*Oeuvres*, 10: 368–70) and rule 11 (10: 407–8). On sensation as modeled after touch, see rule 12 (10: 412).

10. See the *Ethics*, bk. 5, propositions 25–33.

11. See *Meditationes de cognitione, veritate et ideis*, G 4: 422–26.

12. See § 7b below.

The gap between sense and understanding is now unbridgeable. There cannot be any simple transmission between perception and language because a sensible and a discursive form are by no means homogeneous. Sensibility is the receptivity of a manifold, and the understanding's concepts are the *be-greifen* (*con-cipere*) or grasping together of characters, *Merkmale*, or conceptual marks into a unity.[13] Therefore we cannot postulate or take for granted an inertial image as a remnant of sensation. The concept cannot be the skimmed or filtered result of an image that is itself a supposed copy of the percept; that is, a concept is a rule, not a mental image drawn from past experience (as in Hume, for example). To form a concept we need not only logical acts such as comparison, reflection, and abstraction, but also the explicit intervention of a spontaneous and yet blind (it, too!) function of mediation of which we are scarcely aware (imagination), because intuition and concept are heterogeneous.

Even more important than their heterogeneity, however, is their respective negative characterizations. No conflict of interests or tasks is possible between sensibility and understanding because the former cannot think and the latter cannot intuit. They are relatively independent of one another. This means that sensations cannot be concepts in disguise, obscure thoughts, as they were in Leibniz and then Georg Friedrich Meier, Christian Wolff, and Alexander Gottlieb Baumgarten. In turn, concepts cannot function in disguise and accomplish the work traditionally assigned to images and percepts ("see in" or through them). Since the understanding is in contact no longer with things but only with sensibility, concepts are but logical functions. All the understanding has is concepts, all of which equally belong together in principle as the result of a spontaneous thinking. They can all be connected as subjects or predicates in a judgment.

It is not that seeing is now exclusively attributed to either sensation or the understanding. To be more precise, once sensation and perception have been sharply divided, *vision can no longer be the model for sensibility.* Sensibility is the immediate being-presented-to of a sensible plurality of data that, in order to become intelligible, must be ordered in a relation and brought back to—subsumed under, says Kant—a concept. The concept alone gives intelligibility to an intuition that by itself is blind. But by itself a concept is no less wanting. The logical function of concepts disregards all reference and is thus empty.[14]

---

13. Kant himself calls attention to this meaning at *KrV* A 103.

14. A concept without content is an impossible (because contradictory) concept in the Wolffian pre-Kantian tradition. Kant calls it "empty object without concept, *nihil negativum*"

This does not mean, as is too often thought, that an intuition is impossible without a concept or a concept without an intuition, let alone that all intuitions come already conceptualized. Nor does Kant, after blinding intuition and the imagination, choose the understanding as the single bearer of the beacon allowing us to see. The whole relation among these terms needs to be recast. If the understanding is pure spontaneity and not the grasp of an essence or even the analysis of a given (as it still was in Kant's *Dissertatio*), *the analogy with vision should be dropped altogether*.

For what is redefined by Kant is nothing less than *the notion of form* (and its correlate, matter). Form no longer denotes the essence of a thing or the relations among essences. Instead, it is doubled and becomes the unification of the manifold in concepts by the understanding and also the form of appearances (the way the form-of-matter appears to us: "that which allows the manifold of appearance to be ordered in certain relations," *KrV* A 20/B 34, i.e., pure intuition as opposed to empirical intuition). Recognizing this object as a lamp means to unify its several components in one object and bring this appearance back to its concept. In turn, recognizing that it lies at a certain distance from me on the left of my visual field is a pure intuition of its spatial relation to the observer that does not require or involve concepts.

If it were only essences that disappear from the scene, Kant's theory would not be so unprecedented, for it would then seem to belong in the nominalist camp. It does not because, more importantly, it is things that no longer have a right to be as in themselves. If things become appearances ostensibly containing no internal connections that we have not made, all questions turn on our forms of access to them; namely, an intuitive form in which we synthesize the manifold and a conceptual form through which we constitute the unity. Intuitions do not mirror appearances because the understanding and concepts do not depict anything. Intuitions give shape to the manifold, and concepts are discursive rules for the unification of the manifold.

In experience, no matter is given unformed, and form is but the form-of-matter. If form and matter are complementary in appearances, if they indeed constitute appearances jointly, this does not mean that they are themselves empirically identifiable or given as absolute terms. Form and matter are not

---

(*KrV* A 292/B 348: it is without concept but not without a name, e.g., round square). Kant differs from the Wolffian tradition in that he adds a new way to consider concepts empty: when they refer to a noumenon, an *ens rationis*. In this case the concept can be thought and therefore does have a content. What it cannot have is an object. On this point see Caimi, "Gedanken ohne Inhalt."

the fixed and objective *sides* of appearances. They cannot be shown as such. To clarify, contrast this with the bronze statue in Aristotle's *Physics*, in which the form is the figure and the matter is the metal.

Form and matter are not *parts or aspects* of things that we can abstract or point to in their distinctness because things do not offer to our grasp a material and a formal side, each self-subsistent, existing and irreducible to the other. Furthermore, if form and matter were parts, it would be possible to cognize each separately from the other. If they were aspects, they would be distinct and equally worthy perspectives on one single indivisible unity. There is no form or matter that is preexisting and given prior to my activity.

Because things are nothing before our constitution of them as appearances, form and matter are the complementary ways in which we constitute objects as respectively *the determination and the determinability* of appearances. In addition to that, form and matter are functional operators. Not only do they not denote existing sides or parts; neither are they identifiable absolutely as form or matter, for they can even *exchange roles*. For example, pure concepts, as the understanding's forms, can be the matter on which the superior forms, i.e., ideas, are active. In a different example, time as the form of inner sense is itself the object of the understanding's determination in schemata.

While knowing matter separately is excluded, the case of form is slightly but importantly different. Form is not an empty receptacle for a formless matter. And yet form has a relative independence from matter that in turn matter cannot enjoy. This is possible even if the terms are correlative because they are correlative *in experience*. But form can be investigated by transcendental philosophy in itself: that is, as a condition for experience, hence as independent of it. In a different sense, then, form is the essence (*das Wesen der Sachen*) that can be known by pure reason, as a famous *Reflexion* has it.[15] Indeed, form gives the thing its being (although not its existence) and thus is *one part and the whole* at the same time: one element and the unity of contrary elements. It can be insofar as it is not a part or a side but is

---

15. "*Forma dat esse rei*. Denn das Wesenliche der Sache kann nur durch Vernunft erkannt werden; nun aber muss alle Materie der Erkenntnis durch Sinne gegeben sein, also ist das Wesen der Sachen, sofern sie durch Vernunft erkannt werden, die Form." (Erdmann 656). See also *On a Recently Prominent Tone* (Ak 8: 404, ENG 443), and *Reflexion* 3852 (Ak 17: 312). Essence is not a metaphysical but an epistemological notion. It is neither the actuality of a thing, as in the tradition from Aristotle's *energeia* (e.g., the soul as the first entelechy of the living body) to Wolff's *principium actualitatis entis* (*Philosophia prima sive Ontologia*, § 947), nor its possibility. Instead it is the determination of a thing. See Graubner, *Form*, 37ff., and Carl, *Der schweigende Kant*, 111ff.

now equated with an *act of determination*, whereas matter is determinability. Form is not an inert or ideal principle, for it is one with its execution.

If form and matter are correlative, with the former determining the latter, the relation between *form and content* is quite different. In logic, form is separate from all content because it has been preliminarily abstracted and objectivized as thematic in itself. In transcendental logic form is the content itself, the product of my constitution and the condition of objectivization. The product of my constitution—or a priori synthesis—is the form of an object in general as the fulcrum of possible experience. This product is the core from which all determinate categorial relations of appearances irradiate and the anticipated frame within which I will experience whatever appearances can be given to me. This form, one element and the whole, is the 'form-content' that is the object of transcendental philosophy.

In the Amphiboly, which deals with the conceptual pair form-matter thematically in polemics against Leibniz, Kant criticizes the *Intellektualphilosoph* in terms that can well apply also to a metaphysical empiricist. Leibniz assumed, argues Kant, that matter, including the logical matter of basic concepts and universals as the whole of possibles and thus of beings, precedes form (*KrV* A 267/B 323). Form is the relation of conceptual matter in judgments. Monads are assumed as the first datum the way sensible data are assumed by empiricists as the primitive and formless simple elements to be combined by us. This would be right and would justify both Leibniz and Locke if we could know things in themselves. However, we can know only appearances. Being does not follow from ontological possibility but is what accords with the possibility of experience, that is, our acts of determination. Therefore we get the curious result that form (the form of experience, the form in which we apprehend appearances) is not only independent of but also *prior to matter* and the original ground determining it. Matter can only adjust to a prior form. As Kant remarks, "the form is given for itself alone" (*so ist die Form für sich allein gegeben, KrV* A 268/B 324), while matter presupposes the form of intuition in which we apprehend it.

The result is curious for yet another reason. This precedence of form over matter implies that in an appearance we know only relations. In fact, an appearance is "nothing but relations" (*KrV* A 265/B 321), not a thing with internal conceptual properties accessible to the pure intellect.

If form is an act of determination and a spontaneity, not only is it not a substitute for vision. Nor must it be necessarily conscious either. Consciousness, a term often associated with spontaneity by Kant, is not absolute transparency to itself (as in Descartes). In turn, spontaneity is not

deliberate, intentional, and goal-directed activity, but "the faculty for bringing forth representations itself" (*KrV* A 51/B 75). The strange modality of the
expression "the I-think must be able to accompany all my representations"
(*KrV* B 131–32)—the necessity of a possibility—leaves room open for (certainly is not incompatible with) a sort of logical unconscious.[16] It says that
spontaneity belongs to an activity producing representations that at some
point I can in principle bring back to consciousness.

The synthesis is a "blind but indispensable" act "of which we are seldom even conscious" (*KrV* A 78/B 103); my empirical consciousness is ever
changing (*KrV* A 107); I can have a "weak" consciousness of the act by which
I generate a representation (*KrV* A 103). What matters is that I can be conscious of the effect of such act, the unity of the concept. What matters is that
I can go through, take up, and connect (*durchgehen, aufnehmen, verbinden,*
KrV A 77/B 102) the manifold of experience in a unitary act. But I can unify
the manifold—recognize, assimilate, and distinguish impressions—only if
I can bring it back to a norm or rule of my judging activity. *The norm precedes*
whatever relations the given manifold may present.

This act of unification is the identity of a function. This identity presupposes the identity of an original consciousness (the transcendental unity of
apperception), which can realize this identity only insofar as it is conscious
of the function or act (*Handlung*) by means of which the manifold is combined in one cognition (*KrV* A 108). A concept is thus a comprehensive
connection of marks (*Be-griff*) made possible by the transcendental unity
of apperception's operation.

3a. A Priori Synthesis. The Speculative Synthesis

We may harbor all the doubts we want on this notoriously problematic
relation between empirical and original consciousness. The purpose of this
section is to delve deeper into the conception of a priori synthesis as the
activity by which pure reason produces the forms-contents in which we will
experience objects.

We have seen that reason can only unify given materials. But this turns
out to be only partially true. For reason can unify a given manifold only
provided it is capable of handling (organizing, structuring: *forming*) it. For
reason to unify a manifold it must have operated on itself first. That is, reason must have preliminarily prescribed its order to the forms of sensibility

---

16. On the unconscious in the understanding, see La Rocca, "Intelletto oscuro," 2007.

in which we will apprehend objects. In fact, reason unifies a given manifold insofar as it has beforehand unified its own forms.

This is not a contingent fact but a necessary presupposition. Reason is neither an Aristotelian *nous* that cannot have a form of its own because it must be capable of becoming all forms whatever, nor a Lockean empty cabinet or blank slate progressively furnished with items from experience. I can apprehend materials from experience and unify them in meaningful unities only if I first have the forms in which to organize them. But these forms are not ready-made or inborn. I must first *produce* them. This is not the creation of objects out of nothing. It is the way I make possible determinate forms-contents as the conditions for all experience. To revert to the earlier example, I produce the form 'substance' by referring the logical concept of identity to the pure intuition of temporal permanence.

If concepts without content are empty, I need to make them sensible and show they refer to objects, i.e., to give them an object in intuition. This process, which Kant calls *sinnlich machen, darstellen* (KrV A 51/B 75, A 242/B 299), or in Latin *exhibitio* (V-Lo/Dohna, Ak 24: 752, ENG 486), differs according to the kind of concepts involved. With empirical concepts exhibition is not a problem, for they are derived from experience. They are classes with respect to which individual things are instances.

With pure concepts, however, we must raise the question of their objective reality. How do we know they refer to objects in the world? How do I know they are concepts I can apply in my experience and not figments of my imagination or heuristic tools devoid of all reality or meaning? Here we cannot think of a relation of instances and classes. This wooden artifact may indeed be an instance of 'table,' but 'table' is not an instance of 'substance.' Pure concepts have at best examples (KrV A 715/B 743), for they are rules for the constitution of different empirical objects.

In addition to empirical and pure concepts we have mathematical concepts. These exhibit their object in intuition. That is, there is no difference between thinking of a triangle of a determinate magnitude and drawing it, which is an act by which I give it reality. Mathematical concepts thereby have a real definition and objective reality (KrV A 242n).

The crucial question Kant raises is: Can we get *a real definition for pure concepts*, too? This is where the Transcendental Logic becomes key. It is

a *science* of pure understanding and of the pure *cognition* of reason, by means of which we think objects completely a priori. Such a science, which would determine the origin, the domain and the objective validity [*Ursprung, Umfang, objektive Gültigkeit*] of such cognitions . . . has to do . . . with the laws of understanding and reason . . . solely insofar as they are *related to objects a priori*. (*KrV* A 57/B 81, italics mine)

While general logic abstracts from all content and expects that representations will be given to it, transcendental logic "has a manifold of sensibility that lies before it a priori, which the transcendental aesthetic has offered to it" (*KrV* A 76–77/B 102). Space and time contain a pure a priori intuition and belong to the conditions of receptivity of our mind. Therefore, while general logic is the analysis of concepts, *transcendental logic synthesizes its concepts by providing its pure concepts with a content*. It is none other than space and time as the pure intuitions we know from the Aesthetics. This synthesis is thus "the first origin of our cognition" (*KrV* A 78/B 103). All analysis, further intellectual operation, and experience must presuppose it. Transcendental logic is the canon for the "objectively valid, thus true use" of the understanding and the power of judgment (*KrV* A 131/B 170).

The Analytic of Concepts is the deduction of our pure concepts. But concepts consist in the use we make of them in judgments. Therefore it is the Analytic of Principles, which builds on the Analytic of Concepts, that teaches our power of judgment "to apply to appearances the concepts of the understanding" (*KrV* A 132/B 171). The pure concepts of the understanding are not just rules or mere logical forms. Their application or use is legitimate in transcendental logic because it can indicate, in addition to the rule, also the case to which the rule ought to be applied.

General logic is the logic of noncontradiction. It investigates the agreement of a representation with the general and formal laws of understanding and reason in which the understanding attends only to itself. By contrast, transcendental logic is the logic of *truth*, that is, of the relation of our pure concepts with their object (*KrV* A 63/B 87, A 57/B 81, B ix). The rules of the understanding are not simply true. They are the source of all truth, as they contain the ground for the possibility of experience and all agreement between concept and object.

Transcendental logic, in other words, deals with concepts that relate to their objects a priori. Pure concepts relate a priori to their objects insofar as they have an internal reference to their intuitive content. Kant shows that pure concepts have a content in two ways. First he shows the sensible condition under which they can be used (here the implicit intuitive content is time, the form of all appearances whatever). Then he specifies the synthetic a priori judgments that we actually make. These flow from the pure concepts and in turn ground all a priori cognitions (the explicit content is the principle [*Grundsatz*] expressed).

These two ways are respectively the Schematism of pure concepts and the Principles of the pure understanding (*KrV* A 136/B 175). In the former we learn that concepts having a content; an object, objective reality, transcendental truth, and a meaning are all different expressions of the same requirement. Pure concepts have an object once they contain the a priori formal conditions of sensibility under which a category can be applied to any object. The joint activity of a pure concept and a pure intuition (e.g., substance as permanence in time) yields the possibility of experience as an orderly structure from which I can learn and whose lawfulness I can trust. In turn, the principles are fundamental propositions (*Grund-sätze*), synthetic a priori judgments. Experience has "principles of its form which ground it a priori" (*KrV* A 157/B 196). The principles of the empirical employment of the understanding, antecedent to all experience, are the most general laws of nature (e.g., "In all changes of appearances substance persists, and its quantum is neither increased nor diminished in nature," *KrV* B 224).

Transcendental logic's task is to show the possibility of synthetic a priori judgments. Only thus can we determine the extent of the pure understanding, measure its domain, and establish its limits. If giving pure concepts an object is to refer cognitions to a possible experience, the understanding cannot overstep the limits of sensibility. Through this reference to possible experience the understanding has *brought a "transcendental content into its representations"* (*KrV* B 105).

What I have summarized is a theory of the object (and, in dynamic categories, of relations among objects, i.e., events) as a rule for all experience of whatever appearance we will encounter. It cannot tell us anything about this or that object, except that, as an appearance, it will have to conform to the principles, laws, and rules I have constituted a priori. But this constitution, formal though it must remain until I experience, is of the highest importance. For it shows that nothing will be able to speak to us unless reason prescribes this order. *Prescribing this order is pure reason's power*, its a priori synthesis. Whatever affects us is known in advance in the form of determinability dictated by our reason. Experience and its correlate (*natura formaliter spectata*, as Kant calls the affinity or orderly connection of all appearances) are known in advance as a lawfulness prescribing the normative frame for all sensible apprehension of determinate appearances.

If we say that whatever we will experience is subsumed under laws we have constituted a priori and known in advance, we must infer that the time of experience rests on a sort of timeless past (to recall Hegel's suggestion, something like Aristotle's *to ti ēn einai*). Our experience must presuppose ideal conditions it cannot make possible.

This move thus overturns three dogmas of empiricism. It claims: (1) experience is in truth made possible by constitution; (2) the individual is made possible by the universal, the empirical by the a priori; (3) the indefiniteness of experience is in principle intelligible, lawlike, and familiar.

Let me explain. The universality of order is the product of my constitution to which I bring back individual appearances. To be more precise, it is only because I have this orderly connection of all appearances that I can experience individuals meaningfully. What enjoys a prior existence is therefore not the individual (materially), but the universal plane of a theory of objects (only formally). I address myself to the open-ended horizon of what I do not yet know but can in principle apprehend within the lawful scope I project onto what I call experience. Unfamiliarity is thus a mode of familiarity. In this view, ignorance is an *empirical*, not yet filled *gap* within a preexisting *a priori knowledge*, an absence in a pregiven presence, a contingently missing variable in an anticipated spectrum of real possibilities.

This constitution also shows that reason's power is directed to its objects. The proper use of its pure concepts is a schematization in view of experience. Experience, however, is doubled. It is the empirical side in our knowledge of appearances, but it also begins to acquire its more definite meaning as "the first product of our understanding" (*KrV* A 1). Respectively, the two meanings are an endlessly diverse material and a predelineated selfsame form. The former may or may not enter the building prepared by the latter. The latter prescribes the relational form the former must assume to become *meaningful* matter.

Objectivity is therefore this anticipation, this universal and necessary projection we have made. Knowing objectivity is the a priori cognition of a frame in which individual experience, indefinite and varied, may or may not fit. There is, as it were, no dialectic between the one and the many. Both terms (the form and matter of experience, what we produce and what we find) remain what they are. Our everyday and our scientific experiences play themselves out in the space opened by and stretching between them.

Notice three points that we will need to discuss further in the next sections. First, this a priori synthesis is called a cognition. It is not simply the condition for knowledge. It is itself an a priori cognition.

Second, every empirical synthesis presupposes and corresponds to an a priori synthesis (*KrV* A 95). If I can bring representations back to concepts, transcendental logic brings the pure synthesis of representations back to pure concepts (*KrV* B 104). To continue with our previous example, all judgments regarding this table are possible because I employ the concept of substance and refer the empirical representation to a pure schematized concept.

The judgment regarding this table through which I determine its aspects and predicate them of the object (and not of my representations simply, hence the notion of objective validity) is made possible by the transcendental unity of apperception that unifies in its concepts the pure intuition of space and time. The judgment regarding this table has thus two moments: the a priori synthesis of pure concept and pure intuition, and the predication relative to this empirical object.

Third, pure concepts are, as Kant puts it, elementary and original, i.e., underived and uncomposed (*KrV* A 64/B 89). But it is important to understand this properly. We may be tempted to say that the category of substance is an atom of intelligibility. But it is such only insofar as by atoms we mean constituents that relate to and combine with one another to form molecules and more complex products. Unlike a traditional category (and unlike the original meaning of atom as "indivisible"), a category cannot be a simple, unanalyzable atomic constituent of an eidetic alphabet, or one of the highest genera (of being or of thought), or an absolute given existing independently of its combination. In other words, a category is not the ultimate point of arrival of analysis after a conceptual division, or, conversely, the point of origin of all synthesis. Why?

For one thing, pure concepts are themselves the *result* of a pure synthesis (*KrV* A 78/B 104; A 95). For another, they consist in their *use*. They are not, differently stated, fixed abstract points we reach at the end of a *diairesis* or a regress to the ground, because they are a form of activity. They make possible a unification in judgments. By their means we institute relations. A condition of possibility is not an inert atom.[17] Instead, it consists entirely (indeed, has no reality independent) of what it conditions and makes possible. It is therefore quite misleading to describe the condition of possibility that categories are as a datum distinct and separate from what it effects. By the same token, the talk of faculty, typical of eighteenth-century philosophy and of Kant in particular, gives the wrong impression that a faculty might be something apart from what it is the faculty for.[18]

---

17. Still in the *Negative Magnitudes* Kant considers causality an unanalyzable given we can only attest in experience but not explain. Because he still shares with Leibniz and Wolff the theory of judgment as the analytic inherence of a predicate in a subject, the idea of causality as an a priori synthesis has not yet dawned on him.

18. This impression can be quickly rectified if we pay attention to Kant's language. He describes the faculties of the Doctrine of Elements as *Quellen* (sources, origins) and thereby stresses the functional-operative meaning of the notion. He adds, notably in the Amphiboly, that bringing back representations to their source is what transcendental reflection must do. Failing a correct transcendental reflection, Hume can take causality as a product of imagination instead

The object, as the form-content in the frame of which this table makes sense as an ordered unity, is thus not a thing. It is the product of my constitution. It is an appearance, experienceable only in the forms in which I have ordered it in advance. These forms are a pure structure (conceptual and intuitive) in which I can run through, apprehend, and unify the empirical manifold: that is, as relative to my pure intuitions and concepts.

One paramount consequence of this point is yet another paradox. An object does not exist before my experience or knowledge. Indeed, no object is given to me to be later unified and brought back to the understanding's laws. The understanding first produces the object. The appearance "is not given prior to the synthesis, but is given only through it" (*Refl* 5639, *Ak* 18: 278). Through this synthesis we "anticipate the form of a possible experience in general" (*KrV* A 246/B 303). In fact, if we can know anything a priori of the object, it is only because it is given *through* my knowledge of it, not *to* it (*KrV* B 66). It is insufficient to say that my forms alone produce an object; paradoxical though it may sound, we must say that *knowledge alone can produce an object*. Givenness and finitude are crucial, but givenness in itself is dumb. Givenness must be able to speak to us. It does in the forms in and through which we give it objective validity and reality.

The weight Kant attaches to this point can be seen in two complementary ways. One consists in recalling that of all the complaints voiced by Kant about his interpreters, this is the thesis they missed to which he, vexed and almost incredulous, returns most often. The other is a fresh reading of the B Preface. In light of this point, it offers a continuous and sustained argument in favor of this anti-empiricist, or better antirealist, inversion. When Kant laments the shallow reading of the *Critique of Pure Reason* by its first reviewer (the anonymous author of what is to us known as the Garve-Feder review), he objects that "he did not say a word about the possibility of synthetic a priori cognition, which was the real problem, on the solution of which the fate of metaphysics wholly rests, and to which my *Critique* (just as here my *Prolegomena*) was entirely directed."[19]

Later, when Kant vents his frustration over Johann August Eberhard's misunderstandings, none outrages him more (and rightly so, if I may add)

---

of a pure concept, and Leibniz is bound to conflate numerical and specific identity. See Carl, *Die transzendentale Deduktion*, 79–84.

19. *Prol*, *Ak* 4: 377, ENG 164–65. In a letter to Garve (August 7, 1783, *Ak* 10: 339–40), Kant writes that the *Critique* is a science as yet not investigated, the science studying all objects that reason can derive out of itself and to which it relates. What is distinctive about this new science is that unlike any other science it can develop a priori all the judgments we can give on reason's objects.

than the conviction, ascribed to him by Eberhard, that *metaphysics is analytic and mathematics alone is synthetic*. How can Eberhard ignore, asks Kant, that the *Critique* "presents the idea of a complete system of metaphysical, and indeed *synthetic* principles, and establishes them through a priori demonstrations" (*Entdeckung*, Ak 8: 233, ENG 322)? The principle of synthetic judgments is key, and that is precisely what Eberhard overlooked. In a letter to Karl Leonhard Reinhold, Kant writes: "But this principle is completely unambiguously presented in the whole *Critique, from the chapter on the schematism on*" (*Ak* 11: 38, italics mine).

If we now turn to the B Preface (1787), we realize that from the outset it presents the problem of the *Critique of Pure Reason* as that of *a science of reason*. It is difficult for pure reason to enter upon the secure path of science because it has to deal not only with itself but also with its objects (this is the connection we saw in chapter 1 between pure reason's autarchy and its self-transcendence). Reason can relate to its object either by determining it or by making it real (respectively, theory and practice: *KrV* B x). The pure part of this cognition of reason (i.e., both theoretical and practical cognition) is that in which "reason determines its object wholly a priori" (ibid.). The revolution in the way of thinking that took place in mathematics and physics must happen in metaphysics as well. It too must resolve to ascribe to the thing what we have put into it in accordance with its concept. Reason has insight only into what it itself produces according to its own design.

This is all that metaphysics can hope to gain from imitating the models of mathematics and physics. We need to try an experiment in metaphysics (*KrV* B xviii n.), something unprecedented and wholly paradoxical given that metaphysics is nothing concrete and verification seems out of the question. If we suppose that the object conforms to our sensibility rather than that our cognition conforms to the object, we can know it a priori before it is given to us (*KrV* B xvi). As Kant writes, "we can know of things a priori only what we ourselves have put into them" (ibid.).

Our pure concepts, far from being made possible by experience, make experience possible. This means that we approach experience not passively but equipped with questions orienting and guiding our experiments—and equipped, before such questions, with an a priori cognition regarding nature. In the *Prolegomena*, Kant writes against Hume that metaphysics is the thought of all a priori connections of things arising in the understanding (*Ak* 4: 260, ENG 57). This is the a priori knowledge of quality, quantity, and relations allowing us to know before this or that experience that from a given object the search for another is warranted (V-Met/Mron, *Ak* 29: 809, ENG 163). If the pure concept of causality has its origin in the understanding, the particular experience "fire destroys wood" is the example that makes us know it *in concreto* (V-Lo/Wiener, *Ak* 24: 906, ENG 349).

Notice that Kant speaks of the critique of pure reason as if it were metaphysics. As mentioned more than once, "metaphysics" is an umbrella term that can cover vestibule as well as building, propaedeutic as well as system. When Kant speaks of the judgments of metaphysics in the *Prolegomena*, he writes that they are all synthetic. The aim and content of metaphysics are the production of a priori knowledge (*Prol*, *Ak* 4: 273, ENG 66).

Kant's example is striking but at this point perhaps unsurprising: "the proposition: All that is substance in things persists, is a synthetic and properly metaphysical proposition" (ibid.). In the Introduction to the second edition of the *Critique of Pure Reason*, the example is quite different. There Kant says that the intention or end of metaphysics is to extend its cognitions a priori, but we may go so far beyond the possibility of experience that we hope to find meaning in an empty proposition such as "The world must have a first beginning" (*KrV* B 18). This is an example of a *failed* a priori synthesis. In both cases, reason reaches beyond itself and pretends to know something of its object. A priori synthesis thus covers both the positive and immanent part of metaphysics, that is, the production of objectivity in the Analytic, and its negative and transcendent part, that is, the vain pretension to determine the noumenon that we need to censor in the Dialectic.

What defines synthetic judgments is quite simply the extension beyond the given concept that adds to it a property lying outside it. This further element is taken sometimes as an intuition, sometimes as a predicate (*Entdeckung*, *Ak* 8: 232, ENG 321) or a conceptual mark into which I have translated the intuition (*Fortschritte*, *Ak* 20: 339, ENG 416). This has little to do with analytic and synthetic methods (V-Lo/Hechsel Pinder, ENG 418–19), which concern exposition and demonstration in science. But it is not a question of mere logic either.

The case of Eberhard is again telling. He rephrased the distinction between analytic and synthetic judgments into that between identical and nonidentical judgments, which rests on whether the predicate derives from the essence of the subject or not. Thus he did not see that the distinction belongs instead in transcendental philosophy, where we investigate the origin of a priori cognitions of objects (*Entdeckung*, *Ak* 8: 244, ENG 331). The "term *synthetic* judgment . . . immediately carries with it an allusion to an *a priori synthesis* in general" (ibid.), which pertains to transcendental philosophy, not to logic.

This begins to tell us that the form of judgment is not decisive. To be sure, it is difficult not to follow Kant's lead in his thesis on the propositional expression of a priori synthesis in judgments. The very distinction between analytic and synthetic judgments is described as a going out of the given concept to a predicate that was not included in it. Still, I suggest that what is decisive is not the propositional thesis but the more general thesis regarding the extension beyond the given concept.

I insist on this point for three reasons that all boil down to saving the requirement of universality. (1) The expression "a priori synthesis" applies to all instances of a priori extension, while "judgment" does not. For example, in mathematics the extension is made possible by pure intuition, not by a new predicate; in the third *Critique*, the new element is not a predicate but a feeling. (2) Also, Kant's emphasis on judgments consigns his reason to a fixed mode of apophantic expression that need not be always the one valid standard.[20] Logical relations among concepts must be distinguished from metaphysical relations regarding contents irreducible to identity and nonidentity.[21] (3) Finally, the a priori synthesis we have been considering in this section is only one of the forms taken on by this determination of its objects by pure reason. Other a priori syntheses, notably the practical, are the determination of a real world that does use judgments (in the form of laws) but can hardly be reduced to judgments.

What we have considered so far in this section is the a priori synthesis that most interests Kant in the first *Critique*. In the Discipline, he calls it "*a transcendental synthesis*" "with which only the philosopher can succeed" (*KrV* A 719/B 747). But, among others, also the laws of homogeneity, specification, and continuity and the heuristic principles and maxims of speculative reason are synthetic a priori propositions (*KrV* A 663/B 691). The transcendental synthesis yields metaphysical principles that give rise to laws of nature and (as the *Metaphysical Foundations* has it, MAN, Ak 4: 478, ENG 192) give "objective reality, that is, meaning and truth" to its concepts. In turn, the *special* metaphysics of corporeal nature "does excellent and indispensable service for *general* metaphysics, in that the former furnishes examples (instances *in concreto*) in which to realize the concepts and propositions of the latter (properly speaking, transcendental philosophy)" (ibid.). For example, the relation between the Analogies of Experience in the Analytic of Principles and the science of mechanics in the *Metaphysical Foundations* rests on this relation between general and special metaphysics. The pure part of a science of nature (i.e., what is not empirical but rather

20. See Barale, *Kant*, 75–96, and "Rileggere Kant," 129.
21. See, besides Kant's criticism of Eberhard, *Reflexion* 3216 (*Ak* 16: 716–17).

mathematical about it) is an a priori synthesis: a production of fundamental laws that have their origin in the faculty of thought.

3b. A Priori Synthesis. The Practical Synthesis

The speculative production is by no means the only one. It is no less interesting to examine the *practical* a priori synthesis.[22] Here it is easier to show the generative power of pure reason. But it is not simply that reason produces its several empirical effects in the world. What matters to Kant is that in this production pure reason *act on itself* in practice as it does in theory. What matters is its relation to itself—its self-affection—as it constitutes the ground for its relation to its other. All that Kant is interested in is the effects reason produces *insofar as* it wills exclusively the form of rationality, the purity of a universal law it itself issues unmixed with natural inclinations. This is not because Kant's interest is selective, but because that is the only genuine problem and the veritable a priori synthesis. By affecting itself, reason not only motivates itself to action. It even produces a feeling, the respect for the law. Pure reason does not engulf in itself the indefinite multiplicity of matter and passions or pretend to pass as pure what is empirical. Pure reason is concentrated on one problem alone: its a priori synthesis.

The question underlying the *Critique of Pure Reason*, "How are synthetic a priori judgments possible?," has its correlate in the *Groundwork* in the question "How are all these imperatives possible?" (*Ak* 4: 417, ENG 69). By that Kant means more precisely categorical imperatives (*Ak* 4: 419, ENG 71–72; *Ak* 4: 444, ENG 92; *Ak* 4: 453, ENG 100). For hypothetical imperatives concern only the adequacy of means to ends. Because willing the end is also willing the means, this relation is analytic. By contrast, in a categorical imperative I have a synthetic a priori proposition in which I connect a priori the deed with the will of a rational being as something that is not contained in it (*Ak* 4: 420 and n, ENG 72; *Ak* 4: 444, ENG 92–93).

In both the *Critique of Pure Reason* and the *Critique of Practical Reason*, then, Kant has isolated the only element in need of grounding. In an empiricist view, I have no problem accounting for knowledge through experience or action through external causes, such as inclinations and selfish interests. In a rationalist view, purely theoretical and logical cognition is as little a problem as the fact that, once I posit an end, I will the means also. In both cases, relations are analytic. Neither empiricism nor rationalism, however,

---

22. Recall that "it is still one and the same reason which, whether from a theoretical or practical perspective, judges according to a priori principles" (*KpV, Ak* 5: 121, ENG 237).

can account for an a priori synthesis, that is, the power reason has to determine an object in the world out of itself. In the categorical imperative, what I will I can do. Ought (all veritable oughts as universalizable commands) entails can. This is the opposite of what happens when we measure the success of all hypothetical imperatives and especially when we have in view happiness, the empty form of satisfaction of all inclinations. Here our power is limited by the world. In the categorical imperative, instead, the simple thought of duty gives rise to a deed. Autarchic reason does not go out of itself to ground action.

In the practical use of reason all we consider is

> the determining ground of the will, which is a faculty either of producing objects corresponding to representations or of determining itself to effect such objects . . . , of determining its causality. For, in that, reason can at least suffice to determine the will and always has objective reality insofar as volition alone is at issue. (*KpV*, *Ak* 5: 15, ENG 148)

The supersensible concept of freedom, the *ratio essendi* of the moral law, has objective reality and a meaning (*KpV*, *Ak* 5: 48–50, ENG 179–80). The production of an effect out of a form, the objective reality and meaning of the moral law, the realization of freedom, the self-determination of reason, autonomy: these are the notions around which the a priori synthesis of will and deed revolve. As we can see, the correspondence with the first *Critique* is strong. Even in the practical synthesis, the propositions at stake (which determine the will) are *Grund-sätze*, principles or fundamental propositions (i.e., maxims or laws, *KpV*, *Ak* 5: 19, ENG 153).

This raises the question of the import of cognition for practical reason. What is indeed striking in comparison with the first *Critique* is that in practical reason we have not simply *thought* of a noumenal will. We have *determined* it through a law, for the moral law is a law of causality through freedom. For Kant this means that in the second *Critique*, unlike the first *Critique*, we as moral agents extend our cognitions beyond the limits of the sensible world (*KpV*, *Ak* 5: 50, ENG 180). If the objective reality of pure concepts needed a deduction in the first *Critique*, in the second the moral law is a fact of reason of which we are immediately aware and that cannot be demonstrated. This practical (not theoretical) cognition is the ground for the existence of its objects (*KpV*, *Ak* 5: 46, ENG 177).

A priori practical principles need not wait for intuitions in order to have objective reality. They themselves produce their reality (*KpV*, *Ak* 5: 65–66, ENG 193). Practical reason approaches its objects not to know but to produce them (according to its knowledge of them). Because it starts from principles, proceeds from them to concepts (good and evil), and finally reaches sensibility (in the form of moral feeling), the procedure is the inverse of that of the Analytic of the first *Critique*.[23]

In both theory and practice it is necessary to take into account the capacity of our faculty of thought to represent to itself the law. If reason is the source of norms and all order in nature and in our conduct, in both theory and practice we have laws that are valid universally and necessarily.

In these notions there is something unique: only human beings can represent a law to themselves. For Kant universality and necessity exist neither in nature nor in the mind, however sophisticated it may be, of a highly evolved animal, which—even if it is capable of prediction, abstraction, causal reasoning, and choice—cannot have a concept of universality and necessity (*kennen*, not *erkennen* is what animals can do). A law has nothing to do with the representation of a means for an end or of a conduct that responds to needs. A law imposes itself as such. It includes a universal obligation, so that when I subject myself to a command I expect all others to do the same. This is an objective aspect of the law. If it is broken, it loses nothing of its essence (rational universality and necessity) because breaking it is not a defect of the law, but a choice that some make.

Whereas in thoughts regarding nature, the law is valid irrespective of my will and need not receive an assent on the part of the I, in morality my endorsement of the law is indispensable, definitive of and integral to it. While appearances in nature are all equally subject to laws, moral laws are such that they are valid insofar as we subject ourselves to them. We do so when we conceive a law in thought. Here we are both legislators and willful subjects. Whereas the law of nature is constitutive for the object and admits no exceptions, so that a body cannot choose to fall otherwise than with uniformly accelerated movement, the law I freely impose on myself stands or falls with the possibility of its transgression. I can bind myself to an action only insofar as I know that transgressing an obligation is possible. Here necessity (ought) and freedom imply one another. I maintain a difference, a nonidentity or distance from the law, which cannot hold for laws of nature. Like a law of nature, the moral law is indeed constitutive, but of a possibility, because it consists in acting according to freedom. Law, generally speaking lawful conduct, is here a kind of project the rational being thinks

---

23. More explicit examples of a practical a priori synthesis include the principle of the doctrine of virtue in the *Metaphysics of Morals* (*MS, Ak* 6: 396, ENG 526), and the will of the highest good in the world in the *Religion* (*Ak* 6: 6–8n, ENG 59–61n).

and wants for his or her life. It is not the rule identifying the movement of a natural body.

Representing to itself laws with respect to which actions are particular instances is fundamental for the will. Action happens not in conformity with the law, but because I conceive the mere representation of the law as the cause of its being. The will therefore is not a tendency toward something, as in pre-Kantian theses, but the assertion of rationality. It is the choice of universality thanks to which I transform a particular intention into a principle I want everybody to recognize as binding: not because it is mine, but because it is rational. The deed then becomes a consequence of reason's representation.

In this representation, the form of the law alone counts. The will, as causality and the principle of its actualization, is not identical with practical reason. The will is not in itself in conformity with reason and thus inherently good, for it must compel itself to be good. Principles of action such as maxims and laws are not identical because the determining cause for the will is not exclusively reason (*KpV*, *Ak* 5: 201, ENG 153–54). Not all maxims can be universalized and transformed into laws. Once again we need an a priori synthesis, based on a self-imposed duty.

A deed is, as I said, a consequence of reason's representation. Still, it introduces an irreversible change in the empirical world. And this is another difference from the laws of nature. The human world is not an objective and unchanging order. *It becomes what we make of it.* In the third *Critique*, history will be a prominent stage of reason's self-realization. Right is the product of reason and a limitation of individual freedom: an order making possible the coexistence of free wills under a universal law. Even here what counts is not the matter but the form-content of reason's several norms and institutions.[24]

Finally, my respect for the moral law is not a determining factor. It is rather a subjective consequence of rational motivation. This feeling is a feeling like no other because it is not influenced by any given object but generated by the representation of reason when I subordinate my will to the law. In other words, rather than causing reason's choice, it is caused by reason. The feeling is the representation of an unconditional value in me

---

24. In a commercial transaction between two individuals, for example, "no account at all is taken of the *matter* of choice. . . . All that is in question is the *form* in the relation of choice on the part of both, insofar as choice is regarded merely as *free*, and whether the action of one can be united with the freedom of the other in accordance with a universal law" (*MS*, *Ak* 6: 230, ENG 387).

that infringes upon my self-love (*GMS, Ak* 4: 401–2n, ENG 56) and a sign of my supersensible destination.

This characterization of reason as itself practical is a poignant way to express reason's power to produce itself in the world out of its purity. Reason "is really practical, it proves its reality and that of its concepts by what it does" (*KpV* 5: 3, ENG 139). It is itself practical in that it moves itself to action without any incentive other than its own form, the universality and necessity of the laws it issues. Reason's representation of its law is the sufficient motivation for the will, which does not need to draw its motives from expectations, goals, interests, passions, or feelings.

By contrast, in hypothetical imperatives only the representation of a material goal can move reason to operate on the world. For whenever the will has a given object, it is determined through the mediation of an incentive that is the anticipated effect of the action upon it. The heteronomous will cannot determine itself categorically and immediately through the mere representation of a deed, as in the categorical imperative (*GMS, Ak* 4: 444, ENG 92). The ground of morality must be more than a speculative representation. It must have moving force, as Kant writes to Herz (*Ak* 10: 144–45). Incentives effect legality owing to their "power over the mind."[25] Duty must speak to the will and make itself sensible: the feeling of respect for the law is the effect of reason's representation of the law.

It is difficult to overestimate the revolution brought about by Kant with this point. Reason is not instrumental in effecting plans or ends set for it by desire, need, or selfish interest. Instead, it is itself the motivation of conduct. Nobody before Kant in the history of philosophy had come even remotely close to such a thesis on the relation between reason and motivation, which had always been kept external to one another.

Plato opposes truth and eros as the eternal and unchanging is opposed to what is always in motion and has no form of its own.[26] Still, eros (whether as a divine gift, a cosmic drive, or a passion) is a force with respect to which we are passive. It mediates between separate levels, makes us transcend our condition, and puts us in touch with what is above us. While it does not make us divine, it does raise us to a vision of the intelligible reality because it is the longing for the whole. Eros changes meaning depending on

25. This is a phrase that the Doctrine of Method of the second *Critique* uses repeatedly at *Ak* 5: 151–52, ENG 261–62.

26. On this relation between reason and desire and the modern transformation of classical theories of motivation, see my *Hegel and Aristotle*, 345ff.; *Artificio, desiderio* (on Hobbes); *Saggezza, immaginazione*, 79–94. See also Nuzzo, *Ideal Embodiment*, 140ff.

its object, which in turn can be ranked. At its peak (in Diotima's speech in the *Symposium*) eros is love of wisdom, philosophy, i.e., the vision of what surpasses the world of generation. Thus, eros is not an irrational or blind passion, because in the philosophical soul it leads to the good and serves reason's purposes. Nevertheless, it is a power external to reason.

Aristotle dedramatizes and naturalizes Platonic eros. He examines it in terms of the principle for animal movement. Eros loses its manic and un-controllable charge and becomes *orexis*, appetite: reaching out to a goal and moving toward its attainment. Only the object of a drive or the end of an action (*orekton, prakton*) moves an animal to act (*De anima* 3.10, 433b 13–27). The intellect is only directive and identifies the apparent good as its object and thus does not exercise efficient causality on tendencies. Desire is separate from the intellect. As Aristotle puts it, the intellect "by itself moves nothing" (*Nicomachean Ethics* 6.2, 1139a 36).

The moderns, having made Aristotle's naturalization literal and mate-rial, transform desire into a *conatus*, an appetite that demands satisfaction. This desire is not the tendency to an end we actively pursue but a passive being attracted by an object external to us. All finality is rejected as is all rank-ordering of ends, goods, values. The good is now what attracts me. What matters is that I have the means and the power to obtain it. In the definition of desire in Descartes,[27] in Hobbes,[28] or in Spinoza,[29] there is no longer any reference to the apparent good as something independent of our desire. All talk is of the state of commotion and frustration in which desire puts us. Passions are understood as part and parcel of a theory of movement modeled after natural impulse, if not mechanical motion. The good is what we desire (Hobbes, *Leviathan* bk. 1, chap. 6) or hold useful to ourselves (Spinoza, *Ethics* 4, def. 1). For Diotima (*Symposium* 206a–b) and Aristotle (*Metaphysics* Λ7, 1072a 29), instead, we do not think something is good because we desire it, but rather we desire it because we think it is good.

In the moderns, then, reason is literally moved by passions, which are indifferent to ends and external to reason. When Hume writes that reason is inert and powerless, he but sums up the inevitable conclusions of this thesis. Reason is theoretical. Or, if it is practical at all, it is insofar as it is the choice of the appropriate response to an external stimulus. In all such

---

27. *Passions of the Soul*, art. 86, *Oeuvres*, 11: 392: "an agitation of the soul caused by the spirits, which disposes the soul to wish, in the future, for the things it represents to itself as agreeable."

28. "By desire we always signify the absence of the object." Hobbes's definition is in bk. 1, chap. 6 of *Leviathan* (desire is *conatus* or 'endeavour').

29. "This sadness, insofar as it is in reference to the absence of the object of love, is called desire" (*Ethica* 3, prop. 36, note).

instances, the will is not reason's autonomous self-determination to action, but only (at best and if it is free at all) the choice among given objects. The good or end or object of desire is external to reason.

Only with Kant does reason become the incentive to itself, the motivation to realize itself, the sufficient cause and beginning of action. Reason is now a force. Obviously what matters is not deciding whether the motives are internal or external to the subject. A toothache and a state of distress are internal impulses to action, but they are not rational. What matters is that the will be affected by reason and not by an impulse (*conatus, Trieb*, material or otherwise), the only affection that modern philosophy thought possible.

As in the first *Critique*, where it was divided into pure and empirical, in practical philosophy sensibility is likewise divided. It is the matter, not the incentive for the will (only the moral law, for all its formality, is). But sensibility is not only matter. There is a side to it that is not empirical at all but rather generated by reason: the feeling of respect for the law. In this respect, sensibility does not come first as did the immediate relation to intuitive objects in the first *Critique*. It comes last, as the product or effect of reason's formality. It can be known a priori just as can reason's law. Again, the a priori is an a priori synthesis. As such, it is a force, not an abstraction. It is a cognition (*and* an impulse), not a mere condition.

Incidentally, if pure reason's a priori synthesis projects worlds according to ideas, it is a pity that Hegel did not appreciate or fully understand this unprecedented move on Kant's part. In his criticism, Hegel writes that the categorical imperative to return deposits does not imply that reason abides by an unconditional principle. It implies instead that it presupposes a given matter (private property and the institutions and laws governing its existence), which it winds up sanctioning.[30] For Hegel, since maxims are empty forms, the universalization of the maxim is a trivial test that all maxims can pass. Universalization is valid when it comes to the promise to return the deposit as to any other maxim. For him from the outset the form contradicts the content. As a result, the Kantian moral agent, by endorsing and legitimizing external, empirically found contents, lives in a necessary contradiction with the moral autonomy it aspires to safeguard and realize.

Hegel asks, 'What if there were no deposits?,' and wonders why Kant is preoccupied with construing as a contradiction the absence of deposits from the world. What Hegel does not see, however, is that this is not the contradiction that Kant argues emerges if the maxim of returning the deposit is

---

30. See the discussion in *Über die wissenschaftlichen Behandlungsarten des Naturrechts* (1802), *Werke*, 2: 453ff., abridged later in the *Phenomenology* (*Werke*, 3: 322–23).

violated. Instead, it is the self-contradictory *world* in which deposits would disappear because reciprocal trust would vanish. What Hegel does not see then is that the form, as the will's agreement with itself, generates the content. It generates it and does not find it or presuppose it, because reason has the power to transcend itself and produce a world through its legislation.

If the binding promise to return a deposit is a content instituted by a resolution whose form is a relation to oneself (a lasting pledge, loyalty, integrity, or truthfulness to oneself), form and content are aspects of the same. They are not absolutely opposed the way universality and determinateness are. In the practical a priori synthesis the content is not the surreptitiously assumed and empirically found content standing opposed to an empty rational form, but the form's own product. The formality of the imperative is not "the analytical unity and tautology," as Hegel calls it in the *Naturrechtaufsatz* (*Werke* 2: 463), but an a priori synthesis.

Because Hegel misses the form-content, he also misidentifies the "empirical." What remains external and indifferent to the form-content that alone counts is the matter, not the content.[31] It is indifferent, that is, whether it is money I borrowed or a book I was loaned or whatever else I promised to return.

We can lament a missed opportunity for these two giants to have encountered differently. We could also regret the lack of a more detailed consideration of *how* morality needs to concretize itself in specific duties. What for our purposes bears highlighting is that in the second *Critique* Kant has subjected the division of faculties to a dramatic change. The faculty of desire has been severed from the feeling of pleasure and displeasure. When reason is the pure and autonomous determination of the will, it is defined as the higher faculty of desire or practical reason. In turn, the feeling of pleasure is not ousted from morality on account of its irrationality. Nor is pleasure opposed to the will the way the empirical is opposed to the pure. In fact, the year after the publication of the second *Critique* Kant will discover that pleasure, too, has not only a nonempirical side but even an a priori principle. The third *Critique* will be born of that discovery.

It is very reductive, then, to take the third *Critique* as a work on aesthetic and teleological judgment. The *Critique of Judgment* is the missing link, the crown, of the critical project regarding pure reason. Here, to be sure, reason does not determine any object. Still, the third *Critique* shows how

---

31. We can say, with Ferraris (*Documentalità*), that a deposit has the manner of being of a social, not an empirical object. It is instituted by a community of wills, not found in nature. See Orsini, *Il metodo della critica di Hegel*, 200–201.

reason operates reflectively on itself as it evaluates and judges what it cannot bring back to laws: as it deals with the contingent. In other words, reason is directed no longer to "experience in general," i.e., nature as a full-blown mechanism, but to the heterogeneous and multifarious system of empirical laws. Reflective judgment does not legislate over objects but tries to make sense of a rich empirical diversity because it considers nature in analogy with technique. It views its objects as if they were made to fulfill ends and be part of a rational design.

In this self-affection reason is occupied not with objects but with a perception of the harmonious relation between its own faculties, i.e., imagination and understanding (*EE* § 8, *Ak* 20: 223, ENG 25), which generates a feeling of pleasure and the sentiment of being enlivened by the disinterested contemplation of an object whose form we regard as purposive. We regard it, that is, as if it were made to adjust or correspond to our faculties, as if it were made for our enjoyment, as if it were the product of a providential design. If this feeling is as pure as the feeling of respect for the law in morality, it is not a subjective consequence of a law (or the mere concomitant side effect of judgment). It is the product of the reflective judgment without which no judgment of purposiveness is even possible. The third *Critique* is the completion of the system of reason in this sense.

The following passage is about judgments of taste, but it can also be cited to describe the whole third *Critique*. Notice also that here the presumed "predicate" of the synthetic a priori judgment, the additional element that was not contained in the beginning but is added a priori to it, is a feeling: the feeling of pleasure.

> That judgments of taste are synthetic is readily seen, because they go beyond the concept and even the intuition of the object, and add to that as a predicate something that is not even cognition at all, namely the feeling of pleasure (or displeasure). However, that such judgments, even though the predicate (of *one's own* pleasure that is combined with the representation) is empirical, are nevertheless, as far as the requisite assent *of everyone* is concerned, a priori judgments, or would be taken as such, is already implicit in the expressions of their claim; and thus this problem of the critique of the power of judgment belongs under the general problem of Transcendental philosophy: How are synthetic a priori judgments possible?[32]

32. *KU* § 36, *Ak* 5: 288–89, ENG 169. On the teleological judgment, see the passage (§ 79, *Ak* 5: 417, ENG 286) where Kant writes that teleology belongs not to a doctrine but to the critique of that cognitive faculty known as power of judgment. Its a priori principles provide a

4. Mathematics and Metaphysics

How do we reconcile the a priori synthesis in transcendental philosophy of the previous section with Kant's repeated admonition that philosophy should not imitate the contagious example of mathematics? Mathematics is the most impressive instance of pure reason's objectifying production. It is even *a model for all a priori synthesis*, as Kant writes to Reinhold (*Ak* 11: 43–44). In the Discipline he contrasts philosophy with mathematics especially with regard to their respective methods or procedures. Knowledge from concepts, that is, the discursive use of reason in accordance with concepts, is opposed to its intuitive use, knowledge from the construction of concepts (*KrV* A 712/B 740). Mathematics considers the universal in the particular or even the individual, whereas philosophy considers the particular in the universal. In spite of common preconceptions, writes Kant, mathematics and philosophy do not differ as to their object but only as to their form or method (*KrV* A 713–19/B 741–47).

The contrast between philosophy and mathematics dates back to Kant's earliest essays. In *The Only Possible Argument* (*BDG, Ak* 2: 66, ENG 111) metaphysics is "a bottomless abyss . . . a dark and shoreless ocean, marked by no beacons." It is also "a slippery ground," the disregard of which, along with the "mania for method and the imitation of the mathematician, who advances with a sure step along a well-surfaced road, [has] occasioned a large number of . . . mishaps" (*Ak* 2: 71, ENG 117). For a long time metaphysics appeared to Kant as a path to be mistrusted and also a yet unwritten science (*Deutlichkeit, Ak* 2: 283, ENG 255). All attempts at imitating the mathematician in metaphysics, which were quite common among the German scholastics (and in general since the time of the scientific revolution), appeared to him as a dangerous seduction against which we should guard ourselves.

The important *Inquiry concerning the Distinctness of the Principles of Natural Theology and Morality* (*Deutlichkeit*) of 1764, the most explicit tract Kant devotes to the theme of the different kinds of evidence and distinctness of principles employed by mathematics and philosophy, begins with the explicit intention *not to do metaphysics* by relying on the uncertain doctrines of philosophers or on their definitions (*Ak* 2: 275, ENG 247). Only the certain propositions of experience can be allowed in the inquiry. The proper method of metaphysics is the one introduced by Newton in natural sciences (*Ak* 2: 286, ENG 259).

---

method of judging nature according to final causes and have a negative, restrictive influence on the science of nature.

This mention of definitions by itself is sufficient to differentiate the two sciences. Definitions in *mathematics* are arbitrary combinations of concepts. "The concept which I am defining is not given prior to the definition itself; on the contrary, it only comes into existence as a result of that definition" (*Ak* 2: 276, ENG 248). A cone in mathematics is the arbitrary representation of a right-angled triangle rotated on one of its sides. The cone is the result of a synthetic activity. As definitions give rise to their object, it is absurd to ask for their demonstration (*Ak* 2: 281, ENG 254). Whatever propositions are allowed in mathematics are regarded as immediately certain principles presupposed as true.

It goes quite differently in philosophy. Here the concept of things is given, but obscurely and indeterminately. The task is to analyze the concept, separate its characteristic marks, and render complete and determinate an abstract thought (*Ak* 2: 277, ENG 249). As a result, metaphysics, which is "philosophy of the fundamental principles of our cognition," cannot begin with definitions or explanations, which are "the last thing I come to know" (*Ak* 2: 283, ENG 256). Metaphysics therefore must proceed analytically, since it is the analysis of confused cognitions.

The arbitrary character of the signs adopted in mathematics and the synthetic origin of its concepts are hardly the germ of the future notion of construction as the exhibition of a concept in a corresponding intuition. In the *Inquiry* Kant has not yet elaborated the distinction between pure and empirical intuition, and with it the notion of construction as an a priori exhibition in pure, nonempirical intuition essential to the first *Critique*. The distinctive evidence and exactness of mathematics rest on the univocity, immediate verifiability, and visibility of its sensible signs as opposed to the indeterminacy of the words that metaphysics must use. Signs in mathematics (algebraic symbols and geometric figures), unlike signs qua words, which are no more than mediate designations or reminders of meanings, lend themselves well to representing the universal *in concreto*. They are the perfect instrument to promote mathematical knowledge.[33]

---

33. Note that in the *Inquiry* symbols are the genus of which characters as well as figures are the species, and in the *Dissertation* symbols are the means of discursive knowledge. Later, especially in the *Critique of Judgment* (§ 59) and the *Anthropology* (§ 38), the symbol is an indirect figure to be opposed to the discursive characters, not to the intuitive exhibition. The passage on "a symbolic construction" in the Discipline at A 717/B 746 is, I suggest, either a transitional stage before the mature conception or the unintentional residue of an earlier usage of 'symbol' within the new conception of intuitive construction striving to make its way. On signs and symbols in mathematics and on Kant's novelty in comparison with Leibniz and Wolff, see my "Kant's Productive Imagination," 84–87, "Construction and Mathematical Schematism," 133ff.,

In the famous letter to Herz of 1772, as he juxtaposes the passive receptivity of the *intellectus ectypus* and the active creation of the *intellectus archetypus*, Kant writes that in mathematics we do not have the problem of objective reference. The solution is at hand. Objects can be represented as magnitudes in that we *produce* (*erzeugen*) their representation by taking the unity as many times as we need. Concepts are made arbitrarily. They are "active in their own right" (*selbstthätig*, Ak 10: 130–31) or spontaneous.

The constitution of the mathematical object is a quasi-idealistic activity. In the Discipline of the first *Critique*, mathematics can extend its knowledge completely a priori because it is an objectifying production in which the mere representation of the object constructed both contains the actuality of the object and shows its concept by giving its definition. The exhibition of a concept in pure intuition is a synthetic activity that is then the basis for a growth in knowledge. Exhibition *in concreto* is unattainable in philosophy, which can only hope to clarify given concepts. In empirical knowledge it needs to rely on experience. In mathematics instead the a priori construction of the objects in a spatial or temporal intuition is sufficient to determine exhaustively their content. As Kant writes, "while philosophical definitions are never more than expositions of given concepts, mathematical definitions are constructions of concepts, originally framed by the mind itself. . . . Mathematical definitions *make* [*machen*] their concepts" (*KrV* A 730/B 758). A mathematical concept does not exist prior to our definition of it, but once the definition through the synthesis of concept and pure intuition is given, so are the object and its existence. What is striking about mathematics is that arbitrary concepts denote a reality: the reality they have constituted.

A transcendental investigation, recall, shows the origin, domain, and objective validity of our cognitions. And a transcendental investigation is all that interests Kant in his consideration of mathematics in the first *Critique*. Kant connects the synthetic origin of mathematical concepts and their objective reality throughout. "Mathematical definitions can never err. For since the concept is first given through the definition, it contains just that which the definition would think through it" (*KrV* A 731/B 759). Mathematical definitions are not logical or nominal but real definitions, insofar as they

---

from which I am drawing many points in this section, and La Rocca, *Esistenza e Giudizio*, 56–60. Also note that making mathematics rest on the evidence of sensible signs makes mathematical knowledge in the precritical period depend either on the senses, or on "their vicarious representative, the imagination" ("von den Sinnen oder der Vertreterin, der Einbildungskraft," *Refl* 1634, Ak 16: 54; "unsere Sinne oder deren vicaria, die imaginatio," *Refl* 1670, Ak 16: 72). See Capozzi, *Kant e la logica*, 317ff.

show the objective reality of their concepts by providing the corresponding pure intuition, insofar, that is, as they give rise to their object.[34]

Definition and construction are the flip sides of the same coin. A mathematical concept always involves its figurative synthesis, its schematization. I cannot think a triangle without describing it in a space, whether mental or external, just as I cannot think a line without drawing it in thought (*KrV* B 154). Similarly, the mathematical definition of a circle as a curved line on which all points are equidistant from the center[35] involves the necessity to go beyond the concept and show its pure, a priori determination of a spatial intuition. The definition is then the guide for the construction of the object. Conversely, the construction is the realization in pure intuition of the concept expressed in the definition.

For the mathematician, to think is to construct spontaneously, to use the concept as a direction for the construction of the object. The geometer "hurries immediately to intuition" (*KrV* A 716/B 744) and can produce the solutions needed, through a chain of inferences sustained by pure intuition. By contrast, the philosopher is confined to his or her general concepts.

Mathematics offers a shining example[36] of this objectifying production, in which the mere concept of the object constructed makes it actual. So when Eberhard (and Abraham Gotthelf Kästner) object that the mathematician need not say a word on the existence of mathematical objects (*Entdeckung*, Ak 8: 190–91, ENG 286–87), Johann Schultz, inspired by Kant, replies that "in mathematics possibility and actuality [*Wirklichkeit*] are one, and the geometer says *there are* conic sections, as soon as he has shown their possibility a priori" (*Ak* 20: 386; see *Entdeckung*, Ak 8: 191, ENG 287). If mathematics considers the concept *in concreto*, and not empirically but in a pure intuition and a priori, the sense of existence in mathematics differs from empirical existence (*KrV* A 719/B 747). It is an ideal existence that satisfies the exclusive criterion of constructibility in pure intuition. As we saw, in it possibility and actuality are one. By contrast, in "empirical" exist-

---

34. Kant writes to Reinhold: "The definition which Apollonius gives, e.g., of a parabola, is itself the exhibition of a concept in intuition, namely, the intersection of a cone under certain conditions, and in establishing the objective reality of the concept the definition here, as always in geometry, is at the same time the construction of the concept" (*Ak* 11: 43–44).

35. I use Kant's example from the letter to Reinhold (*Ak* 11: 43–44). On the a priori production, the real definitions, and the inseparability of concept/definition and construction in mathematics, cf. also *Deutlichkeit*, Ak 2: 276, ENG 248; Ak 10: 130–31; *KrV* A 241–43, A 713–19/B 741–47, A 731/B 759, B x–xii; Ak 20: 386; *Entdeckung*, Ak 8: 242, ENG 329.

36. The phrase "ein glänzendes Beispiel" recurs many times, e.g., A 4/B 8, A 39/B 55, A 712/B 740. Mathematics exemplifies how far reason can go a priori in its cognitions without help from experience.

ence, the existence of appearances, possibility and actuality are quite apart. But in mathematics possibility and actuality can be one insofar as objective reality regards pure intuition alone: not experience but its possibility.

When Kant speaks of making a concept sensible or giving it a meaning, then, he means that the concept shows *how* the object *can be real*: not *that* it is *given* to us (*KrV* A 241–42 and n/B 300–301). The objective reality and the givenness of appearances differ markedly. Transcendental philosophy focuses on the former alone.

If for the mathematician to think is to construct spontaneously, the mathematician is able to bridge the otherwise insurpassable gap between discursive reason and exhibition in intuition. Thinking and knowing, the identification of which was the primary error of traditional metaphysics, do not seem different in mathematics.[37] If in mathematics rule and exhibition are inseparable, the pure intuition in which we construct our concepts is not simply a means or a ladder to throw away after use, but the demonstration of the objective reality of our concepts. Therefore the question of the syntheticity of mathematics cannot be reduced to the extensive character of its demonstrative procedure. The synthesis here involves the necessity to go beyond the concept and show its pure a priori determination of a spatiotemporal intuition. If pure intuition accounts first of all for the synthetic genesis of *concepts*, what counts as a synthetic *judgment* is not a formal, discursive relation between subject and predicate, but the activity of exhibiting in intuition the real belonging of a property to its object.[38]

Through such an activity mathematics can increase its patrimony of laws and cognitions. This is a point Kant makes with great clarity in a striking passage of the *Prolegomena* (§ 38, *Ak* 4: 321–22, ENG 114). He asks if the properties of geometric figures we learn or demonstrate belong to space and its figures or instead to the understanding. His reply bears quoting:

> that which determines space into the figure of a circle, a cone, or a sphere is
> the understanding, insofar as it contains the basis for the unity of the con-
> struction of those figures. The mere universal form of intuition called space
> is therefore certainly the substratum of all intuitions determinable upon par-
> ticular objects . . . ; but the unity of the objects is determined solely through

37. "With mathematics we can safely avail ourselves of reason without criticizing it beforehand," because "it can exhibit its concepts in intuition. . . . In mathematics illusion is prevented by intuition, but in metaphysics by critique" (V-Met/Mron, *Ak* 29: 766, ENG 127).

38. "If one is to judge synthetically about a concept, then one must go beyond this concept, and indeed go to the intuition in which it is given" (*KrV* A 721/B 749), i.e., not to the predicate, as I argued before. See also A 718–19/B 746–47; *Entdeckung*, *Ak* 8: 242, ENG 329.

the understanding . . . ; and so the understanding is the origin of the universal order of nature.

Thanks simply to the rule for its construction, the mathematical object contains many properties that, from a consideration of the figure produced according to a rule, allow for a synthetic increase of knowledge. The understanding can *learn* what it put into the figure. It can *be taught* properties of the circle it had not thought when it constructed it according to the rule of the equality of the radii. In this sense the subject of a judgment is synthetically supplemented with a new predicate, the demonstrated intuitive property.

The extensive character of mathematics, namely, its synthetic a priori judgments, is grounded on the synthetic origin of its concepts, which makes possible the transition from the representational system of discursive characters or linguistic signs, to use the terminology of the *Critique of Judgment* (§ 59), to the system of ostensive hypotyposes. We can have an a priori growth in knowledge without having to rely on experience because of this twofold synthesis that is unique to mathematics. Neither transcendental philosophy nor any science whatever can have a demonstrative development *and* an ostensive production of their objects in intuition.

Let us recall Kant's discussion of the schema of a triangle (*KrV* A 141/B 180). No image could ever be adequate to the concept of a triangle in general because it would be right-angled or obtuse-angled, that is, always determinate and thereby lacking the universality of the concept. Therefore the triangle cannot exist except in thought, where it has the property of universality. The schema of a triangle is then "a rule of synthesis of the imagination, in respect to pure figures in space" (ibid.). In itself a schema is nothing other than a method, but it is not an abstract or discursive standard. It is a mediation, the procedure by which we assign a concept its sensible representation. As to our mathematical concepts, it is always schemata, not images, that underlie them (ibid.).

This implies that the relation between concept and schema is necessary and immanent to our mathematical concepts. In geometry we disregard the sensible image of the triangle and take it for granted that we must regard it as an instance of the schematized concept. Mathematical concepts qua pure sensible concepts intrinsically relate a priori to intuition or are inherently schematized. This is not, however, in virtue of their own alleged 'nature' but because they always involve my constructive *activity*. When I draw a triangle, the intuitive manifold is not given to me independently of and prior to my act of apperceiving a priori the figure I am drawing: I generate it.

This is possible because intuition here is not just the empty form of our sensibility negatively restricting the use of our concepts, but a determinate pure intuition as the unity of a manifold. It is an actual representation as opposed to a mere condition of possibility of experience such as was portrayed in the Aesthetic. In the words of Kant's and Schultz's reply to Kästner, if metaphysics shows how one *has* the representation of space, geometry teaches how to *describe* a space. Whereas in the former space is considered as "given, before all determinations . . . , in the latter it is considered as it is *generated* [*gemacht*]. In the former it is *original* and only one (single) *space*. In the latter it is derived and there are (many) *spaces*" (*Ak* 20: 419–22). Space, represented as an object ("as we are required to do in geometry," *KrV* B 160–61), contains more than the mere form of intuition, namely, the combination (*Zusammenfassung*) of the given manifold in an intuitive representation. If the form of intuition is something all-embracing, given, one, underlying all intuitions, formal intuitions are limitations on that one intuition.

This is the decisive step. In mathematics space and time are not only the condition for all intuition. In a more fundamental sense, they are themselves the object of our determination. But since space and time are the forms of our sensibility, Kant can say that the figurative synthesis is a *Selbstaffektion*, our spontaneity's determination of our own sensibility. Through the imagination's determination, the understanding exercises its effect (*Wirkung*) on sensibility. Hence, with specific regard to mathematics, our generation in space and time of one whole representation through the progressive combination of their parts is the condition of possibility of our representing an object as a *quantum* or extensive magnitude (*KrV* A 162–63/B 203).

The schema of a triangle cannot be analogous to that of an empirical concept (Kant mentions the schema of a dog) because an intuition of the dog, which exhibits its concept *in concreto*, has to be supplied by experience. An important consequence, which Kant never draws, is that mathematical schematism has no residual matter. There is no radical split between matter and a priori form. The matter is the concrete image of the triangle drawn on this piece of paper, not a jumping dog in flesh and bones. It is something that by and large I have produced and not something I find. Above all it is something irrelevant I naturally disregard and treat as no more than the instance of a concept, the illustration of a rule.

In other words, if in empirical schemata there is a three-term relationship among schema, image, and a given appearance, in mathematical schematism the only relation that counts is that between the two terms of schema and image. The intuition is not of an appearance but of the image as itself representative of the method of its a priori construction. Whereas in mathematics I make a concept intuitive, in an empirical concept discursivity is separate from exhibition. The form is separate from the content. We can have an extensional logic as a formal connection of discursive concepts, but this implies that individual and universal differ in nature. While a dog is synthesized according to independently given (logical and empirical) rules, geometric figures are direct exhibitions of rules and thus there is hardly a gap to bridge.

At the end of the Discipline Kant draws his conclusions. Mathematics begins by positing its real definitions, has axioms as immediately certain synthetic a priori principles, and is capable of apodictic demonstrations insofar as it has intuitive proofs. In none of this can philosophy hope to imitate mathematics. Definitions at best come last, as the crown of a clarificatory effort. Philosophy cannot avail itself of any immediately certain principles. Its apodicticity is at best acroamatic or discursive. The result seems straightforward: philosophy is simply analytic and aims at explanation of given concepts (*Erklärung*). But we have seen that, on the contrary, transcendental philosophy is synthetic. So how do we solve this dilemma?

Some distinctions are first required. Since clearly philosophy is never constructive, it is necessarily a *discursive* account. But of a *synthetic* or an *analytic* enterprise? If there is an obvious difference between the account and the object (and we are interested here in the object), there is also a difference between a synthetic and an analytic exposition of the same material (let the examples of *Critique of Pure Reason* vs. *Prolegomena*, and of the *Critique of Practical Reason* vs. *Groundwork*, suffice as an illustration of the respective methods of exposition of roughly the same material). Still, the contradiction seems to remain. Since the Doctrine of Method is established as a definitive text in the first edition of the first *Critique* (1781), and the second edition (1787) does not change a word of it, the contradiction can be expressed as follows. In 1781 Kant writes that philosophy cannot imitate mathematics. In 1787, in the B Preface, he claims that *metaphysics must imitate mathematics*. Is there a difference between philosophy and metaphysics? No. Here philosophy is the discursive method of metaphysics. So we are back at the question of the syntheticity of metaphysics (as well as of transcendental philosophy, which is its positive, immanent part). The possibility that Kant changed his mind between the first and the second edition of the *Critique of Pure Reason* must therefore be examined in the remainder of this section.

If we study the unpublished notes of the 1770s, we realize that it is during this time that Kant formulates his mature theory of mathematics. The notion of construction, with the parallel separation of pure and empirical intuition, is a discovery that becomes paramount for critical philosophy. It is thanks to his reflection on mathematics that Kant discovers synthetic a priori judgments.

In the *Inquiry*, Kant writes that "[t]he object of mathematics is magnitude" (*Ak* 2: 282, ENG 255). In the Discipline he writes: "Those who thought to distinguish philosophy from mathematics by saying of the former that it has merely *quality* while the latter has *quantity* as its object have taken the effect for the cause. The form of mathematical cognition is the cause of its pertaining solely to quanta" (*KrV* A 714/B 742). This reversal was possible because Kant had meanwhile dropped the reference to sensibility and instead made pure intuition the only object of mathematics.[39] It is because in 1781 he had identified and made available a pure intuition to which we can relate a priori independently of experience that he could elaborate the notion of construction as exhibition in intuition, ascribe to mathematical concepts an objective reality, and focus on the *form* of knowledge as opposed to its subject matter.

If in metaphysics, as we have seen, reason determines its object wholly a priori, mathematical knowledge becomes a model for philosophy. But this notion is potentially quite misleading.[40] First, mathematics cannot be a model for experience and empirical knowledge, even if mathematics for Kant is the best example of science human beings could come up with. In fact, even in natural sciences "there can be only as much *proper* science as there is *mathematics* therein" (*MAN, Ak* 4: 470, ENG 185). It is a shining example of science and of a priori growth in knowledge. And yet, paradoxically, it is not a cognition!

At *KrV* B 147 we read that mathematical concepts are not cognitions because they relate to the form of pure sensible intuition, not to appearances. It is left undecided whether or not the form will be the form of an appearance. In this connection, recall Kant's distinction between the actuality of the mathematical object and its empirical reality. An *actual* triangle is the *possible* form of the side of a pyramid. Until it is met with as such in experience, i.e., until it proves to be more than a form and is seen as the form-of-an-appearance, "it would still always remain only a product of the imagination" (*KrV* A 223–24/B 271).

39. See Capozzi, *Kant e la logica*, 320.

40. In my "Construction and Mathematical Schematism," I was quite misled by Kant's opposition of philosophy and mathematics, so that the extent of the affinity of mathematics and transcendental philosophy on the a priori synthesis had escaped me.

It may make sense to distinguish mathematics from its application to appearances and show how even this application rests on principles. It is perhaps fair to recall that transcendental principles must be able to ground all cognitions, including mathematics (*KrV* B 188–89 and B 198–99), and that this point concerning the insufficiency of mathematics is expressed in the midst of a transcendental deduction (§ 22) of *empirical* cognition. Finally, it is vital to remember that if confusion arises at all, it is to a significant degree due to translations. The German language (admittedly, with help from Latin) has a clear distinction that most other languages cannot render. Kant uses *objektive Realität*, not *Wirklichkeit*, i.e., not actuality, and thus refers to the positive determination of a concept, not to the existence of things.[41]

Still, some of the ambiguities concerning the actuality, reality, and possibility of mathematical objects, pure intuition, and form remain.[42] The status of *prima inter pares* among sciences, or soul of all sciences, ascribed to mathematics, along with its not being a cognition, is baffling. After all, traditionally science has always been the highest instance of knowledge, not a seemingly different genus.

In what ways then is mathematics a model for all synthesis (as Kant wrote Reinhold), and thereby for knowledge? From Schultz, and then Eberhard-Kästner, Jakob Sigismund Beck, to Maimon, Kant's allies and foes have noticed this affinity between mathematics and critical philosophy. Kant himself did all he could to encourage it in his collaboration with

41. See *Ak* 20: 415. *Realität* is a category of quality opposed to *Negation*, while *Wirklichkeit* is a modal category. My point is that objective reality is the possibility of experience and corresponds to empirical possibility, not to actuality or *Wirklichkeit* (think of the analogous medieval distinction taken up by Descartes in the Third Meditation of *realitas formalis* and *objectiva*). Kant writes to Reinhold that Eberhard misses the notion of synthetic a priori judgments because he conflates logical and real ground (*Realgrund*). A real ground, in turn, is either formal (constitutive of intuition) or material (and therefore the ground of the existence of things: *Ak* 10: 35–38). Since construction aims at the extension of the concept in a pure intuition showing a property that was not considered before, a synthetic a priori judgment in mathematics concerns the *properties* of a mathematical object (i.e., of a possible empirical object). Instead a synthetic judgment in experience concerns the *existence* of an appearance (*KrV* A 721/B 749, A 719/B 747). The *Critique of Judgment* says that in pure mathematics "there can never be an issue of the existence of things, but only of their possibility" (§ 63, *Ak* 5: 366n, ENG 239n).

42. For example, mathematical intuition is an experience comparable to perception in *Reflexion* 5661 (*Ak* 18: 319). In the passage from the text of Schultz's review of Eberhard's *Magazin* cited above ("in mathematics possibility and actuality [*Wirklichkeit*] are one," *Ak* 20: 386), the word is indeed actuality. However, an attentive reading of the text that Kant sent Schultz (*Ak* 20: 379–99) *on the basis of which Schultz wrote his review* shows that Kant never uses 'actuality' for 'objective reality.' He only denounces Eberhard's misuse and misunderstanding of *Wirklichkeit* in mathematics. The addition of *Wirklichkeit* is then Schultz's.

Schultz, in his correspondence (with Herz, Schultz, Reinhold, Beck),[43] and in his rebuttal of Eberhard and Kästner. But this does not imply that in mathematics we are like gods, as Maimon put it. Mathematics is not valued as a free creation, an a priori production irrespective of experience that can grow on itself because it disregards intuition. It is valued because it is a synthesis of pure intuition that attains its result (a geometric figure, a number) by the successive addition of homogeneous parts, by the composition of a whole through the repetition of arbitrarily established units of measure.

Mathematics has this privilege because the objects on which it operates are space and time, which are pure intuitions containing a pure manifold we constitute and make determinate in our several constructions. We determine them as we limit an originally given whole, which we take as an infinite magnitude we proceed to articulate in unitary segments. But this mathematical synthesis, an a priori production, is "entirely identical" with the synthesis we exercise in experience as we apprehend the form of an empirical manifold (*KrV* A 224/B 271). For otherwise there would be a gap between what we apprehend and what we construct. We could not apprehend, say, the geometric shape of a rectangular object as identical with the rectangle of which I demonstrate geometrical properties. Mathematics could not be applied to experience. *I would know what I apprehend and what I construct, but not their relation* (their identity or difference).

This is key. As Kant tries to formulate his critical philosophy in the late 1770s and understands we can know only appearances, mathematics begins to appear to him as a model for what he now is first conceiving as transcendental knowledge. The thesis of the *Inaugural Dissertation*, that sensibility and understanding aim at two different worlds, begins to be abandoned in the letter to Herz as Kant shifts his focus to the problem of the real use of the understanding. In the letter (*Ak* 10: 131ff.), Kant advances three possibilities to account for the reference of pure concepts to objects: the empiricist *intellectus ectypus*, the preestablished harmony à la Malebranche, and the Platonic *intellectus archetypus*. No solution, however, seems apt to him. Kant formulates the thesis that mathematical concepts are self-active and constitute a priori their reality as an interesting but inconsequential aside.

In the first *Critique* instead, where sense and understanding are two distinct modes of aiming at the same world, Kant verifies the possibility that

---

43. I find of particular interest in this connection the discussion of the mathematical model of synthesis proposed by Beck (who was himself a mathematician by profession) and Schultz's negative opinion on the misconstrual of the Transcendental Aesthetics implicit in it. On this discussion, see De Vleeschauwer, *La déduction*, 3: 515–30.

pure reason determines its objects as mathematics determines its. The three possibilities of the letter to Herz are then reduced to two: either the object makes the representation possible or the representation makes the object possible (*KrV* A 92/B 125). Vice versa, the understanding can now be archetypal, a possibility excluded in the letter, not in that it creates its objects but in the limited sense that it determines them a priori (ibid.).

Mathematics can work as a model for knowledge because it is the synthesis of a pure succession that underlies all appearances. In fact, this synthesis is exercised a priori even as it is directed to the empirical manifold (*KrV* A 99). It is a progressive synthesis that reaches its whole through and out of its parts, regardless of the object to be unified. This is one of the lessons of the threefold synthesis of the A Deduction, which discusses synthesis as the apprehension of a manifold in which I distinguish the units of time, the reproduction of parts of a line that would never appear as a unity unless its parts were retained in one act, and counting.[44] The category of quantity, differently stated, plays a prominent role as Kant struggles to define the objective validity of pure concepts.[45]

Strikingly, these examples are the same as those Kant uses for the Axioms of Intuition (the Principles of Quantity). Furthermore, the importance of the mathematical model is prominent in all treatment of time and succession, in the figurative synthesis in B, and with it in the notion that a *Selbstaffektion*, the understanding's schematic affection of pure intuition, suffices to determine a form. Once he has established the objective reality of mathematical concepts, Kant realizes he can use the issue of objective reality to solve the question of the reference of pure concepts to possible experience. That is the question of what the famous letter to Herz called the ground of the relation of representations to objects.

This is not to say of course that pure concepts can be constructed. But the a priori synthesis in transcendental philosophy, i.e., the a priori reference of pure concepts to pure intuitions, is philosophy's discursive analogue to mathematical intuitive construction. In both cases reason's a priori synthesis generates a form-content.

In light of this consideration we can now return to the text and verify what Kant says of the different syntheses in mathematics and philosophy. First, in the Discipline itself, where we may expect the contrast to be at

---

44. The empirical examples of cinnabar, the seasons, and word associations are empirical syntheses of reproduction that presuppose the a priori synthesis of time (*KrV* A 99, 101).

45. See my "Construction and Mathematical Schematism," 147–62, and Longuenesse, *Kant and the Capacity to Judge*, 30–44.

its strongest, Kant does not only oppose mathematics and philosophy, he also puts them on a par (which is natural as they are the two kinds of rational cognitions). More important, he even shows the affinities of their procedures, which means of their *synthesis*. Kant writes that "an a priori concept . . . either contains a pure intuition in itself, in which case it can be constructed; or else it contains nothing but the synthesis of possible intuitions" (*KrV* A 719/B 747). The first is the mathematical synthesis, the latter is the *transcendental synthesis* "with which in turn only the philosopher can succeed, but which never concerns more than a thing in general" (ibid.). In mathematics intuition guides my synthesis, "in transcendental cognition . . . this guideline is possible experience" (*KrV* A 783/B 811).[46]

If pure reason's production is the anticipated form of the object of experience, and if transcendental philosophy shows how pure concepts can be made sensible, we must conclude that mathematics and philosophy differ in the *method* they follow, but not in the ambition to *realize* concepts. As Kant writes:

> Mathematics fulfills this requirement by means of the construction of the figure. . . . The concept is always generated a priori. . . . That this is *also the case with all categories*, however, and the principles spun out from them, is also obvious from this: that we cannot even give a *real definition* of a single one of them, i.e., make intelligible the possibility of their object, without immediately descending to conditions of sensibility. (*KrV* A 240/B 300, italics mine)

The conditions of sensibility indeed give pure concepts meaning. As we can see, the objective reality of pure concepts is the aim of a deduction that mathematics does not need both because it can construct its concepts and because it presupposes transcendental principles (the Axioms of Intuition) as its condition. But the task of showing the objective reality (the possibility of referring to experience, of being their form-content) remains the same for pure and mathematical concepts.

This synthesis is something at which *"speculative a priori knowledge"* (*KrV* B 13), rather than a special science, aims (here at B 13 the example of philosophical synthesis is causality). Except that in philosophy the synthesis is indirect and cannot determine its object exhaustively. In fact, it cannot give us an object in intuition to begin with. What it does give us is the principle

46. In the Dohna-Wundlacken Logic the affinity between mathematics and philosophy regards their apodictic and certain cognition (*Ak* 24: 733, ENG 468). For a problem threatening this transcendental synthesis, see below, chapter 3, § 2.

on which all intuitions rest. Here what acquires objective reality is the synthesis of possible objects, not the intuition of real ones.

The dilemma mentioned above concerning whether transcendental philosophy is a synthetic or an analytic science cannot therefore be solved with the resources of *Entwicklungsgeschichte*. We cannot, that is, identify different formulations in chronologically arranged texts, each representative of a univocal thesis, and then discard the earlier ones. We cannot, in particular, treat the Doctrine of Method as a stage later overcome, for within the Doctrine of Method itself we find conflicting positions. In it, for example, we had the Architectonic and the notion of cosmic philosophy with respect to which the mathematician was a mere artist of reason. The high-sounding name "cosmic philosophy" does not necessarily contradict this much more sobering description of philosophy. After all, the privilege of the procedure of artists of reason remains intact. For all their ease and growth in a priori knowledge, their attitude may still be one of cyclopic, partial vision.

The tension is of a different kind. The reason why we must rule out the possibility that Kant has changed his mind on this contrast between philosophy and mathematics and that the Discipline, as such a supposed conceptual unity, bears witness to an earlier layer of his thought is that Kant's ambivalence appears in different parts of the Discipline (as well as elsewhere in the *Critique of Pure Reason*). I think we must conclude that Kant did not distinguish explicitly between, or remained confused about, the relation between synthesis and analysis in metaphysics for some time.

In the Discipline two conflicting theses are maintained: first, metaphysics cannot be more than analysis of given concepts; second is Kant's recently discovered idea, which struggles to assert itself in his mind, of transcendental philosophy's a priori synthesis. By the time of the *Prolegomena* this assertion is complete.[47] In the *Prolegomena* we read in the same paragraph the twofold thesis I think we must take as paradigmatic: metaphysics is an *analysis* of pure concepts, and it is "the *generation* of its a priori cognitions" (*Ak* 4: 273, ENG 66, ital. mine) expressed in *synthetic* propositions. In the B edition it becomes the proud slogan of the Copernican revolution we are asked explicitly to adopt in metaphysics and endorse in a new way of thinking.

Kant initially conceived of metaphysics as analytic for a number of rather obvious reasons, some of which we have seen and some of which we will

---

47. As attested by the passages quoted above on the metaphysical synthesis involving pure concepts of relation and the similar treatment reserved to metaphysics as to mathematics and natural science.

return to below. But one must be noted here: the lack of a sharp distinction between empirical and metaphysical concepts that marks the *Inquiry* and reappears in the Discipline.

Lest we lose our bearings, I strongly suggest that whenever we speak of concepts we specify if we mean pure, empirical, or mathematical concepts, for each of them has different rules of formation, a different exhibition *in concreto*, a different relation between universal and instance, between matter and form. When Kant first introduces concepts for the sake of contrast in the Transcendental Aesthetics and argues that pure intuition is a total form *within* which I intuit singularities whereas a concept is that *under* which I subsume instances, he refers to empirical concepts: concepts as classes, discursive aggregates generated by reflection (*KrV* A 24/B 39). A conceptual aggregate has no core. Our analysis of it knows no end, for I am never certain I have exhausted the essential traits of the empirical concept precisely because it has no ultimate essence I can grasp.[48] I can always adopt a new way to approach an appearance and conceptualize it in an ever different manner, be it a natural thing or an artifact like a ship's clock (*KrV* A 729/B 757).

In the contrast of the *Inquiry*, the deficient distinctness of philosophical concepts had to do with the fact that in metaphysics we draw on the common usage of the words we employ. The example was the concept of gold (*Ak* 2: 285, ENG 257), the same as in the Discipline (and in Locke). To say that an empirical concept cannot be defined or determined more closely because it is bound to remain indeterminate, or, as in the case of artifacts (the ship's clock, *KrV* A 729/B 757), because it is bound to designate our project more than the object itself, is a philosophical point on the inevitable confusions of natural language that Leibniz could have made. But this point on the inevitable confusion of language differs from the difficulty of defining a metaphysical concept such as, for example, causality. The word 'gold' indeed designates an object, but it cannot exhaust its concept because it depends on the characters and properties we know of gold. It is indeed

---

48. When it comes to *empirical* concepts, Kant is heir to a Lockean tradition. By making appearances a combination of matter and form and not of essence and accidents, Kant achieves two results: we can have no ultimate insight into real essences because our concepts are largely stipulative, so that knowledge of objects is an empirical and ever-increasing process of approximation that may be conceptualized differently depending on historical discoveries or new ways to analyze a given; and we approximate a logical essence, not a real essence, because if a concept is the result of an arbitrary combination, then it reveals its content to an analysis of its formation only. When we discover that gold is soluble in *aqua ragia*, then we are in possession of a better tool to identify the metal. But in contrast to the Lockean tradition, pure and mathematical concepts are *not* comparable to empirical concepts. See my "Lived Space," 11–17.

made of such properties, unlike a pure concept. Substance qua permanence in time as a schematized concept that rules experience and therefore has objective reality does not contain anything more than that rule. It does not conceal or inadvertently leave behind notes that mar its completeness or make it indeterminate and confused.

To clarify this point, it is time to focus more closely on the difference between mathematical, empirical, and pure concepts.

5. Mathematical, Empirical, and Pure Concepts

Objective reality, as we have seen, is formal, or ideal. It concerns pure, not empirical intuition and is no more than the schema or possible form of empirical objects. Pure and empirical are not simply distinct. They belong in different realms. From the point of view of objective reality there is little difference between a schema and a pure intuition. They constitute not the *condition* or the *scope* of determination, but the only *object* of determination. In other words, concepts determine not an object *in* pure intuition, but pure intuition itself to which objects, which are appearances to our sensibility, will conform. This determination is pure reason's remarkable power but also where it finds its inevitable limit. Pure concepts give the rule, but only experience can give the empirical instance to which to apply it. While transcendental philosophy stops before the threshold of experience whose form alone is its concern, mathematics separates pure and empirical intuition and stops before its application, which must each time be verified through experience.

Another difference is that transcendental philosophy produces the synthesis, the general form-content, for all possible objects. By contrast, mathematical concepts involve their figurative synthesis. By defining its concepts and exhibiting them in intuition, mathematics produces its objects, which are thus objectively real. Mathematical exhibition can produce both pure and empirical intuitions a priori—except the empirical is quite irrelevant, and we look only to the pure. In the empirical image constructed I consider only the rule that is shown in the image, not the image itself. It makes no difference if in my construction or exhibition of geometry, arithmetic, and algebra I find help in intuitions such as the beads of the abacus, points, fingers, metronomic beats, drawings, different notation systems, an orthogonal plane on paper, or any other help to divide and articulate a homogeneous space, the blood pulse in my veins or any other throb or beat scanning a rhythm, articulating temporal intervals in a homogeneous yet divisible medium. Empirical intuitions of this sort are irrelevant to the mathematician and to Kant. What is relevant, indeed of crucial importance, is that mathematics cannot do without a particular exhibition. For its construction an exhibition is indispensable. If no one exhibition is in itself indispensable and all are *de facto* contingent, the assistance of *some* form of concrete illustration or other is *de jure* needed. And this neediness or dependence is not a defect of mathematics but its strength. For through exhibition mathematics gives reality to its objects. For it certifies that, unlike the transcendent concepts of metaphysics, they are not illusory.[49]

In sum, mathematics is extensive. It is an *ars inveniendi* and a heuristic science with a proof structure. General logic, which has no comparable relation to pure intuition, is a formal and merely analytical explanatory discipline. Transcendental philosophy shares traits of both. It is discursive and not demonstrative. But it is also synthetic in that it constitutes the principles of experience a priori, and its form is not simply logical but a form-content referring a priori to time-schemata and pure intuition. Nonetheless transcendental philosophy is unlike mathematics, Kant tells us, with regard to definitions. We can define only what we have made. Concepts that are arbitrarily thought are always definable, "for I must know what I wanted to think, since I deliberately made it up" (*KrV* A 729/B 757).

One might raise two objections to this point. Artifacts are also arbitrary syntheses of objects that do not exist in nature but are made by us. Why can they not be defined? Kant's reply (recall the ship's clock) is that "if the concept depends upon empirical conditions, then the object and its possibility are not given through this arbitrary concept; from the concept I do not even know whether it has an object, and my explanation could better be called a declaration (of my project) than a definition of an object" (ibid.). Unlike aerospace engineering or genetics, for example, mathematics permits me to rest assured that concepts refer to objects because all they need to refer to is pure intuition rather than empirical intuition.[50]

49. From Hegel to Friedrich Adolf Trendelenburg to Gottlob Frege down to Rudolf Carnap, Jaakko Hintikka, Michael Friedman, and Charles Parsons, the interrelation in Kant's mathematics of objective reality, construction as exhibition in intuition, and syntheticity has been ignored. See my "Pure Intuition in Mathematics."

50. The Aristotelian tripartition of theory, practice, and production is reduced to a bipartition and redefined around the two fundamental concepts of nature and freedom. In sum, production is not free-standing but accessory to theoretical philosophy as the practical side of a science of nature. See the first introduction to the *Critique of Judgment* (§ 1, Ak 20: 196, ENG 3–4), which changes the Stoic tripartition (logic, physics, morality) at the beginning of the *Groundwork* (see my *Saggezza, immaginazione*, 67).

A second objection is neither raised nor met by Kant but is more relevant to our concerns. Had Kant not made the Copernican revolution in metaphysics in his B Preface turn around the idea that we have insight only into what we have ourselves made? If what we have made is the form of experience, can we not define our concepts as can mathematics and thereby call into question Kant's point that only mathematical concepts have a real essence and a definition?

Consider the following two examples of empirical judgments: "yesterday it rained," and "the lamp is to the left of the screen." These are judgments about appearances. They mean to describe or communicate information about facts and events and aim at objectivity. Differently stated, they are not simply shared by other observers but valid of the objects they describe. Such judgments are empirical indeed, but they have a pure counterpart. Not only do the categories of substance and relation structure the objectivity of these judgments. Their pure counterpart lies also in the institution of temporal and spatial relations that measure the lapse or distance between a point of reference I arbitrarily choose ('today,' 'my body and my visual space') and the point occupied by the object described. The two judgments, that is, presuppose a pure intuition, i.e., the minimal requisite relation of spatial or temporal order, which affects not the objects as such but my relation to them. In pure intuition I institute an intuitive order that is at a different level than my conceptual order (the unity of notes) referring to the rain or the lamp.

When mathematics constructs its concepts in pure intuition, intuition is not this pure counterpart to an empirical judgment concerning appearances in space and time, for mathematicians are not concerned with experience. Pure intuition is not a correlate at all, but the *exclusive object or ground* of our intellectual determination. The privilege of mathematics rests on this isolation of pure intuition and on its operations on it. Mathematics legislates over and predicates its conclusions of all intuition.[51]

The privilege of mathematics is therefore that its concepts have a special, i.e., determinant, relation to pure intuition, not that it is an intuitive cognition. The latter is indeed possible (for example, I know the relative position of the lamp). But it is never universal or necessary. The spatial or temporal order of intuition can instruct me on spatial or temporal relations alone, *or* form the basis for the judgment "between two points only one straight line

---

51. "Empirical intuition is possible only through the pure intuition (of space and time); what geometry says about the latter is therefore undeniably valid of the former" (*KrV* A 165/B 206).

is possible." This is an example of a universal and necessary *judgment* whose object or ground is *pure intuition*.

Mathematics then is not simply intuitive because it is a rational science based on concepts articulated in judgments and proofs. It has pure a priori principles "derived from pure intuition . . . (although by means of the understanding)" (*KrV* A 159/B 198–99). But these principles themselves rest on higher principles that are the product not of mathematics but of transcendental philosophy. They run the opposite course: from pure concepts to pure intuition, not from pure intuition to mathematical concepts. According to the principles of the Axioms of Intuition, appearances are intuited as aggregates (the representation of parts makes possible the representation of the whole) but unified through a concept. It is on axioms of intuition that axioms of geometry such as "two straight lines do not enclose a space" rest (*KrV* A 163/B 204). That is, axioms of geometry *refer* exclusively to the pure intuition of spatial relations but *rest on* (are made possible by) the principle of quantity, i.e., the synthesis of the category and the pure intuition.[52] These propositions are synthetic a priori judgments (*KrV* A 165/B 205), and to attempt to derive them from concepts would be futile. You must instead turn to the form of space, give yourself an object in intuition and "ground your synthetic proposition on this" (*KrV* A 47–48/B 65–66).

This is made possible, writes Kant, by the "faculty for intuiting a priori" that "lies in me" (ibid.). In arithmetic as well as in geometry we go beyond the concept to the intuition in which we construct the object. In 7+5, 12 is not contained. The sign '+' implies a task (*Aufgabe*) and therefore an activity. We go out of the given concept and seek the result or evidence for it in intuition. As Kant writes in an important letter to Schultz, given two numbers, the sign '+' indicates a mode of synthesis, the postulate or way to find a third.[53] I turn to the form of space to realize that my concept of 'shortest' is added to my concept of 'straight' ("which contains nothing of quantity, but only a quality," *KrV* B 16) "and cannot be extracted out of the concept of the straight line by any analysis" (ibid.).

---

52. The synthetic judgments of mathematics are determinant judgments that "never consist in mere intuitions. . . . Even the judgments of pure mathematics in its simplest axioms are not exempt from this condition. The principle: a straight line is the shortest line between two points, presupposes that the line has been *subsumed* under the concept of magnitude, which is certainly no mere intuition, but has its seat solely in the understanding" (*Prol, Ak* 4: 301, ENG 95, italics mine).

53. November 25, 1788, *Ak* 10: 555–58. See also the letter to Rehberg in *Ak* 11: 207–10 and the draft (*Ak* 14: 53–55) on the difference between thinking and producing $\sqrt{2}$.

Sometimes, notably in the *Prolegomena* and in the Introduction to the first *Critique*, Kant compares and contrasts mathematical with pure concepts. In the Introduction the argument proceeds as follows. Judgments of experience are synthetic in that we extend our knowledge of something and can attach to it a predicate we did not know belonged to it. The obvious problem is that this cannot guarantee any necessity or universality, since it depends on experience. In synthetic *a priori* judgments, by contrast, we cannot turn to experience for help. The additional element we invariably find combined with the original concept is not analytically included or thought in it. In mathematics it has to be a pure intuition; in metaphysics it is the possibility of experience (the application of a pure concept to experience). At A 9/B 13 the example is this: while "all effect has a cause" expresses an analytical relation, in "everything that happens has its cause" we go beyond what is contained in "everything that happens" and predicate a property of it in a universal and necessary synthetic proposition.

By and large, however, Kant is not so clear or consistent. The problem lies in his comparing mathematical and empirical, not pure concepts, as in the contrasts between the concepts of triangle and gold in the Discipline or of the dog in the Schematism chapter.[54]

The concept of dog is a general class allowing us to subsume particular dogs we experience under their concept. This concept is a universal whose poverty in sensible aspects demarcates it from its living instantiations, but whose virtue is precisely that of allowing me to do without its presence in intuition and use an abstract form instead. I can talk about dogs and relate 'dog' to 'mammal' or contrast it with 'inanimate body' even while I am not perceiving any particular dog. The intuition of a dog and its concept belong in different realms: that of perception and that of the mind's spontaneous activities (in this particular case imagination and thought). By contrast, space and time are intuitions preceding appearances. Space and time are intuited and known a priori as such. They are not a class because they relate to 'this' space or 'this' time not as a universal does to an instance, but as a singular whole to a partial limitation of it.

This space or place[55] is not intrinsically different from space as a whole. An individual space and space in general do not differ in kind the way a dog and its concept do. The whole is not descriptively poorer or in any

---

54. In section 15 of the *Inaugural Dissertation* we find the same contrast between empirical concepts and space.

55. For brevity's sake I will speak only of space, but as is known the same arguments hold also for time (and its successions or intervals).

important way different from the parts. That the shortest distance between two points is a straight line holds of the triangle and of space as a whole in exactly the same way. This truth is intuited, i.e., I do not reach it by reflection. Space is thus a continuum that is divided into partial representations and a whole prior to its parts. Points, lines, and particular ways to describe or apprehend space are so many ways to limit space and generate particular intuitions. Parts do not preexist the whole because they must be understood as limitations of a previously existing and antecedently given whole. Space thus contains the sufficient ground for the several representations of space. An inch is space just like a triangle or the space occupied by the dog (*KrV* A 25).

We read in the Transcendental Aesthetic that space underlies all possible outer intuitions, so that several spaces are intuited as within space (*KrV* A 24/B 39). In the case of concepts, by contrast, the logical constituents or *Merkmale* must be presupposed, and the whole arises only through the mediation and progressive combination of these *Teilvorstellungen* (partial representations, *KrV* A 32). The whole—the dog—is that representation which allows us to identify or reproduce a dog to ourselves but that by itself cannot individuate its object because it must hold for all its possible referents. Space and time are given immediately and as a singularity, while concepts are an indefinite plurality and are given only mediately.

As I pointed out, in his contrast between a total form within which I intuit singularities and a concept under which I subsume instances, Kant is thinking of concepts as discursive aggregates generated by reflection. The fact, however, is that the formation of empirical concepts is hardly ever the object of explicit focus in the first *Critique*, and for a very good reason. The cognition of empirical nature is not its theme. But the main problem is that not all concepts (especially not the subject matter of the Analytic, pure concepts) are aggregates. At the beginning of the Transcendental Logic Kant insists that he is going to deal only with elementary and original concepts, i.e., those that are not derived or combined (*KrV* A 65/B 89). If empirical concepts are rules for the apprehension of appearances, they are themselves ruled by pure concepts, which are guides for the understanding's functions of synthesis and the power of judgment's subsumptions. If space is an intuition and not a concept, it is because it is a singular object given immediately, not because of its opposition to conceptual aggregates. In sum, the defect of this presentation is that it generates confusion about the relevance of empirical concepts for transcendental philosophy, and that, as it underlines the contrast between mathematical and empirical, it seems to thrust aside the affinities between pure and mathematical synthesis. This is the ground for a more serious and threatening confusion concerning exactly what the relation between a priori and a posteriori is, to which I will return in the next section.

The lectures on logic are a precious goldmine supplementing and integrating the account of the first *Critique* with an important theory of concepts and their formation. Deploring the absence of this treatment from the first *Critique*, however, means forgetting that empirical concepts do not belong in transcendental philosophy. It deals only with pure reason's self-determination: i.e., with the general conditions for experience, not with knowledge of determinate and particular empirical objects. What mathematics, transcendental philosophy, and morality share is precisely this legislation through self-affection. Reason determines its forms-contents a priori by operating on its own forms.[56] In the case of empirical concepts, by contrast, reason does act on, indeed constitutes, the logical form, but must reflect on the data with which experience provides it.

General logic abstracts from all content. It therefore must not investigate the *source* of concepts. The source or origin of concepts, what the logic lectures call their *matter*, is the subject of metaphysics or transcendental philosophy. All concepts are universal. As a result, notes Kant, it is mistaken to divide concepts into universal, particular, and individual, for it is only their *use* that can be thus divided. This universality is their *form*.

All concepts as such are then a product, the result of a formation process. Logic studies the logical acts of reflection, comparison, and abstraction thanks to which concepts are produced as to their form. This is to say that *all* concepts find their origin in the understanding. But unlike empirical concepts, pure concepts have their origin in the understanding also with regard to their content. "A *pure* concept . . . arises rather from the understanding even *as to content*" (*Log* § 3, *Ak* 9: 92, ENG 590).

---

56. In some unpublished reflections Kant is much more explicit on this point: metaphysics is a *science of the subject*, not the object. Only thus can reason discover something new (see *Refl* 102 in Erdmann 347, *Refl* 106 in Erdmann 348, *Refl* 109 in Erdmann 349, and *Refl* 215 in Erdmann 377). "Hieraus kann nur eine Wissenschaft des Subjekts entspringen" (*Refl* 103, in Erdmann 347). Perhaps the most telling passage is this quote (*Refl* 5636, *Ak* 18: 267): "In pure sensibility, the pure power of imagination, and pure apperception lies the ground of the possibility of all empirical cognition a priori and of the synthesis in accordance with concepts, which has objective reality. For they pertain only to appearances . . . , so that one properly cognizes only oneself as the thinking subject, but everything else as in this thing. Heautognosy [*so dass man sich eigentlich nur sich selbst als denkende Subjekt erkennt, alles andere aber als in diesem Einen. Heautognosie*]." (Heautognosy means knowledge of oneself.) See also *Reflexionen* 3948 and 4464 in *Ak* 17, the passages on the autarchy of reason in chapter 1, and Velkley's *Freedom and the End of Reason*.

This division of form and matter accounts for a homogeneous treatment of all concepts alike as to their *form*. On the other hand, this dichotomy prefigures another division. When it comes to their *matter*, concepts are either *given* or *made* (*dati, factitii*).

In the *Jaesche Logic*, concepts can be "*empirical or arbitrary or intellectual.*"[57] *Both given and made* concepts are further divided into *empirical or pure*, depending on whether an a priori or an a posteriori operation is their ground.[58]

Given concepts are defined negatively: they are given insofar as they are not arbitrary. In turn, a "concept is made a priori when it is made through pure reflection, without the objects being given through experience. E.g., I represent a 1000-sided figure, without ever having seen it" (*Ak* 24: 914, ENG 356). Given concepts can be defined only through analysis, made concepts through a synthesis. The latter generally are arbitrary. An example here is not a mathematical concept but a representation originating in the will.[59] Made concepts can be defined. Their definition contains only what I have put into it. In the Vienna Logic, unlike the Discipline, artifacts, noumena, and mathematical objects are similar on this score. Still, only mathematical objects have a real essence. Artifacts do not because what is at stake is my project, not the object; noumena have neither an object nor a fortiori an essence.

---

57. § 5, *Ak* 9: 94, ENG 592. Note that here we have a tripartition, but usually Kant proposes a quadripartition, a doubling of the original division between given and made concepts, such that the concept that is here called 'arbitrary' (a made concept) is either the mathematical or the *manufactured* concept. The manufactured concept is the concept of an artifact or of an object that, though deriving its elements from experience, is the result of an act of imagination. For example, on the basis of moats, stone, etc., with which I am acquainted from experience, I conceive of an unconquerable fortress (V-Lo/Wiener, *Ak* 24: 915, ENG 357). This "concept itself is *factitius*. This is how it happens with someone who invents a new instrument" (ibid.). Arguably, imagination's concepts of this sort are reminiscent of Descartes's *ideae factitiae*. But Descartes's tripartition of *innatae, adventitiae, factitiae* does not correspond to Kant's division for a host of reasons, of which I will simply mention three. First, Descartes's ideas are mental representations, unlike Kant's discursive concepts; second, Descartes's adventitious ideas are mostly representations resulting from perceptions (thus violating the gap between Aesthetics and Analytic), unlike Kant's empirical concepts; third, innatism is, according to Kant, the expression of reason's laziness. A priori concepts are originally acquired, not inborn.

58. As a result, in the Vienna Logic given concepts are pure (e.g., causality) or empirical (e.g., dog). Made a priori concepts are mathematical (e.g., triangle) or noumenal (an immaterial thinking being) or imaginative (e.g., a ship's clock, an unconquerable fortress), while made a posteriori concepts are concepts extending given empirical concepts through marks I have collected in experience. No example is given by Kant in this passage of the Vienna Logic (*Ak* 24: 915, ENG 357). Presumably 'gold' or 'water' would fit the bill: through experience I acquire further marks to extend and enrich my concept.

59. "I *want* to represent a thinking being not combined with any body" (*Ak* 24: 915, ENG 357, Kant's emphasis); "I want to think this" (ibid., ENG 358).

For mathematical concepts (I would also argue for noumena, but Kant does not), the definition "precedes the concept, then. It is always so in synthesis" (V-Lo/Dohna, *Ak* 24: 757, ENG 490). I make a concept for myself through its definition. As we know, this implies that definitions cannot err, are complete, give the real essence, and thereby give us "insight into the possibility of things" (V-Lo/Dohna, *Ak* 24: 760, ENG 493). "The mathematician in his definition says: *sic volo, sic iubeo*" (*Reflexion* 2930, *Ak* 16: 579).

Let us pause and notice a few things. The line between a *made a posteriori* and a *given a posteriori* concept is thin. The latter is made a posteriori when we need further marks to identify and explain it, i.e., when we ask for a more complete and precise synthetic definition regarding it. If so, I *make* a concept a posteriori *of a given* a posteriori concept.

Notice, further, the conspicuous absence of ideas. In the *Jaesche Logic*, after distinguishing empirical from pure concepts, Kant writes that ideas are "the archetype for the use of the understanding, e.g., the idea of the *world-whole . . .* to be regarded as a necessary basic concept, either for *objectively completing* the understanding's actions of subordination or for regarding them as *unlimited.*—The idea cannot be attained *by composition*, either, for the whole is prior to the parts" (*Log* § 3, *Ak* 9: 92, ENG 590). Everything that precedes section 56, on the inferences of reason, is about the understanding's concepts. The interesting aside of the Vienna Logic about noumena as made a priori concepts is not picked up here.

And yet, a great deal could be learned about ideas in this connection. For example, how their matter shares some ground with arbitrary and intellectual concepts while not being reducible to either (ideas can be "heterogeneous" to concepts, *Log* § 3, *Ak* 9: 92, ENG 590). Or how their lack of reference to objects is not unlike the concept of 'unconquerable fortress' after all. It is not clear what Kant thought about that. Why would he mention an idea as a made a priori concept if he finds no further use for this characterization? On the other hand, if ideas are sketches of the whole or architectonic plans coming before their parts, the logical origin (the form) of ideas is not comparable to that of all concepts, for these arise through reflection, comparison, and abstraction of marks or partial representations. This is obviously not to say that ideas do not have a logical origin, but rather to stress that the logic of ideas is the logic of totalization, of inferences to the unconditional or to perfection.

Unfortunately, all we can say is this: by contrast with made concepts, given concepts cannot be defined. At the same time, what is most striking in these pages is Kant's insistence that definitions are not needed and that their importance is largely overrated. This holds notably of empirical concepts.

Should I want to define 'water' analytically "as a fluid body without taste or color," one would immediately see "how precarious" the definition is (Vienna Logic, *Ak* 24: 918, ENG 360). Unless I am already acquainted with water, the definition will be of no help.

Rather than being problematic, however, such a definition is indeed useless, for "in the concept 'water' there lies so little that I immediately go outside the concept and have to collect new marks through experience," i.e., synthetically. (This is, I take it, how I make an a posteriori concept of a given a posteriori one.) But 'water' "cannot be defined synthetically either, because we cannot be acquainted with all the possible marks that experience can teach concerning an object" (ibid.). Our definition is then of our concept of the object, not of the object itself; therefore the definition of empirical concepts is "wholly dispensable."[60] If knowing a real essence is equivalent to knowing the entire essence (or nature or internal ground) of a thing, then this goal is simply beyond our powers for appearances (and their relative empirical concepts).[61]

If we can have no real definition of given concepts, then we can have a "nominal" definition of them that serves "to distinguish a thing" (V-Lo/Dohna, *Ak* 24: 760, ENG 493), without, however, being able to achieve completeness or precision and without, more importantly, possessing all the marks or notes that constitute the concept. If we cannot know the real essence of the objects of given concepts, we do know quite easily their "logical essence," i.e., "nothing more than the complex of all marks that first constitute a certain concept."[62]

I find no argument for the completeness of these marks. But the question I want to pursue here is rather this: in what sense is a concept given? The form, as we have seen, is always the product of an intellectual synthesis. Literally, then, a concept is never *given* (though its matter may be). Hegel repeatedly said that Kant uses a barbaric language. His favorite example was the oxymoronic phrase "empirical concept" instead of the more plausible

---

60. V-Lo/Dohna, *Ak* 24: 757, ENG 490. It is also "subjective" in the sense that it aims at our concept alone (ibid.). "I need a definition only if I want to predicate the *definitum* of some other certain concept. E.g., if the question is: What is virtue?, then I only need exposition; but if the question is whether holiness is virtue, then I must know this concept completely" (*Refl* 2962, *Ak* 16: 587–88).

61. V-Lo/Dohna, *Ak* 24: 757, ENG 490, and V-Lo/Wiener, *Ak* 24:, 839, ENG 294.

62. V-Lo/Dohna, *Ak* 24: 757, ENG 490, and V-Lo/Wiener, *Ak* 24: 839, ENG 294. "Through declaration we make a distinct concept. Through exposition we make distinct a given concept. Through definition we make a distinct concept complete and precise" (*Refl* 2925, *Ak* 16: 578). "Explication is of an expression, exposition of a concept" (*Refl* 2931, *Ak* 16: 579).

"concept of an empirical being." Rather than playing Hegel against Kant, however, I prefer to show that Kant himself occasionally uses a sloppy language that other times is far more precise.

Consider some examples regarding what he describes in the Busolt Logic as "the problem of logic," that is, how a concept arises out of intuition (*Ak* 24: 654). He writes that "we cognize things through their marks. . . . Intuition comes from the senses; through marks the understanding dissolves [*löst . . . auf*] intuitions and puts them together. Reason subsequently goes from that which the marks contain to that which the whole concept contains" (*Refl* 2281, *Ak* 16: 298). This passage is relatively unproblematic as it reflects the standard opposition between sensibility and understanding. The transition from intuitions to their presumed 'dissolution' in empirical concepts, however, is left wholly indeterminate and appears as a mystifying, impenetrable core—or, better, an open question.

This other passage we read in the *Jaesche Logic* is more troublesome: "an empirical concept arises from the senses through comparison of objects of experience and attains through the understanding merely the form of universality."[63] It is more troublesome because it suggests (1) that the senses (or the simple comparison of impressions) have the power to generate a concept, and (2) that the understanding somehow finds the concept and simply universalizes it. This is not only reminiscent of the 'transmission of forms' doctrine I described earlier as Kant's polemical target. It is also literally impossible for Kant because, as we have seen, all concepts are such insofar as they are universal. But, before being impossible, it is false.

Elsewhere Kant underlines the *synthetic* activity behind all empirical concepts, which do not at all reproduce sensible data but are the product of spontaneity. Before returning to that, let us note that in his unpublished notes Kant is more attentive and precise: "the concept is then not given, but rather the matter is" (*Refl* 2947, *Ak* 16: 584). Recall the motto of the introduction: "A reason that were determined sensibly would be no reason" (Eine Vernunft die sinnlich bestimt wär wäre nicht Vernunft, *Ak* 23: 17).

Having intuitions is not enough to get conceptual marks (*Merkmale*), and through mere marks we do not get a concept. First, no intuition is in itself sufficient to strike me and make me turn it into an individual representation

---

63. § 3, *Ak* 9: 92, ENG 590. Compare this other note from the *Reflexionen*: "rational cognitions [*Vernunfterkenntnisse*] are *given in the senses* as to their matter and have only the form of reason, e.g., universal concepts; or they express the form of reason itself," and are pure concepts (*Refl* 269, Erdmann 396, italics mine). Again, the givenness of rational cognitions (and a cognition is more than a simple concept) in the senses is a quite misleading phrase.

and then a relevant mark unless I bring it into relief, isolate it, focus on it, and relate it to other intuitions. An intuition is not a self-subsistent representation with its own conceptual meaning. Second, a mark cannot be the logical tag attached to an intuition, once we have shown that sensibility and understanding function according to different rules. An account of the transformation of an intuition into a mark is sorely needed. Third, even isolating an intuition or mark would not be enough to generate a concept, for marks need to be coordinated and subordinated through an ordered synthesis.[64] A concept is never reached through the generalization of impressions or the association of intuitions.[65] Instead, sensible traits are isolated, not simply reproduced, to be then compared and reflected upon. This operation is far more complex than a mere translation from intuitions.

On the one hand empirical acts presuppose pure acts. Therefore the supposed particular impressions of empiricism are already integral to the organic unity of general and lawful procedures in both intuitive and conceptual terms. On the other, at the empirical level a determinant judgment presupposes a preliminary reflection that inductively and synthetically produces a generality. This generality is an anticipation to which I will eventually give my assent in a determinant judgment.

This brings to light yet another presupposition. A concept cannot be an isolated unity. The formation of empirical judgments presupposes also a web of mutually related empirical cognitions and beliefs, such that the more developed this web is, the more distinct the empirical concept will be. The child who is learning about different trees must first possess the general concept of tree and then learn what different trees have in common (trunk, leaves, etc.) on the basis of which they can be compared and distinguished. The botanist's knowledge differs from the child's knowledge not in nature but in degree: in precision, distinction, and the wealth of particulars. This means that the concept can be considered under a subjective and an objective perspective. On the one hand my concept of gold and the chemist's or

---

64. See *Refl* 2959, *Ak* 16: 587. On Kant's very rich and elaborate notion of marks, see Capozzi, *Kant e la logica*, 483–540.

65. Against Meier's notion of an evolution (*evolutio, Auswickelung*) of an original representation in the transition from obscure to clear cognition, Kant stresses the synthetic origin of clarity (cf. La Rocca, *Soggetto e mondo*, 132). As La Rocca puts it, a mark is a mark only insofar as I assign it a function and a meaning (*Soggetto e mondo*, 135). The masterful chapter on empirical judgments in La Rocca's book is a uniquely painstaking and instructive study I wholeheartedly recommend to the reader. Incidentally, it appeared in an English translation ("How Are," 265–93), but the title of the essay in English is the result of an unfortunate typographical error: it should read "How are synthetic a posteriori judgments possible?"

the goldsmith's differ insofar as they reflect our respective cognitions and beliefs. On the other, this is irrelevant for the concept itself: a concept cannot be reduced to our knowledge of its matter because it is normative, a rule for judgment.

If a concept is always one among many concepts with which it shares a thematic affinity, that is, a concept is one among many, its only use is in judgments. In one of the earliest (ca. 1776) formulations of this thesis we read: "A concept, by means of its universal validity, has the function of a judgment. It is related to other concepts *potentialiter*. The actual relation of one concept to others as a means for their cognition is the judgment" (*Refl* 3045, *Ak* 16: 630).

There are many lessons to draw from these considerations.

1. One concerns the gap between logic and metaphysics (and the correlative gap between logical and real essence and between nominal and real definition). While only mathematical objects have a real essence, all concepts have a logical essence and are made of marks. But these are the product of our reflection, not traits of the object. Logic deals only with the form of concepts, while metaphysics deals with their origin, their reference, object, and content.[66] One important consequence of this is that the completeness available in logic is not the same as that required in metaphysics. Whether or not there are pure concepts at all is the business not of logic but of metaphysics to establish. Logic regards them as any other concept.

2. The second lesson regards the reflection involved in synthesis. According to Kant the three logical acts through which I produce a concept as to its form are comparison, reflection, and abstraction. Kant presents these acts in this order in the *Jaesche Logic*.[67] As to abstraction, Kant corrects the traditional usage[68] according to which we abstract something from something. He stresses that abstraction has a solely negative function (*abstrahere ab aliquo*, abstract *from* something). Through abstraction no concept is produced, but rather we deliberately leave out or ignore marks or differences

66. When we read that logic considers only the form of concepts, and therefore regards them "subjectively" (*Jaesche Logic* § 3, *Ak* 9: 92, ENG 590), "subjective" obviously has here the meaning of "form without a content" as opposed to how an intellectual source can reach out of itself to objects, i.e., as opposed to the "science of the subject" and *Heautognosie* we saw in the passages quoted in note 56 above.

67. § 6. See also the Vienna Logic (*Ak* 24: 909, ENG 352, and *Refl* 2876, *Ak* 16: 555–56). Notice, however, the contrast with the V-Lo/Dohna (*Ak* 24: 752–54, ENG 486–87) and the V-Lo/Pölitz (*Ak* 24: 566).

68. As in popular views on induction, but also in Meier's *Auszug* (§ 259, *Ak* 16: 549–50: "*conceptus per abstractionem logicam formatus*").

that are not relevant to our concept. This negative act is indispensable if we are to consider a partial representation the ground of cognition and set its limits, but comes after the positive and formative conditions: comparison and reflection. Kant's example is famous (*Log* § 6): I see a spruce, a willow, a linden. First I compare them and see their differences (with regard to trunk, branches, leaves, etc.); next I concentrate and reflect on what they have in common; finally, I abstract from quantity, figure, and so on, and acquire the concept of a tree (ibid.).

Heidegger aptly remarks that in order to take note of the differences, we must take a look in advance at their trunk and branches. We therefore need a preliminary bringing into view of the several objects before we can compare them in the respects selected. *Pace* Kant's presentation, reflection "has the leading role"[69] since it makes "transparent the unity which contains commonness in itself and *thus* is related to the many."[70] Comparison and abstraction are instrumental to it. "Comparison prepares for reflection, though never without reflection; abstraction brings reflection to completion and concludes it."[71]

Reflection has the upper hand in that it is an initial unification of a view that gets progressively refined through comparison and abstraction. Actually, elsewhere Kant expresses himself in similar words.[72] In mine, I would say that I cannot abstract from something unless I have established an invariant core first, which only reflection can isolate and which comparison can operate on and make progressively distinct.

More important is what Heidegger does not say. Reflection stands or falls with concepts of relation, identity, and difference in particular. They are

---

69. Heidegger, *Phenomenological Interpretation*, 158.

70. Ibid., 161.

71. Ibid., 159. According to Longuenesse (*Kant and the Capacity to Judge*, 116), reflection and abstraction do not follow comparison, but "each depends on the others and all proceed simultaneously." Similarly Allison (*Theory of Taste*, 22). For a criticism of the circularity of Kant's theory, see Pippin (*Kant's Theory of Form*, 112–14) and Ferrarin ("Construction and Mathematical Schematism," 158–60). La Rocca (*Soggetto e mondo*, 139–48, and "How are") distinguishes two senses of logical reflection, so that we have four, not three logical acts, which safeguards the consistency of the theory (in his earlier *Esistenza e Giudizio*, 148ff., he advanced a useful distinction of five meanings of reflection, among which the logical reflection is only one). On the relation of these acts to attention and to Wolff's use of it (as *collatio* and *conferre*) in the *Psychologia empirica*, see Capozzi, "La teoria kantiana dei concetti," 122–24.

72. See *Refl* 2865 (*Ak* 16: 552): "Durch abstraction werden keine Begriffe, sondern durch reflexion. . . . Die comparation und abstraction bringt keine Begriffe hervor." See also the progression in *Refl* 2876 (*Ak* 16: 555–56): "1. apprehensio variorum (Auffassung). (comparatio mit dem object zum Erkentnis). 2. Reflexio: Überlegung des Zusammenhangs zur Einheit des Begrifs. 3. abstractio. von dem Übrigem." Cf. Carl, *Der schweigende Kant*, 108–11.

crucial not only for pure intuitions themselves, but also for the selective focus we have on intuitive marks we isolate and work on to acquire conceptual marks and for the formation of empirical concepts. Nothing becomes an object of knowledge unless I make it stand out of the undifferentiated flow of experience through my several relational acts.

3. The third lesson regards pure concepts. Kant is far less univocal about them, and his uncertainty is telling. His hesitations are reminiscent of the treatment they receive in the first *Critique*. There Kant writes as if he were carefully following his own cautious admonition not to put definitions at the start of a philosophical tract. At best definitions will crown the work at the end. Accordingly he introduces the categories by saying: "I deliberately spare myself the definitions of these categories" (*KrV* A 82/B 108). Later, once the job is done (towards the end of the Analytic, *KrV* A 241), he writes: "This [sparing the reader the definition] was no excuse, but a not inconsiderable rule of prudence, not immediately to venture a definition and seek or pretend to completeness or precision."

There is a conspicuous oscillation, though. At first (in 1781, at *KrV* A 241–42), contrasting the issue of real definitions in mathematics to that of pure concepts, Kant writes that "now it turns out that the ground of this precaution lies even deeper, namely, that we could not define them even if we wanted to." Then (in 1787, at *KrV* B 129), *before* and by way of *introduction* to the Transcendental Deduction, he writes: "I will merely precede this with the *explanation [Erklärung] of the categories*. They are concepts of an object in general, by means of which its intuition is regarded as *determined* with regard to one of the *logical functions* for judgments."[73] Recall also the quote from A 240/B 300 in section 4 on the *real definition* of pure concepts, consisting in the reference to conditions of sensibility, which runs directly opposite to the "prudence" of the A 241–42 passage.

Likewise, speaking of pure concepts in the Vienna Logic, Kant says that "concepts that are given a priori independently of experience can be defined analytically" (*Ak* 24: 917, ENG 359), only to reformulate his version one page later: "With concepts of the understanding, and in particular with ones that are given, a proper analytic definition is likewise impossible, which is due not to the thing, however, but to us, since it is hard to set forth the marks of a concept precisely."[74]

---

73. Explanation is here synonymous with definition, as the manifest goal of the second sentence in the text attests.

74. *Ak* 24: 918, ENG 360. The Dohna-Wundlacken Logic has the same enigmatic inconsistency but in the same continuous passage: "*Conceptus dati* can usefully be defined only insofar

However that may be, what remains clear is that we can never be sure that we have given a complete exposition of a concept other than in mathematics. Again about pure concepts, in the Dohna-Wundlacken Logic we read: "how can we ever be certain whether we have expounded a concept perfectly? In such cases one must be very cautious, e.g., in those of substance and cause . . . not to be conscious that something is lacking is quite different from being conscious that nothing is lacking" (*Ak* 24: 758, ENG 491).

In sum, we can infer that philosophical definitions of pure concepts, since they cannot be synthetic like the mathematical but can be only analytical, are always marred by an uncertainty regarding their completeness. (Obviously the completeness of the table of categories is one thing, the complete definition of each category quite another.) Still, pure concepts, though given a priori, originate in the understanding as to both their content and their form.

With regard to their form, pure concepts do not differ from other concepts. If we take this point seriously and the categories are not atoms of intelligibility or primary conditions but are themselves a product, the very important consequence is that reflection (together with comparison and abstraction) plays an indispensable role in their formation. In this view the Amphiboly is not simply instrumental to the criticism of Leibniz but integral to the Analytic and should be valued vastly more than it usually is.

Again, the expository order of the first *Critique* ends up dictating its conceptual order. Because the Amphiboly comes after the Analytic of Principles, it is typically thought that transcendental reflection has nothing to contribute to the production of the principles and of pure concepts (and of pure intuitions). Instead the couples of mutually related concepts, especially identity-difference and form-matter, are functions of reflection overarching the pure synthesis that produces the categories (*KrV* B 105). For we must be able to reflect on what constitutes identity and difference in the categories, to compare and contrast them, to reflect on their interaction and how they not only limit each other, but in fact are constituted in opposition to one another (just as substance is defined through its relation to what changes, or the third category is the combination of the first two of its class). Finally, we must be able to abstract from matter. Without all these presuppositions,

---

as they are given a priori. My definition never becomes complete in regard to the object and *eo ipso* never becomes a definition" (*Ak* 24: 757, ENG 490).

the transcendental apperception could not generate any one of its pure concepts for the unification of experience.[75]

The inevitable question that emerges from the considerations above is this: How can pure concepts be at once original and a product? How can they be at once formed and given? To be more precise, considering that categories are all interrelated as are the forms of judgment, the question should be rephrased as: How are nonindependent concepts of this sort to be arrived at if not in a systematic and interconnected way? Pure concepts are given and original not because they are intelligible atoms but, to reiterate one of Kant's *Reflexionen*, insofar as they cannot be changed or produced differently (*weil keine synthesis ihn erzeugen oder verändern kan, Refl* 2936, *Ak* 16: 581). The understanding contains pure concepts a priori in itself (*KrV* A 80/B 106), and yet they are not innate or inborn in us but an original acquisition, i.e., they arise on the occasion of experience as directive for (and in this sense logically prior to) the several empirical concepts we make.[76]

With regard to their content, pure concepts demand a comparative/contrastive answer to the question of their synthesis. The answer we can summarize by way of conclusion of this section is this.

The *synthesis* involved in the formation of *empirical concepts* is a necessary but preliminary basis for reflection whose activity, rather than constitutive, is the search for the right concept. The empirical concept, whose matter is given, is made as a work in progress and a partial approximation. It can be modified as our cognitions regarding the object change and is but a description of what we know of the object. Experience, though structured by few general principles that we can know in their completeness, is open-ended and indefinitely rich in its particularity.

The synthesis in *mathematics* is wholly arbitrary. By freely defining its concept it produces its object. Mathematics is an a priori synthesis through and through, as its concepts arise through an activity of construction and have objective reality.

---

75. La Rocca (*Esistenza e Giudizio*, 143–72) offers a very interesting and unorthodox interpretation. The concepts of reflection precede the categories and even the forms of intuition, as respectively logical and intuitive relations. The modes of relation precede their terms, so that only the logical concepts of reflection applied to space and time can give rise to intuitive relations, which the Transcendental Aesthetics, owing to the restriction of its isolating exposition, which must abstract from all conceptual unity, must presuppose in order to make sense but cannot yet introduce.

76. This anti-innatist position has been Kant's since the *Dissertation* (*Ak* 2: 406). See also *Entdeckung, Ak* 8: 221–23; V-Met/L1/Pölitz, *Ak* 28: 233; V-Met/Schön, *Ak* 28: 468; V-Met/Mron, *Ak* 29: 763.

Pure concepts do not have objective reality per se. The only bridge across thought and reality is transcendental apperception's synthesis of pure concepts and time. Once so synthesized, pure concepts produce an objectively real form-content, the schema for making experience possible as a systematically ordered whole of cognitions. Concepts are logical forms of connection that become schematized under the condition of time. That is to say that in experience pure concepts are transcendental conditions and forms-contents presiding over all other concepts, while in logic their form does not enjoy a special status and does not differ from that of all other concepts.

6. The A Priori

The mathematician obviously need not look to appearances to construct intuitive objects. There is nothing like mathematical abstraction from experience. When, contrasting mathematical and philosophical knowledge, Kant writes that the mathematician constructs both the empirical image of a triangle and its pure intuition, he stresses that he/she does so "in both cases completely a priori, without having had to borrow the pattern [*das Muster*] for it from any experience" (*KrV* A 713/B 741). It is natural to infer that the mathematician constructs a priori the triangle, whereas in my experience of triangles, i.e., when the geometric form is applied to an object (the side of the pyramid), *I neither see anything a priori nor construct a triangle*. I am as passive with regard to the perception of the given appearance as mathematics is wholly active in its activities and constructions. The philosopher does not enjoy the mathematician's privilege and can hope to explain only the concepts involved in experience.

This apparently natural conclusion is mistaken.

1. Were it so, mathematics would give rise to a world of forms, if not separate from then surely independent of the world of experience. Reconciling the two worlds would be a subsequent but distinct problem, one that would consist in accounting for not simply the ("top-down," as it were) possibility of applying mathematics to appearances but also the inverse problem, the "bottom-up" possibility of the mathematical apprehension of objects. For in everyday and scientific experience it so happens that I apprehend appearances according to geometric forms (as in "this table is rectangular"). How that can happen if mathematics is an a priori construction while experience is experience of given objects is bound to remain unintelligible. As with Aristotle's criticism of Plato's mathematical forms, forms (mathematical or otherwise) are not independent of matter. Forms are always forms-of-matter, principles of spatiotemporal or conceptual organization

of appearances. To be sure, for Kant mathematical objects are not Aristotle's *hulē noētē* (intelligible matter), nor does the mathematician abstract forms from matter. But certainly mathematical objects do not exist in the mind (or in a Platonic plane of truth). Construction speaks against this givenness of mathematical objects. If we drove this wedge between a priori mathematical knowledge and a posteriori empirical knowledge, the purity of rational mathematical cognitions would be distinct from but in truth irreconcilable with our access to empirical reality. Between a priori and a posteriori there would be an *alternative* rather than a duality, for they would denote two mutually exclusive worlds.

2. Were it so, mathematical knowledge would be opposed to empirical knowledge and to transcendental philosophy alike. We would get the amazing result that the first *Critique* would not even come close to—indeed has probably even forgotten along the way—a major part of the problem it set out to solve. That is, it could not reply to its leading question—how are synthetic a priori judgments possible?—through an explanation of the lawfulness of experience. Instead of the fundamental investigation of the principles making possible all forms of knowledge alike, philosophy would be analysis of concepts and forever suffer from envy of the privileges of mathematics.[77]

3. Were it so, empirical knowledge and transcendental philosophy would complement each other, the one in giving us what the *Prolegomena* calls the indispensable fruitful lowlands of experience, the other in clarifying it by isolating the subjective forms explaining all knowledge. (Indeed, this is what the debate on 'transcendental arguments' often looks like.) In this case, the a priori transcendental conditions would be another world unto itself, populated, unlike the mathematical world, with fixed representations one is free to dub as one will: innate ideas, original conditions of possibility, necessary abstract concepts, categories as highest genera. Whatever their name, their function is instrumental to the organization of data that can come only from without. If we judged by the very vivid description of the inanity of the philosopher's efforts in a striking passage,[78] transcendental

---

77. In a *Reflexion* (282, Erdmann 401), Kant writes that the happy fate of pure mathematics is the object of admiration and envy ("ein mit Recht bewundertes und bisweilen wol beneidetes Glück").

78. "Give a philosopher the concept of a triangle, and let him try to find out in his way how the sum of its angles might be related to a right angle. He has nothing but the concept of a figure enclosed by three straight lines, and in it the concept of equally many angles. Now he may reflect on this concept as long as he wants, yet he will never produce anything new. He can analyze and make distinct the concept of a straight line, or of an angle, of the number three, but he will

philosophy, sobered by the admonition not to pretend to be like mathematics, would be not what constitutes the principles making reason's use possible in both mathematics and experience, but the mere explanation of the basic requisites for experience to which it would ascend through an analytical regress starting from experience (or the sciences).

We know it cannot be so. We have seen that Kant does not have the problem of the application of mathematics to experience because the same form of intuition underlies both mathematics and appearances, which allows us to treat mathematically the objects of our experience.[79] We also know that if mathematics produces both empirical images and pure intuitions a priori, and we disregard the empirical because we consider it the exhibition of the pure, then empirical and pure are much more closely interrelated than might appear.

We also know that constructing and apprehending are the complementary sides of the same process. In fact, they are "entirely identical" (*KrV* A 224/B 271). The process is the act of unification of an extensive magnitude through the successive addition of a homogeneous manifold in which the imagination is responsible both for the apprehension of the manifold in a unitary form and for the construction in a pure (or empirical) intuition. This obviously does not make the two acts or scopes symmetrical or interchangeable. I can apprehend the mathematical form of objects in experience, but mathematics exceeds experience thanks to its prerogative of

---

not come upon any other properties that do not already lie in these concepts. But now let the geometer take up this question. Since he knows that two right angles together are exactly equal to all of the adjacent angles that can be drawn at one point on a straight line, he extends one side of his triangle, and obtains two adjacent angles that together are equal to two right ones. Now he divides the external one of these angles by drawing a line parallel to the opposite side of the triangle, and sees that here there arises an external adjacent angle which is equal to an internal one, etc. In such a way, through a chain of inferences that is always guided by intuition, he arrives at a fully illuminating and at the same time general solution of the question" (*KrV* A716–17/B 744–45). Notice all the verbs used to describe the mathematician. He/she is feverishly active whereas the philosopher seems resigned and frustrated at the futility of reflection. The passage almost reads like a contrast between a hyperactive brilliant youth and a depressed adult. It is also reminiscent of Descartes's rhetoric (after the endless futile and sterile debates internal to schools shaped by the Aristotelian model of contemplation, we are finally called to solve problems and make progress in our understanding of nature), except that Kant's philosopher is not the contemplator of a *kosmos* but has internalized one aspect of Descartes's program: the transformation of metaphysics into a *science*. See below, chapter 3, § 5.

79. I mean primarily *quanta*, the number and the form of appearances. But appearances can be treated mathematically not only as to their form, but even as to their matter in sensation or quality (e.g., the intensity of radiation of the moon's light, the momentum of velocity, the degree to which a color strikes our eyes) in intensive magnitudes (*mathesis intensorum*) and thanks to infinitesimal calculus.

considering construction and all exhibition of its real objects *in themselves* and of exploiting this isolating consideration of its objects for extending a priori its cognitions. The problem here, however, is this: how can we have "the identical synthesis" if mathematical synthesis occurs a priori?

Is it possible that *apprehension of an empirical manifold occurs likewise a priori*?

After all, is this not what we read at B 144? "[T]he empirical consciousness of a given manifold of one intuition stands under a pure a priori self-consciousness, just as *empirical intuitions stand under a pure sensible one, which likewise takes place a priori.*"[80] Kant is telling us here that there are intuitions a priori. These are of nothing else than given appearances. "Of these [appearances] alone are we capable of an intuition a priori" (*KrV* B 151).

In the progressive *Absonderung* (dichotomic procedure) of the Aesthetics, empirical intuition is composed of matter and form, i.e., sensation and shape. This is the summary to be found in the Mrongovius Metaphysics: "There is something empirical for all empirical intuitions, i.e., sensation, and something that can be represented a priori. . . . [I]f with chalk I omit the intuition, only the form remains, size, shape, that is a priori. . . . I will call the form of intuition that which remains of extended beings when I omit all the matter of perception" (*Ak* 29: 796, ENG 150).

The a priori intuition is the result of an omission, of a division, performed on one underlying act of perception. In perception of appearances, then, there is an a priori as well as an a posteriori intuition. A priori and empirical occur together. They are different ways of access to what presents itself as a unity.

This may come as a surprise to many readers. We could claim that the concept of a priori has many and apparently diverse meanings as well as grammatical forms. For example, Kant uses the phrase as both an adjective and an adverb, as in 'an a priori intuition,' 'I construct a concept a priori,' and so on. Besides, often the terms 'pure' and 'a priori' seem equally and therefore indistinctly opposed to 'empirical,' and thereby interchangeable.[81]

---

80. Italics mine. Guyer and Wood have "which likewise holds a priori," which weakens the claim. Kemp Smith has "takes place a priori," which I find more faithful to the German ("die gleichfalls a priori Statt hat").

81. 'A posteriori' is seldom used by Kant. Perhaps it is not needless to repeat that one of the sources of confusion is Kant's penchant for fine distinctions he cannot hold fast to. When he introduces the terms at the very beginning of the first *Critique* (*KrV* B 3), he explains that 'every alteration has a cause' is a pure but not a priori principle, whereas at B 4–5 he claims the opposite (now 'every alteration has a cause' is a pure a priori judgment, a necessary and universal connection that would be lost if one were to derive it, with Hume, from association). This

The concept of a priori definitely is linked to subjectivity, but in exactly what ways it is hard to pin down.

Take this striking passage: "only the understanding (and the will insofar as it can be determined by the understanding) is free and a pure *self-activity* that is not determined by anything other than itself. Without this original and unalterable spontaneity we would know nothing a priori. . . . *The faculty of thinking and acting a priori is the only condition of possibility of the origin of all other appearances*" (*Refl* 5441, *Ak* 18: 182–83, italics mine).[82]

There are many points to stress. Let me note some we have already come across: the mention of understanding for what elsewhere Kant would have called reason, and his claim that self-activity[83] and freedom identify reason (i.e., understanding, the will). Let me also note, more curiously, the necessity for a free self-activity and spontaneity not only in order to know but also to act a priori. If anything, the phrase 'to act a priori' should also lend credence to the equation of a priori and pure. Last but not least, our free spontaneity is literally the origin of all other appearances. A priori seems to designate unequivocally the subjective source of knowledge and action.

But this identification cannot go unspecified. My sense of touch, for example, is such a source, but it is determined and not free. Logic is also a subjective source and logical thinking is free, and yet it does not produce anything. Once again, what Kant means by *a priori* is a *free self-activity that produces forms-contents*; that is, "all other appearances" in the passage of *Reflexion* 5441 cited above.

---

contradiction was noticed by an anonymous critic in a review of 1787, and admitted by Kant himself in the essay *Über den Gebrauch teleologischer Pinzipien in der Philosophie* of the following year (see Vaihinger, *Commentar*, 1: 211). Another contradiction is this: in these same pages, as an illustration of the dichotomic procedure he is introducing, Kant first mentions impenetrability along with hardness, color, and weight as the properties we must eliminate progressively so as to remain with the pure intuition of space (*KrV* B 5); a few paragraphs later (*KrV* A 7/B 12), instead, impenetrability is an example of a mark analytically contained in the concept of space. Were this not enough, in the *Prolegomena* impenetrability is the basis for the empirical concept of matter (§ 15, *Ak* 4: 295, ENG 90).

82. "der Verstand (und der Wille, so fern er durch Verstand bestimmt werden kann) ist frei und eine reine Selbstthätigkeit, die durch nichts anderes als sich selbst bestimmt ist. Ohne diese ursprüngliche und unwaldenbare Spontaneität würden wir nichts a priori erkennen. . . . . Das vermögen, a priori zu denken und zu handeln, ist die einzige Bedingung der möglichkeit des Ursprungs aller anderen Erscheinungen."

83. Self-activity returns a few lines below, in the same *Reflexion*, to designate reason's going from the universal to the particular. Recall that *selbstthätig* in the 1772 letter to Herz denoted the nature of mathematical concepts *before* Kant realized that the mathematical a priori synthesis was the model he had to think through more deeply to understand pure reason's a priori synthesis in its speculative and practical legislation.

Consider these two notable examples of identification of subjective and a priori. First is this entry in a philosophical dictionary, which I single out because I find it representative of a general reading. "Kant's notion of a priori is . . . the same as that of Leibniz and the Wolffians. 'There are,' says Leibniz [at the beginning of the *New Essays*], 'ideas that do not come from the senses and that we find in ourselves without forming them.' The originality of Kant's notion" consists in the a priori "not being an isolated scope or dominion of cognitions, but the *condition* of all objective knowledge. The a priori is the *form* of knowledge, whereas the a posteriori is *the content*. . . . The a priori is not in itself a cognition.*"[84]

In this view of the a priori, which I will call "subjective endowment," a priori and transcendental are identified as referring to the ultimate subjective condition of all cognition. I think this view must be thoroughly criticized.

1. Before Kant, 'a priori' and 'a posteriori' designated modes of logical demonstration. But Kant's a priori has nothing to do with the priority of principles over consequences. His distinction is quite different from that of Leibniz and the German scholastics.

2. On this "subjective endowment" view, furthermore, knowledge is reduced to empirical knowledge. Yet we know 'knowledge' has a much broader meaning in Kant than the conception he defends in the Transcendental Deduction of the first *Critique*.

3. On this view, the transcendental knowledge we have discussed as pure reason's a priori synthesis, i.e., the constitution of forms-contents and the

---

84. Abbagnano, *Dizionario*, 63. Here I do not discuss the incorporation of Kant's a priori in evolutionary epistemology at the hands of Karl Popper and Konrad Lorenz because of its manifest anti-Kantian results. Obviously I object neither to the use of Kantian concepts for scientific purposes nor to the possibility that successful induction over millennia has made certain cognitive attitudes almost ingrained in our organs or that instinctual expectations are so strong and habitual that they seem innate. But I do object to attributing to Kant, as do Lorenz ("Kants Lehre vom apriorischem") and Popper (*Conjectures*), the notion that the a priori is the inborn schema of responses to the environment philogenetically inscribed into the human mind over the course of evolution. Causality becomes no more than the instinctual expectation of regularities in experience. Kant's formal requirements for experience become biological and psychological facts regarding our perceiving apparatus. This is a description of human nature, not a transcendental investigation into laws. The tendency to turn Kant's a priori into a neurological or mental apparatus has resurfaced pervasively in cognitive science. See vol. 14 of *Trends in Cognitive Science* (2010) and the articles by Palmer and Lynch ("Kantian View of Space"), Langston ("Development of the Spatial Representation System in the Rat"), and Wills et al. ("Development of the Hippocampal Cognitive Map"). They all speak of spatial representation and the hippocampal cognitive map as a Kantian synthetic a priori system (by which they mean that we can represent some patterns or schemes without having had a prior experience of them).

principles of experience, is effaced because the a priori is a subjective form opposed to contents found a posteriori. It suffices to think of pure intuition of appearances "taking place a priori" to realize that this juxtaposition of a priori and a posteriori cannot hold.

4. As already pointed out, a condition of possibility cannot be a given principle existing in us the way innate ideas would: as abstract, fixed, empty, inert subjective forms waiting to be filled with contents coming from experience.

5. If this were the a priori, Kant's progress over Locke's empty cabinet would consist merely in the choice of the right hangers in the right number we put in the closet before we access experience, as if we could only then turn to experience to find the clothes that we best fancy or that would fit us individually and store them in an orderly fashion.

6. If this were the a priori, we would know what we know because we are so constituted. Kant would have no reason to lament that this is precisely what Hume wants and he does not want. The concept of cause "would be false if it rested on a subjective necessity, arbitrarily implanted in us. . . . I would not be able to say that the effect is combined with the cause in the object (i.e., necessarily), but only that I am so constituted that I cannot think of this representation otherwise than as so connected; which is precisely what the skeptic wishes most" (KrV B 168). In general, I think that reading the first Critique as a response to Hume necessarily leads to misunderstanding the a priori. As we saw in chapter 1, Kant is not a naturalist.

To take a second misreading of the a priori, consider Husserl's interpretation. For Husserl, Hume unlike Kant has an authentic concept of the a priori, as a relation grounded in the universal essence of concepts and intuitable in evidence.[85] Kant limits himself to introducing principles other than habit to organize experience, but that does not make them less subjective. Kant's theory winds up being no less skeptical than Hume's. After all, asks Husserl, do we not find in Hume's idea that the unity of experience conforms itself to thought the Copernican turn that Kant later made explicit?[86] Is Kant not a subjectivist and a phenomenalist if he transfers all lawfulness to our faculties while claiming that things in themselves are forever beyond us? Because Kant does not grant sensibility any independence, and because connections for him are first established through our apprehension, his

85. Husserl, Gesammelte Werke, 7: 354; see also, in 1915–16, the essential necessity in the vision of essences missed by Kant (ibid., 7: 402).

86. Ibid., 7: 354.

conception of sensibility does not differ markedly from Hume's.[87] Kant's general attitude is prejudiced. He favors naturalism as he takes for granted, indeed even starts from, the validity of natural sciences, mathematics, and physics in his grounding of experience.

Husserl takes Kant's manner of questioning as an analytical regress to the ultimate condition starting from given and unquestioned sciences because he reads the *Critique of Pure Reason* in terms of the *Prolegomena*, where it is easy to be misled about the extent and importance of Kant's pronouncements on the dogmatic slumber interrupted by Hume. My conjecture—that Husserl is bound to read the a priori as the faculties human beings are naturally equipped with because he understands Kant as a Humean—appears to be strengthened if we consider this point. Husserl rightly identifies the fundamental problem of the *Critique of Pure Reason* as that of synthetic a priori judgments, but misunderstands the very meaning of this problem.[88] It is striking that he repeatedly and with few exceptions calls it the problem of Kant's *Critique of Reason*.[89] The excision of 'pure' is significant and not for the sake of brevity. Reason is Husserl's name for an intentionality directed toward reality and aiming at evidence and intuition, not for the pure principles of all speculative and practical legislation, let alone for reason's striving for the unconditional totality of its concepts. Reason is the reason of experience, not a pure reason independent of it.

If Husserl is another victim of the "subjective endowment" view of Kant's a priori, Heidegger seems to push this line of reasoning even further. He uses Kant's extension and regrouping (in the *Jaesche Logic*) of the three questions of the Canon under the fourth one, "What is man?," to understand the first *Critique*'s metaphysical question as an analysis of *Dasein*'s finitude and as fundamental ontology.[90] On this view, the a priori is what grounds experience and general metaphysics.

Yet Heidegger differs from the two previous views in that he emphasizes that the a priori forms are not abstract and inert forms we are endowed with but rather, as he puts it, "enabling."[91] That is, they are an anticipation of the form of experience and a preliminary pre-understanding that alone makes possible all encounters with objects. Synthetic a priori judgments "are al-

87. Ibid., 7: 358.

88. See the MS A I 36 quoted in Kern, *Husserl und Kant*, 185; cf. 179–87. I give a detailed interpretation of Husserl's relation to Kant in my "From the World to Philosophy."

89. *Gesammelte Werke*, 25: 4–5, 7: 285, 373; *Krisis, Gesammelte Werke*, 6: 272, 455.

90. Heidegger, *Kant and the Problem of Metaphysics*, §§ 36–45; *Phenomenological Interpretation*, 49, 213)

91. *Phenomenological Interpretation*, 73.

ready asserted in all scientific judgments. They are pre-judgments [liter-
ally: prejudices, *Vor-urteile*] in a true and necessary sense."[92] For Heidegger
thought is in service of intuition and all Kantian apprehension is *in nuce*
phenomenological. In the second edition of the *Critique of Pure Reason*, according to Heidegger, Kant retreats comfortably back to the understanding
and betrays his brilliant discovery: the original unity of time and imagination. Heidegger is therefore uninterested in Kant's correlation between
apprehension in categorial form and application of the understanding's categories to the intuitive grasp of objects. Thus the a priori is not the complementary side of the a posteriori in empirical cognition. Even pure intuition
is fundamentally a preliminary view and has a temporal connotation: as an
in-advance projection, it makes all apprehension possible.[93]

The temporal understanding of the a priori is a crucial question that
seems only to add to our perplexities. Take the point I criticized above, that
the a priori construction of mathematics is wholly other than apprehension in experience.[94] Were it so, in mathematics productive imagination
would produce a schema for the triangle irreducible to all images, while
for empirical concepts our active contribution would seem to boil down
to the making of the unity of the concept out of its marks. Still, we are in
for more surprises. For recall that Kant speaks of the schema of a dog: the
schema of a sensible concept "is a product and as it were a monogram of
pure a priori imagination" (*KrV* A 142/B 181). *A pure a priori schema of a dog,
itself the product of a pure a priori imagination?* We may blame Kant for a very
careless phrasing or for being plainly wrong, or we may prefer the theory
of the *Critique of Judgment* according to which only our pure concepts have
schemata, while empirical concepts have only examples (§ 59, *Ak* 5: 351,
ENG 225). Either way, this passage cannot be simply ignored or brushed
aside. Nonetheless it remains puzzling for the advocates of the temporal
precedence of the a priori.

92. Heidegger, *What Is a Thing?*, 180, 166.
93. Another example of a mistaken interpretation of the a priori is Fichte's. He interprets a
priori and a posteriori as the two points of view (philosophy and common sense) on the same
phenomenon (*Sämmtliche Werke*, 2: 474; *Werke*, 3: 31). Idealism gives the deduction of the a priori in pure consciousness as the anticipation of experience. The philosopher is like the chemist
who can deduce the elements combining in a metal, which common sense experiences as given.
94. I believe this position is widespread in the secondary literature. Rather than denouncing
scholars and philosophers and naming interpreters for missing what it took me a long time to
understand, this sense of a priori and the productivity of reason, I might as well cite my essay
("Construction and Mathematical Schematism") as an example of wrongheaded and yet standard interpretation.

We could try to finesse and qualify this thesis by saying that all that productive imagination could do with an empirical concept is produce a figurative synthesis: the apprehension of the dog as the unity of its characteristics in an image. Were this the case, productive imagination would not at all produce a priori the schema for the apprehension of a dog in an image but be limited to apprehending the particular dog as the image of a member of a class. This would radically differ from mathematical schematism, because, to put it bluntly, we fail to see how it could be a priori. In fact, no pure a priori concept or schema of a dog seems to make sense. The schema of a dog would be not a method (as schemata are), but at most the admonition to interpret and picture the dog as a member of its class and to take all particular images as irrelevant to and derivative from our ability to picture a dog in general.[95]

The problem is evidenced further if we consider that regarding mathematical schematism, familiarity is not an issue. The construction of a triangle and of a chiliagon are equally rules for exhibition in intuition and do not differ in kind, for I can invent all shapes I want to provided I can realize them intuitively. Everything is equally removed from my personal interests (equally familiar or equally alien), for I move about in a world of rules. Now take the dog. We are all more or less familiar with dogs. We may love them, be afraid of them, or prefer cats to them, but we recognize them when we run into them.

But what happens the first time we experience something new that we cannot bring back to familiar objects, for example, the first time Europeans meet a platypus, as Umberto Eco asks?[96] It surely is impossible to claim sensibly that we possess an a priori schema of a platypus. Unbeknownst to us, our mind would be suffering from overpopulation, overflowing with all possible 'unknown cognitions.' Our mind would look like the mockery of omniscience: the admittedly finite and unconscious microcosmos reflecting God's infinite *omnitudo realitatis*.

What is wrong is not Kant's schematism but construing the question of the a priori in this manner, and, further, using it to criticize Kant. This is the damage caused by the "subjective endowment" view of the a priori, which is only aggravated by the thesis, call it "subjective prior endowment," of the temporal precedence of the a priori.

95. This was my suggestion in "Construction and Mathematical Schematism," 158–59.
96. *Kant and the Platypus.* See also Ferraris, *Good-bye Kant,* and my critique in "Good-bye Is Too Good a Word."

It could be objected that Kant should not be taken literally regarding the schema of a dog. We should, accordingly, correct his explicit wording. We could then say that the a priori retains different meanings, and the schema of the dog, if a priori at all, is so in a manner different from that of the a priori intuition of space or the pure concept of causality. This is to some degree true, but this strategy would be no interpretation. It would rather be an arbitrary, ad hoc circumvention of the problem to make a troublesome point square with a presupposed reading of the a priori as precedence in the mind.

The a priori has different nuances, not different meanings. We are not left with a hopeless homonymy, for there is one fundamental sense of this concept in its different applications to intuition, schema, and concept. The thesis I want to defend is that we have no a priori forms that are not the production of a pure spontaneous synthesis. The a priori does not identify given forms but is used to distinguish from the receptivity involved in perception and empirical apprehension the kind of activity we perform when we construct or apprehend mathematical forms, when we perceive appearances, when we intuit the space occupied by this table, when we schematize categories, when we act freely, when we produce rational forms-contents. The a priori is that constituent of our experience which cannot derive from experience, i.e., our constitutive activity. The a priori is *the a priori of the empirical.*

Still, it could be objected that the "subjective endowment" view of the a priori is one thing, while the thesis of its temporal precedence is quite another. Conflating them for the sake of criticism without a prior examination of temporal precedence is unfair. In the Mrongovius Metaphysics, Kant first says that if I omit the empirical in experience, I remain in intuition with the size or shape, and in the empirical concept with the form of the concept (which he would call the pure concept in the Transcendental Analytic). He claims that we can represent both a priori (*Ak* 29: 796, ENG 150). He adds that such cognitions of the form of intuition and of the form of empirical concepts are "the basis of synthetic a priori judgments," so that these concepts not only are synthetic but also come "before all experience" (*Ak* 29: 796, ENG 150). He then says that once we have abstracted from the matter of perception, we are left with the intuition of space that is in us a priori. Finally, two pages later he concludes that we "can know a priori how we will be affected by things that are mere shapes, e.g., if I omit everything empirical from a die, then *I still retain the shape. . . . I can know that a priori, for that is pure intuition*" (*Ak* 29: 797–98, ENG 152, italics mine).[97]

---

97. "I can say something a priori about space without an object being there. . . . Thus I do have a priori intuition" (*Ak* 29: 797–98, ENG 152).

As we can see, an a priori intuition, far from being preliminary to experience as a preparatory act, is the result of an omission, a separation. The a priori is the way to represent and know a form I have reached through progressive elimination. The a priori basis of experience is synthetic and active, as it produces judgments that extend our cognitions. In this passage the pure intuition of space is not a condition of possibility of knowledge but the object of an a priori cognition. Recall that all pure representations are "originally acquired" and produced by reason a priori (*Entdeckung*, Ak 8: 221–23, ENG 311–13), while empirical concepts are acquired "derivatively" (ibid.). But there is in us an a priori *ground* to intuit in space and time that is an inborn capacity;[98] this a priori ground is quite unlike pure concepts, determinate spatial representations, and all pure intuitions, which are the result of an original acquisitive activity.

And yet, having this "ground" a priori, namely, the form of space, means that we can *relate spontaneously* to what is outside us: orient ourselves in space, draw lines, measure distances, and so on, i.e., *trace* the basic, nonconceptual oppositions up-down, right-left, front-back, for which our body is the point of origin. The *preintellectual awareness of orientation* in space is the presupposition for the distinction between right and left, and therewith for recognizing the spatial incongruity that *no conceptual description of internal relations* can capture. These basic, nonconceptual oppositions in space are represented as the three planes intersecting each other at right angles with the body as the first *originating* ground of directions.[99] The activity of acquiring representations, in turn, is what we do with this natural, inborn disposition.

None of that should strike us as new, for it rephrases what we read in the Transcendental Aesthetic. Sensibility is not passivity or mere receptivity, as is often said in the literature on Kant that appeals to the unilluminating opposition of blind intuitions and empty concepts, receptivity and spontaneity.[100]

---

98. *Dissertation* § 8, Ak 2: 395, ENG 388, and § 15, Corollary, Ak 2: 406, ENG 400; *Entdeckung*, Ak 8: 221, ENG 312.

99. See *GUGR*, Ak 2: 378–79, ENG 366–67, and my "Lived Space," 23–30. Hence the distinction between numerical and logical identity and the criticism of Leibniz's intellectualization of appearances.

100. By passivity I mean the mere capacity to be affected without any contribution on our part. My thesis is that Kant denies that such is our sensibility. Pure intuition does not simply play a role in our application of pure concepts to experience, as neo-Kantians (including Cassirer) thought. It is the form that makes the manifold be apprehended in certain orders and relations. The form is "positive" (as Kant writes in *Entdeckung*, Ak 8: 240, ENG 327), not a simple negative condition restricting our concepts. For this reason Kant dubs sensibility *receptivity, not passivity*.

The Aesthetic, "the science of all *principles of a priori sensibility*" (*KrV* A 21/B 35, italics mine), is ushered in at the end of the Introduction. Here we read that sensibility "*contains a priori representations*, which constitute the condition under which objects are given to us" (*KrV* A 15/B 29–30, italics mine). The form of appearance is "that which allows the manifold of appearance to be *intuited as ordered in certain relations*" (*KrV* A 20/B 34, italics mine). "*The pure form of sensible intuitions in general is to be encountered in the mind a priori, wherein all of the manifold of appearances is intuited in certain relations.* This *pure form* of sensibility itself is also called *pure intuition*" (ibid., italics mine). "Extension and form . . . belong to the pure intuition, which *occurs a priori*" (*KrV* A 21/B 35, italics mine). Appearances have *a form*, "which is the only thing that sensibility can make available a priori" (A 22/B 36). About appearances, then, "much may be said a priori that concerns their form" (*KrV* A 48/B 66, A 42/B 60).

All these passages are unequivocal. In fact they wreak havoc on all cautious, balanced, well-meaning, commonsensical interpretations. They leave us no choice. They cannot be twisted or minimized in their import. They show that *the form of what is given to me is known a priori.* That is, the form of intuition can only be the form of appearances, and the form of intuition or pure intuition is a priori. (Hard as I have tried, I could not find in these or other passages any significant difference between pure, a priori, and formal.) Since intuition differs from concepts in that the whole lies in its every part, the form of intuition and determinate intuitions are isomorphic. Intuition can be inflected, i.e., declined in the plural or the singular (for space in general and this space, for this rectangle and the space occupied by this table, the same intuition holds).

Incidentally, this shows that in the Transcendental Aesthetics Kant is torn between anticipating what he must in order for sensibility (and especially pure intuition) to make sense, and censoring this tendency, because the *unity* of the intuitive manifold is not yet thematic. That is, he would like to introduce only the pure form of intuition but cannot, because a form cannot be given or *represented* (or expounded, metaphysically or transcendentally) without being *pluralized and objectified.*

There is one exception: when Kant writes the Refutation of Idealism (and generally when he faces the problem of the existence of reality outside us), he intends to show that things existing outside us determine our existence in time. Outer sense is prior to inner sense *a parte objecti,* even if *a parte subjecti* all apprehension takes place as a modification of inner sense. In that context (which does not contradict this), it is understandable that sensibility should be passivity. It is even understandable that a *Reflexion* (5653, *Ak* 18: 307) calls sensibility "original passivity."

The form of intuition, as we just read, is a pure intuition. So when Kant later (in 1787, at *KrV* B 160–61n) contrasts "the mere form of intuition" of the Transcendental Aesthetics, which "merely gives the manifold," with what he then calls formal intuition (an actual and determinate intuition that can be declined in the plural in geometry, where it is "represented as an object"), he is muddling his thought and giving us a tremendous retrospective simplification of the Aesthetics, even as he is adding to it very important qualifications: namely, that intuition presupposes an intellectual synthesis that could not be introduced in the Aesthetics.[101]

In any case, whether in the singular or the plural, space is *not an empty form* because it is itself a *determinate object of a priori knowledge*. For how would it be known otherwise? Not only is pure intuition a priori. It can only be a priori, for it is as senseless to have a pure intuition a posteriori—we can and do have at the same time an empirical and a pure intuition of appearances, but empirical intuition cannot be at the same time pure—as to presume that I can intuit a color a priori.

Strange though it may sound, therefore, in "the lamp is to the left of the screen" we must acknowledge that I do have an empirical judgment regarding the lamp and the screen. At the same time, however, I have an a priori or pure intuition of their mutual spatial relation, and of their relation, jointly as a group of items, *to me* as their observer. (If my friend sitting across the desk were to utter his empirical judgment, it would be "the lamp is to the right of the screen.") Space is the form of *Neben- und Aussereinandersein*. This obviously does not mean that the a priori intuition of the space occupied by the screen takes place *before* the apprehension of the screen. It means that the a priori intuition is the pure *correlate* of my perception, given along with it.

Yet sometimes Kant expresses himself as if temporal priority were relevant. The a priori, then, would be not only what is absolutely independent of experience (as it is defined at *KrV* B 2–3), but also what precedes all experience (e.g., *KrV* B xvii–xviii, A 159/B 198). The least we can say is that if Kant had wanted to avert the danger of a temporal interpretation of the a priori, he would have been much more careful in the choice of his words. He did not in fact see any such danger. The exit strategy that denies all

---

101. The picture is blurred even further if we consider that the phrase 'formal intuition' was used in place of 'form of intuition' in the first edition of the antinomies (*KrV* A 429: a passage retained in the second edition at B 457), where instead the opposition between the two is stated clearly. Even the *Prolegomena* uses 'formal intuition,' but as equivalent to 'image'! (note I to § 13, *Ak* 4: 287, ENG 83).

temporal connotations of the a priori because transcendental philosophy is opposed to all *quaestio facti* and all psychology is then too facile to be taken seriously.

If one examines the German text attentively, one realizes that Kant almost invariably uses temporal adverbs (*vorher-, vorausgehen, im voraus, bevor, ehe, vor*). In a *Reflexion* Kant goes to the point of connecting the a priori with prophecies.[102]

Should we then assume a duality of meanings, a temporal precedence and a transcendental presupposition, possibly respectively linked to a priori intuition and pure concepts?

In the *Prolegomena* Kant returns to this point. His question is: "But how can the *intuition* of an object precede the object itself?" (§ 8, *Ak* 4: 282, ENG 78). If pure intuition were of things in themselves, "it would not take place a priori, i.e., before the object were presented to me. . . . There is only one way possible for my intuition to precede the actuality of the object and occur as an a priori cognition, *namely if it contains nothing else except the form of sensibility, which in me as subject precedes all actual impressions through which I am affected by objects*" (§ 9, *Ak* 4: 282, ENG 78). Pure intuition is a priori because it contains nothing but my form of sensibility, which precedes all sensible impressions (*KrV* A 267/B 323). To assert that we know a priori the form of appearances in our form of intuition, all that Kant needs is his thesis of transcendental idealism, the identification of spatiotemporal appearances with representations (*KrV* A 102, A 109, A 191/B 236, A 563/B 591; *Prol, Ak* 4: 288, ENG 83). If things are appearances conforming to our sensibility, it is no problem to understand why, of all appearances given to us, we know a priori the intuitive form. By having the object conform to our intuition instead of having our cognition conform to objects, we can know it a priori *before it is given to us* (*KrV* B xvi). The problem, rather, is how an object of representations can be distinct from apprehension and representations generally. That will be the subject matter of the Transcendental Deduction.

"The intuition of the object precedes its actuality" means that its form is my sensibility, nothing but the way I am affected by my positing my

---

102. "A priori heisst . . . im voraus, so wie bei den Wahrsagungen" (Erdmann 81/395). In the *Anthropology* (§ 28), Kant writes that imagination, as the faculty of intuitions without the presence of the object, is the original presentation (*exhibitio originaria*) of space and time, and as such it precedes experience. Kemp Smith claims there are two conflicting views of the a priori: an early psychological version for which a priori intuition antedates experience, and a later version for which a priori intuition precedes experience as a potential disposition (*Commentary*, 88–90). Ewing (*Short Commentary*, 31–33) favors a different interpretation: a temporal sense is not needed, for a logical presupposition is all that matters and Kant was careless in his text.

representation in my inner sense.[103] Pure intuition is a form of self-affection, knowledge of which (i.e., self-knowledge, reached at the end of an abstracting and isolating process of elimination) at the same time precedes and grounds knowledge of appearances. Pure intuition and empirical intuition lie on different planes. Without the former I could not have the latter. The a priori intuition of the space occupied by the table does not take place before the apprehension of the given table. As a pure intuition, however, it is independent of it.

To conclude, a pure intuition is independent of perception. It is given with it, but it can also be isolated (in mathematics or when I think away all matter) and known as it is imagined.[104] If we say that this intuition is given prior to all experience, if, that is, Kant insists on knowing pure intuitions a priori, consciously, and before experience when he says that I know a priori the form of what I *will* experience (not only the form of what I experience), this should not trouble us or tempt us with an interpretation of the a priori as temporal precedence.

To be precise, this is indeed a temporal understanding, but one quite different from the "subjective prior endowment" view of the a priori. Literally I do appeal to a temporal precedence when I say that I know a priori the form of what I will experience. The present "grounds" the future. Still, this is different from the "subjective prior endowment" view because I am not claiming that forms lie ready a priori in the mind, but simply repeating what we have seen under the rubric of the a priori synthesis. "Preceding" means that the a priori representation makes the object possible. In a priori cognitions I cannot ascribe to the object anything "except what the thinking subject takes out of itself" (*KrV* B xxiii). If no object exists before my synthesis, if the object comes to be only thanks to my synthesis and activity, then I am entitled to say that my activity precedes it. But what I mean is that every empirical synthesis presupposes an a priori synthesis and that experience is made possible by the transcendental unity of apperception, which unifies in

---

103. "Since it does not represent anything except insofar as something is posited in the mind, [it] can be nothing other than the way in which the mind is affected by its own activity, namely this positing of its representation" (*KrV* B 67–68).

104. "We cognize the real only a posteriori, but the formal a priori. The representation of the impression of the object on us is sensation, thus is something subjective that we all must cognize a posteriori. . . . [*The forms of space and time instead*] are the form how objects will appear to us when they affect us, therefore we can *imagine* much that we have never seen, e.g., cones and pyramids as in geometry; *accordingly* one can *cognize space and time a priori*" (V-Met/Mron, *Ak* 29: 829, ENG 187, italics mine).

its concepts the pure intuition of space and time. I mean neither a psychological thesis nor judgments with timeless truth values.

The formulation of the *Prolegomena* states this clearly. We cannot find in experience any lawfulness. Our pure intuitions and pure concepts are the a priori cognition making *lawful experience* possible. I can judge that air is elastic "because certain judgments occur beforehand" (*Prol* § 20, *Ak* 4: 301, ENG 95). When all appearances are subsumed under pure concepts they form "a system of nature, which precedes all empirical cognition of nature and first makes it possible, and can therefore be called the true universal and pure natural science" (*Prol* § 23, *Ak* 4: 306, ENG 100). This system of nature makes it possible for me to cognize a priori *that*, given an alteration, I infer *generally* that an effect has been determined by an antecedent cause and follows in accordance with a constant law. But only *determinate* experience (a posteriori, empirical cognition) can tell me that sunlight melts wax while it hardens clay (the example at *KrV* A 766/B 794). At the same time, determinate experience is lawful and objective because perception of appearances is subsumed under pure concepts.

Once again the gap between a system of nature as a system of forms-contents (the principles on which reason exercises its a priori legislation) and empirical, determinate experience cannot be effaced. *Knowledge of objectivity* (the universality and necessity of the system of nature) differs from *objective knowledge* (the universal and necessary validity of an empirical judgment). But notice that empirical cognition *is* objective, as we will see more in detail in a moment.

Furthermore, as I have been claiming, the contextualization of this point should not be lost sight of: objective knowledge and knowledge of objectivity are a major yet subordinate part of the critique of pure reason. For transcendental philosophy investigates origin, principles, and extension of a priori cognitions, and is thus aimed at reason's self-knowledge. Pure reason's powers and limits, including its capacity for experience, are available only to its reflexive examination.

7a. The Relative Independence of Intuition. Judgments of Perception and Judgments of Experience

The misunderstanding to be avoided regards a supposed possession of ready-made representations prior to all experience. But if there is no object before an a priori synthesis that gives rise to it, temporal priority and transcendental presupposition appear relatively intertwined—as intertwined as are intuition and concept for the constitution of the object.

In the Introduction to the Transcendental Deduction (which, recall, must show the objective validity of pure concepts, which therefore underlie all empirical concepts), Kant distinguishes the *vorausgehen* (the verb 'to precede') of the forms of intuition from the *Voraussetzung* (presupposition) of pure concepts, the a priori condition of experience (*KrV* A 93–94/B 125–26). I am not sure how intentional this distinction is, i.e., whether or not it aims at contrasting pure intuition's temporal precedence to the transcendental presupposition of pure concepts and at being taken as a standard usage. Since intuition is the immediate relation to objects while concepts are mediate representations referring to intuition, it is fair, indeed plausible to assume such difference.

Whatever our interpretation, all our exegetical efforts so far seem to be in vain once we turn to the *Prolegomena*. The passage just cited at the end of section 6 (I can judge that air is elastic "because certain judgments occur beforehand," *Prol* § 20, *Ak* 4: 301, ENG 95) refers to the transcendental presupposition of pure concepts, except that it is embedded in the notoriously difficult difference between judgments of perception and judgments of experience. This difference is difficult not because unintelligible or hard to grasp, but because it seems to conflict with Kant's doctrine as it is expounded elsewhere and, worse, appears also as internally incoherent. The topic has been discussed at length in the literature.[105] Here I intend not to propose a new comprehensive interpretation but to clarify the distinction and discuss two points. The first aims at enlarging our perspective on the issue of the a priori as precedence. The second aims at bringing to fruition the considerations of the earlier sections on the difference between pure and empirical concepts.

The thesis proposed by Kant is that not all empirical judgments are judgments of experience. What is needed for the transformation of the ones into the others is a priori concepts allowing us to subsume perception under them (*Prol* § 18). Judgments of perception do not need pure concepts and are valid only subjectively.

To begin with, let me remark that the perceptions which are valid only subjectively can be of different sorts. Kant's first examples are poorly chosen, but even worse is their grouping ("the room is warm, the sugar sweet,

---

105. See, among others, De Vleeschauwer, *La déduction*, 2: 131–36, 454–96, 3: 137–40; Prauss, *Erscheinung*, 190ff.; Hoppe, *Synthesis*, 29–58; Allison, *Idealism*, 178–85; Kotzin and Baumgärten, "Sensations"; Thöle, *Kant und das Problem der Gesetzmässigkeit*, 90ff.; Longuenesse, "Kant et les jugements empiriques"; Longuenesse, *Kant and the Capacity to Judge*, 167–209; *Kant on the Human Standpoint*, 23–26; La Rocca, *Soggetto e mondo*, 79–119.

the wormwood repugnant," *Prol* § 19, 4: 299 and n, ENG 93 and n). Kant himself seems embarrassed by them, as he immediately confesses they have a merely introductory function but are not a good illustration of what is at stake. That these examples do not fulfill the function desired is not just avowed by Kant himself but also prima facie obvious. They cannot, says Kant, become judgments of experience. *Why* they cannot, however, is more debatable. One could argue that the reason is that those are all secondary qualities and that Kant, much like most modern philosophers from Galilei, Descartes, and Locke on, thinks that primary qualities have an objectivity denied secondary qualities and can be subjected to scientific treatment. Some notable passages from the first *Critique* are evidence of this belief ("secondary qualities are only changes in the subject, changes which may, indeed, be different for different men," *KrV* A 29–30/B 45).

I think this is wrong. This revitalization of the modern opposition between primary and secondary qualities rests on a precritical conception of appearances. Even sensible qualities (*realitas phenomenon*), as we have seen, can be known a priori in their degree and continuity in the Anticipations of Perception. More importantly, judgments of experience pretend to be objectively valid of given empirical objects here and now. The issue is not the scientific status of qualities but the transcendental question of the reference of intuitions, which are directed either to the subject or to the object. In fact, primary and secondary qualities should be treated on a par, not because of their scientific status but on account of the fact that they equally belong to appearances—on account, that is, of Kant's transcendental idealism.[106]

Judgments of experience such as how warm the room is (but not how sweet the sugar is or how repugnant the wormwood) are standard and typical.[107] So, as I pointed out earlier, it is a serious misunderstanding to claim that the objective validity of judgments shown in the Transcendental Deduction or in these sections of the *Prolegomena* pertains only to laws and universal judgments with timeless truth values, i.e., to science. The objective

---

106. Consider this passage in the *Prolegomena* (note II to § 13, *Ak* 4: 289, ENG 84): "That one could, without detracting from the actual existence of outer things, say of a great many of their predicates: they belong not to these things in themselves, but only to their appearances and have no existence outside our representation, is something that was generally accepted and acknowledged long before Locke's time, though more commonly thereafter. To these predicates belong warmth, color, taste, etc. That I, however, even beyond these, include" space and what depends on it, means that we can know only appearances and not things in themselves.

107. In the first *Critique* (*KrV* B 69–70n), Kant writes that secondary qualities, as opposed to illusion (*Schein*), can legitimately be attributed to the object itself as its predicates: "The predicates of appearance can be attributed to the object in itself, in relation to our sense, e.g., the red color or fragrance to the rose."

validity of judgments is not meant originally or even mainly as a grounding of necessary laws of experience—say, of Newton's laws of motion. Instead, it grounds, but is quite independent of, empirical truth and falsity.

What makes objective validity possible is not the universality and necessity of its objects but the form of judgment and the fact that all intuitions stand under the original unity of apperception. Recall that objective validity is validity predicated of the object, i.e., neither intersubjective validity (the claim to a shared consensus based on the postulate of a *sensus communis*) nor the validity of the general laws of a system of nature. What matters for Kant is the relation between principles and objectively valid statements on empirical facts. Conversely, what matters is how empirical judgments rely on pure concepts; how the decision on empirical truth and falsity presupposes the objective validity of judgments as its condition. The objectivity of judgments of experience is distinct from and no less important than Kant's demonstration that a system of pure laws underlies our experience of nature, which is meant to bring back the several empirical judgments to a systematic framework.

Differently stated, there is an important difference between *knowledge of objectivity and objective knowledge*: the former is a priori and universal, the latter is empirical. The former, nature as a system of laws, is the answer to the question: what can pure reason produce a priori? This, i.e., the Principles of Experience, is one of the fruits of the Transcendental Deduction of the Pure Concepts of the Understanding (as the Analytic of Principles is the consequence of the Analytic of Concepts).

But the latter, concerning judgments of experience, is the answer to a different question. It concerns the truth value I can claim for my empirical judgment "the room is warm."[108] While the former question concerns reason's a priori synthesis, the latter concerns the transcendental presupposition of pure concepts for the objective validity of judgments of experience.[109]

---

108. "The objective validity of a judgment of experience signifies nothing other than its necessary universal validity. But also conversely, if we find cause to deem a judgment necessarily, universally valid . . . , we must then also deem it objective, i.e., as expressing not merely a relation of a perception to a subject, but a property of an object; for there would be no reason why other judgments necessarily would have to agree with mine, if there were not the unity of the object—a unity to which they all refer, with which they all agree, and, for that reason, also must all harmonize among themselves. Objective validity and necessary universal validity (for everyone) are therefore interchangeable concepts" (*Prol* § 18 and 19, *Ak* 4: 298, ENG 92–93).

109. In the Hechsel Logic we read: "Judgments of experience are such insofar as they are given only *a posteriori* and we *judge without proof*" (V-Lo/Hechsel Pinder, 88, ENG 382, italics mine).

In other words, it is possible to have experience without science. Experience and science have their distinct ways. Conflating knowledge of objectivity and objective knowledge, and thereby principles as forms-contents and empirical cognitions, comes down to confusing reason's a priori synthesis as a criterion of truth with the empirical truths grounded by it. Accordingly, refuting a principle (whether or not this is at all possible in Kant is a different, and debatable, question) is totally different from refuting a law of nature or a judgment on an empirical state of affairs (which is obviously possible).[110]

If in both cases our pure concepts are operative and therefore both cases presuppose an a priori cognition, whatever certainty experience produces is not the result of its resting on a fully developed a priori science. I need not, that is, have developed a system of laws of nature to claim objective validity for my empirical judgment "the room is warm."

The difference between judgments of perception and judgments of experience, then, does not rest on a fully developed science. Nor is the theme of secondary qualities as mere changes in the subject (KrV A 29–30/B 45) relevant for it. What is relevant is that when I bring sensation under categories, that is, when I think it through, it becomes amenable to a conceptual structure and can be valid of the object. Feeling cannot aspire to such validity, in principle. Sensation, in non-Kantian terms, has an intentionality. It can contribute to knowledge, whereas feelings of like and dislike cannot be universalized. Even the third *Critique*, which discovers an a priori principle behind the feeling of pleasure, excludes judgments regarding sugar or wormwood from its scope.

In the so-called *Stufenleiter* (the progression of the kinds of representation at KrV A 320/B 376), Kant writes that sensation is a conscious perception, but only as a modification of one's state. "[A]n objective perception is a cognition (*cognitio*). The latter is either an intuition or a concept (*intuitus vel conceptus*)" (as we can see, intuition is a cognition even without a concept).

It is therefore insufficient, even if literally true and obvious, to claim that judgments of perception pertain only to subjective psychological states. A feeling is private whereas judgments of perception refer to what can be

---

110. A good example of such a confusion, which I take to be paradigmatic especially in philosophy of science, is Popper. In *Conjectures* he writes: "Kant proved too much. In trying to show how knowledge is possible, he proposed a theory which had the unavoidable consequence that our quest for knowledge must necessarily succeed, which is clearly mistaken. When Kant said 'Our intellect does not draw its laws from nature but imposes its laws upon nature', he was right. But in thinking that these laws are necessarily true . . . he was wrong" (48).

perceived also by others and *become* objective: to potential objects, as it were. It does not make sense to apply the concept of an object in general to a feeling; to a percept, it may or may not. In fact, turning a sensation into an experience would amount to applying the pure concepts producing the concept of an object in general to the percept (expressed conversely, to subsuming the percept under it). What is missing from judgments of perception seems to be this subsumption, this conceptual determination.

That we can have intuition without concepts is clear not just from this passage, but in general. We regularly pass judgments we do not pretend to be binding for everyone. Take "I am cold" when "you are warm." Undoubtedly these are judgments and there is no normativity to such assertions. Surely Kant does not want his theory of the objective validity of judgment to invalidate such common and ordinary judgments. Just as he denounces the error of those who pretend to have their taste dominate over that of others and distinguishes between the objective validity of judgments of experience and the intersubjective validity of judgments of taste, he must also acknowledge that certain judgments have no claim to validity at all.[111]

Intuitions (even judgments) without concepts are exemplified in Kant's philosophy by these two instances: (1) Judging without concepts is the everyday experience of aesthetic appreciation. (2) The spatial relation in the judgment "the lamp is to the left of the screen" is an independent intuition and a cognition.[112] Obviously I *do use* concepts and the form of judgment in these two examples. But what I *aim at* is respectively an aesthetic judgment and a pure intuition. In other words, concepts can very well be involved. The question is whether or not they are determinant, i.e., whether I subsume an intuition under a concept.

Take the second example: noticing that 'x is to the left of y' yields an independent intuitive cognition expressed in a judgment. But if I want to understand what x and y are and what it is that I predicate this spatial relation of, unless I have the concepts of lamp and screen the intuition is blind. To have an *empirical cognition* of this fact, intuition and concept are jointly required. By contrast, to *intuit a spatial relation*, intuition is sufficient unto itself. In sum, intuition is blind when it works in independence of

111. He does at least in the Mrongovius Metaphysics: "We also have a posteriori judgments; these are either judgments of perception or of experience, the latter presuppose the former,— the first have only subjective validity; I say, e.g., *I am cold*. The latter have objective or general validity" (*Ak* 29: 815, ENG 169, italics mine).

112. In the *Dissertation* Kant writes that only the nonconceptual act of pure intuition can notice and grasp spatial diversity and incongruity (*"quadam intuitione pura diversitatem, nempe discongruentiam, notari posse,"* Ak 2: 403, ENG 396).

determinant concepts. Establishing a sense of distance, depth, and all spatial relations does not aim at concepts, while object identification aims at bringing objects under concepts.

To repeat: What is missing from judgments of perception? And what is incoherent about this distinction? The incoherence is easily articulated. In the space of a few sentences Kant argues that pure concepts, and with them a priori judgments, precede empirical judgments, and then that judgments of perception precede judgments of experience.

An argument in defense of Kant would maintain that judgments of perception are discussed here because in contrast to the first *Critique* we proceed analytically and start from given sciences—including in the case at hand a system of laws of nature—in order to ascend to their conditions. But this consideration is of little help. The distinction remains problematic for several reasons.

1. It is paradoxical to say that judgments of perception are valid only subjectively in the context of the demonstration of the objective validity of knowledge made possible by the logical form of judgment and the necessary unity of original apperception in its predication. If the form of judgment is what gives objectivity, then in calling the relation of perceptions a judgment Kant works against himself, for he pretends, in the midst of the introduction of his specific sense of judgment, to appeal to the common-sensical understanding of judgment.

2. The example in the note ("If the sun shines on the stone, it becomes warm," *Prol* § 20, *Ak* 4: 301n, ENG 95n) is quite misleading and shows the opposite of the judgment of perception Kant wants it to exemplify, namely, the objective causal connection in a hypothetical argument.

3. Furthermore, the thesis that judgments of perception "do not require a pure concept of the understanding, but only the logical connection of perceptions in a thinking subject" (*Prol* § 18, *Ak* 4: 298, ENG 92) seems to contradict the fundamental aim of the Transcendental Deduction, including in particular the principle that Hume's association is actually ruled by pure concepts.

4. For the a priori the major problem, however, is that the antecedence relation is inverted. Kant writes: "All of our judgments are at first mere judgments of perception; they hold only for us, i.e., for our subject, and only afterwards do we give them a new relation, namely to an object" (*Prol* § 18, *Ak* 4: 298, ENG 92). Kant has just finished explaining that synthetic a priori judgments are the principles that constitute nature as a system of laws ruling appearances, and that all empirical synthesis presupposes a pure synthesis. Here, instead, he uses adverbs that contradict his teaching and this time

unequivocally involve a temporal precedence (*zuerst . . . und nur hinten-nach*). Kant even claims universality for this thesis.

Is it wrong, then, to talk of the transformation of a judgment of perception into a judgment of experience? It is if we say, as does Kant, that the former always precedes the latter.

Another problem is that I can distinguish between these two kinds of judgment only provided I presuppose the pure concept (in the background, so to speak, as an available resource). For without it I could not pass from the judgment of perception to the judgment of experience thanks to the subsumption that only the pure concept makes possible. That is, I can first distinguish between judgments of perception and judgments of experience because I possess something (the pure concept) that in one case I decide to omit from my consideration. If so, judgments of perception are reached *by subtraction*. So why does Kant say that it is possible to have perceptions without categories?

The point here is not to be charitable to Kant and see what we can rescue from this muddled conundrum, for there is something genuinely Kantian and therefore worth preserving about this distinction. As we have seen, we often have impressions that we articulate in judgments of sorts that precede our actual objective judgments. Admittedly, the very distinction between sensation and perception in the *Stufenleiter* just recalled means precisely this (and not in the *Prolegomena*, but in the *Critique of Pure Reason*). Accordingly, point 3 above could perhaps be rephrased in more flexible terms. It is true that association is ruled by pure concepts *provided I assert* what I think and claim validity for my judgment as I normally do. If so, my yet unasserted judgment is merely tentative. (It may always remain such, or instead be appropriated, confirmed, or possibly rectified by my actual objective judgment.) My stance on it differs from the normal/normative objective attitude I link to my judgments.

If we accept this point, however, we must conclude that the judgment of perception *sometimes* precedes the judgment of experience while at the same time the latter is transcendentally presupposed *necessarily* by the former. But this necessity is not recognized as such, or is suspended. Since Kant is no Aristotle and for him the distinction between first in itself and first for us hardly holds, accepting this point drives a wedge between temporal and transcendental. The temporal precedence, not the judgment of perception, has inadvertently been turned into a psychological or genetic priority, which is contingent and quite different from the priority we saw at the end of the previous section (which was problematic but after all legitimate and integral to a transcendental investigation).

Everything hinges on the meaning we attribute to the absence of categories. Kant writes that they are "not required." Is it possible to have a judgment without categories? Not in the standard view. The absence of empirical concepts is one thing, that of categories quite another. We can very well have a judgment that presupposes pure concepts and yet does not have the empirical concepts available, as we are going to see presently.[113] But a judgment that is not the objectifying relation between subject and predicate through the copula and does not require pure concepts is what Hume, not Kant, would recognize as standard.

Is there another possible view? A judgment of perception must be admitted by transcendental philosophy as a noncommittal, recalcitrant judgment: i.e., when I deliberately withhold from my judgment its natural claim to validity and hold fast to the percept and consider it independent of and indeed prior to the pure concept. I suspend (objective) judgment on it insofar as I do not bring it back to concepts. The suspension is revoked when I do (which may also never happen). The percept is my certainty, but not a truth. I am merely "persuaded" by it. As long as I am not ready to determine the percept, I limit myself to accepting it uncritically, possibly even reflecting on it but in a nonbinding way. In other words, I exercise the freedom of not applying categories. Such judgments are preliminary to the objective assertion a judgment typically produces. I prescind from the object and refer the judgment to the modification of my subjective states (*Refl* 5923, *Ak* 18: 386): not because I want to describe my states, but because I abstain from taking a stance or have not yet verified or sufficiently tested my judgment to be willing to present it as objective.[114]

If so, a natural, interesting, yet potentially troublesome consequence of this point would be the modalization of Kant's assertorial or categorical thesis I have called the flexible rephrasing of (3). Instead of saying that our experience presupposes pure concepts, we should say that it 'typically' does. After all, this would square well with the difference between empirical consciousness and consciousness in general (*Prol* § 20, *Ak* 4: 300, ENG 94), and with the distinction in the first *Critique* between subjective validity and objective unity of apperception (*KrV* B 141–42). Therefore it should be allowed in critical philosophy. But because it is a self-denying judgment not determining its object or asserting what it says, it does not undermine Kant's

---

113. In § 7c below. Meanwhile we can think of the platypus.

114. These judgments are not to be confused with either problematic judgments or prejudices or *judicia praevia* (and the related question of preliminary and provisional judgments that serve to prepare an investigation, familiar to students of Kant's logic).

notion of objective judgment. I should *not* say that "experience 'typically' presupposes pure concepts," both because this judgment does not aim at talking about experience and, more importantly, because in it I still have the pure concepts constituting an object in general, but simply do not *apply* them. My pure concepts do not determine their object because what I have is a *potential* object, one I have suspended (or not yet recognized) as such. If so, a judgment of perception does belong to transcendental philosophy: not to its constitution of objective knowledge, but rather to a different question, that of its *certainty* and modes of *Fürwahrhalten* (taking to be true).[115]

Many interpreters consider this distinction of the *Prolegomena*, which is neither proposed in the first edition of the *Critique* nor picked up again in the second, a temporary loss of rigor on Kant's part. This distinction, however, is not a transitional incident. As I have argued, there are solid reasons to defend it, only not quite in the way Kant does. The judgment as a connection of perceptions is—has the logical form of—a judgment. Its function cannot be belittled as that of a limiting case or a contrast.[116]

Besides, the distinction is not a hapax legomenon of the *Prolegomena*, for it reappears under different titles in the second edition of the *Critique* and subsequently as well. At B 142, Kant writes that if the relation of representations had only subjective validity, I could say "'If I carry a body, I feel a pressure of weight,' but not 'It, the body, is heavy,' which would be to say that these two representations are combined in the object, i.e., regardless of any difference in the condition of the subject, and are not merely found together in perception." There is thus no repudiation in 1787, but only a retrieval of the distinction under a different name. In two *Reflexionen* dated by Adickes between 1790 and 1804 (*Refl* 3145, 3146, *Ak* 16: 678–79), Kant picks up

115. See the section "Opining, Knowing and Believing" in the Canon. One of the reasons why I incline toward this solution lies in this passage: "I cannot *assert* anything, i.e., pronounce it to be a judgment necessarily valid for everyone, except that which produces conviction. I can preserve persuasion for myself if I please to do so, but cannot and should not want to make it valid beyond myself" (*KrV* A 821–22/B 849–50). I do not believe that if categories are not required then Kant is here close to Husserl's passive synthesis, a minimal activity before the onset of the I. This conclusion would contradict the necessity of the transcendental unity of apperception and the aim of the Transcendental Deduction with its pure concepts. (I wish to thank Pierre Kerszberg for this suggestion.)

116. De Vleeschauwer is right that the Metaphysical Deduction does not include the epistemological distinction of the *Prolegomena*, but is wrong in concluding that judgments of perception are not judgments (*La déduction*, 2: 132ff.) because they do not really unify (2: 458). Also, judgments of perception do not serve as mere contrast, as a foil to judgments of experience (2: 455; see, before him, Vaihinger, *Commentar*, 1: 353–55).

Meier's concept of judgment of experience[117] and uses the same words as in the *Jaesche Logic* (*Log* § 40, *Ak* 9: 114, ENG 608–9):

> A judgment from mere perceptions is not possible except insofar as I assert my representation as a perception. I, who perceive a tower, perceive the red color in it. I cannot, however, say: the tower is red; for that would not be merely an empirical judgment, but rather also a judgment of experience, i.e., an empirical judgment whereby I acquire a concept of the object. E.g., *"In touching a stone I sense warmth"* is the former: but *"the stone is warm"* is the latter.

In *Reflexion* 3146 the example is this: "'I sense warmth in touching the oven' is a perception: 'The oven is warm' is a judgment of experience" (*Ak* 16: 679). These examples and this doctrine generally seem relatively uncontroversial, are coherent, and should settle the matter once and for all. But they do conflict with the *Prolegomena* and the interpretation of the judgment on the sun and the stone in the note discussed at (2) above. What is striking about that note, it now turns out, is that two notes below Kant himself rectifies his interpretation.

> That this warming follows necessarily from illumination by the sun is indeed contained in the judgment of experience (in virtue of the concept of cause), but I do not learn it from experience; rather, conversely, experience is first generated through this *addition* of a concept of the understanding (of cause) to the perception. (*Prol* § 22, *Ak* 4: 305n, 99, italics mine)

We could object to Kant's unfortunate use of the term "addition" (*Zusatz*), which suggests that the judgment of experience, instead of being a unitary operation, is a sum of distinct moments of which one (the decisive) may be missing. Subsumption would be optional and contingent. But this is precisely what is argued in the passage from § 18 from which we began: to attain judgments of experience a priori, "special concepts must yet be added" (*hinzukommen müssen*, *Ak* 4: 297, ENG 92). Instead of presenting the judgment of perception by subtraction, as I have read it, Kant presents the judgment of experience by addition, which is possible only if one looks at the distinction from the vantage point of perception.

Still, the conclusion is clear. This addition does not take place when I decide not to claim validity for my judgment. The note ends with a reference

---

117. See section 323 of his *Auszug aus der Vernunftlehre* ("Ein Erfahrungsurteil ist ein jedes Urteil, welches durch die Erfahrung gewiss ist," *Ak* 16: 678).

to the Doctrine of Judgment in the first *Critique*. When Kant recalls that chapter elsewhere he means primarily the power of subsumption and the mirror terms subsumption-application (and secondarily the schematism as its means). A judgment of experience is a posteriori and regards perception; perception is subsumed under pure concepts. The judgment is thus *necessary* in two distinct ways: (1) because the empirical relation asserted between warmth and sunlight presupposes pure concepts (causality), the form of judgment, and transcendental apperception, and thereby becomes an experience, and (2) because experience as a net of systematically interrelated principles is made possible by pure reason's synthetic a priori judgments.

The twofold sense of the necessary presupposition of judgment is reflected in, albeit not identical with, a twofold sense of subsumption. It is one thing to subsume this table under the empirical concept 'table' (or 'table' under 'artifact'), quite another to subsume it under the pure concept 'substance.' It is with regard to the latter that the *Prolegomena* speaks of the possibility that categories might not be "required," which is evidence that in judgments of perception we still have the concept of an object in general but fail to apply it to perception.

Many years later, in a letter to Johann Heinrich Tieftrunk (December 11, 1797), Kant distinguishes between logical and transcendental subsumption. In the former we bring a concept back to a superior concept thanks to the rule of identity: the two concepts are homogeneous. The latter is the subsumption of an empirical concept under a pure concept through an intermediate term that mediates between two heterogeneous concepts (*Ak* 12: 224–25), i.e., the schema.

This distinction may not be that helpful. In fact it changes once again the issues at stake, for it speaks no longer of the subsumption of an appearance under a concept as did the first *Critique*, but of concepts under higher concepts. But with it we now obtain a special name, 'transcendental subsumption,' for how judgments of experience differ from and exceed judgments of perception.

7b. The Relative Independence of Intuition. Pure Intuition

Kant criticizes all positions that equate the a priori with truth as well as synthesis with experience on the grounds that, whether they are empiricist or rationalist, they oppose empirical and pure. For example, Hume opposes relations of ideas to matters of fact, while Leibniz opposes necessary truths of reason to contingent truths of fact. The a priori synthesis (with the new concept of form) overcomes precisely such an opposition. Kant's mathematical construction itself rests on this very distinction. All readings that take the intuitive to be synonymous with the 'visible,' all reductions of intuitions to images, are off the mark.

Kant's thesis holds only if he can show the reality of pure intuition and all its difference from empirical intuition. It is striking to notice how often the importance of pure intuition is simply neglected in interpretations of Kant. Pure intuition and empirical intuition must not be construed as opposed, and yet must be kept sharply distinct. Empirical intuition rests on pure intuition. Even here, I suggest, the relation is one of matter in distinction from form, which is an activity of ordering a pure manifold. My interpretation of pure intuition relies on the notion of *receptivity*, which must be sharply separate from all senses of *passivity*. This thesis is defended in this section.

Sensibility is divided into sensation (matter) and pure intuition (form). Matter is always apprehended in its proper form. Sensibility is the faculty of receiving representations through the mode in which we are affected. As such, it is the very *source of givenness*. Receptivity and givenness are mirror terms. Receptivity is that through which objects are given to us, because it is in immediate relation to appearances (*KrV* A 19/B 33). It is contrasted with the absolute spontaneity of the understanding, but its form admits of "a science of the rules of sensibility" (*KrV* A 51/B 75). For receptivity's own form "contains a priori representations" (*KrV* A 15/B 29). If sensibility is a mode of receiving, this mode is the form we know a priori.

It is therefore quite clear that if sensibility were passive, receptivity could not contain a priori representations and could not make possible the order and relation of the manifold. If sensibility were passive, then it could not take place a priori in us and give us a pure cognition, nor could we have a science of the a priori principles of sensibility. If it were passive, then mathematics could not be built on its ground. If it were passive, space and time would not be pure but empirical intuitions.[118]

The a priori of sensibility, irreducible to sensation, functions as a criterion of the truth of experience. For example, because Berkeley did not make any such criterion underlie his appearances a priori, his idealism was dogmatic and treated the world as illusion. But Berkeley is just one example in Kant's vindication of his discovery because, as he proudly says, before the

---

118. The a priori ways in which sensibility can be modified precede all sensation and affection. They are the a priori cognition that is the object of the Transcendental Aesthetics, while the principles of a priori cognition are the object of Transcendental Logic, as the Metaphysics L2 reads (*Ak* 28: 576, ENG 339).

first *Critique* "it did not occur to anyone that the senses might also intuit a priori."[119]

The only viable option is to conceive of *pure intuition as a formal, nonconceptual activity of ordering the intuitive manifold, even as we receive the given*.[120] In fact, we can receive the given only insofar as we order it in our pure forms. The *Dissertation* stated this clearly: in a sensible representation we distinguish the matter (sensation) and the form, which "is a relation in what is sensed" to an act of the mind "by means of which it co-ordinates for itself that which is sensed" (*Ak* 2: 393, ENG 385). The way we *receive* the manifold coincides with the way we *order* it, so that even of sensation passivity cannot be predicated without qualifications.

Passivity is properly speaking an *attitude*. In the *Anthropology*, in a section significantly entitled 'Apology of Sensibility,' Kant anchors his defense of sensibility against its detractors by arguing on behalf of its indispensability for superior faculties. The passive side of sensibility, its opposition to freedom and resistance to the understanding's rule, is the real cause of the evils we ascribe to it (*Anth* § 8). This evil, however, is no fault of its own because sensibility is not in itself passive. It is alogical, not irrational. That is, it is not rational (implicitly or otherwise), but this does not mean that it works *against* reason. Unlike the black horse in the *Phaedrus*, sensibility is not a thrust downward: it is we who let ourselves be made passive when we abdicate rule. In fact, sensibility has many virtues. In this section, it has a central aesthetic function, not just concerning the beautiful but also with regard to cognitive representations (the emphasis and vigor of expression, the luminosity of conscious representations, the pregnancy and density of thoughts).

The notion of the virtues (or, in strict eighteenth-century parlance, *perfections*) of sensibility is discussed by Kant before he discovers the a priori of sensibility, but is closely related to it. As Alfred Baeumler reminds us, it is

119. *Prol, Ak* 4: 375n, ENG 163n. This statement is more than reminiscent of one that antedates it by two years. At *KrV* A 120n, Kant wrote: "No psychologist has yet thought that the imagination is a necessary ingredient of perception itself." The relation between these two claims raises all sorts of questions on the relation between sense and imagination into which I cannot go here. The relation could be interpreted, as does Nuzzo (*Ideal Embodiment*, 345), to mean that sensibility should be understood in a wider sense to include functions that the *Critique*, and especially the secondary literature on it, ascribe to the imagination. Or it could, as I would say, be taken to mean that no intuition can come to be without a synthesis. Whether or not we want to call such synthesis, as does Kant, the product of a blind but indispensable imagination is a different matter to which I will come back.

120. "Wenn wir im Raum und in der Zeit etwas setzen, so handeln wir; wenn wir es neben und nach einander setzen, so verknüpfen wir," as *Reflexion* 4634, *Ak* 17: 619, has it.

at the intersection of logic and aesthetics that the question of the worth of sensibility becomes central in the evolution of German philosophy.[121] The idea, shared by Wolff and Meier, that all representations are concepts and that sensations can be reduced to indistinct or confused concepts is for Kant the deplorable consequence of Leibniz's philosophy (*KrV* A 270/B 326). Opposing sensibility and the understanding as the sources of indistinct and distinct representations means treating sensibility as a lack of clarity and a source of confusion, but also as an inferior faculty continuous with the understanding and teleologically directed to it. What Leibniz does not see is that the difference between sensibility and understanding does not depend on the logical form. It is a question not of degree but of the content of representations.[122] Both intuitions and concepts are wholes, complete representations in their own right, and each can be clear and distinct in different ways. The difference is that the intuition is a coordinated whole of intuitive parts, while the concept is a whole of partial marks that subordinates its conceptual and analyzable parts under itself.

I have a clear intuition when I am conscious of the whole. In turn, a distinct intuition occurs when I can distinguish the constitutive parts of the whole intuition.[123] Kant's point is that a sensible representation that becomes distinct does not for this reason stop being an intuition. In the *Jaesche Logic*, distinctness can be intellectual or sensible. The former is exemplified by the case of virtue, of which I can isolate the marks without which it could not be, i.e., freedom, duty, rule over inclinations. Distinctness here comes down to analysis and explanation and regards the form. Sensible distinctness, in turn, "consists in the consciousness of the manifold in intuition. I see the Milky Way as a whitish streak, for example." The representation "becomes distinct only through the telescope, because then I glimpse the individual stars contained in the Milky Way" (*Ak* 9: 35, ENG 546). As is evident, this intuition becomes distinct not because it is conceptualized but because it is technically empowered in its apprehension of details.

Thanks to intellectual and sensible distinctness, we achieve respectively a logical and an aesthetic perfection of knowledge. The aesthetic perfection in the Vienna Logic is based on "the universal and necessary laws of sensibility. Herein lies the concept of the beautiful" (V-Lo/Wiener, *Ak* 24: 806–7,

---

121. *Kants Kritik*, 167ff.

122. *Anthropology*, § 7. Why then the *Metaphysical Principles of the Science of Nature* (*Ak* 4: 507, ENG 218) suddenly speaks of Leibniz as a "great man" who has not been understood by his followers, when both before and after 1786 Kant has criticized his theory of space, is quite unclear. That he should distinguish Leibniz from Eberhard in *On a Discovery* is less puzzling.

123. On this topic, see Capozzi, *Kant e la logica*, 366–76.

ENG 266). This sudden reappearance of aesthetic concerns should not surprise us. As human sensibility has its own nature (which cannot be universalized to other beings), the beautiful is about form, symmetry, and harmony, the contemplation of which is appropriate for us as human and gives us a pure pleasure. The *Critique of Judgment* uses this universal consensus on beautiful forms, as opposed to what pleases in sensation, for the a priori principle of purposiveness underlying the aesthetic judgment.

According to Giorgio Tonelli, Kant in the mid-1760s, under Baumgarten's inspiration and following the impulse of Crusius and Lambert and his own reading of British empiricism, speaks of the concretization of the abstract in terms of examples or individual instances.[124] Taste acquires the positive function of providing concrete examples that enrich rational concepts. Aesthetics has a cognitive function because sensibility has one. The essay on the regions of space (1768) finally gives a theoretical ground to the cognitive independence of sensibility first elaborated on an aesthetic basis. The order of sensibility, as mentioned, is the order of coordination rather than the conceptual order of subordination. The richness of the particular intuition is sensible and alogical and necessarily escapes the understanding. Sensibility and understanding have their respective scopes irreducible to one another, each with its own laws, forms, and criteria for clarity and distinctness.

Kant clearly seems to be introducing *a nonconceptual cognition*. But how is it possible if intuition without concepts is notoriously blind? And how is a nonconceptual cognition supposed to work?

As we saw, mathematical cognition cannot be understood as such nonconceptual, intuitive knowledge. Kant does say that "[t]ime and space are two sources of cognition, from which different synthetic cognitions can be drawn a priori, of which especially mathematics . . . provides a splendid example" (*KrV* A 38–39/B 55). But mathematical construction, which is indeed exhibition in intuition, is exhibition of concepts, in judgments, in a proof structure. Intuition is its ground, but its content is the universal results it yields.

Intuitive knowledge, by contrast, is the a priori knowledge of intuitive forms, which can apply to empirical objects. It is thus objective knowledge. Recall the examples of "Yesterday it rained" and "the lamp is to the left of the screen." Rain, lamp, screen—all empirical objects—are the variables saturating forms that refer to time and space alone. The intuition is the object

124. *Kant*, 309–15, 338–43, 375–76.

the judgment aims at. The intuition is an objective representation (*KrV* A 320/B 376), which means that it is valid of the object (it *represents the object,* unlike feeling) but is not yet true or false. The judgment is the only touchstone of truth (*KrV* A 293–94/B 350), but that does not alter the fact that intuition is a specific mode of access to and cognition of the object, one that is alternative to concepts. As the essay on the regions of space shows, the relation "to the left of" can be apprehended only through spatial intuition. It is in no way a concept. And, after all, it is pertinent to recall that according to Kant animals do have such empirical cognitions and an orientation in space, while they do not have concepts.

Still, it is difficult not to admit that "knowledge" is employed in different ways here, as we will see in the next chapter, which may be one of the reasons why Kant himself is at time confused about the cognitive nature of intuition. Pure intuitions are cognitions according to the numerous passages I have been quoting, but not all.[125] Besides, an important passage from the B Deduction also denies intuition the status of cognition. At B 137 Kant writes: "The mere form of outer sensible intuition, space, is not yet cognition at all . . . in order to cognize something in space, e.g., a line, I must *draw* it."

I think that this passage is misleading. *Every* manifold in intuition must be synthesized in order not simply to be cognized, but to be in the first place. Therefore the opposition between a mere form of sensibility and an intuitive manifold is introduced so as to stress the requirement of a synthetic activity, but what is left of space without synthesis is no more than the availability of the manifold.

The form of intuition is not a "mere" form of intuition. It is not an inert form we are endowed with, separate from its application. The form of intuition comes only in the form of an activity. Pure intuition is possible without concepts but not without a synthesis, as it is a forming—relation and unification—of a manifold for which the mere availability of the manifold

125. To the passages we have seen so far defending the cognitive status of intuition we can add *KrV* A 320/B 376; V-Lo/Dohna, *Ak* 24: 701; *Log, Ak* 9: 33; *Refl* 1693, *Ak* 16: 85. But I should mention the two following examples as exceptions. In the Metaphysics L2 Kant writes that intuitions and concepts in themselves "give no cognitions at all" (*Ak* 28: 547–48, ENG 314). This passage is in the section on ontology, which, like the Transcendental Deduction prefaced by the passage on blind intuitions and empty concepts, aims to prove that experience is made possible by sensibility and understanding jointly. In the *Stufenleiter* of the Dohna-Wundlacken Logic (*Ak* 24: 752, ENG 458), Kant says the opposite of the *Stufenleiter* of the first *Critique* (and of the Vienna Logic, *Ak* 24: 904, ENG 348: "cognition is of two kinds, *intuition, concept*"): "*intuitus*—this is not yet a cognition."

cannot suffice. It takes a synthetic activity, although not a conceptualization, to collect, run through and relate the sensible manifold and make intuition cognitive.

The objective of the Transcendental Aesthetic is to prove the transcendental ideality of space and time. Therefore it turns on their metaphysical nature as forms of receptivity. This is gained at a price, though, the same price as that paid by the linear reading of the *Critique of Pure Reason*: the impression it gives the reader that intuition can do without the synthesis, first introduced later at A 77/B 103, in which alone it acquires meaning. For the Aesthetic cannot strictly speaking present relations without a "synopsis of sense" (A Deduction, *KrV* A 94) or an act of unification (*KrV* B 160–61n). But assuming this much amounts to going beyond the external arrangement of the Doctrine of Elements and reflecting upon what is anticipatory, on the inseparability of basic and more advanced levels, and on the relation between intuition, synthesis, unity, and concept.

In a baffling note in the B edition I have already partly recalled (*KrV* B 160–61n), Kant addresses the unity of intuitive representations: "In the Aesthetic I ascribed this unity merely to sensibility, only in order to note that it precedes all concepts, though to be sure it presupposes a synthesis, which does not belong to the senses but through which all concepts of space and time first become possible."[126] No intuition is determinate and can become a cognition without a synthesis. Kant himself blames the expository order of the *Critique*.[127] His doctrine, he now says, is that a synthesis underlies intuition and that it does not belong to the senses.

But if the synthesis does not belong to the senses, to whom or what does it belong? The continuation of the note is puzzling: "For since through it [*synthesis*] (as the understanding determines sensibility) space or time are

126. The footnote has been discussed at length in the literature. For two examples of an instructive treatment, see Allison (*Idealism*, 112–16), and Longuenesse (*Kant and the Capacity to Judge*, 212–27).

127. This reminds of Hegel's criticism in the 1830 *Encyclopaedia* (§ 60, Remark): "In any dualistic system, but in the Kantian system particularly, its fundamental defect reveals itself through the inconsistency of *uniting* what, a moment earlier, was declared to be independent, and therefore *incompatible*. Just as, a moment before, what is united was declared to be what is genuine, so now it is said that *both moments* (whose subsisting-on-their-own was denied by asserting that their unification is their truth) have truth and actuality only by being separate. What is lacking in a philosophizing of this sort is the simple consciousness that, in this to-ing and fro-ing, each of the simple determinations is declared to be unsatisfactory; and the defect consists in the simple incapacity to bring two thoughts together." For Hegel the defect is one (and radical and sweeping). I am trying to keep the defect in exposition separate from the unitary meaning of Kant's philosophy.

first *given* as intuitions, the unity of this a priori intuition belongs to space and time, and not to the concept of the understanding (§ 24)." We learn, that is, that space or time are first given as intuitions through the synthesis. But which space and time? Those that the beginning of the note called the mere form of intuition (the availability of the manifold, our capacity to apprehend it) or the formal intuition (the unity of the intuitive representation)? It seems we should reply "the latter," or space and time as such would be the product of the imagination, while in fact only their several determinate representations, produced by a figurative synthesis, are.[128]

More fundamentally, however, we should question the very meaning and independence of the former, indeed deny any effective difference between the former and the latter. The capacity for intuiting is an abstract concept waiting to be filled with content and meaning. In fact, the form of intuition is nothing without determinate intuitions: singular and plural in intuition are indistinguishable.

The note seems to contradict itself. Kant usually opposes the synthesis of imagination to the unification of the understanding. (He is not, however, entirely consistent, for in B he speaks of an intellectual synthesis as well). Here the synthesis—recall the phrase: "as the understanding determines sensibility"—is the effect of the understanding on sensibility. And yet Kant immediately denies that "the unity of this a priori intuition belongs to . . . the concept of the understanding," for it belongs to space and time themselves. It seems either that the understanding, the faculty of concepts, is capable of a nonconceptual activity or that its name (as it often does in the revised edition of the Deduction) replaces that of imagination—but, alas, only in the first case ("the understanding determines sensibility"), not in the second (as implied by "not to the concept of the understanding").

The note concludes with a reference to section 24. Here Kant wrote that the motion or act by which the subject in its self-affection unifies the manifold in space can be considered in abstraction from this determination. If "we attend solely to the action in accordance with which we determine the form of inner sense, [this motion or act] first produces the concept of succession at all. The understanding therefore does not *find* some sort of

---

128. That space and time should be the product of the imagination (this is, as is well-known, the core of Heidegger's interpretation, *Kant and the Problem of Metaphysics*, 102, *Phenomenological Interpretation*, 90, but is found also in Waxman, *Kant's Model of the Mind*, 33–116, and Longuenesse, *Kant on the Human Standpoint*, 73–74) is a thesis that Kant criticizes explicitly and ascribes to Leibniz at B 57. In the first *Critique* imagination works intuitively, that is, on space and time, which are its elements, whereas on the contrary space and time are constituted by the imagination in the *Opus Postumum* (see De Vleeschauwer, *La déduction*, 3: 635).

combination of the manifold already in inner sense, but *produces* it, by *affecting* inner sense" (*KrV* B 155). Self-affection is a figurative synthesis that involves the imagination under the influence of the understanding.

The lesson is not that space and time are imagined. (That they should be *made* by the understanding is explicitly denied.) It is instead that time, i.e., temporal succession, is produced by the imagination through a schematization, and that the production of space is made possible by this original production of time as the determination of inner sense we perform as we experience.

Typically, a schematization is of concepts. But later, in the third *Critique*, it is not. Before we analyze whether in the first *Critique* it is or not, let us push the relation between time and space a bit further.

The relation is undoubtedly complex, and here I can list only a few relevant points. Time presupposes space and appearances in space in the Refutation of Idealism, for example, and in the Analogies of Experience. But as we know, the a priori synthesis that produces schematized categories needs only to bridge the logical plane of concepts and the intuitive plane of time, not space. When we say that time is produced as we experience, we imply a synthetic activity in our apprehension. It is not the case that all representations are time-indexed and come with a temporal tag attached to them. Instead, all representations are such for a consciousness that apprehends them in time. I.e., consciousness temporalizes them. Things are not by themselves temporal. By being apprehended, they are turned into appearances. In sum, apprehension, as activity within receptivity, is the original position of representations. And temporal succession is the way apprehension originally produces diversity as such.

In inner sense the manifold consists of the activity of the I who posits and thereby temporalizes representations while abstracting from their content. As far as external sense is concerned, on the contrary, the manifold is brought into the form of space by sensation, which is itself the effect of things on our sensibility.[129] While in outer sense cause and object of the modification (the *affizierende* and the *apprehendierende*) are different, in inner sense they are two different sides of the same I, the active and passive, the I as subject and the I as object. The possibility of actual sensation of outer objects presupposes the possibility of apprehension, which takes place along two lines: one regarding the object (and the information we can get about it) and the other regarding the very act by which we apprehend it.

---

129. See Vaihinger, *Commentar*, 2: 482.

This is what I have been referring to as self-affection, an activity on ourselves that makes possible the apprehension and cognition of appearances.[130]

Now, it is one thing to discuss the difficulties of a dichotomic exposition of sensibility, quite another to rewrite the first *Critique* altogether. In his correspondence with Kant and in his interpretation of the *Critique*, Beck tried to go beyond the internal division of the Doctrine of Elements. He thought that in it Kant had wanted to accompany the reader from the dogmatic level of sensibility to the proper transcendental level consisting in the synthetic unity of consciousness.[131] Beck had therefore started from the Analytic and the original apperception, but had thus minimized the role of intuition in cognition. Like Reinhold, Beck demanded the unity of a starting point. He found it in what he called the *original act of combination (Zusammensetzung), the only truly a priori function*, so he thought, in cognition.

If Beck were right, the original synthetic activity of consciousness would produce the object. But there would be no room for an independent synthesis or for any independence at all of the intuitive manifold. Even Beck, then, misses the import of pure intuition.[132]

In his replies to Beck between 1792 and 1794, Kant emphasizes the role of a priori intuition and of the transcendental schematism. He insists that the composition or synthesis of the manifold must harmonize the *two* elements of empirical cognition: the intuition through which the object is given and the concept through which the same object is thought (letter of January 20, 1792, *Ak* 11: 313–16). Time, the schematism, and the subsumption of the percept under the concept through judgment disappear from Beck's reconstruction. Kant must call Beck's attention to this absence.[133]

---

130. In the *Anthropology* (§ 22), inner sense is a consciousness of what man undergoes (*leidet*), not what he does (*thut*), insofar as he is affected (modified) by his representations. It follows that there is an inner division within the subject, so that the question: 'who affects whom in inner sense?' implies *ein doppeltes Ich*, an I as subject and an I as object (and these are *ein und dasselbe Subjekt: das Gemüth wird durch sich selbst afficiert*). See the discussion of these passages from the *Lose Blätter* by Vaihinger, *Commentar*, 2: 480–81.

131. These points are made explicit in the letters of June 17, 1794, and September 16, 1794 (*Ak* 11: 490–91 and 505), even though the correspondence with Kant had started three years before. For a fuller treatment, see his *Einzig möglicher Standpunkt*, 1796.

132. Hegel is strikingly Beckian: he praises the footnote at B 160–61 in *Glauben und Wissen* (*Werke*, 2: 361–64) as an excellent way of understanding the apriority of sensibility (*das Apriorische der Sinnlichkeit*). Unfortunately Hegel entirely misses pure intuition and conflates it with perception, as can be seen by his treatment in the *Science of Logic*. See *Werke*, 5: 223, and 1830 *Encyclopaedia* § 231, and my discussion in "Pure Intuition in Mathematics" and *Il pensare*.

133. He reiterates the point also in the letters of July 3, 1792 (*Ak* 11: 346–48) and December 4, 1792 (*Ak* 11: 394–96).

In defense of Beck, however, we could point out that Kant himself, perhaps out of dissatisfaction with the exposition of the Doctrine of Elements of the first *Critique*, progressively tries to revise that presentation. As we saw, the note at B 160–61 is evidence of a shifting consideration. Immediately thereafter, in the *Critique of Practical Reason* (1788), as he speaks of the first *Critique*, Kant writes: "The Analytic of pure theoretical reason was divided into transcendental Aesthetic and transcendental Logic. . . . The Logic in turn was there divided into Analytic of concepts and Analytic of principles" (*Ak* 5: 90, ENG 212). This is an incredible turnaround.[134]

"Analytic" is used homonymously, as it is at once the genus of Aesthetic and Logic, and the object of Logic. More importantly, the Aesthetic, instead of giving the first element and, qua immediate and intuitive relation to appearances, the foundation for the Doctrine of Elements, is part of the Analytic. And the Logic, instead of being divided into Analytic and Dialectic, suppresses the Dialectic altogether. The Analytic no longer simply occupies the central position in the partition but becomes central thematically, to the point that the understanding almost effaces sensibility and reason.

We will return to this passage in chapter 3, for it harbors more surprises. Perhaps even more shocking is a different fact, more relevant in this context. In the manuscripts for the *Fortschritte*, that is, *during* his exchanges with Beck (1792–94), whom he criticizes for missing the importance and independence of the Aesthetic, and at the same time as he stresses the "two hinges on which it [metaphysics prepared by critical philosophy] turns: *First*, the doctrine of the ideality of space and time . . . ; *second*, the doctrine of the reality of the concept of freedom" (*Ak* 20: 311, ENG 397) without which neither a speculative nor a practical a priori synthesis would be possible, Kant ends up adopting *literally* Beck's exact standpoint in his own remodeling of the *Critique*. Instead of starting from the division of Aesthetic and Logic or recalling the fundamental role of pure intuition, Kant begins with the notion of *Zusammensetzung*. He goes to the point of calling it the only a priori element! "The concept of a *compounding . . . is in the end the sole basic concept a priori*, which is the original foundation in the understanding for all concepts of sensible objects."[135]

Kant's objection to Beck sounds then almost like an automatic and perfunctory defense mechanism. He has clearly grown unsure about a position he now considers past, even as he defends it from Beck's reductionism. He

134. Noted by Brandt, *Die Bestimmung des Menschen*, 40 and 362.
135. *Ak* 20: 271, ENG 363. See De Vleeschauwer, *La déduction*, 3: 466–70.

is ever more tempted by this reshuffling. Indeed, in his heart he thinks that yes, the first *Critique* needs rewriting. But, as we will see in the next chapter, rewriting it is actually what he has been doing since the *Prolegomena*, in a process culminating in the third *Critique*.

Paraphrasing what Jacobi said of things in themselves, we can argue that without the relative independence of sensibility we cannot enter the system, but with it we cannot stay inside it. At least Kant could not. With Kant gone, that left the stage completely empty of "strict" Kantians around 1790.[136] The parable of the first *Critique*'s integrity lasted really less than ten years. It was such a rich and fruitful book that it left a desert around itself, and all its fruits were harvested elsewhere—even by Kant, who incessantly recast the interrelation of faculties and the inner articulation of reason, as we will see in detail in chapter 3.

7c. The Relative Independence of Intuition. We Are All Savages

We have distinguished several cases: mathematical construction, pure intuition, empirical cognition. In the first, intuition is the object of construction, which however is a conceptual activity. In the second, intuition is both the object and the ordering activity independent of concepts. In the third, we have pure and empirical intuition, and an empirical concept presupposing a pure concept.

Intuition seems possible as a determinate cognition without concepts, but not without a synthesis. But what does it mean to say that intuition can function without concepts in the case of experience? In the case of judgments of perception, we fail to apply categories. It is important to specify what kind of concepts are not applied. When we say that pure concepts are not required, we have a difference between thinking and judging (in Kant's sense of these words), i.e., we have concepts but do not apply them.

There are cases, however, in which we think and judge but do not know. That is, we do not judge informatively because we miss the knowledge required to subsume objects under our concepts. This is a discrepancy between pure and empirical activity. If empirical cognition presupposes pure cognition, in turn pure cognition *exceeds* empirical cognition. More precisely: if in judgments of perception assertion is missing, what is missing here is the empirical concept, everything else (all moments of pure cognition) being equal.

---

136. With one exception: Schultz. See note 43 above.

Let me clarify and illustrate this point with Kant's example. In the *Jaesche Logic*, as he tries to explain the difference between matter and form in cognition, Kant writes:

> If a savage sees a house from a distance, for example, with whose use he is not acquainted, he admittedly has before him in his representation the very same object as someone else who is acquainted with it determinately as a dwelling established for men. But as to form, this cognition of one and the same object is different in the two. With the one, it is *mere intuition*, with the other it is *intuition and concept* at the same time. (*Ak* 9: 33, ENG 544–45)

The savage has the same matter as we. His[137] form, i.e., the way in which he knows the object, differs from ours. He can only intuit the matter we also intuit. But unlike him, we know what the house is for. The savage has an intuition but not a concept. This has nothing to do with a colonialist view of the savage's intelligence. Kant's point is that we are all foreigners somewhere, we are all savages sometimes: that is, when we do not have an empirical cognition regarding the object in front of us. The savage does not have the competence to judge, the ability to subsume a percept, because he has never before encountered a house, just as Europeans before discovering Australia had never before encountered a strange creature like the platypus, which did not seem to fit into any of their known kinds.

In the Bauch Logic (V-Lo/Hechsel Pinder 47–48), Kant says that we can know (*erkennen*) something through intuition without having a concept for it. Although he obviously could not mention the platypus of which he was not aware, the example is that of a monstrous animal never encountered before, which we can even represent in distinct ways. This is another case in which sensible distinctness is independent of and prior to concepts (and intellectual distinctness). To have a concept is something else: a concept is a *repraesentatio communis*; therefore we must experience more than one occurrence of the same species (ibid.). This requirement is explained in the Vienna Logic. "If someone were such that in the case of the expression *house* what occurred to him was always just the *tavern* that he had seen, he would always preserve an *intuitus*" (*Ak* 24: 909, ENG 353). Knowledge of individuals is impossible other than as an intuition.

To Kant, this shows that with only abstraction and without comparison and reflection a concept is not reached. It also leads us to wonder, though, if

---

137. Kant uses the example of a man, and so will I.

the requisite plurality should not be that of the marks unified in the concept rather than that of the instances of the kind. Moreover, we wonder if this abstraction is the negative and eliminative shape of the concept we have seen before or instead the hasty misidentification of one familiar intuition with a kind, and of this familiarity with a concept and a cognition. For this man would subsume 'house' under 'tavern' falsely, but he would still believe his to be a genuine subsumption under a concept.

However that may be, the savage does not know the house. So what does he intuit? *An as yet indeterminate object* (*KrV* A 20/B 34). It is quite important to describe it in these terms because there are many steps taken by the savage leading him to the concept of an object in general that are not at all made explicit by Kant and need unpacking.

To begin with, an as yet indeterminate object has sensible features, an intuitive form, spatial and temporal relations, relations between parts and whole, and is distinct from other similar indeterminate objects around it. The savage facing this indeterminate object can learn its function or essence. He can learn, that is, what a house is (as Europeans can learn what a platypus is). He can give his intuition a name once he has a concept for it available. The concept he is missing is an empirical concept.

But is he missing also pure concepts? Is an as yet indeterminate object all he has? A simple look at the title of § 20 of the B Deduction would declare it impossible ("All sensible intuitions stand under the categories," B 143). Notice that Kant speaks of categories or pure concepts; he is not claiming that intuitions stand under concepts generally. For Kant the B Deduction as a whole proves that we cannot have intuitions without categories (e.g., B 136), for all intuitions stand under the categories and the original synthetic unity of apperception.

Let us move beyond the letter, however, to verify on the basis of this concrete example the consistency of Kant's point. If the savage were prone to animism and faith in magic, if he or she were to think that the house can suddenly melt like snow or fly away into thin air or be the deceiving materialization of Harry Potter's mother, he would be missing also pure concepts. But in that case he would live in animal terror, in a totally senseless chaos with infinite particulars without identity, in which only intuitions would be available to him: no kinds, no objects, no order.

Typically this is not the expectation. Presumably instead the savage is initially in a state of wonder but does not try to find out about the house by attempting to pass through its walls or smashing his head against it. Why? Because he thinks the house is something, a bodily object with its solidity and material structure. He believes it is there to stay. Walking *around* it to inspect it is an option, but *through* its walls is not. This means that the savage *knows and judges* that the house has a temporal and spatial existence, but on top of that also a quantity, a quality and a substantiality and causality that he knows determine appearances.[138] That is, the savage judges the house as an object in general: he subsumes the former under the latter.

His pure reason has produced its a priori syntheses all along. The *Critique of Pure Reason* applies to the savage and to us equally, it seems. For it has to do not with our empirical knowledge but with what all empirical knowledge presupposes. The savage thus shares in principle our same a priori knowledge about the world. What he misses is the same thing we miss most of the time: experience, empirical concepts, and names for them.[139]

Besides, the savage understands the independence of his intuition from his concept very well. He is not necessarily telling himself, as is the transcendental philosopher, that there are rules for the formation of concepts, which belong in the understanding, "rules for the formation [*dichten*] of an idea which belong in reason, and *rules* for the formation of images belonging in sensibility" (*Ak* 25/1: 98–99). But nor are we in our ordinary experience. He is aware of the gap between what he sees and what he knows.

For this independence of sensibility from concepts to prove tenable, however, it must still pass the test of the A Deduction. Recall my earlier thesis that pure intuition is a formal, nonconceptual activity of ordering the intuitive manifold, even as we receive the given. The threefold synthesis begins with a passage that the interpretation of sensibility as passivity finds difficult, but that on the reading of pure sensibility as activity in receptivity is not problematic. Kant writes: "If I ascribe a synopsis to sense, because it contains a manifold in its intuition, a synthesis must always correspond to

---

138. Notice that the judgment need not be verbalized. It is a subsumption and an assertion. This is a crucial point to recognize if we want to understand what some call propositionalism and Kant calls discursivity.

139. If I open the hood of a car, or go to the hardware store, the percentage of things I can name or know the function of is ludicrously minimal and makes me feel smaller than do the starry heavens (without a corresponding sense of sublimity, even if I do feel some awe for engineers). Differently stated, my experience sounds like the opposite of Heidegger's thesis on the meaningful familiarity of the world of tools. In fairness to Heidegger, it must be said that he contemplates, as he discusses an example very similar to that of the savage, the case where the meaningfulness (*das Bedeutungshafte*) directing our experience is the complete alienness and absence of meaning. In *Zur Bestimmung der Philosophie* (71–72), Heidegger discusses the example of the experience of a desk in a university classroom for us, for a peasant from the remote hills of the Black Forest, and for a man from Senegal. We all see the same thing, but understanding it depends on the meaning we attribute to the thing. It is not a conceptualization independent of it. For Heidegger's Senegalese, "not knowing what to do with the desk" is probably going to be the response.

this" (*KrV* A 97). Yet again, no intuition can come to be without a synthesis. Because receptivity and spontaneity work together, spontaneity can exercise its activity in three syntheses: the apprehension in intuition, the reproduction in imagination, and the recognition in a concept. Indeed spontaneity is the ground of all apprehension. It is with regard to apprehension that Kant writes that "*receptivity* can make cognitions possible only if combined with *spontaneity*" (*KrV* A 97).

These three syntheses are exercised on the pure manifold, in abstraction from everything empirical belonging to appearances. We are focusing not on this or that object but on the object in general insofar as it is an object of possible experience, e.g., a substance in time. Whatever I apprehend, I apprehend in time, and my representations belong in inner sense. In time representations are ordered, connected, and related. As we have seen, however, this means that time is not an order of succession before my apprehension. Apprehension produces succession as such insofar as I distinguish time in the succession of impressions apprehended (*KrV* A 99). All appearances are apprehended as extensive magnitudes, successively. If all appearances are the result of a combination or successive synthesis of the manifold, I must be able to run through it and distinguish the parts of my apprehension. Nothing is graspable as simple. A whole form, as it is not a monad but the one of a many, presupposes a synthesis of its manifold in succession. This means that on the transcendental level I cannot have an instantaneous grasp of the appearance (even if on the psychological level I may take the figure as an immediate and primary datum, whether in a Gestaltist or other fashion). To claim the opposite for Kant would be equal to assuming an intuitive understanding.

Furthermore, the manifold must make sense to me as a determinate something. It would not if I could not hold together the several parts as I go through them. In order to combine the manifold, I must be able to retain the parts as parts of one whole. Representations have no inertia, as already noticed. They are not assumed to persist in me. They need to be actively reproduced from one moment to the next.[140]

Notice that memory has nothing to do with this reproduction in imagination, for reproduction is directed not to the past but to the present.

---

140. "If I draw a line in thought, or think of the time from one noon to the next, or even want to represent a certain number to myself, I must necessarily first grasp one of these manifold representations after another in my thoughts. But if I were always to lose the preceding representation (the first parts of the line, the preceding parts of time, or the successively represented units) from my thoughts and not reproduce them when I proceed to the following ones, then no whole representation . . . could ever arise" (*KrV* A 102).

Notice also that here imagination is not, as it typically is when it steps in in the absence of intuitions (*KrV* B 151), the presentation or presentification of the absent, but the effort at keeping together the apprehended parts of something present as parts of a whole.

Let me emphasize a few more points. One is that Kant does not rely on—in fact, he puts out of play—traditional theories of memory and images. Another is that nothing whatever, even sensation, would come to be in me unless spontaneity were to operate actively to apprehend a manifold, reproduce it, recognize it. Time is the element of our consciousness. If pure intuition involves a minimal spontaneity in receptivity, all pure concepts are made possible by the activity of an abiding self, the consciousness of an identity.

The two syntheses of apprehension and reproduction are inseparably bound together (*KrV* A 102). That is, I can never apprehend something unless I can also reproduce it in one whole. The first moment cannot be without the second. What is the third moment? The recognition in a concept. I recognize the sameness or identity of my acts. I am conscious that what I am thinking of at time T1 is the same as what I am experiencing or imagining at T2. The recognition is the consciousness of the identity of the synthetic act. Is the third synthesis as inseparable from the first two as these are from one another?

As we know, we can have concepts without intuitions. These are irremediably empty. We can also have intuitions without empirical concepts, whereby what is missing is cognition. An intuition without pure concepts (in judgments of perception) is also possible, whereby what is missing is their *application* and the *assertion* of the judgment: but the pure concepts of an *object in general* are not missing. If, however, we cannot have a synthesis of apprehension without the possibility of reproducing the manifold to ourselves, we cannot have these two syntheses without the rule that presides over them, the pure concepts and their correlate, the object in general. In the only case contemplated by Kant where categories are not applied (i.e., "the stone feels heavy"), we cannot say anything of the object because, having suspended the categories, *we do not even aim to refer* to one. All we assert is the percept as it affects us.

To conclude, what we intuit and what we think are essentially distinct. The savage intuits the house, but not qua house, because he does not possess the concept. The architects to whom Kant compares the architectonic reason, as we saw in chapter 1, do have the concept of house. As they plan an edifice, they have, in addition to the concept, also an idea, a project. They know that there are rules of symmetry and proportion; rules of volume and light; and rules (more conventional and culturally changing) regarding functions and ends. What they make with their sketches must respect such rules and bend to their style whatever additional constraints (concerning materials, budget, landscape and surroundings, regulations on urban planning, etc.) they face. The rules of space are the first object of consideration. But they are themselves instrumental to the ends and functions of the construction. Differently stated, the architect uses the space as he or she sees fit but knows all too well that this use of space, however indispensable, is no more than a presupposition for his or her project. Considerations of space naturally differ from considerations of functionality. Intuition is the primary datum, concepts follow, and all are in service of an idea.

The upshot of this simile, predictably, is that for Kant the order of concepts and that of intuition differ. The former does not influence or shape the latter, which has its own form and rules. We may be at a loss on the application of pure concepts, but this is a problem for the power of judgment, for which they remain indispensable. When we say that concepts *determine* intuitions, we do not mean that intuitions are concepts in disguise, i.e., that concepts *shape* intuitions. We mean that empirical concepts help us interpret empirical intuitions and pure concepts rule pure intuitions. Subsumption under empirical concepts means identifying and giving a name. Subsumption under pure concepts means bringing under a lawful order, be it knowledge of objectivity or objective knowledge.

Let me close with two remarks on positions widely debated in recent years regarding this relation between concepts and intuitions. The first is about Kant's presumed "conceptualism." Slogans are hardly ever useful in philosophy. Certainly the principle that concepts without content are empty,[141] intuitions without concepts are blind (*KrV* A 51/B 75) has not helped Kant's cause. As we will see in the next chapter, it is not necessarily the case that knowledge is the unification of intuition and concept. According to many interpreters, however, Kant must take intuitions as conceptualized. Intuitions cannot represent objects unless they stand under or are informed by concepts.[142] I do not mean to downplay the influence that the understanding has on sensibility, but I do want to emphasize that it is

141. *Begriffe ohne Gehalt* is the expression. Often one reads in the literature on Kant, I suppose for love of symmetry, that concepts "without intuitions" are empty. This is a serious mistake that even the best Kant commentators have made (for example Cassirer, *Essay on Man*, 56). There are different ways in which concepts can be empty for Kant, and the lack of intuition affects only one mode of cognition, empirical knowledge. I will return to this in the third chapter.

142. A famous advocate of the conceptualist position is McDowell (*Mind and World* and *Having World in View*). See also Kitcher (*Kant's Transcendental Psychology*, 80ff.), Heidemann

one thing for an intuition to be without pure concepts, quite another to be without empirical concepts. Kant denies the former but not the latter. We have seen that an object has intuitive as well as conceptual marks and that we can represent it according to its intuitive appearance or its logical marks (for example, in the schematism chapter, Kant writes that roundness can be intuited as a circle and thought as a plate: *KrV* A 137/B 176). Recall the formation of empirical concepts: experience of different trees takes place before we have their concepts. We reflect, single out, compare objects without possessing their concepts. This means that intuitions are not only that which gives content to concepts, but also that which allows us to form concepts. This would be impossible if intuitions came already conceptualized. Furthermore, I must be able to recognize intuitively the appearance to be able to talk about it in discursive terms. This means that the apprehension of an object takes place at two distinct levels that should not be conflated.

The second remark is this. Much post-Kantian philosophy from German Idealism to hermeneutics, from pragmatism to many postmodern theories in both analytic and continental philosophy (but not, for example, phenomenology), claims that intuition is an intellectual construction or a conceptual norm in disguise, itself deriving from culture, language, or history. If you can intuit only what you already are familiar with as it is filtered through language, cultural practices, a tradition, then the mediation of inference and interpretation guides and constrains intuition and with it our access to reality. An independent intuition is an illusion. From Kant's perspective, this view conflates empirical and pure concepts and transfers the cultural, linguistic, historical stratification of layers constituting empirical concepts, the result of a long and laborious process, to pure concepts. By making pure intuition the product of history, it understands intuition as solely empirical.

From a historical perspective it is quite reasonable to claim that the return to realism in the late nineteenth and twentieth centuries was a direct reaction to Kant. It is less obvious that contemporary advocates of realism, working to undermine postmodernism and its claim that there are no facts but only interpretations, should take Kant as their target.[143]

("Vom Empfinden zum Begreifen"), Hanna ("Kant and Nonconceptual Content"), and Ginsborg ("Was Kant a Nonconceptualist?").

143. Ferraris, *Good-bye Kant.*

CHAPTER THREE

Kant on Kant

Trust no-one.
—Patti Hewes, *Damages*

1. Science and Knowledge. The Combination Thesis

In this chapter I will try to shed light on one last piece of the puzzle of the difficulty inherent in Kant's texts. Complaints about the obscurity of Kant's convoluted prose are a dime a dozen and have been since the appearance of the first *Critique*. The main problem, I suggest, is not Kant's style, terminology, or the length and complexity of his sentences. The sometimes awkward syntax or the abundance of Latinisms may seem distasteful to purists, but do not pose a conceptual problem. If the problem were Kant's obscure prose, we would need only to find a proper key to decipher his meaning consistently, so that his works, translated into an accessible language (whatever that meant), would speak to us clearly. We saw in the introduction that this was Friedrich Schlegel's ambition. It must instead be acknowledged that the many different and widely diverging interpretations of Kant's thought in general, and of the first *Critique* in particular, seem justified by passages and concepts whose authenticity we cannot deny.

The major stumbling block for a correct and rigorous understanding and consequently a fruitful reading of his philosophy is sometimes, alas, Kant himself. The oscillations, constant wavering, at times contradictions on some crucial points, especially on what he wants or claims the first *Critique* to have accomplished and on the relation between critical philosophy and metaphysics, are confusing enough. Possibly even more troublesome is the equivocity of some key terms. Even more damaging are Kant's unrelenting shifts in his judgments on his own work. Kant simply cannot be trusted as an authority on himself. He is hardly fair to himself in his retrospective summaries and reconstructions. The perspective of what he is presently focusing on can dictate his priorities and tends to engulf, distort, or even efface the perspective—the concerns, questions, solutions—from which he completed his previous works. To clarify this point let me turn in this section to the equivocity of the term 'knowledge.'

I have argued against the interpretation of the first *Critique* as a work in the theory of experience or knowledge. The discussion of the conditions of knowledge is subordinated to and undertaken as a part of the wider concern for pure reason's powers of extending itself in the world. And yet at the same time I have shown how even the grounds of morality lie in the necessary and universal form of pure reason that only a fundamentally cognitive faculty can establish. Because in action thought can represent to itself the law and this is binding, *thinking* of the law and *determining* the will purely are one. Thereby reason exercises its powers beyond the limits of the sensible world. Only pure reason can be the source of all norms, whatever the object it applies itself to.

We have also seen in chapter 1 that cognitions are inferior to the maxim of thinking on our own. There is a gap between the maxim and the method on the one hand, and the several determinate products of reason's activity on the other. Metaphysics and philosophy embody the maxim as they concern the principles of a priori knowledge. And yet, at the same time, the legislation of pure reason—pure reason's highest activity—is not only an objectivization of the maxim but also a cognition.

This notion has generated several paradoxes that we have already discussed. Recall the case of mathematics. However science was defined in our Western tradition, it has always aspired to be an exact, rigorous, possibly deductive, architectonic system of cognitions (if not the highest instance thereof). Sometimes science has been subordinated to wisdom, a move with which Kant is sympathetic. Now, Kant is convinced that mathematics is the science par excellence. And yet it is not a cognition. But this claim in that context cannot be understood as if knowledge were now higher than science, for Kant does not intend to distinguish between the two terms or invert their order. Instead, he is demonstrating the insufficiency of mathematical knowledge *for experience*, that is, for empirical cognition of the natural world. Science and knowledge, then, apparently cannot be taken as absolute terms.

Is there a criterion that helps us to make sense of their relation in different contexts? Is there a univocal meaning to 'knowledge'? Unfortunately, there is no such criterion or univocity in Kant. Only a discerning contextualization can clarify his views. Our power of judgment must find its way without the assistance of a superior guide. The fact, however, is that this issue is of interest not simply in assessing the status of knowledge and that of the several sciences discussed by Kant. It turns out to be deeply consequential for how we understand critical philosophy itself and even Kant's idea of reason. If we are not clear on the relation between critical philosophy and knowledge in general, we are bound to miss a fundamental aspect of the critique of pure reason: its claim to scientificity.

The First Introduction to the third *Critique* begins by introducing the notion of a system of the higher cognitive faculties on which philosophy rests. We intend to divide not philosophy itself, writes Kant, but our higher faculty of a priori cognition through concepts (§ 2, *Ak* 20: 201, ENG 8). This does not imply we should subordinate all faculties of the soul to the faculty of cognition. Wolff, whom Kant has in mind here (§ 3, *Ak* 20: 205–6, ENG 11), is guilty of such reduction. It is futile, for no *vis repraesentativa* can unitarily account for the distinct faculty of cognition, the feeling of pleasure, and the faculty of desire. About these three different faculties Kant writes: "The exercise of all of them, however, is always grounded in the faculty of cognition, although not always on cognition (since a representation belonging to the faculty of cognition can also be an intuition, pure or empirical, without concepts)" (§ 11, *Ak* 20: 245, ENG 44). The exercise of the three faculties, in other words, is grounded respectively in the understanding, the power of judgment, and reason proper, which together constitute the faculty of cognition that is called 'pure reason.'

Bringing back the feeling of pleasure to the power of judgment and the faculty of desire to reason, however, is as arbitrary as reducing the faculty of cognition to the understanding, as we are going to see. But these passages may be puzzling and misleading also on account of the kind of cognition they refer to. A mere few months after this passage was written—it was not published, as is well-known, until Wilhelm Dilthey rediscovered the 'First Introduction'—Ludwig Heinrich Jakob called Kant's attention to the fact that the first *Critique* employs the word *Erkenntnis* in two different ways (May 4, 1790, *Ak* 11: 164). In one sense it is a genus of which intuition and concept are the species. In another, it is the representation composed of both intuition and concept. For his part, Hans Vaihinger noted "a certain ambiguity" to 'cognition' but went on to argue that it could be solved very easily if we assume a broad and a narrow sense of cognition.[1]

---

1. *Commentar*, 2: 2.

Unfortunately, Vaihinger's optimism is unwarranted, and Jakob's remark, while quite apt, is insufficient. The situation is reminiscent of the endless debate in the Aristotle scholarship on the scientificity of the *Metaphysics* and of all the disciplines founded by Aristotle. Briefly put: there is hardly a science that fulfills the definition of science in the *Posterior Analytics*, that is, a science is such when it pertains to one genus, demonstrates properties syllogistically starting from the intuition of its essences and their definition, proceeds through causes, is universal, and pertains to what is necessary. Mathematics does not because it deals with accidents (*to poson*, the quantitative), not substances. Logic is not listed by Aristotle in the formal division of the sciences. The practical sciences deal with things that come to be through our activity and are therefore dependent upon it. The natural sciences, including psychology, do not fulfill the requisites either. They are superior to mathematics insofar as they account for the principles of substances, but inferior as to the status of knowledge. For they investigate the *hoti*, not the *dioti*, i.e., the facts, not the reason for the facts, and deal with what is by and large the case: necessity does not rule the sublunar world.

Most importantly, first philosophy, the most noble, important, and directive science (*epistēmē kuriōtatē*), culminating in theology, does not proceed syllogistically or demonstratively. Besides, it certainly does not pertain to one genus since being is transcategorial and cuts across genera. In the case of the *Metaphysics*, the only way out is to assume a nonunivocal meaning of being (variously referred to as a unity *pros hen*, *tōi ephexes*, focal meaning, and the like). The *general* solution is to assume a conception of science as a rigorous (necessary and universal) demonstration of per se accidents (*sumbebēkota kath'hauta*) from given premises through a causal chain. This conception is no less genuinely Aristotelian.

Likewise with Kant. If we took our bearings from the famous definition of knowledge as the combination of intuition and concept, a good deal of what Kant claims would be immediately deprived of all sense. The difference from Aristotle is that I doubt that paronymy (Aristotle's middle course between strict univocity and mere homonymy, allowing for a unitary treatment of the different senses of being) applies to the several meanings attributed to knowledge by Kant. Equivocity seems more adequate to describe Kant's usage of the term. Let us see why.

If knowledge were science (implicitly, potentially, in disguise, etc.) and if the purpose of the Transcendental Deduction were to ground objectivity and along with it the judgments of science, then judgments of experience such as "The room is warm" would never attain objectivity and hold of the object but instead would be subjective and hold only for the subject.

To be sure, Kant himself is not directly responsible for the conflation of knowledge and science (what I called objective knowledge and knowledge of objectivity). In fact, responsibility largely falls in the camp of some of his interpreters. However, other requirements Kant imposes upon knowledge do indeed contradict one another.

That this is so in mathematics we have already seen. It can be denied the status of cognition only if we adopt the point of view of experience. It is not that mathematics falls short of the combination of concept and intuition. In fact, the science of mathematics is a paramount case of such combination. What is missing (from mathematics and from objective reality) is *empirical* intuition. Unfortunately, however, if empirical intuition were indispensable, indeed the touchstone of cognition, then the claim that a priori cognitions, alone universal and necessary, are the highest forms of knowledge (*KrV* B 3–4) would be senseless. We could reply on Kant's behalf that experience counts not insofar as it is empirical and contingent but insofar as the empirical is grounded in the pure. The counterreply would have to be that this is undoubtedly what interests transcendental philosophy, but also that it is empirical intuition qua empirical whose absence makes mathematics count as knowledge. Simply put, mathematics is one step removed from experience.

If establishing objective reality or real possibility—the conceptual result common to mathematics and transcendental philosophy—is not enough to qualify a set of cognitions as knowledge, then the critique of pure reason and a critical theory of experience would not only not be knowledge but also not qualify as a science of rules. Instead, they would merely be an explanatory analysis of conditions. In that case, the pure would not be reason's a priori product and the result of an activity. It would be implicit in the empirical. Kant would be a liberalized empiricist rather than a transcendental idealist.

If intuitions without concepts were blind and knowledge consisted only of intuition plus concept, as Kant says, how could pure intuition be a cognition? Kant could not claim that he wants to have, in the Aesthetic, a *science* of the senses and their a priori representations (*Ak* 29: 802, ENG 156), a science of all the a priori principles of sensibility (*KrV* A 21/B 36). If sensibility makes possible the order and relation of the manifold, takes place a priori in us, and gives us a pure cognition, how could the science of these rules come about if only together are concept and intuition a cognition? "Hence we distinguish the science of the rules of sensibility in general, i.e., aesthetic, from the science of the rules of understanding in general, i.e., logic" (*KrV* A 52/B 76). Sensibility and understanding are indeed distinct, but this distinctness also implies a relative independence of their functions and results.

Does this hold for concepts, too? If intuitions are a cognition in themselves, there is no disputing the fact that by and large they are best described as constituents, that is, subordinate and instrumental elements of the empirical cognition at stake in the combination thesis. Concepts are by and large instrumental to empirical cognition as predicates of possible judgments. They have to be asserted of the object in order to hold as cognitions. A concept, as a unity of marks, denotes something determinate but is no more than the problematic representation or thought of an object.[2] And yet there is a different sense in which concepts are cognitions: not insofar as they refer to an as yet undetermined object (*KrV* A 69/B 94), but qua pure concepts.

The combination thesis, the requirement that concept and intuition jointly give rise to a cognition, is at odds with the relative independence of functions and results. It even seems to contradict the *Stufenleiter* itself (the progression within the genus 'representation' at *KrV* A 320/B 377). The two points appear in the same section of the first *Critique*, the Transcendental Analytic. Let us take a closer look at this progression.

Intuition is that through which an object is given to us. Hence it is the immediate representation of the object. The concept is that in which that immediate representation is thought. Hence it is the mediate representation of it. That is, intuition and concept are both related in a progression and subspecies of one species (*objektive Perzeption, Erkenntnis*) belonging to the overarching genus, namely, representation.[3] Nonetheless, Kant is hardly a representationalist. In fact, the whole purpose of this progression is to counter the use (rampant in the Wolffian school, but we might as well say in Descartes or in common parlance) of 'idea' as a representation, for example of the color red. Kant is addressing polemically the notion

---

2. A very explicit and clear expression of this point occurs in a letter to Beck (July 3, 1792, *Ak* 11: 346–48), where Kant distinguishes between the unification of representations in a concept ('the black man') and the unification of representations in a judgment ('the man is black'). The former thinks the concept as determinate, the latter thinks the action of my determination of the concept. The first unity is subjective, the second, thanks to the copula, objective. The first predicates a quality of my representation, the second of the object. Things are different in the case of pure concepts, as we will see presently. Categories, which should be even more clearly instrumental to cognition and not a cognition per se, instead *are* cognitions—obviously, in a different sense.

3. *KrV* A 320/B 376–77. As we have seen, the ambiguity (and it is a major problem, into which I cannot go) is that representation can stand either for a modification of consciousness or for an appearance.

that representations are mental contents differing by degree of clarity and distinctness. For Kant representations instead are forms, that is, processes guided by rules and activities with a specific reference (to the subject or the object).[4]

To Wolff's and Meier's conception that every representation is a cognition in one way or other, Kant objects that often representations are obscure and we ignore the fact that we have them (*Refl* 1677, *Ak* 16: 79). The set of representations is therefore larger than the set of cognitions. Accordingly, Kant proposes a taxonomy of representations excluding unconscious ones. He begins with perception, i.e., a conscious representation. Perception referring to the subject alone is *sensatio*, but when it refers to the object it is *cognitio*. Cognition "is either an intuition or a concept (*intuitus vel conceptus*)"[5] (*KrV* A 320/B 376–77).[6]

The progression continues with the distinction of pure and empirical concepts and with the concepts of reason, namely, ideas. Here Kant does not say that ideas are not cognitions, and yet this point is implicit when he says that ideas go "beyond the possibility of experience" (*KrV* A 320/B 376–77). Still, we may wonder what the criterion for this progression is. In it ideas are introduced less homogeneously than the previous representations, all of which not only follow from the previous ones but also according to the ramification of a tree-like principle. For example, we have divided representation into those that are with and those that are without consciousness. Conscious representations are divided into those that refer to the subject and those that refer to the object. The latter are cognitions, divided into immediate and mediate (intuition and concept). The latter, i.e., concepts, are

4. For a brilliant analysis of thirteen meanings of representation, see §§ 44–45 of Husserl's Fifth *Logical Investigation* (*Gesammelte Werke*, 19/1).

5. Unlike the Latin *vel*, the German *entweder-oder*, correctly translated by Guyer–Wood as a disjunctive *either-or*, suggests an alternative. But this is not, it seems to me, Kant's meaning (the fact that otherwise he would have used the Latin *aut* is part of the problem but is not decisive, for Kant often uses also the Latin *vel* as disjunctive: see, for example, *Ak* 16: 79). Differently stated, this passage implies not that cognition is either intuition or concept, but that it can be considered as the one or the other or both. This passage does *not* contradict, that is, the combination thesis. But nor does it put in question the relative independence of intuition I have emphasized in chapter 2, § 7.

6. As we can see from the presence of *sensatio*, if the distinction between judgments of perception and judgments of experience is to be discarded or considered spurious, then so is this progression. This progression returns, substantially unaltered, throughout Kant's lifetime. See *Refl* 2394, *Ak* 16: 342–43; *Refl* 2835 and 2836, *Ak* 16: 536–39; the *Jaesche Logic* in *Ak* 9: 91, ENG 589; the Vienna Logic, *Ak* 24: 904, ENG 348, and 24: 846, ENG 299–300. See Rumore, *L'ordine delle idee*.

further divided into empirical and pure. The latter, pure concepts, give rise to ideas as concepts of reason.

Here for the first time in this progression we get an element without a contrary or a correlate. Kant does not specify if ideas are conscious representations made of pure concepts referring to objects, as the progression implies, or conscious representations made of pure concepts not referring to objects (because no intuition can correspond to it), as we know they are. But if they do not refer to objects and here Kant has silently deviated from the criterion of cognition or objective reference and opted for the sense of representation as an element in pure reason, then we should take notice of this shift explicitly.

Further, we should ask why schemata are not included in the progression. For, like ideas, they are not a cognition in themselves, and yet they are the sensible concept of objects in accordance with the categories (*KrV* A 146/B 186), an indispensable element and mediation for concept and intuition to work together.

Consider the following reply we can offer on Kant's behalf: unlike ideas, schemata are *exhausted* by their bridging heterogeneous elements. A schema is not an additional representation over and above time and pure concepts. That is, the function of schemata is instrumental and mediating. Therefore they have no reality in themselves, whereas ideas are quite real at least from a practical point of view. Besides, if they are instrumental at all, it is in that they are regulative for empirical cognition: their function and identity do not consist solely in the mediation between two heterogeneous elements.

Or we could say this. If the concept of representation is wider than knowledge, it is because we have obscure representations. This is why one branch of the tree of this progression, the one we start to divide, begins with conscious representations. We need to perceive representations in ourselves for them to become cognitions. The difference is that ideas are conscious whereas schemata are a hidden art of which we are scarcely ever conscious.

These, unfortunately, would not be successful replies, the former because the reality (certainly the practical reality) of ideas is ostensibly not on Kant's mind here, the latter because schemata and ideas are equally denied the status of independent cognitions and can be equally obscure. Rather than appeasing us, in fact, this added requirement of awareness in the *Stufenleiter* raises a host of different interesting questions.

First, ideas are not necessarily conscious. We have seen that an idea differs from a schema of the idea in that the former guides us unbeknownst to ourselves, while the latter is what we contribute to produce. The idea of cosmic philosophy, in particular, is compared to a seed precisely in view of this aspect. Recall that it grows in us irrespective of our consciousness of its unobtrusive and impersonal action.[7]

Second, consciousness and understanding do not overlap. As we saw in chapter 2, it would be wrong to equate consciousness with understanding and obscurity with sensibility. This is the position of Wolff, Meier, and Baumgarten. For Kant, instead, obscurity and lack of consciousness span different faculties, including the understanding (Ak 25: 31–32). A lot goes on in us, as it were, before we are ready for a conscious decision such as the assertion of a determinant judgment. For example, provisional judgments, described much like the schematism as a "secret procedure of the mind" (Ak 25: 481), accompany our perceptions and guide our judgment without our awareness (PhilEnz, Ak 29: 24).

Likewise, our reflection on sensible impressions is a relentless work of which we are mostly unaware. It has become natural to us through habit, and we mistakenly attribute it to sensible intuition (V-Met-L1/Pölitz, Ak 28: 233–34, ENG 52) or feeling. In the B Deduction itself, Kant speaks of the combination of a manifold as the product of spontaneity "whether we are conscious of it or not" (KrV B 130), suggesting that even intellectual synthesis may be unconscious. This is a very curious result if the understanding is the faculty of concepts for knowledge and if cognitions are a subset of representations because they exclude from their group unconscious representations.

But the thesis of awareness or consciousness is problematic for other reasons as well. Without going into the famous problems about Kant's theory of self-consciousness, let me note that if consciousness is defined as the representation that a representation is mine or is in me,[8] consciousness is also somehow derivative of the concept 'representation.' Still, consciousness does not appear in the Stufenleiter. The reason ostensibly is that consciousness is here thought of as a predicate of representation, not as one kind thereof. Representation is divided into conscious and unconscious, and further into representation related to the object and representation related to the subject. The progression regards the relation of representations to the object. It aims at the definition of cognition. Consciousness is not a cognition because it is a representation related to the subject.

---

7. Whether or not it is unconscious, an idea is rarely for Kant the object of distinct knowledge. He says repeatedly, for example, that in our most elementary decisions we all take our bearings by a certain idea of justice that we do not usually question. But to ascertain what it is we need much thought, even a fully developed Science of Right.

8. As in V-Met/L1/Pölitz, Ak 28: 227, ENG 46, and Log, Ak 9: 33, ENG 544.

Nevertheless, can this representation of a representation be a case of intuition plus concept? Cases such as, for example, "I am aware that my math is not up to speed for the solution of this problem," whereby awareness is construed as intuition and math as a concept, do not fit the bill. Awareness is never an intuition. In this example, it is equivalent to a mode of knowledge. Statements relative to self-consciousness are of the form "I *know* that I . . . ," except that this cognition is hardly a case of combining intuition and concept.

In the central sections of the Transcendental Deduction, a thought is contrasted with a cognition (*KrV* B 146), which needs an intuition. Transcendental apperception's self-consciousness is not an intuition (*KrV* B 157) but an act of spontaneity and a thought, unlike self-knowledge. I can know myself only as appearance in my inner sense. Here concept and intuition cooperate as they typically do for knowledge of appearances. Is my being conscious of a representation as mine a cognition? If it is, it is a cognition of my empirical objectivized self, whereby, however, it becomes unclear how a relation of belonging (the representation that a representation is in me) can be brought back to the model of combination. If, instead, it is the thought of the original synthetic unity of apperception or the I-think that may accompany my representations, this creates a gap between the transcendental apperception's self-consciousness and my empirical self-consciousness. The latter is treated as one appearance among others, and the former is more like a cognition of rules and the empty even if primary condition of experience than a self-consciousness. What is worse is that the *thought* of the original synthetic unity of apperception is precisely that which Kant denies should be a cognition.

With a yet different and bewildering twist of the sense of 'knowledge,' Kant now writes that the original synthetic unity of apperception is "the first pure cognition of the understanding" (*das erste reine Verstandeserkenntnis, KrV* B 137). This statement is at loggerheads with (1) the combination thesis of the Analytic and (2) the specific difference between thought and knowledge in these very pages. Still, it is not difficult to explain, in particular by Kant's concern in the same section, that is, to account for *knowledge of principles* (*KrV* B 138). It cannot be confused with the self-knowledge of me as appearance to myself regarding which points 1 and 2 were set. It means that because the unity of combination of the manifold performed by the understanding is the supreme principle of all cognition (*KrV* B 135), the universal condition of all knowledge is not itself a cognition like knowledge of appearances.

And yet it is a cognition of a different sort, one not contemplated in any definition given so far. Once again if we want to stick to the familiar usage of the pair condition-conditioned, we must at least make an effort at taking the condition in a less abstract sense. In this case, to know the original synthetic unity of apperception means to know that every unity presupposes a prior synthesis. The a priori synthesis of thought makes possible the unity of concepts. Unities are the result of an activity of synthesis, and this original a priori synthesis can be known—except, as I pointed out, not in the same sense as appearances, but as a principle and an act.[9]

What makes this point even stranger, however, is that contrary to Kant's anti-Cartesian and anti-Leibnizian strategy in his critique of traditional theology and in his thesis that existence is not a predicate and cannot be drawn from a concept, Kant now says that the representation I-think entails *that I-am* (*KrV* B 157). To be sure, this is a thought, i.e., not a concept but an act of determination whereby I determine only *that* I am, not *what* I am. It can be known not in experience or as an appearance but only as the primary and most universal act of positing (ibid.).[10]

If 'knowledge' is perplexing, we do not fare better if we turn to 'science.' A science is an architectonic, not a technical unity. It is a system guided by an idea, which the *Jaesche Logic* opposes to common knowledge as an aggregate (*Ak* 9: 72, ENG 575). In view of this definition, we can well understand how the systematic knowledge of Right should be called "juridical science" (*iurisscientia*) in the *Metaphysics of Morals* (*Ak* 6: 229, ENG 386). Because the power of judgment is key in the application of laws, it is also understandable how such science is inferior to *iurisprudentia* (legal expertise). It is also understandable that Kant should say that we *know* that a Louis XIV once lived (*Ak* 18: 288–89). Here knowledge means conscious assertion of unalterable truths as opposed to belief (e.g., in the seven kings of Rome, for which all documents are lacking).

9. In the V-Met/L1/Pölitz (Ak 28: 225, ENG 45), Kant distinguishes between two senses of the I: as soul and as intelligence. The soul interacts with the body, and therefore has even a location, while "as intelligence I am nowhere" (ibid.). The soul says: 'this is my body,' or 'I am a body,' whereas intelligence says: 'what attaches to me is a body.' The I of intelligence is a logical principle of unification. It makes no sense to ask questions about it regarding, among other things, death and immortality that we can legitimately ask about the soul. See Fabbrizi, *Mente*, 198–240.

10. In the *Prolegomena* (§ 46, Ak 4: 333n, ENG 125), Kant goes so far as to say that the I is not a concept, but the "feeling" of an existence without a concept! In the refutation of Mendelssohn in the Paralogisms he even says, "The I-think is an empirical proposition" (*KrV* B 422n)! In the V-Met/L1/Pölitz (Ak 28: 233–34, ENG 52), consciousness as representation of my representations is "a self-perception, a perception [*Perception*]"! As Henrich has shown, Kant's theory of self-consciousness is of incalculable importance (see my "Autocoscienza"), but there is no denying its confusion. The confusion in these pages stems, I believe, from treating self-consciousness as a representation.

But it does strike me that knowledge is grounded in one case on reasons (in Aristotle's terms recalled before on *to dioti*, the 'why'), in the other on the attestation of facts (on *to hoti*, the 'that'). Kant's assertion that such knowledge of past facts grounds history as "true science" (ibid.) is harder to grasp (and swallow), for I fail to see what idea or system should be behind my supposed science of Louis XIV.

In the first *Critique* what Kant calls practical knowledge not only is understandable but even accords with the combination thesis. If I refer to my object in order to realize it (*KrV* B ix–x), and in it I represent to myself what ought to be (*KrV* A 633/B 661), then I have both a possible intuitive object and a thought through which I determine it. It is a pity that this is not sufficient to substantiate the combination thesis, because we are talking about not appearances in experience, but *noumena*. But at least it is clear that both are required.

It is not as clear how Kant, speaking of Moses Mendelssohn, can call 'knowledge' (and not, say, 'belief') the "ever increasing cognition of purposiveness in everything we see" (*KrV* B 426). But it is even more shocking to read in the Mrongovius Metaphysics that ideas are "cognitions of reason"![11] More than anything else, what cannot square with the combination thesis, and in fact introduces a whole new concept of knowledge, is the *Erkenntnis nach der Analogie* of the *Prolegomena* (§ 58, *Ak* 4: 357, ENG 146).

Here Kant writes that reason can find completion and satisfaction only in those noumena it cannot know, an immaterial being and an intelligible world. In the attempt to satisfy its need for unity, reason finds "a real connection" (*eine wirkliche Verknüpfung*) of the known to the unknown (*Prol* § 57, *Ak* 4: 354, ENG 144), the relation that the world may have to a principle outside it. Thereby reason does not attribute to God any properties, for that would be "*dogmatic* anthropomorphism" (*Ak* 4: 357, ENG 146). Instead, it attributes properties to the *relation* of this being to our world and allows itself "a *symbolic* anthropomorphism" (ibid.). What I *know* is not a divine being, but "what it is for me, that is, with respect to the world of which I am a part" (ibid.). This is *analogical cognition*, "which surely does not signify, as the word is usually taken, an imperfect similarity between two things, but

---

11. "But there are also cognitions of reason, which cannot be given in experience. These arise from the cognitions of the understanding, but reason extends them so that they never can be given in experience" (*Ak* 29: 875, ENG 245).

rather a perfect similarity between two relations in wholly dissimilar things" (*Prol* § 58, *Ak* 4: 357, ENG 146–47).[12]

If one has in mind the critique of traditional theology (the analogy with nature, physical theology, and moral theology, *KrV* A 631–32/B 659–60) in the Transcendental Dialectic, it is very strange to see this analogical knowledge described as a cognition barely two years after the first *Critique*. If once again, as in the difference between judgments of perception and of experience, we minimized the importance of the *Prolegomena* on this point, we would not only choose arbitrarily one version of Kant over another owing to its greater notoriety (possibly success, plausibility, or proximity to our historical situation and taste). We would also blind ourselves to the first important occurrence of what in the third *Critique* will be the as-if of purposiveness and of ethicotheology in relation to the notion of symbol. There are other concepts present in the *Prolegomena* but absent from the first *Critique*: for example, the discussion of the handedness of space and of incongruent triangles does not appear where it could have, in the Transcendental Aesthetics or the Amphiboly. Regarding symbolic anthropomorphism one may wonder why in the first *Critique* there is no trace of it: if not in A (1781), then in B (1787), wherein Kant could have easily fitted it. But before we can even ask this question we need to settle preliminarily the issue of the compatibility of these positions.[13]

Upon closer investigation, in the chapter "On the Final Aim of the Natural Dialectic of Human Reason" in the Transcendental Dialectic, what is criticized is ascribing properties to God and naming this illegitimate move a cognition. No tension there, then. In fact, if symbolic anthropomorphism is missing, the notions of analogy and its 'as-if' are not. When I assume a divine being, writes Kant there, I do not have the slightest concept of it. Yet through it reason can approach the contingent with a regulative principle in its hands and "obtain the most perfect satisfaction in regard to the greatest unity for which it is searching in its empirical use" (*KrV* A 676/B 704). Thereby I do not know God, but only think God "in order to make it into the schema of a regulative principle for the greatest possible empirical use of

12. The examples in the footnote include such analogies as this: "the causality of the highest cause is that, with respect to the world, which human reason is with respect to its works of art. Thereby the nature of the cause remains unknown to me: I compare only its effect (the order of the world), which is known to me, . . . with the effects of human reason that are known to me" (*Ak* 4: 360n, ENG 148).

13. On the metaphysics of analogy in Kant, see Marty, *La naissance de la métaphysique*; Faggiotto, *Introduzione alla metafisica kantiana dell'analogia*; Melchiorre, *Analogia*; Munzel, "Beautiful"; L. Bianco, *Analogia e storia*; Callanan, "Kant on Analogy."

my reason" (*KrV* A 679/B 707). The *"purposive* unity of things" opens up for reason "new prospects for connecting up things in the world in accordance with teleological laws, and thereby attaining to the greatest systematic unity among them" (*KrV* A 687/B 715). This is all in the interest of *speculative* reason (ibid.). *"Without any doubt"* must we presuppose a divine being (*KrV* A 697/B 725) in analogy with the empirical concept of an intelligence. But this is *"by no means"* a cognition (ibid.).

So one may wonder why that which both A and B called the schema of a regulative concept, i.e., thought or faith as opposed to knowledge, is in the *Prolegomena* called a cognition. True, this is analogical cognition. I do not know God in Him/Herself but I do know the relation of God to the world. But do I? Or do I merely *think* or represent to myself one relation between the supreme being and the world as the one I favor based on my faith? For example, take the relation mentioned by the Athenian in Plato's *Laws*: we are the gods' playthings, puppets on a string.[14] Or consider the myth in the *Protagoras* (320d–322a): our gifts are Prometheus's belated attempt, obtained through a crime, to compensate for the absentminded and incompetent distribution of powers on the part of Epimetheus (whose name means 'the one who thinks after the fact,' after the mess he has made).[15] Would a senseless creation of this sort be counted by the *Prolegomena* as a good instance of symbolic anthropomorphism? If it were not, is it perhaps because Kant is presupposing a benevolent omnipotent creator granting us hope in immortality? If it were, why call it a cognition?

Also, it is strange that the 'known' in the relation of the known to the unknown should be "the world" and not nature. And that when Kant claims that I know an object directly and know only indirectly its relation to other terms he seems to suggest that direct knowledge is a form of complete determination, a notion that he criticized in the Transcendental Ideal as untenable. Finally, it is even stranger to recall that in the Amphiboly Kant wrote that appearances are known as "nothing but relations" (*KrV* A 265/B 321). In the analogy between reason and its works of art, Kant says we do not pretend to know a cause in itself; a cause is known to us only through its effects. But do we ever know a cause in itself?

Plausible though these questions may be, these points can perhaps be reconciled to different degrees with the spirit of the different contexts in which they are uttered. Whatever we think about them, however, objective

---

14. 1: 644d ff. The image is also used by Aristotle to illustrate physical motion in *De generatione animalium* 2.1, 734b10ff. and *De motu animalium* 7, 701b 2–4.

15. See my "Homo Faber.".

knowledge as well as knowledge of objectivity as the hallmark of true cognition definitely is called into question by this new understanding of knowledge. The model of a reduction of all knowledge to the intellectual synthesis of a given manifold expressed in an objectively valid, if not categorical judgment cannot possibly apply to this use of knowledge.

The following interpretation is rather common in the secondary literature. After the first (and second) *Critiques*, Kant discovers the lawfulness of the contingent and is led to investigate a power of judgment that cannot be resolved in the determination of its objects. Reflection becomes central. Indeed, if all thought is judgment, in the third *Critique* Kant discovers the originally reflective mode of judgment, which is therefore a search for the appreciation of singulars as bearers of possible universal meanings in a multifarious experience not reducible to science and its objectivizing attitude.

Much of this interpretation is sound, of course. The first and third *Critiques* are clearly linked through the relation between judging and reflecting, searching and determining, regulative and constitutive functions. The continuity between power of judgment, schematism, Amphiboly, and Appendix to the Dialectic in the first, and reflection, power of judgment, disinterested pleasure, and purposiveness in the third, is crucial. As I said before, only a superficial reading can rest content with the idea that the first *Critique* has to do with scientific knowledge and the third with aesthetics and teleology.

Still, this interpretation presupposes some unwarranted assumptions. It invites us to set aside the *Critique of Pure Reason* and pushes us to look for the true and/or better (i.e., emancipated from the letter and truer to his inspiration) Kant in the *Critique of Judgment*. The third *Critique* is the liberation from the fetters of an objectivizing reason and the discovery of the indefinite and contingent variety of species and forms that cannot be brought back to readymade concepts. The problem with this reading, however, is that the third *Critique* aims not at replacing or correcting the first but at investigating the a priori principle of a different faculty of pure reason, the feeling of pleasure and displeasure. If this reading were correct, Kant would have to admit to abandoning many of the key points of his first *Critique*, which he does not. (In fact, in the 1790s he relentlessly reelaborates the first *Critique* and its results without forsaking its main inspiration.) Instead what he discovers is a deeper rather than an altogether new link between reflection and determination in the constitution of reason.

If therefore this interpretation does not restore a *true* Kant, then perhaps it can give us a *better* Kant. In fact, however, all that it does is simplify the first *Critique*. In the third *Critique* Kant does not suddenly discover reflection, the ideas, and all that cannot be covered by the model of determination and the constraints of a rigid understanding. Instead, these concepts live, albeit in a somewhat muted fashion, in the *Critique of Pure Reason* along with what for Kant is its core, the Transcendental Deduction of the Pure Concepts.

Significantly, the symbolic anthropomorphism of the *Prolegomena* is embedded in the discussion of the limits of reason. We do not transgress them but "hold ourselves" (*Ak* 4: 357, ENG 146) to them if we judge the relation alone and do not pretend to talk about the object. In other words, this new sense of 'knowledge' is introduced in the midst of pure reason's reflection on itself. As a result, it becomes less strange. We know that the critique of pure reason is a science of the limits of reason. Cosmic philosophy in particular is a science of the relation of pure reason to its ends. In its autarchy, reason is an organic unity that plans an architectonic order for its scopes of legislation. But its gaze is on itself, on the limited totality that it is. Reason can aspire to complete self-knowledge because it is a self-enclosed system.

It is this knowledge of pure reason's a priori principles insofar as they make possible experience (and with it the combination of intuition and concept) that is at odds with the combination thesis. That is, it is transcendental philosophy that contravenes the constraints of that which the combination thesis makes possible, constraints that all too often are taken as Kant's exclusive sense of knowledge, if not of rational activity. Transcendental philosophy as a peculiar and fundamental type of knowledge is the paramount example of violation of the combination thesis.

Consider these passages. Given what we have just seen, it is no wonder that *philosophy* is called *knowledge* (*KrV* A 714/B 742). As a knowledge of its ignorance it is indeed a *science* (*KrV* A 758/B 786). Transcendental logic is a *science* of the pure cognition of objects (*KrV* B 81–82). Its *knowledge* alone, in the form of an a priori synthesis, can produce experience and the concept of an object. Its *knowledge* is the ground of experience itself (*Fortschritte*, *Ak* 20: 274, ENG 375). The pure cognition of the understanding with its categories is *knowledge*; it is not the regress to a condition (*KrV* A 62/B 87): that is, the transcendental logic is not a discourse on the conditions of possibility, a "that without which not," but the very solution of the problem of metaphysics. Categories are "pure a priori *cognitions*" (*KrV* A 119, italics mine) and not empty forms or conditions for a priori sciences other than philosophy. Indeed the science of the principles of sensibility and reason is an *a priori knowledge* through which objects are possible (*Ak* 28: 77–78). *The possibility of experience is a cognition through which objects are given to us* (*KrV* A 217/B 264).

2. The Synthetic Knowledge of Transcendental Philosophy

If the Doctrine of Method of the first *Critique* is cast aside, rarely read and discussed in the literature, the chapter "The Discipline of Pure Reason in Regard to Its Proofs" is virtually unknown.[16] In the "proofs of transcendental and synthetic propositions," reason "may not apply itself directly to the object by means of its concepts, but must first establish the objective validity of the concepts and the possibility of their synthesis a priori" (*KrV* A 782/B 810). Their proof does not show that the given concept of an event leads directly to the concept of its cause, but "rather it shows that experience itself would be impossible without such a connection" (*KrV* A 783/B 811).

Kant presents the three rules of a proof in transcendental philosophy: (1) the preliminary examination of the principles on which to build and the right we have to use them, (2) the uniqueness of the proof (only a single proof can be found), and (3) its ostensive character (proofs should be always ostensive, not apagogic and negative: *KrV* A 789/B 817). An ostensive or direct proof both merits the conviction of truth and gives insight into its sources, whereas the apagogic proof is based on contradiction and is therefore less satisfying for reason. True, philosophical proofs are discursive, not intuitive, and cannot be *mathemata*. But they cannot be *dogmata* either, i.e., synthetic proofs through concepts alone. What is Kant's third way?

If he is not inconsistent, surely Kant oscillates on whether or not this proof is direct. Often he will use the mediate syntheticity of real possibility or objective reality (the fact that its pure concepts refer a priori to possible intuitions) as a *second-degree ostensive* proof rather than as an indirect or apagogic one. Even if it proceeds from concepts alone, transcendental philosophy is thereby mediately or indirectly synthetic.

This, however, appears to mask a fundamental problem.[17] Reason is synthetic because it constitutes a priori the form of an object in general to which all experience will have to conform. Kant writes that it is "transcendental cognition" (*KrV* A 783/B 811) that produces objectivity. *Transcendental synthesis* is something "with which . . . only the philosopher can succeed, but which never concerns more than a thing in general" (*KrV* A 719/B 749). The difficulty is that forms-contents, objective reality, the possibility of experience, are reason's production for every user of reason, but not every user of reason is a transcendental philosopher. Were it so, we would have to charge

---

16. A notable exception is Barale, *Kant*, 204–55.
17. I wish to thank Richard Velkley for his comments on this point.

Kant with conflating reason's production of objectivity, active in all rational agents, and the transcendental philosopher's synthesis.

This problem arises only if we set up an opposition between reason and philosophy. But Kant does not mean that reason produces whereas philosophy reflects. The fact is that transcendental philosophy is nothing but reason's self-knowledge. The opposition, if any, is between the synthetic principles all rational agents spontaneously and unreflectively employ and the isolation and independent knowledge of those principles that transcendental philosophy aims at (*KrV* B 13). When it comes to transcendental philosophy I think we need to question the standard opposition between reflection and synthesis. Reason's self-knowledge qua transcendental philosophy's reflection is synthetic, i.e., its production is the exhibition of the principles at work in every use of reason.

In this chapter Kant writes that philosophy's proof is not a theorem, but a principle (*KrV* A 737/B 765). A principle produces its objective reality and is *its own ground*. It "first makes possible its ground of proof, namely experience, and must always be presupposed in this" (ibid.). Reason produces possible experience, which in turn makes philosophical proofs apodictic.

A principle is wholly unlike a judgment regarding appearances or an objective cognition. In a principle, reason reflects on, indeed, sees how it acts. In a principle, reason has insight into its own constitution. It understands that a production and a condition are not mutually exclusive but in fact are jointly its inner movement, its activity. A principle of reason exists in the manner of an activity of positing that at once comprehends itself as such, rather than as an inert first datum. Reason's self-knowledge is not simply the cognition of the categories and the understanding's constitution of objects; it is a comprehensive organic totality made up of reflection and determination, regulative and constitutive principles, ideas, concepts, and intuitions.

Among the many implications of transcendental philosophy's proofs, two are very important. First, if knowledge is a term used in different senses for both empirical cognition and reason's transcendental reflective knowledge of its own procedures, a qualification regarding cognition and truth becomes necessary. In its ordinary understanding truth is the correspondence of empirical judgments with objects. We have seen in chapter 1 that the mark of empirical truth is reason's idea of unity (*KrV* A 651/B 679); its contents are the rules of the understanding, which is the source of all truth (*der Quell aller Wahrheit, KrV* A 237/B 296). Transcendental cognition is a kind of knowledge that results not in empirical evidence of any sort, but in its very possibility. Does it aim at truth? And if it does, is there an analogous touchstone of truth for it? Kant writes that he seeks the truth of a priori rules that "contain the ground of the possibility of experience" (ibid.).[18] This truth is not the truth of empirical judgments. It cannot be tested for correspondence to its object. Nevertheless, it is truth in a different, more fundamental sense: the truth of reason's own self-examination. Once again, the discourse on the conditions of possibility remains abstract and analytical only if we take them to be indifferent and neutral with regard to what they make possible. Kant instead confers upon them, and upon transcendental philosophy in general, the claim to a specific sense of synthesis, knowledge, and truth.

A second implication is that the criterion of possible experience, which is a product of pure reason making objects possible, cannot also be used to evaluate reason's self-knowledge. The combination thesis on knowledge as experience cannot be applied to reason's knowledge as the a priori synthesis and production of the possibility of experience. For reason is not an appearance or an object. It cannot be experienced or judged by the understanding. This is why in chapter 1 I spoke of the danger that reason's tribunal drama may end in a mistrial.

Kant's prophetic announcements of the advent of a new era are not just a programmatic manifesto for a future science. He is convinced that, thanks to his critique of pure reason and the knowledge of limits, metaphysics is finally a science, a finished system. Unlike a boundary, which is merely negative, a limit is positive and as constitutive of reason as are its ideas. Ideas are not constitutive of any object but do articulate reason's internal unity and show reason's innermost tendency toward totality. Recall that reason's knowledge of limits results not in a negative prohibition, but in a positive cognition: reason knows why it cannot know the in-itself. It knows it has ultimate questions that drive its every concern.

And yet note that 'ultimate' does not mean 'doomed to inconclusiveness.' Ultimate questions are not bound to remain beyond our grasp, for reason is not powerless over what it makes. In particular it is not powerless over its being in itself dialectical. Once all errors have been eliminated (*KrV* A xii), Kant's philosophy gives a final juridical adjudication, a permanent solution comparable to a state of perpetual peace (*KrV* A 777/B 805), a lasting and peaceful rule of reason over understanding and sensibility (*KrV* A 465/B 493). This is because, unlike other rational sciences, metaphysics has "the rare good fortune . . . that it can fully embrace the entire field of cognitions

18. Guyer and Wood refer us to a correction Kant added to his copy of the first edition of the book. The text said that the rules of the understanding are true a priori and even the source of all truth, and it is not enough to have expounded what is true. He now adds: "what is true, as little as it may be, but also to expand his cognition" (*KrV* A 237/B 296).

belonging to it and thus can complete its work and lay it down for posterity as a principal framework that can never be enlarged" (*KrV* B xxiii–iv).

In a passage that seems to echo and indeed embody the three rules of synthetic and transcendental proofs (*KrV* A 3–5), Kant tells us that metaphysics builds its edifice after having assured itself of its foundations, having brought back its concepts to their sources. The critique leads thus necessarily to science (*KrV* B 22–23). All conflicts of reason with itself are entirely over (*KrV* A 516/B 544). The certainty of the critique of pure reason rests on the same self-sufficient totality or systematic unity on which the analysis of the faculty of the understanding relies (*KrV* A 64–67/B 89–92): the unity of the organism formed by a principle, which can grow only internally and to which no further part or element can be added.

The definitive elimination of errors is not always asserted so bombastically. Elsewhere, transcendental illusion (*Schein*) is considered inevitable and does not cease even when it is uncovered (*KrV* A 297/B 353). Reason's dialectic is an adventure we cannot free ourselves from (*KrV* A 236/B 295), nor will it cease to lead our reason on with false hopes (*KrV* A 298/B 354). When it comes to metaphysics, the image of the seduction of innocence is recurrent. Sometimes it happens through no fault of reason (*KrV* A vii), other times because of its inner dialectic. But even when reason is a poor innocent thing led astray by a superior malicious force, what invariably prevails is the appeal to responsibility in the conflict, aiming not just at a truce but at the production of enduring peace. Reason must take upon itself the task of giving a permanent solution to its problems.

Because the questions originate from the same sources from which answers are drawn, ignorance is no excuse. In a section bearing the revealing title "The Transcendental Problems of Pure Reason, Insofar As They Absolutely Must Be Capable of a Solution," Kant writes that in contrast to the natural sciences, where much remains uncertain and some issues are insoluble owing to the givenness of objects independent of our concepts, "there is no question at all dealing with an object given by pure reason that is insoluble by this very same human reason" (*KrV* A 477/B 505). In another passage (recalled in the introduction), which the interpreters of Kant keen on the inescapable finitude of our faculties could use, Kant writes:

> Thus we cannot evade the obligation of giving at least a critical resolution of the questions of reason before us by lamenting the narrow limits of our reason and confessing, with the appearance of a modest [*demutsvollen*] self-knowledge, that it lies beyond our reason to settle whether the world has existed from eternity or has a beginning, whether world-space is filled to

infinity with beings or is enclosed within certain boundaries [etc.]. . . . For each of these questions concerns an object that can be given nowhere but in our thoughts, namely the absolutely unconditioned totality of the synthesis of appearances. (*KrV* A 481/B 509)

This does not imply that our questions on, say, a future life admit of a detailed speculative answer. Instead, it means that the critique has shown that they cannot be answered speculatively and that a practical faith is both legitimate and justified. The critique has given our power of judgment a criterion to distinguish knowledge from illusion. All dogmatic assertion has been shown to be impossible. As Kant writes: "The critical solution, however, which can be completely certain, does not consider the question objectively at all, but instead asks about the foundations of the cognition on which it is grounded" (*KrV* A 512/B 484).

We are sent back to the reflexivity of reason and to its tribunal. In the final words of the Doctrine of Elements, the critique has concluded the trial it has undertaken and drawn up "an exhaustive dossier, as it were, of these proceedings and store[d] it in the archives of human reason, so as to prevent future errors of a similar kind" (*KrV* A 704/B 732).

3. Metaphysics, Critical and Transcendental Philosophy

Throughout his life Kant never tired of exploring, recasting, returning afresh to, and shifting positions on his basic theses. Most important in this regard is his central concern: the meaning he attaches to a critique of pure reason. The sixteen tables reconstructed by Tonelli, presenting diagrams with as many different (often vastly diverging) classifications of the sciences, of philosophy, of knowledge over seventeen years, are the best evidence of these continuous transformations.[19] I think that never before has the critique of pure reason appeared so obviously and dramatically as a work in progress.

Metaphysics, critical philosophy, and transcendental logic or philosophy relentlessly shift their function and relative position. Sometimes they are separated neatly; other times they are identified and then distinguished again as the meaning of one term is revised or qualified, or a general scheme is reformulated wherein they can no longer fit together the way they did. As Kant's work progressed over the years, they hardly ever referred to the same object. But they are not isolated stars, each with its own mass, luminosity,

19. As is Tonelli's masterful analysis in *Kant's Critique*, 236–341. The tables are at 325–41.

and velocity, that allow us to orient ourselves. Though distinct, they form a constellation whose weight, movement, and light are unitary.

The comparison to a constellation may not be fully adequate because it underlines the unity but minimizes the active cooperation definitive of the interrelation of the relata. Consider then how they work as a team. As one advances, withdraws, or attacks, the other two will alternately cover, reposition themselves, rest in the trenches, bask in a consolidated vantage point or a newly vanquished place, or retreat to their former boundaries. Kant's hesitations and changes regarding their mutual relations are little short of incredible.

Take metaphysics. That Kant was the Robespierre of metaphysics, as Heine thought, or that before him Mendelssohn called Kant the all-destroyer (*der Alles-zermalmende Kant*), makes sense, if at all, only for one of the five or six meanings of metaphysics we find in Kant. This is a meaning we would be well advised to contextualize. Metaphysics cannot be approached independently of a pure reason, of which we can in turn emphasize the knowledge of experience, the a priori synthesis, the drive to trespass limits, the legislation, and so on. A critique of pure reason as a study of the conditions of possibility of experience is possible not as alternative to, but because it is undertaken as, a solution of the problem of metaphysics. The solution can only be comprehensive and must take into account the totality of its meanings. The architectonic unity of thought ultimately shapes and determines what we mean by metaphysics.

Metaphysics has several different understandings attached to it. It is in turn a natural disposition; a science; a science of the a priori principles of reason; a metaphysics of nature or of morals; an access to the supersensible; a metaphysics expressing the priorities of the Canon and the postulates of practical reason; and the traditional metaphysics Kant aims at delegitimizing once and for all.

If these are examples of its possible objects, its predicates are also varied. Metaphysics is general and special; immanent and transcendent; positive and negative; speculative and practical. No less diverse are its *functions* or *ends* as the critique comes to the fore as its ground: a pathway to wisdom; knowledge of the supersensible; a canon or an organon; a discipline or a doctrine, in particular a system of pure reason or a propaedeutic to one.[20] Let us address some of these characterizations in turn.

---

20. At times the connection among these different functions and ends is thematic, as in *Refl* 4849 (*Ak* 18: 5–8). Metaphysics here is the absolute unity of reason as the concordance of all ends (condition for wisdom). Its steps are (1) the origin of synthetic a priori knowledge, (2) the

1. A Natural Disposition

The *Prolegomena*, having stated at the outset that metaphysics is the production of synthetic a priori cognitions such as "All that is substance in things persists" (*Ak* 4: 273, ENG 66) and investigated its possibility as a science, comes eventually to the "Solution to the general question" (*Ak* 4: 365, ENG 154). As we know, the analytic method of the *Prolegomena* starts from the actuality of sciences and proceeds to inquire about their a priori principles, i.e., their possibility. Metaphysics before Kant is indeed actual, but as a natural untested disposition of reason left to grow on its own, it is dialectical and deceitful (*KrV* B 21–22). For metaphysics to become a science, it must be preceded by a critique of reason aimed at setting forth

> the entire stock of a priori concepts, their division according to the different sources (sensibility, understanding and reason), further, a complete table of those concepts . . . and then, especially, such a critique must set forth the possibility of synthetic cognition a priori through a deduction of these concepts, it must set forth the principles of their use, and finally also the boundaries of that use; and all of this in a complete system. Therefore a critique, and that alone, contains within itself the whole well-tested and verified plan by which metaphysics as science can be achieved. (*Ak* 4: 365, ENG 154)

The Transcendental Dialectic, which occupies more than half of the Doctrine of Elements and is at times proudly exalted by Kant for its results, is here reduced to a mere "finally also the boundaries" after the long and detailed recapitulation of the Analytic. This is the beginning of a dramatic change in Kant's retrospective evaluation to which we will return in the next section. Furthermore, a disparaging sense of metaphysics derives from a more basic trait, namely, its being a natural and inevitable tendency of our reason. Natural dispositions should not go unchecked. The past is obscure, but now bright times are ahead of us. As Kant writes, "Critique stands to the ordinary school metaphysics as chemistry stands to alchemy, or astronomy to the fortune-teller's astrology" (*Ak* 4: 366, ENG 154). What counts more than progress and enlightenment is that metaphysics is a science and a system because its source—pure reason—is an organism and a subjective system of a priori syntheses guided by ideas.

---

restriction of the use of reason to empirical conditions, (3) the independence of reason from these conditions, (4) the extension of the use of reason beyond the sensible, albeit negatively only, (5) the absolute unity of reason as the complete principle of practical unity.

When Kant describes metaphysics as a natural disposition, he does not (always) describe it as an error that can be extirpated *à la* Bacon. Metaphysics is so ingrained in us that we cannot pretend to do without one, because reason's questions, which drive us beyond the sensible, animate human reason in all of its activities. In a passage from the Mrongovius Metaphysics lectures, which is especially poignant now that metaphysics is taken by so many contemporary philosophers as a dispensable baggage, Kant says: "All the despisers of metaphysics, who wanted thereby to give themselves the appearance of having clearer heads, also had their own metaphysics, *even Voltaire*. For everyone will still think about their own soul" (*Ak* 29: 765, ENG 126, italics mine).

Metaphysics is in disarray. The battlefield of endless controversies has been ravaged by bitter fights, but we can never become indifferent to its destiny (*KrV* A vii–x). Reason has never been able to do without a metaphysics (*KrV* A 842/B 870), which it needs to give voice to its essential ends. As Kant puts it, we can be sure that "we will always return to metaphysics as to a beloved from whom we have been estranged" (*KrV* A 850/B 878). A system of a priori principles is (to use Hegel's description) the inevitable diamond net woven into everything we do or say, whether or not we know it. But not only is this metaphysics inevitable and a need, as we saw in the opening pages of chapter 1, it is also indispensable and even, as the *Metaphysics of Morals* has it (*Ak* 6: 216, ENG 371), an explicit *duty*. Since it innervates all our judgments, it had be better be good and we had better know it is there.

Note, finally, that reason's natural disposition is the source both of dogmatic metaphysics and of the critical metaphysics as science of the laws of human reason.[21] Both tend to be systematic because reason itself is.

2. Dogmatic

The negative sense of metaphysics is especially strong in the 1760s as Kant, convinced that despite its best efforts metaphysics was heading nowhere, undertakes to reform its method. Metaphysics is the most difficult of sciences, as Kant remarks in the *Deutlichkeit*. But the fact is that so far no metaphysics has even been written (*Ak* 2: 283, ENG 255). All extant examples of metaphysics are futile and vain chatter. In them, self-appointed philosophers idly give themselves the pomp of supreme importance and the air of utter arrogance. This irritation, even rancor, which Kant confesses first

---

21. There is a difference, reads a *Reflexion* (4984, *Ak* 18: 51), between thinking metaphysically and thinking about metaphysics: "das erste thun alle" (everybody does the former).

to Lambert and then to Mendelssohn, led him to write the *Dreams* (*Ak* 10: respectively 54–57, 69–73). The emphasis in this essay is on the vanity of metaphysics's self-righteous attempt to unveil the inner essence of things as through an illumination. But Kant does not on that account think we can simply dismiss metaphysics. On the contrary, because it is a science of the principles of reason on which depends "the true and lasting welfare of mankind" (the words of the letter to Mendelssohn), it must undergo a complete reform.

Unrequited love persists in its pursuit, but not out of faithfulness or disinterested and selfless passion. The lover hopes to receive his or her benefit in the form not of an eventual reciprocation but of improved self-understanding. In Plato's *Phaedrus*, Lysias's speech reduced love to utility. Similarly Kant writes: "Metaphysics, with which, as fate would have it, I have fallen in love but from which I can boast of only a few favors, offers two kinds of *advantage*" (*Ak* 2: 367, ENG 354, italics mine). The first is the solution to the problems of the inquiring mind, but this is all too often unsatisfying. The disappointing outcomes of metaphysics must not, however, be misunderstood because the elimination of useless and futile certainties is quite important. "I have deceived my reader in order to benefit him. And although I have not furnished him with any new insights, I have, nonetheless, eliminated the illusion and the vain knowledge which inflates the understanding" (*Ak* 2: 368, ENG 354).

This is the second advantage of metaphysics. It consists in knowing "whether the task has been determined by reference to what one can know, and in knowing what relation the question has to the empirical concepts, upon which all our judgment must at all times be based. To that extent metaphysics is a science of the *limits of human reason*" (ibid.).[22]

In the *Deutlichkeit*, the method of metaphysics had to be the same as Newton's method in the natural sciences (*Ak* 2: 286, ENG 259). Kant announces to Lambert his forthcoming work due to appear on Easter of 1766 on "the true method of metaphysics" (*Ak* 10: 51). The problems to be solved by this method are the relation between the universal and the individual in metaphysics, the relation of causality (which in the 1760s Kant still thought empirical), and the distinctness of sensible cognition (in view of the antinomies).[23] In the *Dissertation* a method understood in light of these

---

22. This same sentence returns in the *Bemerkungen* (*Ak* 20: 245). Later, in his letters to Herz, Kant says that the title he is thinking of for his work is *The Limits of Sensibility and Reason* (June 7, 1771, *Ak* 10: 121–24, curiously repeated on February 21, 1772, *Ak* 10: 129–35).

23. Tonelli, *Kant*, 347–48.

questions precedes metaphysics itself as the determination of reason's laws (§ 23, *Ak* 2: 411, ENG 406).

The transcendental philosopher will take the question of method to heart so deeply that he or she will read the Doctrine of Method as the soul and form of the *Critique*. Finally, in 1787 Kant will even call the first *Critique* a treatise on method.[24] That this is said after the brilliant pages on the Copernican revolution and Kant's illustration of what the *Critique* is going to deliver is bizarre. For it leaves the reader who has glanced at the table of contents wondering about the redundancy of a treatise on method divided into a Doctrine of Elements and a Doctrine of Method. But this is less paradoxical if we keep in mind that the problem of metaphysics is more and more strongly linked to the problem of what we can know a priori of things (see, for example, the famous 1772 letter to Herz, *Ak* 10: 129–35).

We could almost say that metaphysics is progressively transformed into the question of reason's knowledge. But that would be a hyperbole. The problem of reason's knowledge is preliminary for metaphysics, not all that into which metaphysics can be resolved. The first *Critique* is the preliminary examination of pure reason's powers indispensable for metaphysics to start. The *Prolegomena* reads: "there can be no such science unless the requirements expressed here, on which its possibility rests, are met, and, as this has never yet been done, there is as yet no metaphysics at all" (*Ak* 4: 257, ENG 54). Most fundamentally the critique is a propaedeutic to metaphysics whose complementary functions include clearing the ground of rubble and preparing the proper terrain on which the new science will grow; i.e., the criticism of traditional, transcendent metaphysics and the establishment of the immanent metaphysics of reason's a priori principles.

3. Ontology

A justly famous passage from the third chapter of the Analytic reads: "the proud name of an ontology, which presumes to offer synthetic a priori cognitions of things in general in a systematic doctrine (e.g., the principle of causality), must give way to the modest one of a mere analytic of the pure understanding" (*KrV* A 247/B 303). The days of an ontology as the

---

24. "The concern of this critique of pure speculative reason consists in that attempt to transform the accepted procedure of metaphysics, undertaking an entire revolution according to the example of the geometers and natural scientists. It is a treatise on the method, not a system of the science itself; but it catalogues the entire outline of the science of metaphysics, both in respect of its boundaries and in respect of its entire internal structure" (*KrV* B xxii).

description of the essential and accidental traits of things are undoubtedly over. Ontology as the science of the universal properties of all beings or the science of beings in general (*Refl* 5936, *Ak* 18: 394; VMet-L2/Pölitz, *Ak* 28: 541, ENG 307) made categories the predicates of things. As a result, it paid no attention to the functional nature of pure concepts (products of a unifying activity, not reproductions of the structure of things) or to their restriction to possible experience. More fundamentally, transcendental logic or philosophy, concerned about the sources, extent, and validity of pure reason's concepts, does not occupy itself with objects at all. "For that reason it is wrong to call it ontology. There we consider things already according to their general properties. Transcendental logic abstracts from all that; it is a kind of self-cognition. . . . It thus concerns not the objects, but the subject— not things, but rather the source, extent, and boundaries of reason in its pure use" (V-Met/Mron, *Ak* 29: 752, ENG 116).[25]

But this passage must not be read unreflectively. Ontology is naive rather than proud, and Kant's enterprise is hardly more modest. It is scientific be-cause it is itself the principle for a new science and not an uncritical doc-trine, but it is not a humble attempt at deflating a pretension, that of saying something a priori about objects, for that ambition remains intact.

In a sense it is right to deny that Kant wants an ontology. In another, it is striking that the Introduction to the third *Critique* calls the pure concepts of the understanding "ontological predicates" (*Ak* 5: 181, ENG 68). We should read again what Kant says about transcendental logic and ontology in the Mrongovius lectures (V-Met/Mron, *Ak* 29: 811, ENG 165; V-Met/Pölitz, *Ak* 28: 20–21): Baumgarten starts from possibility and impossibility but might as well have started from being and nonbeing. For if two concepts are op-posed, they stand under a superior concept: opposition is the disjunction of an original concept. The concept of an object in general is the highest con-cept of ontology, the only one that does not have a contrary (and the one of which being and nonbeing, possibility and impossibility are predicated: see the Amphiboly at *KrV* A 290/B 346). If the concept of an object in general is the proper object of ontology, and if transcendental philosophy deals with the a priori cognitions we can have about objects, then transcendental philosophy is what is ordinarily called ontology.[26] Because cosmology and

25. See all the *Reflexionen* quoted by De Vleeschauwer, *La déduction* (1: 62), on the object of metaphysics: not ontology, but the subject and its a priori cognitions.

26. V-Met/Mron, *Ak* 29: 811, ENG 165; *Ak* 29: 752, ENG 114; V-Met-L1/Pölitz, *Ak* 28: 18; *Ak* 28: 541, ENG 307; *Refl* 5936, *Ak* 18: 394; V-Met/Dohna, *Ak* 28: 679, ENG 381.

theology deal with one particular kind of object, they also belong in ontology (V-Met/Mron, *Ak* 29: 875, ENG 245).

Aristotle believed that his first philosophy, insofar as it dealt with being qua being and its causes and principles, was the most universal and comprehensive science. For Kant, who knows Wolff's derivative formula,[27] it is not. Causality does not apply to being. Principles are reason's principles as it addresses itself to objects. Being qua being is not general enough. Ontology, says Kant in the *Fortschritte* (*Ak* 20: 260, ENG 354), has not made much progress since Aristotle. But note that for Kant what since Aristotle has been called metaphysics is actually rational physics, the pure doctrine of nature (V-Lo/Dohna, *Ak* 24: 699, ENG 437).[28] This is necessarily narrower than transcendental logic. Furthermore, ontology (as well as theology and cosmology) belongs in transcendental philosophy, which is the only discipline that considers pure reason in its entirety (*Refl* 5644, *Ak* 18: 286; *PhilEnz* 11–12).

In sum, ontology is not the same as transcendental philosophy, not only because it is not descriptive, but also because transcendental philosophy's object is broader and includes all cognitions of reason, even ideas and principles that cannot be given in experience (V-Met/Mron, *Ak* 29: 875, ENG 245).

Transcendental philosophy, which studies pure reason and its principles, is pure metaphysics and needs a critique of reason's powers (or "is the result of critique," V-Met/Mron, *Ak* 29: 785, ENG 140). But all this is a preparation for metaphysics proper or in the strict sense, i.e., nothing other than applied metaphysics (V-Met/Mron, *Ak* 29: 751–52, ENG 113–14), i.e., rational physics (to which *PhilEnz* 11–12 adds rational psychology).

4. Critique and Transcendental Philosophy

The scheme of the Architectonic of the first *Critique* is one of the most comprehensive representations of the order of pure sciences in Kant's work and of the relation between critique, transcendental philosophy, and metaphysics in particular. It is itself the result of many years of gestation of the project that the *Dreams* called the science of the limits of human reason.

27. "*Ontologia seu Philosophia prima* est scientia entis in genere, quatenus ens est" (*Philosophia prima sive Ontologia methodo scientifico pertractata*, § 1).

28. Actually Kant oscillates on this judgment. If Aristotle's is an ontology, then it should be more than rational physics. That is what Kant implies in the *Fortschritte* (*Ak* 20: 260, ENG 354) as well as whenever he speaks of ontology. For ontology is one branch of pure metaphysics, while rational physics is applied metaphysics.

In the *Dissertation*, metaphysics is first philosophy regarding the principles of the use of the pure understanding (§ 8, *Ak* 2: 395, ENG 387). It is preceded by a propaedeutic science drawing a firm boundary between sensible and intellectual cognition. In the letter to Herz of June 7, 1771 (*Ak* 10: 121–24), Kant sketches his plan for a work on the limits of sensibility and reason aimed at the determination of the fundamental concepts of a science regarding the sensible world. It will be presented along with the principles for the doctrine of taste, metaphysics, and morals. The two cardinal principles of metaphysics are, as one late *Reflexion* (6344, *Ak* 18: 669) and the passage cited in chapter 2 from the *Fortschritte* (Ak 20: 311, ENG 397) claim, the ideality of space and time and the reality of the concept of freedom.

The relation between critique and transcendental philosophy changes over the years and not because Kant is slowly but surely heading in one direction and overcoming or dismissing the previous path. Instead, he alternates repeatedly on this issue. Sometimes critique and transcendental philosophy are identified as the science of the a priori principles and cognitions of reason, while at others critique precedes transcendental philosophy. The *Prolegomena* (§ 5, *Ak* 4: 279, ENG 75) upholds the former view, the first *Critique* the latter: here the critique is a special science that determines the sources and limits of pure reason and is thus a propaedeutic to the system of pure reason (*KrV* A 11/B 24–25). "Transcendental philosophy is here the idea of a science, for which the critique of pure reason is to outline the entire plan architectonically, i.e., from principles. . . . It is the system of all principles of pure reason" (*KrV* A 13/B 27).

The critique is "the complete idea of transcendental philosophy, but is not yet this science itself" (*KrV* A 14/B 28), since it deals only with the complete determination of synthetic a priori cognition. Transcendental philosophy is the *Weltweisheit* of speculative and not practical reason. For the practical "contains incentives, is related to feelings, which belong among empirical sources of cognitions" (*KrV* A 15/B 29). Its a priori is not pure. Later, for example in the *Fortschritte* (*Ak* 20: 272–73, ENG 364), the critique will prepare the way for metaphysics of nature and of morals and will not differ from transcendental philosophy. In this initial division of the Architectonic, transcendental philosophy is not mentioned.

Now the philosophy of pure reason is either *propaedeutic* (preparation), which investigates the faculty of reason in regard to all a priori cognition, and is called *critique*, or, second, the system of pure reason (science), the whole (true as well as apparent) philosophical cognition from pure reason in systematic connection, and is called *metaphysics*; this name can also be given to all of pure philosophy including the critique, in order to comprehend the investigation of everything that can ever be cognized a priori as well as the presentation of that which constitutes a system of pure philosophical cognitions of this kind, but in distinction from all empirical as well as mathematical use of reason. Metaphysics is divided into metaphysics of the *speculative* and the *practical* use of pure reason, and is therefore either *metaphysics of nature or metaphysics of morals*. (*KrV* A 841/B 869)

Kant adds that metaphysics of morals is equivalent to pure morality without any empirical cognition. Therefore even if metaphysics in the strict sense should be only of speculative reason, we can retain the term 'metaphysics' also for the metaphysics of morals insofar as it stems from philosophical cognition. Later (*KrV* A 845/B 873) transcendental philosophy does appear and is equated with ontology: that is, no longer with pure metaphysics or with all a priori cognitions of reason including ideas and principles that cannot be given in experience (V-Met/Mron, *Ak* 29: 875, ENG 245). Transcendental philosophy is contrasted to physiology of pure reason, i.e., the rational science of the sum total of given objects. Physiology is then divided according to immanent or physical (rational physics and rational psychology) and transcendent or hyperphysical (rational cosmology and rational theology). As a result, the whole system of metaphysics comprises here (1) ontology, (2) rational physiology, (3) rational cosmology, (4) rational theology (*KrV* A 847/B 875).

This constant oscillation between Kant's own meaning and the traditional meaning of metaphysics is confusing enough. But that Kant himself generously allowed both senses of the word to infiltrate his writing is worse, especially because it introduces sciences that do not fit his usual classification. Indeed, many perplexities arise regarding this division. Let me mention four.

1. Transcendental philosophy does not include all a priori cognitions, for example the fundamental principles of morality. We have already seen the first oddity regarding wisdom and the mutual priority between metaphysics and ethics in chapter 1. We have not yet seen that what goes with it is the motivation for restricting the use of transcendental philosophy to the speculative use only (assuming that the system of which Kant speaks at A 11–13/B 24–26 roughly overlaps with this scheme of the Architectonic). The practical contains incentives, feelings, and is mixed with empirical sources.[29]

29. The practical is not yet the self-determination of pure reason, which is impulse and motive to its action. The practical here is the object of pleasure and pain (*KrV* A 801/B 829n). The

If this were true, with all due caveats about the fact that Kant has not yet arrived at the conception of morality we find in the *Groundwork* or the second *Critique*, the risk is that this could lead to difficulties in the projected metaphysics of morals. It is not a risk but a certainty, however, that it leads to the exclusion of practical reason from transcendental philosophy. With this exclusion the parallel between theoretical and practical legislation we have been emphasizing in the first *Critique* might then find a place only in the system of reason's a priori cognitions, i.e., in metaphysics. But this is not the case in the scheme at hand.

2. Another point left unqualified is this. We have noticed the broad and narrow senses of metaphysics: respectively, system with and without critique. Now, this *narrow* sense (system without critique, but in the form of a metaphysics of nature and of morals) is *not* the same as metaphysics in the *strict* sense, which is speculative metaphysics.

3. Another ambiguity is the difference, affirmed, then revoked, then affirmed again, between critique and transcendental philosophy. Sometimes transcendental philosophy is reduced to transcendental logic (with the exclusion, that is, of the Transcendental Aesthetics), sometimes even to the Transcendental Analytic alone (*KrV* A 66/B 90–91). Does the reduction to the Analytic imply that therein transcendental philosophy is the theory of objectivity through the understanding's pure concepts? If so, why neglect the critique of transcendent metaphysics and exclude it from transcendental philosophy? Differently put, why reduce transcendental philosophy to positive speculative metaphysics or ontology? Does 'transcendental logic' here possibly not refer to the section of the Doctrine of Elements comprising Analytic and Dialectic but allude to critique's belonging to logic in a broad sense? Either way, why does Kant forget that the Transcendental Aesthetics "belongs to transcendental philosophy" as he said there (*KrV* A 15–6/B 30)? Regardless, and whatever their relation, critique and transcendental philosophy together are contrasted (once Kant has narrowed down his examination to the metaphysics of nature at *KrV* A 845/B 873) to physiology.

4. Concerning physiology (the a priori knowledge of a given nature), it is unclear why the fair-minded treatment of rational psychology on the one hand and cosmology and theology on the other in the Transcendental Dialectic should be now altered. In particular, why should rational psychology be *immanent* physiology (as opposed to transcendent physiology)? It is not clear, in sum, why rational psychology should now seem any more

---

faculties of desire and feeling have not yet been severed, and the distinction between pure and empirical is not affirmed as it will be in the second *Critique*.

legitimate than cosmology and theology as a metaphysics of the soul or rational cognition of thinking nature.

If it were because rational psychology is admitted simply as the establishment of the proposition "I-think," then it must be stressed that the sense of 'soul' in the metaphysics of the soul (here at *KrV* A 846/B 874 as the object of inner sense), to be equated with the thought of the transcendental apperception, is irreconcilable with that of the Paralogisms, which opposes the transcendental apperception to the soul as substance.[30]

In general, this confusion has exercised a profound and divisive effect on interpreters, who have used one or the other of the senses of metaphysics in its relation to critique to support partisan readings and instituted competing and adversarial parties (Kant as metaphysician, as epistemologist, as philosophical founder of the Newtonian sciences, as ontologist, etc.).

Needless to say, the problems to which this confusion gives rise are of major importance. What appear as picky and fine distinctions of interest solely to those who have systematic minds intent on classifications and taxonomies are actually very serious conceptual questions. A few examples:

1. It is not clear whether the sciences mentioned by Kant are ones he planned to carry out or eventually write, or ones he thought were impossible or dogmatic. The addition of "apparent" in "the whole (true as well as apparent) philosophical cognition from pure reason" is very important because it indicates that both successful and failed a priori syntheses are included. But it raises the question as to whether the critique of theology, cosmology, and rational psychology Kant had undertaken in the Transcendental Dialectic was all that he thought we could say about them, or whether one or more of those sciences were going to be the object of an independent treatment (as Kant suggests the physiology of thinking nature might be).

2. There is the cognate, albeit somewhat different problem regarding the reality, self-sufficiency, and completion of transcendental philosophy. We know that Kant thinks he has provided the solution to the problem

---

30. The *Metaphysical Foundations of Natural Science* takes up the distinction between a physiology of outer and inner sense, qua extended and thinking nature (*Ak* 4: 467–71, ENG 183–86). Here we find the possibility of a natural description but not of a science of the soul (understood as the sum total of appearances in inner sense). It is not a science because mathematics cannot be applied to inner appearances (this is not going to be possible until the rise of experimental psychology and the measurement of psychological phenomena, i.e., until Johann Friedrich Herbart and Jakob Friedrich Fries, who react precisely against this Kantian negative characterization of psychological mechanisms). A science of nature, however, presupposes a metaphysics of nature. As a result, this physiology cannot be conflated with the rational physiology of the Architectonic.

of metaphysics. What is left to do is to carry out its system. If the *Critique of Pure reason* is a propaedeutic to metaphysics, does Kant believe that his *Metaphysical Foundations of Natural Science* (1786) and his *Metaphysics of Morals* (1797) are the realization of his system? It would appear so. Yet Kant's later stance on the *Metaphysical Foundations of Natural Science*, from the strange dismissal that came a mere year after its publication to his suddenly urgent preoccupations with a theory of matter in the *Opus Postumum*, indicates otherwise.[31]

More importantly, if the first *Critique* is a propaedeutic, why was Kant so vexed with and contemptuous of the many post-Kantians (Reinhold, Beck, Maimon, Fichte) who thought they were fulfilling his promise? Why does he have to remind them that his system was complete?[32]

3. Also, given this ambiguity of 'metaphysics,' it is not immediately clear if ethics should belong to metaphysics (and if so to which of the kinds of metaphysics) or vice versa. Again it is not a matter of classification. At stake is the definition of the essence of morality as rational and the ultimate destination of transcendental philosophy as a whole.

4. Critique can be a propaedeutic to or already a part of metaphysics. But it is not clear if critique is metaphysical because it is a need and a drive or because the system presupposes it. That is, how metaphysical (and in what sense) is the propaedeutic to metaphysics? For it is not conceivable that a propaedeutic to metaphysics should somehow be "pre-" or other than metaphysical, as if critique and a theory of experience were the external epistemological preparation for metaphysics. Critique *is* metaphysics, for it

31. At *KrV* B xliii he writes: "Since during these labors I have come to be rather advanced in age . . . I must proceed frugally with my time if I am to carry out my plan of providing the metaphysics both of nature and of morals." According to Ottaviani (*Possibilità ed esistenza in Kant*), the *MAN* and the announced metaphysics of nature differ because the former is an application of principles that presuppose the empirical concept of matter and with it a metaphysical foundation of the theory of bodies serving as example for a later, completely pure science that Kant never completed but that the *Opus Postumum* attempts to elaborate.

32. I am thinking of Kant's increasingly irritable reactions, indeed stiffening and closure, in his correspondence of the 1790s, and especially of the nasty public statement on Fichte (*Ak* 12: 370–71). All truth be told, in the *Fortschritte* Kant understands metaphysics as the transition to the supersensible, so that if critique and transcendental philosophy are on the one hand indistinguishable, on the other they are no longer a propaedeutic to metaphysics but themselves an integral part of the system of metaphysics. If this shift was deep-seated in Kant's mind as he took this position in his letters, it must be said that Kant simply forgets that before the *Fortschritte* critique was invariably the indispensable propaedeutic to metaphysics. Besides, since this late phase of Kant's thought was not made public at the time, obviously nobody could have known about the intervening changes.

deals with the principles of pure reason and draws the boundaries between legitimate and illegitimate uses of pure reason.

5. Even more striking, indeed contradictory, is the relation between critique and transcendental philosophy in this scheme. The critique as a *propaedeutic* to metaphysics is the vestibule of the edifice, while curiously transcendental philosophy as *ontology* is the main hall of the subsequent division internal to the meanwhile well-grounded house of speculative metaphysics. But if critique (in which reason gives the principles of a priori cognitions, *KrV* A 11/B 24) and transcendental philosophy (our a priori mode of cognitions of objects, *KrV* A 11/B 25) are virtually indistinguishable, are we not finding the same content in two alternative places, one in the propaedeutic and one in the full-blown speculative metaphysics? Are we concerned about the foundations or the house itself?

As we just saw, that "this name [metaphysics] can also be given" to one part or the whole as we please is not helpful. And as appealing as Heidegger's remark may be that the critique reproduces the relation typical of the school metaphysics (viz., Baumgarten) between general metaphysics (Transcendental Aesthetics and Analytic) and the three branches of special metaphysics (psychology, cosmology, theology in the Dialectic),[33] the situation seems substantially more complicated.

6. More fundamentally, this scheme shows Kant's two agendas: the critique of reason's limits, and the ambition to erect a new metaphysics in a positive sense. The shifts regarding ontology are quite revealing of these tendencies. Ontology is criticized because it objectivizes reason and presumes to know objects directly when in fact, Kant argues, we can know only the source, boundaries, and validity of pure reason and not things. Then ontology reappears in the guise of transcendental philosophy as the speculative metaphysics internal to the system of pure reason.

Very clearly Kant wants to understand reason's legislation as integral to reason's self-knowledge. What is sometimes less clear is how critique and system can live together. Or, to be more precise, it is less clear if system is a critical invitation to metaphysical sobriety, as I said in chapter 1, or also a doctrine.[34]

The ambiguities regarding metaphysics are by no means unique. In fact, 'critique' shares the same destiny. It sometimes means critique of pure

---

33. Heidegger, *What Is a Thing?*, 108–19.

34. The Preface to the third *Critique* ends with these words: "Thus with this I bring my entire critical enterprise to an end. I shall proceed without hindrance to the doctrinal part" (*Ak* 5: 170, ENG 58).

reason and sometimes critique of pure reason's transcendent products (traditional, dogmatic metaphysics): *either* an investigation of the internal divisions, limits, and organization of reason, that is, critique as discrimination (as in the Greek verb from which it comes, *krinein*) of internal limits, *or* critique of reason's drive to trespass its limits, that is, critique of the limits that externally define what meanwhile has emerged as the touchstone of truth, the possibility of experience. Reason is always the judge of itself and cannot admit any authority above itself. But, in light of this duality, the 'of' in the 'critique of pure reason' can respectively be the expression of a subjective genitive (reason reviews itself critically) or an objective genitive (reason denounces the dogmatism of its supersensible use).

"Transcendental philosophy" also admits of several meanings. It can be the whole of, the recognition of, or the examination of the possibility of a priori cognitions;[35] also, as we have just seen, transcendental logic; or only the Transcendental Analytic.

What remains after all these questions and difficulties? The critique is a canon rather than an organon that extends knowledge.[36] It is a discipline before it can be a doctrine. The first *Critique* is so rich because it reflects the complexity of these different functions and meanings. Perhaps we can say that what begins as reason's tribunal progressively advances in the 1780s, in the three *Critiques* taken jointly, to a more comprehensive self-knowledge to include reason as the source of all cognition, desire, feeling.

In all of this it is striking that what never changes in Kant's mind are the intentions and ends of metaphysics. Metaphysics cannot be a scholastic cognition and a dogmatic doctrine. The science of the laws of pure reason is the condition for the absolute unity of reason and the pathway to the sum total of its ends. Even qua system, Kant's metaphysics incorporates a global rethinking of metaphysics in a cosmic sense (a "metaphysics of metaphysics" Kant calls it in a 1781 letter to Herz, *Ak* 10: 268–70). All speculative metaphysics is brought back to a practical teleological philosophy that has in view the supersensible and our final destination.

In the Introduction to the first *Critique*, pure reason's problems are God, freedom, and immortality (*KrV* A 3/B 7). All theoretical-dogmatic metaphysics gives way to what is variously called a practical cognition, a moral faith, a practical-dogmatic metaphysics of the highest good (which

35. See Vaihinger, *Commentar*, 1: 467–76.

36. The critique is a canon, and thereby the preparation for an organon. But it seems to me a mistake, hinting at ulterior levels and risking a possible multiplication of meanings, to call it the preparation for a canon as Kant does at A 12/B 26.

is not, mind you, dogmatic assertion but moral interpretation or reflective judgment). The *Methodenlehre* of the *Critique of Judgment* (§ 86 on ethico-theology) and the *Fortschritte* (*Ak* 20: 260, 272, 294–95) are the best evidence of the "authentic interpretation" of the world as the voice of God of which *The Miscarriage of Philosophical Trials in Theodicy* speaks (*Ak* 8: 264).[37]

Even Kant's nautical metaphors, on which he seems to rely confidently since he strikingly has them open many of his works or chapters, reflect this ethico-theological concern. Metaphysics is "a bottomless abyss . . . , a dark and shoreless ocean, marked by no beacon" (opening page of *The Only Possible Argument*, *Ak* 2: 66, ENG 111); "a shoreless sea, in which progress leaves no trace behind" (opening page of *Fortschritte*, *Ak* 20: 259, ENG 353); a "broad and stormy ocean, the true seat of illusion, where many a fog bank and rapidly melting iceberg pretend to be new lands and, ceaselessly deceiving with empty hopes the voyager looking around for new discoveries, entwine him in adventures" (opening page of the chapter on phenomena and noumena in the Analytic of Principles, *KrV* A 235/B 294).

Whether it is impossible to orient oneself ("no beacon") or to change anything in the world and know it ("no trace behind": you cannot write on water, and progress cannot *make* a new land materialize out of nothing), dogmatic metaphysics is a deceiving place where we risk losing ourselves. In the last passage we almost have a stepmotherly nature deceiving us. But notice that it is mankind's curiosity and hunger for new discoveries that receive the punishment of false hopes.

Still in 1781, Kant wishes that "the voyage of our reason may proceed only as far as the continuous coastline of experience reaches, a coastline we cannot leave without venturing out into a shoreless ocean" (*KrV* A 395).[38]

37. "Das ist aber alsdann nicht Auslegung einer vernünftelnden (speculativen), sondern einer machthabenden praktischen Vernunft, die, so wie sie ohne weitere Gründe im Gesetzgeben schlechthin gebietend ist, als die unmittelbare Erklärung und Stimme Gottes angesehen werden kann, durch die er dem Buchstaben seiner Schöpfung einen Sinn giebt."

38. Tetens uses the same images. He writes that the understanding in physics navigates close to the coastline. Experiences are like shores and lighthouses keeping us from getting lost. Reason is a fragile boat when it ventures into the vast ocean of the divine. According to Schneiders (*Aufklärung*, 8ff.) and Ciafardone ("Introduzione," 49), the source of reason's uncertain navigation in metaphysics may well be the picture in the frontispiece of Samuel Grosser's *Pharus intellectus sive logica electiva* (1697). In it, reason's ship enters the citadel of truth (*Alethopolis*) after the perils of ignorance and prejudices. At the end of book 1 of the *Treatise*, pondering the voyage undertaken, Hume compares himself to someone who, "having narrowly escap'd shipwreck . . . , has yet the temerity to put out to sea in the same leaky weather-beaten vessel, and even carries his ambition so far as to think of compassing the globe" (*Treatise*, 264 [1.4.7]). But in Hume there is no Alethopolis. Growing "apprehensions" at the sight of dangers (enmity and personal isolation, "forlorn solitude") prevail and recommend prudence (264). In fact, "nature

But fear is no argument. The solution is not to close down harbors as if there were a permanent hurricane, or surrender out of fear in the face of dangerous emergencies. Nor, finally, is it in the long run sufficient to take a closer look "at the map of the land that we would now leave and to ask, first, whether we could not be satisfied with what it contains" and see if it is solid enough (*KrV* A 235/B 294).[39] On the contrary: two years later Kant will introduce a significant change.

> These *Prolegomena* will bring them to understand that there exists a completely new science. . . . Hume foresaw nothing . . . , but deposited his ship on the beach (of skepticism) for safekeeping, where it could then lie and rot, whereas it is important to me to give it *a pilot*, who, provided with *complete sea-charts and a compass*, might safely navigate the ship wherever seems good to him, following sound principles of the helmsman's art from a *knowledge of the globe*. (*Ak* 4: 262, ENG 58–59, italics mine).

It is now knowledge of the globe, not of the small island of truth, that must guide us. Navigation is not foreclosed. The map of the inhabitable land is replaced by a complete sea chart, for staying on the firm land of experience cannot satisfy reason. The Transcendental Analytic is not sufficient because the sensible points beyond itself to the supersensible. No positive metaphysics in any guise—a revolutionized ontology or a physiology or a speculative metaphysics—can be understood outside the entire circle of reason: the true *as well as apparent* a priori synthesis (immanent and transcendent metaphysics). No land is conceivable outside its relation to the world surrounding it. In 1786, in *Orientation in Thinking*, Kant calls the compass allowing us to orient ourselves a pure rational faith (*Ak* 8: 142).

The best summary of reason's essential unrest is given by Kant himself again in a *Reflexion*. The critique of pure reason is "the prophylaxis against a malady of reason," its nostalgia or homesickness, a desire to lose itself and cover other worlds.[40] In this brief text there is an *ante litteram* romanticization

---

herself cures" reason of its incapacity to dispel its own clouds by obliterating its chimeras and providing *distraction* from the melancholy of idle philosophical subtleties (269).

39. The passage on deceiving hopes was preceded by this claim: we have surveyed the land and concluded it is no more than an island, "enclosed in unalterable boundaries by nature itself," the land of truth (*KrV* A 235/B 294).

40. *Refl* 5073, *Ak* 18: 79–80: "Die Critik der reinen Vernunft ist ein Präservativ vor eine Krankheit der Vernunft, welche ihren Keim in unserer Natur hat. Sie ist das Gegenteil von der Neigung, die uns an unser Vaterland fesselt (heimweh). Eine Sehnsucht, uns ausser unserm Kreise zu verlieren und Andre Welten zu beziehen."

of pure reason (recall Novalis's definition of philosophy as homesickness) in the form of a hunger for the new and the vertigo of sailing out to open sea, while leaving behind all familiarity. But what is even more striking is Kant's counterintuitive use of *nostalgia*. It is not directed at a *nostos*, a return home. Instead, as with the cyclops, Kant bends analogies against their anticipated associations in order to suit his purposes. The *Weh* of *heimweh* (the 'sickness' in 'homesickness,' the *algos* in 'nostalgia') is not the acute pain of estrangement or of a feared loss, but the bittersweet desire of adventure. The *Heim* of *heimweh* (the 'home' in 'homesickness') is not our small but solid and familiar home, our motherland, but the vast ocean in which we desire to lose ourselves in pure reason's exploration. Pure reason's desire and neediness defy the admonition to stay safely at home because pure reason cannot tolerate being told to keep within its limits. Its spontaneity and freedom cannot repress its adventurous vocation.

In this *Reflexion* it is not imagination that is *heimatlos*, as Heidegger remarked, but reason that is homeless. This Odysseus does not regain his wife and son, his home and kingdom at the end of a twenty-year-long journey. Reason's journey can never end. Restlessness, dissatisfaction, relentless movement and voyages of discovery are reason's lot.[41]

4. Kant's Retrospective Judgments on the *Critique of Pure Reason*. The Interrelation of Faculties Recast

The unity of reason, which has been defended throughout this book, is not usually addressed or sufficiently valued in the standard reading of Kant. Without a relative independence from sensibility and the totalizing drive of ideas, concepts lead nowhere. Indeed, they cannot even be formed. If we consider the comprehensive critique of pure reason in its relation to metaphysics (i.e., the three *Critiques*), we realize that the first *Critique* is a preparation for a larger project, its initial and founding stone. Neither the plan nor the execution of such a project belongs solely to theoretical and speculative philosophy or can be reduced to a theory of experience or an

---

41. About these notions of home and homelessness, it seems pertinent to recall the following exhibition, which will not surprise those familiar with the darkness and harsh, uncompromising humor (or lack thereof) typical of the Danish cinema of the last twenty years. In the Danish Pavilion of the Venice Biennale di Architettura of 2009, in an interior meant to evoke the elegant comfort, intimacy, and coziness of a middle-class living room, hung a small white knitted fabric in a frame. Embroidered in fine needlework meant to evoke maternal sweetness was a jarring message reminding us (so I read it) not to fool ourselves with sentimentality. It said: *"home is the place you left."*

epistemology. The first *Critique* is not about an I as opposed to objects but about pure reason's self-knowledge (in theoretical and practical terms, and for ends that transcend knowledge).

Still, the comprehensive approach to Kant's thought recommended in this book may very well be doomed—not because it is not grounded or does not adequately reflect Kant's deepest-reaching intentions, but because it is obscured by Kant himself. It is not simply one-sided interpretations breaking apart the unity of reason that militate against this reading. Instead, it is Kant who encourages this dislocation, this separation, this disjoining after 1781. If the first edition of the *Critique of Pure Reason* is a culmination of the intense work of over a decade of silence, it is no less a springboard for a journey that will conclude in the third *Critique*. The shape of Kant's thought consigned to the A edition lasts the fleeting moment in which one tries to fixate the crystals of a snowflake before it melts in one's hand.

The idea of a critique of pure reason implies a work in constant progress. Kant not only very soon substantially alters, almost leaves behind fundamental theses of the A edition such as the centrality of imagination highlighted by Heidegger, but reconfigures the *Critique*'s very function. In fact, the problems of Heidegger's thesis, however important, are *derivative*. They are secondary with respect to the shifting conception of a critique of pure reason as it progressively asserts itself in different forms and under different pulls in Kant's mind.

Recall the passage from the opening of the third *Critique* in which Kant identifies the first *Critique* with an examination of the understanding in a theory of knowledge. We must now realize that this tremendous simplification is not merely a slip. In fact, it is the result of a long transformation in Kant's own understanding of the function of the first *Critique* that runs parallel to the evolution of his thought in the other *Critiques* and the writings of the 1780s. If there are no gains without losses, it appears that the misinterpretation of the first *Critique* allowed—indeed suggested—by Kant is the price to be paid for the new groundbreaking acquisitions of the 1780s. This section chronicles this transformation.

Because it does not attempt to reconcile many interrelated cruxes, the version of the first *Critique* as confined to an epistemology of natural sciences is at first blush a lot easier to absorb, command, and assess than the version presented here. The immense literature on Kant, much of which is an often very sharp and intelligent discussion of issues in epistemology, logic, mathematics, and the philosophy of nature, is largely based on this segmentation. Yet, I believe the reading I have presented is more systematic and consistent as well as true and faithful to Kant's revolutionary inspiration. When push comes to shove, textual analysis shows that alternative readings are compelled to throw away too much of Kant's philosophy to remain tenable. They adopt too partial and truncated a perspective to account for Kant's philosophy comprehensively.

One reduction in particular is responsible for the misapprehension of the unity of reason: the condensation of the positive teaching of the first *Critique* in the Analytic, and the Transcendental Deduction in particular. This is not, however, a sudden inexplicable discovery, or a complete turnaround on Kant's part after 1781. After all, the criterion of objective reference is formative of the Transcendental Dialectic itself and essential for the critique of ideas. I would rather call this reduction a recurrent and lingering temptation, already surfacing, along with a comprehensive approach to reason incompatible with it, in the A Preface (*KrV* A xvi–xvii). But it is only after 1781 that the most important result he thought he had reached in the silent decade, the solution to the problem of the relation of representations to objects, is disproportionately emphasized and tends to engulf the rest. Reason is more and more often reduced to the understanding.

To put this point as sharply as possible: taking the *Critique of Pure Reason* as a theory of knowledge of appearances with the Transcendental Deduction as its core does not only restrict knowledge, which has a substantially wider and irreducible meaning, to knowledge of appearances in experience. It also takes reason as the predicate of an I or ego (consciousness, the understanding, I-think, transcendental subjectivity, etc.) as opposed to appearances. This reduction has been widely accepted, indeed almost taken for granted since Hegel's criticism of Kant (and before that since Fichte's transformation of self-consciousness). It is not without basis in Kant's texts, but it cannot take into account the themes we have seen in this book—the architectonic of reason, cosmic philosophy, the positive role of ideas, transcendental philosophy's production of principles—because it is a one-sided version of reason's a priori synthesis.

As I see it, this reduction rests on the following syllogism: reason is an I; but the I is a thought and not a cognition; therefore knowledge is the I's empirical knowledge made possible by a transcendental self-consciousness of which we can say only *that* it is. This syllogism is fundamentally misguided and based on equivocation, as I have argued throughout this book and specifically in this chapter regarding transcendental philosophy's production of principles as reason's specific kind of self-knowledge. Let us see why reason is distinct from consciousness and how the reduction of the former to the latter, which is not ungrounded but risks being problematic for Kant's thought about reason, is suggested by Kant himself.

The literature (but not Kant) often does treat thoughts as properties of an ego-pole. In this view, constitution is its attribute. This ego is presupposed as a pole identical to itself, independent of and prior to its activity that would *in addition* constitute its objects: as if the I were here, the world there, and their relation mediated between them as between two readymade poles. But reason is not one member in a relation. If the world is its idea, reason is the source of the world and thereby the whole correlation. It is nothing before or independently of the process of giving laws to a world of its own making. Of course, this is true only insofar as 'world' means the world of reason's laws, which remain wholly other than the indefinite and diverse empirical givenness outside reason, that is, as external to reason as matter remains to reason's forms-contents. This is the difference—and it is a crucial and huge one—between Kant's and Hegel's idealism.

The problems of thought and of individual consciousness are not to be conflated. If, instead, thought is reduced to the unity of consciousness, and this is equated with the I and the understanding as in the Transcendental Deduction, then there is no way around it: Hegel is right when he says that Kant understands thought in the guise of consciousness, a finite and subjective I as opposed to the world.

But this is only partially true. Thought is world-forming. Reason, as the unity of its faculties (and through the understanding), forms an object in general. Consciousness, in that it brings back all thought to a finite I, is the *reflective result* of reason.[42] Consciousness, aiming at the determinacy of objects of experience and its own individuation, is the unity of sensibility and understanding standing opposed to objects. Thus it is the isolation and division of the original act on which it rests. By contrast, reason is *prior to*—in fact, it is the original unity of—all opposition. Opposition arises out of the unity of reason because reason is internally divided into different faculties with conflicting requirements and criteria.[43]

Even when consciousness and reason tend to be indistinguishable, they are not identical. Reason is not constituted; it is *unconditional* and acts on itself. Consciousness instead is *finite* because it defines itself as the relation to given objects and aims at the manifold of experience.

---

42. One interpreter who acknowledged this problem is De Vleeschauwer (*La déduction*, 3: 292).

43. For example, theoretical reason cannot succeed in many acts in which practical reason does. Or, ideas use concepts to claim that the world is infinite, but the necessity to match this claim with the restriction to space and time, i.e., to harmonize concept and intuition, voids it of meaning.

The bridge between reason and consciousness, essential to both, is transcendental apperception. If we introduce, as well we should, this mediation, we realize that *self-knowledge* also shifts meaning in the three cases of reason, transcendental apperception, and empirical consciousness. Reason's self-knowledge results in the transcendental cognition of principles and of a priori syntheses we have seen so far (and especially in section 2 of this chapter). Like reason, transcendental apperception is a pure source, a first condition, transindividual, neither in space nor in time. Qua self-consciousness, however, it is an undivided thought but not a determinate cognition, let alone a self-knowledge. Empirical consciousness's self-knowledge, in turn, is knowledge of nothing more than an appearance.

Reason functions logically as I but is not reducible to an I. The I-think is not an I who happens to think. It is instead the way thinking occurs, the way the original unity of apperception realizes itself. Consider the B Deduction. The representation I-think is "produced" by the original apperception (*KrV* B 132). If the I is the existence of thought, then it is not an individual self-same substance that owns its thoughts, but rather a function: the combination "of given representations *in one consciousness*" (*KrV* B 133). "I call its unity the *transcendental* unity of self-consciousness in order to designate the possibility of a priori cognition from it" (ibid.). The conclusion is clear: the *consciousness of a synthesis and the production of a priori cognition make possible the identity of the I, not vice versa.*

Consider also the limited role of the I in practical and purposive contexts. For reason an action from duty or a reflective judgment matters in itself. Naturally the individual I is the subject of these acts, for it is the I that universalizes a maxim and feels respect; it is the I that is enlivened by the spectacle of purposiveness and judges an object as if it were made to fulfill a purpose. But the I is entirely involved in the fulfillment of these acts and does not regard them as if they originated in consciousness. The I is all in its object, which it does not view as external and opposed to it.[44]

---

44. For example, it is from the reality of the moral law that I become aware of my freedom. In Mary Gregor's Cambridge edition of Kant's moral writings (*Practical Philosophy*), words such as 'I' or 'self' are not even indexed. When Kant does use this concept in the second *Critique*, he means the I as noumenon, "my invisible self" (*KpV* 5: 162, ENG 269). The moral view "infinitely raises my worth as an *intelligence*" (ibid.). It is interesting to see Kant's wording when he claims that the subject of laws *makes itself subject* to nature as a phenomenon. In this passage (*KpV*, *Ak* 5: 6, ENG 142) Kant mentions the problem of the requirement "to make oneself as subject of freedom a noumenon but at the same time, with regard to nature, a phenomenon in one's own empirical consciousness," but thinks the paradox is only apparent. It would be quite misleading, however, to conclude that the I as noumenon is opposed to the I as appearance: the embodied self is an appearance, but the I, which can never be intuited, is not.

Reason is an original synthesis that is not an I but occurs as and works through an I. Reason is not temporal or finite and yet it temporalizes itself. To borrow a concept from grammar, which distinguishes verbs from their conjugations and nouns from their declensions (case, number, gender), we can say that reason, the unity of thought, inflects or *declines* itself into transcendental apperception, all the way down to the I-think and empirical consciousness.

This is in many ways a problem. To begin with, a distinction between reason's actualization as I-think and embodiment becomes suddenly urgent. That reason declines or inflects itself as I-think is a logical necessity that regards the faculty of concepts. That reason embodies itself in an I means instead that my whole self, body and mind, functions unitarily. My body, that is, my sensibility, is no longer simply an object but a subject of knowledge. Recall, for example, the intuitive knowledge of regions in space that relies on my body. As we saw above,[45] Kant is proud to have discovered pure intuition as the a priori form of sensibility.

The problem with embodiment is that Kant is not evenhanded when he applies this principle to theoretical and practical reason. When it comes to knowledge, Kant has divided reason into sensibility, understanding, and reason proper and shown their respective a priori principles. It is therefore wrong to take reason as consisting of only the two higher faculties, as does Hegel. Hegel excludes sensibility from reason's faculties because it is, as our access to appearances, no more than the vehicle of presentation of appearances to thought. It is therefore indistinguishable from empirical appearances.[46] This reduction is yet another proof (after mathematical construction)[47] of Hegel's confusion about and disregard for the notion of pure intuition and the independence and novelty of Kant's sensibility.

In a different sense, however, Hegel may not be that far off after all, for in the second *Critique* Kant treats reason's determination as due to understanding and reason alone. As we saw in chapter 2, reason is not an abstract faculty; it does take into account tendencies and incentives (it makes itself practical), but not because sensibility has an a priori principle. In fact, sensibility must be bracketed when we determine a motive for morality. The internal division of practical reason differs from that of theoretical reason. The division is for practical reason a *cause* of its necessity, indeed of its very being. If the I were not divided and sensibility's inclinations and passions

---

45. In chapter 2, § 7.
46. *Glauben und Wissen, Werke* 2: 317–18.
47. See chapter 2, § 7, n. 132.

did not threaten the integrity of the subject's motivation, there would be no need for reason's moral determination. In cognition of nature, principles are at the same time laws, whereas in morality, as the second *Critique* reads, "the principles that one makes for oneself are not yet laws" because we need to make reason's rule an *imperative* (*KpV*, *Ak* 5: 20, ENG 153–54).

As a result of the distinction between declension and embodiment therefore I propose to introduce a distinction of three moments within a unity: reason, its inevitable logical and practical declension as an I, and reason's sensible existence as embodied in an individual I. I call them moments because they have no reality in themselves and exist only together (reason is not an activity supposedly residing somewhere apart that at some point embodies itself) but refer to distinct issues. Reason is the subject of thought and rules, and the I is the way it operates. Both transcend the individual I who is the consciousness of rules it finds and has not made.[48]

Also the problems threatening the internal consistency of reason and consciousness respectively are quite distinct, even if often conflated. The problem of reason's identity lies in the necessity to think together its unconditional origin and its self-objectivization. Put even more fundamentally, reason must be at the same time spontaneity and transparency to itself. For reason the task is to think together *activity and self-consciousness*.[49] The problem of consciousness's identity, by contrast, is that of reconciling itself and its opposite, the unconscious (in Kant's sense). For according to Kant the conscious I turns out to rely on an unconscious synthesis, on a blind agent doing its job for it: imagination. With regard to consciousness, which believes it is the origin of the cognition of objects opposed to it, the task is to bring it to see its constitution, the concepts and rules of reason that operate

48. When I say that reason is irreducible to the I but embodies itself in an individual I, I mean that my several cognitions and actions are made possible by rules of which I as an individual am not the author. If I add 5 to 7, or buy an apple, the rules governing my addition and my purchase exist only in function of my operation and commercial transaction, but are nonetheless independent of all activities they make possible. On reason's embodiment, see Nuzzo, *Ideal Embodiment*.

49. This problem was identified with remarkable clarity by Fichte. He started from the recognition of the problem of circularity in Kant's I. He thought that according to Kant the I should be a product of reflection, while instead reflection presupposes the I. If the I must be both the position of itself and the knowledge of itself, this seemingly impossible identification is called in the 1801 *Wissenschaftslehre* the necessity for an activity to have an eye (*ein Auge*) built into it. But even that would be insufficient, for an eye cannot see itself. Hence Fichte's enduring dissatisfaction with his philosophical results. For a brilliant study of this, see Henrich, "Fichtes ursprüngliche Einsicht," 202–9.

behind its back and often unbeknownst to it. Consciousness must realize, in other words, that it is a result, not an origin.

We have just seen that reason is not the property of an I. Its essence is not attributive, but, conversely, reason is also not a substance. It lives in its several functions and has no independent reality other than as this self-actualization. Still, the continuity stretching from reason to empirical consciousness is beset by paradoxes regarding reason's phenomenalization more intractable than the only apparent riddle of the double I feared by Kant (the I as constitutive and the I as an appearance constituted by its activity: *KrV* B 153–56). It is no wonder that post-Kantians took such diverging directions out of this conundrum.

Let me summarize it as follows. We must distinguish the moments of reason while at the same time taking the distinctions as fluid and far from sharp or steadfast. For example, we must *distinguish* the moments of reason as did Beck and Fichte when, having charged Kant with the fatal confusion of accepting a Cartesian slippery slope, they found it necessary to drive a wedge between the question of subjectivity and that of thought.[50] On the other hand, the distinctions must be *fluid*. For example, the apperception's I as a logical universal function cannot be opposed to the empirical I as neatly as Kant believes, because the empirical I is in itself universal, and the universal I is in its actuality individual.

Let these indications suffice merely to flag the problem. What most matters to me here based on these points is to reiterate that *reason cannot be reduced to understanding or consciousness. Likewise, thought cannot be reduced to judgment.* Sound and intelligible discourse cannot be reduced to apophantic predication. And yet it is true that when they engage in knowledge, reason and thought take on the form of understanding and judgment. In cognitive statements the categorical determinant judgment is the model we try to approximate, the implicit aim of every judgment. But this model, as we have seen, extends its claims to the Transcendental Dialectic itself: not so much qua determinant judgment, but in that it is made possible by the discriminating criterion of sensible reference. It is only because they do not have objective reality, i.e., because no object corresponds to them and they fall short of the realistic *desideratum* of sensibility, that ideas are more and more

---

50. Respectively, J. S. Beck kept apart the status of a subject from the original faculty of representation, Fichte from the I (obviously Fichte's absolute I is not Kant's I). Beck criticized Reinhold and Schulze for failing to see that the highest principle is "the postulate of original representing" (*Einzig möglicher Standpunkt*, 120–22). In turn, Fichte criticized Beck in the First Introduction to the Doctrine of Science of 1797 for drawing the laws of thought from logic, like Kant (*Gesamtausgabe*, 1/4: 210ff. [§ 7]).

identified with their deceiving and empty character, rather than as reason's indispensable guides.

Many changes intervene between the first and the second edition of the *Critique of Pure Reason*. As announced, I do not want to focus on the revision of the Transcendental Deduction (from the threefold synthesis in A to the objective unity of apperception and the new definition of judgment in B), of the Paralogisms, on the new chapter on the Refutation of Idealism, or the other important changes in the text. I want instead to dwell on the picture of the content and role of the A edition and the *Critique* as a whole that Kant lets pass (silently, uncritically, *naturally*, likely without realizing all the consequences) even while he is retrospectively projecting his ever new take back onto it. We have seen the passage at B 21–22 and its demotion of the Transcendental Dialectic. We have seen the recasting of sensibility and the notion of formal intuition in the footnote at B 160–61. These passages are evidence that Kant increasingly questions the primacy of sensibility and the necessity to presuppose the Aesthetic to the Logic as he works on the other two *Critiques*. Why?

If we take a closer look, sensibility is actually broadened in scope in the B edition. It is not demoted the way the Dialectic is divided and displaced, as we will see presently. In A,[51] the restriction of the use of reason to possible experience is instrumental in affirming the thesis of transcendental idealism, that is, the ideality of space and time and the reduction of things to appearances. Subsequently, however, Kant is more and more convinced that the critique has a positive function to fulfill as a propaedeutic to a moral metaphysics. When he writes in 1787 that he has to restrict knowledge to make room for faith (*KrV* B xxx), his understanding of morality has gained far greater importance and clarity than it had in the A edition. He has meanwhile published the *Groundwork* and written most of the *Critique of Practical Reason*. The concept of freedom is now his central concern. In A, metaphysics has a shape similar to what it had in the *Dreams*, i.e., an empty and futile dogmatism. In B, metaphysics is a science comparable to mathematics and physics. What has happened in the meantime?

The *Prolegomena* (1783) introduces the memorable pages I have commented on in chapters 1 and 3 on limits and on the metaphysics of analogy. The discussion of the antinomies, though succinct and much shorter, is very clear, but its relevance lies in its being the gateway to the metaphysics of limits and of analogy. The room for a metaphysics in a positive sense

---

51. From now on, let the simple A stand for the 1781 edition and B for the 1787 edition of the first *Critique*.

is greater than it was two years before. This does not yet have anything to do with morality. Instead, it is motivated by Kant's wider reflection on the scientific nature of metaphysics. Given the new and alternative (analytic) method of exposition that begins from given sciences and rises up to their conditions, the *Prolegomena* can, much more unambiguously than the first *Critique*, claim to be a scientific metaphysics. Indeed, this becomes its central theme and is announced at the very outset (in fact, in the title).

But what is more important is that after the opposition of mathematics and metaphysics from the *Deutlichkeit* to the Discipline (the acroamatic or discursive character of philosophy as opposed to the intuitive exhibition in mathematical construction, suggesting a merely analytical procedure in philosophy), and after the several admonitions not to follow mathematics or a deductive method in the *Critique*, here in the *Prolegomena* they are compared and put on a par with respect to their syntheticity (see section 2 in this chapter). The a priori synthesis of the Analytic of Principles, in turn, is treated under the rubric of a pure science of nature (*reine Naturwissenschaft*, Prol § 14) closely related to physics. The *Critique* appears now as a foundational work on the scientific study of *nature*. (After this, the *Metaphysical Principles of Natural Science* of 1786 seems to follow naturally from Kant's supposed "ontology.")[52]

Freedom is pushed to the side not because it is less relevant, but, on the contrary, because it now requires a separate treatment.

In 1781 morality was "foreign to transcendental philosophy" (*KrV* A 801), and the critique of pure reason was the *one* propaedeutic for all cognitions. The legislation over nature and freedom were the two parts of a metaphysical system in the Architectonic. The critique laid the ground for freedom, of which the third antinomy in the Dialectic showed the possibility. This freedom, however, was only negative. The antinomy showed the compatibility of freedom with the mechanism of nature. It was just a matter of dividing appearances and noumena and assigning the former to nature, freedom to the latter, and the antinomies were avoided. But the reality of freedom indispensable for the moral law was not thereby proven.

The *Groundwork* (1784) deduces the autonomy of the will from the concept of freedom. In so doing, however, it comes up against two problems. It contravenes the explicit teaching of the Transcendental Analytic of the

52. The seamless continuity between the Principles of the Understanding and Newton's laws of nature is then taken (by Hermann Cohen and an unceasing host of followers to this day) as indicative of Kant's original attempt at founding physical laws on a transcendental ground. This is, I fear, a conflation of different purposes and scopes.

first *Critique* in that it uses the categories outside the realm of experience. It asserts that freedom is *real* and that the will exercises its *causality* through a law. Furthermore, the concept of freedom is still presupposed and not deduced, which threatens to make the whole foundation of morality circular.

The changes introduced by the *Groundwork* in the scheme of the 1781 Architectonic are important. The concept of freedom suddenly becomes the most urgent problem to solve. Imperceptibly, the propaedeutic role of the first *Critique* also begins to be undermined. For Kant presents the *Groundwork* as parallel to the *Prolegomena* (both follow the analytical method of exposition and are preparatory, *Ak* 4: 391, ENG 47). More importantly, Kant for the first time speaks of a critique of pure practical reason (ibid.), which in 1781 was not needed or even conceivable.

He immediately minimizes this novelty by pointing out that practical and speculative reason must have a "common principle," since they are "one and the same reason, which must be distinguished merely in its application" (*Ak* 4: 391, ENG 47). He construes the moral law as another instance of the common problem of a priori synthesis, parallel to, for example, $7 + 5 = 12$. Reason shows the possibility and objective validity of the principle of morality.

And yet this irreversible change is undeniable. Kant writes that he is going to publish a metaphysics of morals to be preceded by a foundation, "a critique of pure practical reason, just as that of metaphysics is the critique of pure speculative reason, already published" (*Ak* 4: 391, ENG 47). He adds that the former is not as urgent as the latter, for in speculative and theoretical matters reason is "wholly dialectical" and must be disciplined. The Transcendental Dialectic is now understood as transcendent and dogmatic only. At this stage the *Groundwork* seems sufficient to address the need to apply the common understanding, less prone to sophistry than speculative reason, to the clarification of the pure grounds of duty. It seems sufficient, that is, as a critique of pure practical reason, save for the discussion of the "common principle" shared by speculative and practical reason. The propaedeutic role of the first *Critique* is undermined because the reduction of its scope to speculative (as opposed to practical) reason denies its fundamental and universal preparatory character.

The *Critique of Practical Reason* confirms this definitive point of no return. The metaphysics of morals is postponed once again. Now, however, Kant needs a critique of *practical* (not a pure practical) reason (*Ak* 5: 3, ENG 139). Freedom is the only idea we know a priori (*Ak* 5: 4, ENG 140). We no longer need to deduce it. Since no derivation of the law is possible and its consciousness is undeniable, the solution of the problem of freedom is the "fact of reason" (*Faktum der Vernunft*), i.e., the immediate consciousness of the moral law as the ground of our knowledge of freedom. Freedom is in turn the ground of the possibility of the law (*Ak* 5: 32, ENG 165). Now the parallelism is no longer between *Prolegomena* and *Groundwork* qua analytic expositions of the principles of theory and practice resting on one propaedeutic, namely the *Critique of Pure Reason*, but between the *Critique of Practical Reason* and the *Critique of Pure Reason* (*Ak* 5: 3, ENG 139). The first *Critique* is no longer the only propaedeutic. We need a specific one for morality—and here it is.

As summarized above in chapter 2 (§ 3 b), the procedure of the second *Critique* is inverse to that of the first (sensibility, concepts, principles). As reason approaches its objects not in order to know them but to produce them, it starts from principles, proceeds from them to concepts (good and evil), and finally reaches sensibility (in the form of moral feeling). But if we now turn to the explicit wording of this shift (anticipated at the end of chapter 2, § 7b, which speaks of Beck), we are flabbergasted to read what follows.

> The Analytic of theoretical pure reason was divided into transcendental Aesthetic and transcendental Logic; that of practical reason, reversely, into Logic and Aesthetic of pure practical reason . . . ; the Logic in turn was there divided into Analytic of concepts and Analytic of principles, here into that of principles and concepts. The Aesthetic there had two parts, because of the twofold kind of sensible intuition; here sensibility is regarded . . . only as feeling." (*KpV Ak* 5: 90, ENG 212)

Which instructor would pass a freshman exam containing such a sloppy summary of the pillars of the first *Critique*? Everything is upside down. Aesthetic and Logic are here said to be contained in the Analytic, whereas in the first *Critique* the Aesthetic was the preliminary basis for Transcendental Logic whose first part was the Analytic. The Logic is said to be divided into the two books of the Analytic, whereas in the first *Critique* the Logic contained Analytic and Dialectic—which here is not even mentioned!

Why is Kant driving his readers insane? Is it an unbelievable mistake, an unfortunate blunder? Did he lose his thread, if only for a moment?

I do not think so. I believe this is part of the recasting of the structure and order of the first *Critique*. If we go back to another passage (*Ak* 5: 42, ENG 174), we read that "the first datum that made a priori cognition possible" in "the Analytic" (*sic!*) of the "Critique of pure speculative reason" (*sic!*) was "not principles but instead pure sensible *intuition*."

This is of utmost interest. Recall that the Transcendental Aesthetic gave us the immediate contact with givenness and constituted the first premise for the understanding. This passage shows that Kant is now systematically planning to suppress the Aesthetic's function of basis for the Analytic. This is evidenced by what he did in the footnote at B 160–61 of the first *Critique* on formal intuition (which most likely antedates these pages by only a few months), as well as by what he will do in the *Fortschritte*.[53]

Reinhard Brandt, who notices this point, connects it with another one.[54] The *Groundwork*, he argues, eliminates all preliminarily given content and starts from the purity of the will. The second *Critique* starts from the formal law of an autonomous will. This move is parallel to the transformation of the intuition of the Aesthetic as the indispensable givenness into formal intuition (and thus as already integral to the Analytic). But between the *Groundwork* and the second *Critique* there is yet another change. The former makes morality depend on the distinction between things in themselves and appearances established by the third antinomy of the first *Critique*, whereas the latter emancipates morality from all cognition.[55]

If we turn to one last passage from the second *Critique* (*Ak* 5: 141, ENG 253), we realize that reason's pretensions to grasp what turn out to be chimeras in theology and morals is thwarted not by the Transcendental Dialectic, but by the deduction of the categories.[56] The Transcendental Dialectic, even in its minimal negative import, has ostensibly disappeared from Kant's horizon along with the Doctrine of Method (Canon and Architectonic). All immanent use of ideas, indeed all positive contributions of ideas, are expelled from the picture. If a deduction is no longer needed in morality (in the second *Critique*, unlike the *Groundwork*), its very idea is now identified with its paramount and exclusively theoretical version, the Transcendental Deduction in the Analytic of Concepts of the first *Critique*. The result of that Deduction is now summarily broadened by Kant as consisting not only in the restriction of the categories to objects of possible experience, but also in the application of pure practical reason to objects. So applied, catego-

53. Recall his correspondence with Beck in chapter 2, § 7b. The second *Critique* is completed in June of 1787, as the second edition of the *Critique of Pure Reason* has just come out. See the letter to Schultz, *Ak* 10: 467.

54. *Bestimmung des Menschen*, 362–64.

55. Ibid., 524. Brandt concludes, as I would not, that the emancipation of morality from knowledge shows that it is no longer the prerogative of an elite.

56. "By these reminders the readers of the *Critique of pure speculative reason* will be perfectly convinced how extremely necessary, how salutary for theology and morals that laborious *deduction* of the categories was" (*Ak* 5: 141, ENG 253).

ries "serve for a determined thought of the supersensible" (ibid.). In other words, the Transcendental Deduction now takes on tasks originally alien to it and belonging to the Transcendental Dialectic.

Notice that by "deduction" Kant now means once again a synecdoche, a *pars pro toto*. He thinks, it seems to me, of the Transcendental Deduction as standing for the whole Analytic of Concepts and Principles: that is, for the constitutive theoretical a priori synthesis. Schematized concepts, inclusive of the reference to intuition and now apparently self-sufficient, tend to take up the space, if not the role, of ideas. This is a crucial problem that deserves an independent treatment I cannot give here.[57]

As just mentioned, these pages are contemporaneous with the Preface to the B edition of the first *Critique*. Here we read that the metaphysics of nature and morals on which he is going to focus next will be "the confirmation of the correctness of the critique both of the theoretical [*spekulativen*] and practical reason" (*KrV* B xliii). This is a claim, identical to that of the second *Critique*, that he could not have staked before 1787.

5. The A and B Prefaces to the First *Critique*. A Destitute Queen and the So-Called "Copernican Revolution"

Nothing is more instructive for a better grasp of the changes from 1781 to 1787 than comparing the A and B Prefaces to the first *Critique*. Each stipulates programmatically what the book is intended to do with regard to the status of transcendental philosophy, the conception of metaphysics, its relation to science, its syntheticity: the very definition of reason to be introduced at the entrance of the edifice.

Famously, in the B Preface we are supposed to find the so-called "Copernican revolution." In truth, and as the secondary literature has amply recognized, Kant never speaks of a Copernican revolution.[58] He does speak about

57. On the dilemma regarding the use of categories independently of intuition, see the Appendix.

58. See these titles: Natorp, "Die kosmologische Reform des Kopernikus"; Kemp Smith, "Meaning of Kant's Copernican Analogy"; Kemp Smith, *Commentary*, 22–25; Paton, *Commentary*, 370ff.; Russell, *Human Knowledge*; Hanson, "Copernicus' role"; Engel, "Kant's Copernican Analogy"; Kaulbach, "Die Copernicanische Denkfigur"; Blumenberg, *Die Genesis der kopernikanischen Welt*; Bencivenga, *Kant's Copernican Revolution*; Gerhardt, "Kants kopernikanische Wende"; Kerszberg, "Two Senses of Kant's Copernican Revolution"; Bonevac, "Kant's Copernican Revolution"; Miles, "Kant's 'Copernican Revolution'"; Capozzi, "Kant on Heuristics"; Schulting, "Kant's Copernican Analogy"; Schönecker, Schulting, and Strobach, "Kants kopernikanisch-newtonische Analogie"; Carl, "Kants kopernikanische Wende." These are only a fraction of the titles on the topic (the ones I have read). By contrast, there is almost nothing on the A Preface and nothing

a revolution[59] as a sudden breakthrough of a new method ("die veränderte Methode der Denkungsart," *KrV* B xviii). He significantly speaks of the light that unexpectedly flashed upon the minds of those who adopted an unprecedented way of thinking in mathematics and physics.

But scholars are still debating the role of Copernicus in Kant's argument on the new science, the meaning of the reference to "the first thoughts of Copernicus" (*KrV* B xvi), and its relation to the footnote at B xviii. A few points seem to me beyond dispute. One is that Kemp Smith and Bertrand Russell are quite wrong in believing that, given the anthropocentric and subjectivist turn of Kant's philosophy, his should actually be dubbed a Ptolemaic counterrevolution.[60] For Kant's supposed Copernican revolution has nothing to do with perspectivism, subjectivism, or context-dependence. Nor, as Hans Blumenberg points out, does it appeal to a presumed freedom to change our point of view.[61] Kant never mentions and certainly does not have in mind the heliocentric hypothesis. Instead, when he introduces the analogy with Copernicus, he means the commutation of the relation between motion and rest and the transformation of a purely passive spectator on the basis of the methodological relation between hypothesis and confirmation.[62]

It would seem that metaphysics is not amenable to experiments the way sciences are. And yet, even if metaphysics cannot test its objects, it can test its concepts and principles. As a result, its adoption in metaphysics of the experimental model consists in the verification of its concepts as regards the intuition of objects (*KrV* B xviii–xix n.). The experiment proves "the

---

I am aware of on what interests me in this context, a comparison between the A and B Prefaces with respect to the structural changes in the organization of the Doctrine of Elements. The only exception I know is Förster ("Die Vorreden"), who argues that A stands under the sign of Locke, B under that of Bacon.

59. Six times, according to Miles's counting ("Kant's 'Copernican Revolution,'" 1).

60. Kemp Smith, "Meaning of Kant's Copernican Analogy," 549–51; Kemp Smith, *Commentary*, 22–25; Russell, *Human Knowledge*, 9.

61. *Genesis of the Copernican World*, 609, 761.

62. Ibid., 599ff. As Schönecker, Schulting, and Strobach also argue ("Kants kopernikanisch-newtonische Analogie," 498), the analogy should be a Copernican-Newtonian analogy. I disagree with Miles's and Schulting's otherwise interesting articles insofar as they find a disanalogy between the apodictic laws of metaphysics and the falsifiable laws of physics. They share Popper's criticism of Kant, which, as I have explained in chapter 2, misses the difference between knowledge of objectivity and objective knowledge. Also, I fail to see why Schulting insists (twice at p. 62 of his "Kant's Copernican Analogy") on the Copernican revolution as an increase in rationality in solving a "technical" problem. Here as elsewhere, I find worth mentioning Blumenberg's outstanding intelligence and the lamentable rarity with which scholars make use of his insights.

invisible force (of Newtonian attraction) that binds the universe . . . in a manner contradictory to the senses yet true" (*KrV* B xxii n.).[63]

Rather than offering a new interpretation of the "Copernican revolution," what I want to do now is proceed to a comparison of the two Prefaces in view of the changes introduced by Kant in the interrelation of reason's faculties. Many changes from A to B are indeed dramatic and conspicuous. In both, philosophy is a *necessary* enterprise. The A Preface describes reason's peculiar destiny as one of being burdened with (or bothered by, *belästigt*) questions it cannot dismiss (*KrV* A vii). To echo the opening sentence of Aristotle's *Metaphysics* ("pantes anthrōpoi tou eidenai oregontai phusei"), it is not *by nature* that human beings *desire* to know and *enjoy* it. It is by *work*, by a deliberate and painstaking effort, that reason sets out to fulfill its *task* and solve its *problems*.

The ground plan of nature, if there is such a thing, is hidden from us. Rather than being left to its own devices, reason is delivered over to the solitude of its fate and unrest. Finding lawfulness in nature only partially reduces contingency and alleviates reason's dependency on an ultimate moral outcome beyond its control. After all, nature is in itself dumb and cannot be saved other than as appearance. Reason is the only source of lawfulness. At the same time through this very lawfulness and the cognition of its limits reason eventually assumes (*KrV* B xix–xxxi) the role of grounding rational faith in the world (the world is now wholly unlike nature, as I showed in chapter 1).

After the opening sentence on reason's destiny, the 1781 Preface begins a narrative on the fate of metaphysics. It revitalizes the rhetoric of the passage from dogmatism to skepticism familiar since the time of Sextus Empiricus, which will two years later, in the *Prolegomena*, translate into Kant's remark crediting Hume with awakening him from dogmatic slumber.

The A Preface sets up the tribunal of reason, the highest possible authority, with strong political overtones. Neither church nor political absolutism

---

63. In a private correspondence, Wolfgang Carl points out to me that *Versuch* and *Experiment* do not overlap. I believe that while he has a point in general (in the current use of the German language), he does not in the specific sense of *Versuch* that Kant adopts in these pages. To me it seems Kant is using the word in its seventeenth-century sense, as in, say, Galilei's *The Assayer*, where 'to essay' (with its Italian, French, and German—*versuchen*—equivalents) means 'to test through an experiment' or through experience. For corroboration of my interpretation, see the understanding of *Versuch* as an attempt at verification (confirmation or refutation) of a priori principles in the practical use of pure reason at *KrV* A 804/B 832.

can exercise power over it. Enlightenment and freedom of inquiry go hand in hand.[64]

The B Preface is inspired by quite a different model, that of the scientific revolution. The vision, no longer political, is rather the utopia of a "total revolution" (*KrV* B xxii) finally realized by the scientific method. The tribunal of A xi survives in B mostly in the figure of the appointed judge (*KrV* B xiii) who forces nature to answer quite unnatural questions. These questions are devised in the scientists' experiments, for it is arbitrary hypotheses that allow them to formulate such questions, not a desire to contemplate or inspect what nature can show of itself. Notice that if in A reason was both defendant and judge of itself and of its claims, now it is the judge (a fairly aggressive prosecutor, to tell the truth) of the sufficiency of nature's extolled confession as an answer to its queries.

The new motto in 1787 is from Bacon, who inspires the revolution in the way of thinking (*KrV* B xii) and announces the end of an era. But the prophet must wait for a messiah to bring the revolution about. In geometry this hero is Thales, in physics Galilei, Torricelli, Stahl, perhaps in astronomy Copernicus;[65] in metaphysics, Kant. The key narrative here is a combination of Hegel's world-historic individuals and Kuhn's paradigm shifts in scientific revolutions. A sudden revolution takes place thanks to the happy and daring invention of an individual that subverts the "style" the scientific community takes for granted.[66] Of course what counts is the audacity of the

---

64. In the A Preface Kant appeals confidently to the reader's judgment (*KrV* A xv, xxi) because "our age is the genuine age of *criticism*, to which everything must submit" (*KrV* A xi n.). He even expects from his reader the cooperative spirit of a fellow worker when he presents his Metaphysics of Nature (*KrV* A xxi). In "What Is Enlightenment?" (1784), Kant is less confident in the reader's ready agreement with his purposes and in the quick and assured spread of the new ideas: "a public can achieve enlightenment only slowly" (WA, Ak 8: 36, ENG 18). The spread of critique depends on the freedom allowed by the State to exercise the public use of reason. Enlightenment aims at "a true reform in one's way of thinking" (*wahre Reform der Denkungsart*, WA, Ak 8: 36, ENG 18; on this, see Blumenberg, *Legitimacy*, 431). Notice that the contrast between a political revolution overturning despotism and Enlightenment's *reform* disappears in the "apolitical" B Preface, where change in the way of thinking (*Denkungsart*) is brought about by a *revolution* in *method*.

65. Blumenberg aptly points out that after the B Preface Kant has the sequence of names "Galilei, Kepler, Huyghens and Newton" (a sequence never beginning with Copernicus or including Bacon) replace the idea that an individual can singlehandedly bring about a scientific revolution (*Genesis of the Copernican World*, 601). But nor does Kant make this point about exceptional individual scientists *before* the B Preface. To me this is more evidence of the unique character of its rhetoric.

66. By "a general invariant style" I refer to the basic beliefs, worldview, and attitudes forming the fertile background shared by a scientific community. The phrase is borrowed from Husserl's *Crisis* (§ 9b), which I believe is indebted to these Kantian pages.

thought, not the person, and what matters is making it possible to embark upon the secure path of science. Here the triad of mathematics, physics, and metaphysics always appears in this order. Kant reassures us that if one of those sciences is successfully made scientific before the others, it is only a matter of time before all are united again, for they are not heterogeneous efforts of reason.

Notice that they are not heterogeneous *provided* the method adopted is that of experimental sciences. Recall that mathematics and metaphysics were opposed as alternative species of the genus 'rational knowledge' in that they were respectively cognitions from the construction of concepts or from concepts. Now instead the division internal to rational sciences is no longer applied.

If we recall, further, that the B Preface (but not the A) calls the *Critique* a treatise on method, we can notice one more point. In A, metaphysics used to be the queen of sciences and is at present destitute. In B, it is on a par with mathematics and physics insofar as it adopts their method. A queen, however destitute, remains a queen, i.e., a leader, whereas in B she finds herself in a subordinate position. She is ancillary to sciences that have meanwhile gained their superior power through the method they originally devised. It is the method that Kant insists metaphysics must imitate and import, as it were, from without (*KrV* B xvi).

In the A Preface the mention of well-grounded sciences such as mathematics and physics is followed not by metaphysics but by the praise of Kant's century as "the age of criticism" (*KrV* A xi n.). This shows that the first edition has metaphysics follow a scientific path only insofar as it is a *discipline* and a negative restriction. In this earlier account metaphysics has none of the close methodological affinity with mathematics and physics acknowledged in B. In A, metaphysics is understood negatively as the treacherous field from which we must eliminate errors, whereas in B we find the twofold use of the police we saw in chapter 1: positive insofar as it is negative.

In addition, there is a slight but telling difference in emphasis and an impressive one in language. In A, metaphysics is the systematically ordered inventory (*das Inventarium, KrV* A xx) of pure reason's possessions. In B, it must follow the example of geometers (*KrV* B xxii) and undertake a revolution similar to the one initiated by Copernicus. In A it is like the overview of a catalog, in B the manifesto for a revolution and a call to activism. In B there are proud, enthused, almost intoxicating overtones more typical of a Bacon than of an otherwise moderate and sober Kant, which are absent in A. Indeed A opens with the sense of mourning over metaphysics's fallen destiny and deplores indifferentism to the forlorn and despised Hecuba's demise. It is after all exhilarating to take one's destiny into one's own hands, and Kant almost seems carried away.

In B dogmatism is by now a defeated enemy and there is no need to be so combative and visceral. The series dogmatism–skepticism–indifferentism–critique in service of denouncing the despotism of reason of the dogmatists and calling forth a self-reflective critical attitude is replaced by a more nuanced statement. Critique is opposed not to the dogmatic procedure ("for science must always be dogmatic, i.e., it must prove its conclusions strictly a priori from secure principles," *KrV* B xxxv), but only to a dogmatism not preceded by critique.

These changes may be minimal, but they are not minor. As I said, this is in part a matter of rhetoric.[67] But rhetoric is not nothing. It does affect the content. In this case the most important change it introduces is that while in A metaphysics is mostly identified with the deflation of pretensions and the tracing of reason's boundaries, in B the experiment "promises to metaphysics the secure path of a science *in its first part*, where it concerns itself with concepts a priori to which the corresponding objects can be given in experience" (*KrV* B xviii, italics mine). In other words, metaphysics becomes a science insofar as it is identified with "this deduction of our faculty of cognizing a priori in *the first part of metaphysics*" (*KrV* B xix, italics mine). This deduction, in turn, epitomizes the whole of the critique of speculative reason. The "second part of metaphysics" is the practical treatment of the noumenal (*KrV* B xix–xx).

This is the provisional outcome of a shift the *Prolegomena* started. The scientific status of metaphysics in 1783, more accentuated than in 1781, was accompanied by a neat partition. Metaphysics in a positive sense (for brevity's sake: ontology, or what corresponds to the Analytic of Concepts and Principles) was the pure science of nature, while dogmatic metaphysics corresponded to the Dialectic, which in addition opened up the metaphysics of limits and of analogy. Now, in 1787, metaphysics retains, and flaunts, the scientific character heralded by the *Prolegomena*. But metaphysics now becomes a science comparable to mathematics and physics insofar as the first and second parts of metaphysics belong together. The former, the a priori synthesis I have discussed in chapter 2, makes room for the latter (at

---

67. Among the consequences of the rhetorical character of this shift, the accusation that Kant continues the presumed modern project, announced in Descartes's words, aimed at becoming masters and possessors of nature, rings hollow—or, at best, is pertinent only to the *tone* of the B Preface. For this charge is irreconcilable with the gap between philosophy and artists of reason and with the gap between philosophy and *techne*. The novelty of the B Preface is a tendential recasting of the structure of the first *Critique*, not a desire to master nature.

KrV B x Kant writes that the "theoretical cognition of reason" is the part in which "reason determines its object wholly a priori"). As he himself now understands, Kant devises the experiment of a Copernican revolution to safeguard the "twofold standpoint" of reason (*KrV* B xix n.) and thus the reality of freedom (*KrV* B xxiv–xxx).

As usual, however, for Kant defining a concept means also looking beyond it to what is related and opposed to it: in this case, ideas as merely illusory. In 1787 the sense of metaphysics, after the (negative-) positive function of the Analytic, which limits the bounds of a meaningful discourse by giving us a theory of objectivity, has also undergone a change.

It is finally time to ask: what happens to the Transcendental Dialectic (and the Doctrine of Method) in B, and as Kant approaches the third *Critique*? What happens to ideas?

In 1787 the ideas of God and immortality, which constantly change their status and here are joined by freedom, are given a decidedly practical character as the postulates of practical reason. Without them the will cannot determine itself to will the highest good. Thus the ideas of speculative reason "receive objective reality" (*KpV*, *Ak* 5: 135, ENG 248), although not as determinate cognitions of their object.[68] If reason is forced to grant "*that there are such objects*," "they become *immanent and constitutive* inasmuch as they are grounds of the possibility of *making real the necessary object* of pure practical reason (the highest good), whereas apart from this they are *transcendent and merely regulative* principles of speculative reason" (*KpV*, *Ak* 5: 135, ENG 249).

Notice that the criterion of objective reality differs deeply from the reference of pure concepts to sensibility of the first *Critique*. Notice also that the transcendental ideas are still three, but freedom takes the place of the world. In the Transcendental Dialectic world and freedom were closely related in the antinomies, the third of which showed the possibility of transcendental freedom within the causal mechanism of nature. In the contemporaneous B Preface to the first *Critique*, Kant proceeds likewise. He speaks about the practical knowledge of reason as it extends beyond the sensible. Here (*KrV* B xxi) the practical value of the extension is stressed along with what the *Fortschritte* will identify as metaphysics's primary aim: the passage from the sensible to the supersensible.

---

68. "Theoretical cognition, *not indeed of these objects but of reason in general,* is extended by this insofar as objects were given to those ideas by the practical postulates, a merely problematic thought having by this means first received objective reality" (*KpV*, *Ak* 5: 135, ENG 248).

Kant also speaks of the difference between knowing things in themselves and thinking them, but now by means of a discussion of freedom and its causality (*KrV* B xxvi–xxix). What is amazing in regard to freedom at this point is that in the second *Critique* Kant presents its problem as the *original* one: "it is *practical reason* which first poses to speculative reason, with this concept [i.e., freedom], the most insoluble problem so as to put us in the greatest perplexity" (*Ak* 5: 30, ENG 163). Not only does he make it sound as if the Transcendental Dialectic had been written solely to address the problem of freedom; he also blatantly inverts the priority between practical and speculative reason he previously declared was decisive.

One last difference between the A and B Prefaces is striking and concerns the opening definitions of the critique and of the notion of transcendental. In A Kant wrote that the idea of the special science he is introducing "could be useful to the critique of pure reason" (*KrV* A 11). In B this quote is replaced by: "can be called the critique of pure reason" (*KrV* B 24), without alluding to anything over and above it: without residues.

The following modifications are even more important. In B we read: "a critique of pure reason, and its utility *in regard to speculation* would really be only negative" (*KrV* B 25). Notice that the second edition has added the italicized words and alludes to what is now a divided, and twofold, propaedeutic (of speculative and practical reason). The words italicized in the following passage in A will be changed: "I call all cognition transcendental that is occupied not so much with objects but rather *with our a priori concepts of objects in general*" (*KrV* A 11). In B this is what takes their place: "I call all cognition transcendental that is occupied not so much with objects but rather *with our mode of cognition of objects insofar as this is to be possible a priori*" (*KrV* B 25).

This subtle difference has a momentous consequence. The "a priori concepts of objects in general" of A 11 comprehend ideas (regulative ideas of speculative reason are transcendental, *KrV* A 650–61). "[O]ur mode of cognition of objects insofar as this is to be possible a priori" of B 25 restricts its reference to objects of experience, i.e., to schematized concepts with the *exclusion of ideas*.

6. The New Conception of Reason and the Power of Judgment

Ideas are not suppressed, however. They have migrated. They now regard *almost exclusively the practical sphere*. I say "almost" because it would be reductive to take the second *Critique* as the last word on ideas and on freedom in particular. For freedom has yet a wide scope to discover for its own use.

Reflective judgment is impossible without freedom. In the third *Critique* Kant writes that our faculty of knowledge has two domains, nature and freedom, on which it legislates a priori (*Ak* 5: 174–75, ENG 62). But the territory on which it exercises its legislation is one, the realm of appearances. Now, despite the "incalculable abyss" (*unübersehbare Kluft*) between the two domains, between sensible and supersensible, "the latter *should* have an influence on the former, namely the concept of freedom should make the end that is imposed by its laws real in the sensible world; and nature must consequently also be able to be conceived in such a way that the lawfulness of its form is at least in agreement with the possibility of the ends to be realized in accordance with the laws of freedom" (*Ak* 5: 176, ENG 63).

Nietzsche says that some concepts are like rainbows thrown over an abyss.[69] The power of judgment is precisely that. The two self-standing domains remain absolutely separate, but they somehow meet on the territory of experience. In the two domains, the critique that identifies the principle gives rise to a doctrine, whereas in the case of the power of judgment, which does not have a domain of its own, we have only an a priori principle for its exercise, not a doctrine. The domains meet impalpably, i.e., they do not issue a doctrine. It seems as if only the shadow of words can describe this meeting. But unlike a rainbow or a shadow (unlike, say, Odysseus's mother's shadow), this meeting does have a concrete, palpable result. The two domains are ultimately *harmonized* by the power of judgment. It interprets nature as if it were the effect of freedom and bridges the gap between "the manner of thinking" (*Denkungsart, Ak* 5: 176, ENG 63) according to the principles of nature and that according to the principles of morality. For this reason the third *Critique* concludes with moral teleology, history, and culture, which are understood as if they were the realization of a supersensible end.[70] Thus the "power of judgment makes possible the transition from the domain of the concept of nature to that of the concept of freedom" (*Ak* 5: 196, ENG 82).

Furthermore, when I say "almost exclusively the practical sphere," the "practical sphere" may actually mean different scopes: morality in a narrow sense but also a wider interpretation of the world as if it were the result of a wise (good and just) creation. In the ethico-theology of the third *Critique* as well as in Kant's later writings on religion, the ideas will find a new room

---

69. Fragment 419 (1885) of *Der Wille zur Macht.*

70. "The effect in accordance with the concept of freedom is the final end [*der Endzweck*], which (or its appearance in the sensible world) *should* [*ought to*] exist, for which the condition of its possibility in nature . . . is presupposed" (*Ak* 5: 196, ENG 81).

that compensates for and tends to recast their indispensable projection of a maximum and a totality and the role they had in the idea of cosmic philosophy in the architectonic idea of a system of sciences, in the regulative ideas in the sciences, and in cognition in general. The third *Critique* transforms the hypothetical imperatives of the *Groundwork* into technical-practical principles and reduces them to a theoretical corollary of the philosophy of nature (*KU, Ak* 5: 172, ENG 60). Hypothetical imperatives are accordingly expelled from morality, which now contains only categorical imperatives. This *restriction of morality* is the result of the new concept of a *technique of nature* struggling to carve out a space for itself at the expense of and between theory and practice. The purposiveness of nature is merely formal finality. As such, its ends differ from practical ends, even though they are thought in analogy with them (*Ak* 5: 180–81, ENG 68). In morality, that is, ends contain the ground of the reality of things. In the technique of nature, ends are considered as if they contained them.

But ideas will also reappear as aesthetic ideas and in beauty. For beauty is the purposive mode of being of that which escapes the understanding's determination in appearance and must therefore be considered the symbol of the supersensible (*KU* § 59).

So what has been or begins to be suppressed? The positive character of ideas seems to be gradually eliminated. Is it really, though? The "immanent use of transcendental ideas" (*KrV* A 643) as necessary guidance for the fruitful extension of the understanding and for reason's self-knowledge, in particular the regulative use of ideas for science and cognition that was discussed in the Appendix to the Dialectic, has been ousted from the realm of scientific metaphysics. Thus, of the two modalities of reason's procedure in science in the Transcendental Dialectic, *the apodictic and the hypothetical*, the apodictic alone remains. It is naturally all the more dogmatic, so that the identification of the Transcendental Dialectic's exclusive purpose of denouncing the vain pretensions of metaphysics is smoother.

By contrast, the hypothetical use, in which reason projected a maximum that was used as a heuristic instrument to find particular cognitions, far from being suppressed at all, becomes now the principle for the power of reflective judgment. The hypothetical use is the privileged terrain for the power of judgment as it approaches nature in a purposive rather than a mechanistic manner. Regulative ideas become the guidance the power of judgment needs to make sense of the infinite variety and contingency of nature. They become the heuristic maxims to inquire about what cannot be reduced to physical laws under which our determinant judgment simply subsumes events.

In turn, if theoretical reason is identified with the understanding and determinant judgment in particular, reflection is opposed to it. But the neater the opposition, the less independent its relata. Determinant judgment, in order to have a universal from which to start, needs a preliminary reflective activity constituting an empirical generality. Observation is made possible by the presupposition of uniformity. Induction, analogy, empirical investigation are made possible by principles that the first *Critique* called regulative ideas and maxims of reason, and that now are maxims of the power of judgment. The first *Critique*, which was the interrelation of all its moments, is now reduced to a *fragment* of the totality it was: the understanding. It cannot stand on its own feet and would collapse if it could not lean on to its peers flanking it on either side (sensibility and reason proper). For this reason the first *Critique* now vitally depends on the third to be even only a minimally consistent theory of the understanding's concepts.

Determination presupposes reflection. Now Kant presents this as if it were a late discovery he has stumbled upon in the third *Critique*. In parallel fashion, he presents the determinant judgment as if it were a mechanical and thoughtless subsumption. The first *Critique* is less and less sufficient unto itself as it is looted from every quarter, broken apart and dismembered. This is a ransack, not an even battle. Without Kant, who now speaks only from the perspective of the third *Critique*, the first *Critique* has no advocate left. What we get in return is a new conception of reason, which purports to be the result of a more comprehensive self-examination on reason's part.

That this is so finds easy textual support. For it is about the integration of the critique of judgment in the critique of reason that the introductions to the third *Critique* speak (*EE* § 11). Specifically in the published Introduction, *Kant calls the three Critiques together the critique of pure reason* (*KU* § 3, *Ak* 5: 179, ENG 66). The power of judgment mediates between the legislations of understanding and of reason (*KU* § ix, *Ak* 5: 195, ENG 80–81). Now "pure reason" is simply the name for the *faculty of desire (sic)*. What is so striking here is not only that reason is now the practical reason of the second *Critique*. That we have seen; what we have not seen is that it is now called simply *pure reason*. Be that as it may, the third *Critique* is the unity of the first two as they were configured in 1790.

The methodological consequences for the study of Kant are major. Not only, as I said, do a linear and piecemeal reading of the *Critique of Pure Reason* and a selection of individual parts as its supposedly decisive core lead us to a dead end. The first *Critique* must be studied also for what its original idea (plan, design, conception) becomes in the subsequent works, which in turn must be approached comprehensively, as a unitary plan in constant reshaping, a work in relentless progress.

If in A the idea of a system is the highest, although purely methodological, idea that regulates the use of the understanding and represents the world as if it were a totality accessible to us (*KrV* A 672–73), in the third *Critique* purposiveness becomes the a priori principle of reflective judgment. It guides the search for systematic unity in a now particular and contingent nature replete with heterogeneous forms. Systematicity is subordinated to formal purposiveness as one of its aspects. The several laws that the Appendix to the Transcendental Dialectic called the principles of homogeneity, specification, and continuity (*KrV* A 657–58) are now the "transcendental expression of the power of judgment in establishing a principle for experience and hence for its own needs" (*EE* § 4, *Ak* 20: 210, ENG 14). Readers of the Transcendental Dialectic are dumbfounded as they find out that "neither understanding nor reason can ground such a law of nature a priori" (ibid.).

In its third, finally unifying part, the new reason is less rigid and less modeled after the apodicticity and necessity of sciences than before. It is more attentive to finding the universal in the particular and not subsuming the particular under the readymade universal. It is still sensitive to the moral view of the world without being the simple agent of the realization of the categorical imperative.

If now we concentrate on intuitive presentations (*Darstellungen*) that we judge reflectively, we do use concepts but judge independently of them. Imaginative freedom takes center stage. Harmony and purposiveness cannot be found either in morality or in theoretical reason, for they pertain to a newly independent understanding of sensibility and presentation. Accordingly, this new reason is meant to advance a different conception of sensibility as well. Indeed the move parallel to the displacement and impoverishment of the Dialectic and the Doctrine of Method is the broadening of sensibility. Recall that in morality the order of faculties is reversed: instead of going from sensibility to understanding to principles, it proceeds top-down and ends in feeling.

As I said before, the position of the third *Critique* is the result of a recasting of the relation among faculties. Through the discovery that we have a rational feeling that belongs in the faculty of desire (not in the feeling of pleasure and displeasure), Kant separates practical reason from the feeling of pleasure. Now practical reason is the higher faculty of desire sufficient to determine itself to action purely. The feeling of pleasure turns out now not to be exclusively empirical but to have its own a priori principle in purposiveness, which opens up the room for a third *Critique*. In the B edition of the first *Critique* Kant revises his position toward Baumgarten. Kant now wants to share Baumgarten's term 'aesthetics,' which he criticized in A.

In Angelica Nuzzo's excellent reconstruction of this transition, "[t]he term aesthetics is now permitted not only for a transcendental but also for a psychological inquiry. And yet . . . , Kant is decisively moving away from the view of aesthetics as an exclusively cognitive doctrine."[71] In the Doctrine of Method of the second *Critique*, Kant addresses reason's activity of judging the practical and discovers that judging has a strange effect on our feeling. For judgment puts us in contact with ourselves. It makes us feel ourselves.[72]

Reflection in the third *Critique* puts this discovery to use. It is a metafaculty that judges what other faculties do. The power of judgment that Kant now studies is the result of the modification of our state as we judge the purposiveness of forms. This is another momentous discovery: a reflective judgment affects the body and its sensibility. We feel elated and enlivened when we judge something as purposive, as if it met our need to find in it a sign of an intelligent design of nature. Discovering a beautiful form that seems as if it were made for our enjoyment shows that we do have pure, as opposed to empirical, feelings indifferent to the material existence of the object.

Now that we have seen the implications of the retrospective reduction of the first *Critique* to the narrow scope of the understanding in a theory of knowledge, we can take up again the lines of the Preface to the third *Critique* from which we began this section. They will I hope appear more understandable, even if no less shocking. They will also appear as a convenient scheme to be easily memorized in schools—possibly the result of Kant's love of nice and clean symmetries that Schopenhauer denounced as baroque.

Reason is exclusively practical. The first *Critique* concerns only the understanding. Now we move on to the third part, actually a *Mittelglied* (intermediary) between reason and understanding. The Preface to the *Critique of Judgment*, recall, claims that by critique of pure reason "only reason in its theoretical use is understood" (*Ak* 5: 167, ENG 55). The critique concerns solely the faculty of cognition, and

> among the faculties of cognition it concerns itself only with the *understanding* in accordance with its a priori principles, excluding *the power of judgment* and *reason*. . . . Thus it was strictly speaking the understanding . . . which was to be

71. *Ideal Embodiment*, 205.
72. Ibid., 214–15.

established in secure and unique possession against all competitors by means of the critique of pure reason. (*Ak* 5: 167–68, ENG 55–56)

The scheme is convenient because it is functional to Kant's goals. They consist in recalling in simplified, quick, even curt terms an opposition (nature-freedom) whose intricate complexity he has no interest in reconstructing faithfully. All he wants is to introduce the intermediary term, the power of judgment.

This simplification completely forgets the positive character of ideas in the first *Critique* and amounts to the dismissal of the Transcendental Dialectic and Doctrine of Method. This passage undermines the fundamental internal unity of pure reason as an organism prior to its distinctions. It provides support for all truncated readings of the first *Critique* and all positivistic readers of the first *Critique*, from Cohen to Husserl and Heidegger down to most analytic interpretations after Strawson.[73] Rather than approaching reason as a complex unity that can find satisfaction of its needs only in the unconditional totalities of ideas, they limit themselves to repeating the merely negative result that ideas cannot be cognitions and find in the nexus Transcendental Aesthetics–Transcendental Analytic the core of the work.

But Kant's words may also be shocking on different counts. They claim more than the already problematic thesis of the reduction of the first *Critique* to a critique of the understanding in a theory of knowledge. Start from the end of the quote: the understanding *never* needed to be established in its secure possessions. It was reason that used the understanding's concepts for its transcendent ideas and its illegitimate conclusions. Before the third *Critique*, the critique of pure reason was never, to the best of my knowledge, said to be a critique of the understanding. Were this and the alleged exclusion of reason from the first *Critique* not enough, now we find something no less unsettling. The power of judgment, we read, was also excluded from it.

This is more than puzzling, for it dismisses not only the Transcendental Dialectic and Doctrine of Method but also the second book of the Analytic, which is but a *canon for the power of judgment* (*KrV* A 132/B 171). The Principles of the Understanding are the synthetic a priori judgments that structure experience. They are the realization of the Analytic, the application of reason to experience. Obviously Kant *now* (in 1790) thinks that those pages did not

---

73. None of those authors is a positivist, obviously. I use that term deliberately to indicate the theoretical futility of ideas, the impossibility of rising above the phenomenal level, and the exclusively meaningful use of reason in regard to experience.

adequately account for the reflective power of judgment whose centrality he has meanwhile discovered. In fact, now the power of judgment is identified with reflection per se, even if naturally Kant has to admit that the power of judgment is divided into determinant and reflective (*KU, Ak* 5: 179, ENG 66). But it is as if the determinant judgment, now the exclusive concern of a proprietary understanding claiming (better: vainly presuming) it can take care of itself, were treated like history, a thing of his past to be shrugged off or cast out like a beggar of whom Kant in this context hardly even bothers to be reminded. It is as if that understanding were now identified with the most derogatory aspect of the name the Architectonic used to address an artist of reason: cyclops.

When Kant now defines judgment as the relation between universal and particular (*KU, Ak* 5: 179, ENG 66), he forgets some of the most poignant pages of the Transcendental Analytic. He forgets that purposiveness, the a priori principle of the power of judgment that he now introduces, belongs to what was there the natural talent of relating universal and particular he so brilliantly explained (at *KrV* A 132–36/B 171–75). He forgets that the power of judgment through the imagination mediated between sensibility and understanding and made possible the understanding's a priori reference to pure intuition. He forgets that the power of judgment is the schematization of pure concepts relating two heterogeneous planes to one another. He forgets that as a result transcendental logic differs from general logic because in addition to the rule, the understanding can indicate a priori the instance to which the rule applies. He forgets that he defined the understanding as the faculty not only of thinking and of rules, but also of judging if and when those rules apply.[74]

74. A 126. If Kant is reluctant to give a definition of categories (*KrV* A 81/B 108), he gives a remarkable plethora of definitions of the understanding. Common to A and B are the following definitions: at A 51/B 75, the understanding is the spontaneity of knowledge. Later on the same page, it is the faculty of thinking. At A 65/B 90 it is the faculty of a priori concepts. At A 68/B 93 it is the faculty of discursive knowledge. At A 69/B 94 the faculty of judging. When we then come to the Transcendental Deduction, we find more definitions. In A the understanding is first defined as the unity of apperception in relation to the synthesis of imagination (*KrV* A 118). At A 126 Kant says that the understanding is the spontaneity of knowledge, a faculty of thought, of concepts, of judgments, of rules (in this order). In the B Transcendental Deduction he also presents several definitions. At B 130 the understanding is the spontaneity of the representational faculty responsible for combination. At B 134n it is equated with the synthetic unity of apperception. At B 135 it is the faculty of combining a priori and bringing under the unity of apperception. At B 137 it is the faculty of cognitions. At B 172 the faculty of rules. *At this point* Kant distinguishes it from the power of judgment: "If the understanding in general is explained as the faculty of rules, then the power of judgment is the faculty of *subsuming* under rules" (*KrV*

True, the power of judgment is peculiarly amphibious. Its intermediate position between understanding and reason was after all discussed in the first *Critique*. In the section of the Transcendental Dialectic on the logical use of reason (*KrV* A 303/B 359ff.), Kant writes that in inferences I assume a rule through the understanding, subsume a cognition under that rule through the *Urteilskraft*, and determine finally my conclusion through reason (*KrV* A 304/B 360–61).[75] But this is another case of subsumption and relation between universal and particular, i.e., it belongs to the schematization of pure concepts and the relation between concepts and intuitions. In the first *Critique*, this is precisely the business of schematized concepts, which have a constitutive role now forgotten by Kant. In other words, the power of judgment is both between reason proper and the understanding and between understanding and sensibility.

Perhaps I need not remind the reader that there is something healthy about forgetting. Living needs forgetting as much as it needs remembering. Forgetting is looking ahead, not remaining comfortably moored in our harbor or brooding resentfully over the past. Kant's forgetting is in part the antihistorical gesture of the Enlightenment revolutionary keen on voiding tradition and turning a page for good. In part it is also an attitude of detachment: witness his careless, almost indifferent revision of the second edition of the *Critique*. If he had omitted or changed passages no longer consistent with his new positions, he would have improved the clarity and consistency of his works and aided the interpreter. But revolutionaries do not work for scholars.

Kant, however, is a revolutionary *malgré soi*, for his temperament is that of a moderate man. Judging from the allegiance to his thought he sought in his pupils and in those who aspired to be considered his friends and the touchiness he showed as he felt suddenly betrayed by most of them, if he had been faced with the choice of pursuing his thought relentlessly regardless of the consequences or remaining faithful to his word, I am not sure he would have been in favor of a permanent revolution. That is to say: I am not sure he would have valued his own forgetting.

A 132/B 171; see also *EE, Ak* 20: 201, ENG 8). But since no concept is objective unless it is combined with other concepts in a judgment and no rule is such unless it is applied, *the power of judgment is treated as an application of the understanding* (as it is literally called at *KrV* A 132/B 171). Finally, the understanding is the source of principles (*KrV* A 159/B 198).

75. The same can be found already at A 131/B 169. See also the letter to Beloselski of 1792 (*Ak* 11: 344–46).

Another possibility is that this is not forgetting at all but the lack of realization on Kant's part that the many little changes intervening between 1781 and 1790 add up to a significant transformation of his thought. This possibility is worth mentioning only because Kant himself compels us to consider it. For as he introduces the revised edition of the first *Critique* in 1787, he writes that he hopes this "is a more comprehensible presentation, which fundamentally alters *absolutely nothing* in regard to the propositions or even their grounds of proof" (*KrV* B xlii, italics mine).

The tensions between reason's activity and its products and between an organic and a constructive model I stressed in chapter 1 prove deep-seated and persistent. They can be invoked even to make sense of Kant's shifts on and forgetting of his own thinking. The first tension is rooted in the fact that sooner or later thinking insensitively becomes doctrine until it is replaced by what we call tradition. The second tension can be rephrased in the following dilemma: does reason work *through* us, including through Kant the philosopher, as an anonymous force, or is it to be equated with the I's *subjectivity*? If reason is a seed, that is, a power independent of individuality (of the will, of human subjectivity, of consciousness), a gap between reason's and Kant's own self-knowledge is always possible, indeed inevitable, for pure reason is not Kant's possession.

It is true that revolutionaries do not work for scholars, but neither do they work for themselves. They break ground and open up possibilities that do not belong to them. Pure reason escapes our command and sometimes even our consciousness. Reason overlaps with human reason but also transcends it. If, instead, reason is a voluntary and conscious setting of ends, Kant is left with the problematic identification of reason with transcendental apperception and the I-think. As we have seen, reason and thought cannot be reduced to understanding and judgment. In particular, reason cannot be reduced to the subjectivity of individual consciousness or to an I's predicate.

We have thus come back full circle to the questions from which we began. Let us conclude with a reformulation of the problem of the transformation of the power of judgment from one last perspective. The third *Critique* does not only use the *disjecta membra* of the Transcendental Dialectic and the Doctrine of Method and feast on the leftovers of reason proper thanks to the new conceptions of sensibility and of the supersensible substrate of nature and freedom. On many crucial points, Kant attributes to the power of judgment what in the first *Critique* would be distinct functions and aspects of *imagination* (whether as executor of the power of judgment or in itself).

They range from presentation (*Darstellung*) to bridging the gulf between universal and particular to the symbol, from aesthetic ideas to the genius, from the technique of nature to the new conception of form as purposive and the sign of a sought-for harmony.

Unfortunately this discussion would take us too far afield. I had better close with this question and leave it open for another investigation.[76]

76. See my *Kant on Imagination*.

These heterogeneous elements, the subject which is the particular and in the form of being, and the predicate which is the universal and in the form of thought, are at the same time absolutely identical. It is reason alone that is the possibility of this positing, for reason is nothing else but the identity of heterogeneous elements.
—G. W. F. Hegel, *Faith and Knowledge*

We have seen that Kant is more revolutionary than is generally recognized. Despite his rhetoric flaunting the scientific style of his thought, it is not the culmination of modern philosophy or the hidden telos of a trajectory inaugurated by the scientific revolution. Reason is not simply the tool for mankind's progress. Kant is the philosopher of reason, but his reason does not have a scientistic, logical, or instrumental function. Reason is the institution of order and laws in its scopes of application for the sake of ends it sets itself.

In this conclusion I would like to dwell on the problems internal to the definition of reason as faculty (§ 1), and finally give an overview of the results of this book (§ 2).

1. What Is a Faculty? The Facticity of Reason

To illustrate one last time the powers of reason and the compatibility between our finitude and reason's essence as a priori synthesis and activity, let us imagine the following fictitious scenario and consider its implications.

It is dark and rainy outside. The wrist with which John is typing is badly aching from a recent fall. This morning he accidentally dropped his mother's old porcelain cup. To top it all, he needs to write comments on a dissertation he finds more disappointing than expected. Yet he does not feel sad or gloomy. He is listening to the Allegretto ma non troppo of Beethoven's piano sonata opus 101, the only thing that makes him think straight and keeps him sane. Despite being somewhat uneasy and anxious, he also feels quite resolute, for soon he will see his friend. A clarification is sorely needed after their bitter exchange yesterday. He is almost surprised but glad to realize that this incident has not affected him irremediably, for despite everything he is still looking forward to a quite exceptional event tonight, Maurizio Pollini's piano recital.

What I have described is the stuff we are made of. Things happen to us. We have little power over them. They determine us. We live surrounded by things and people that escape our grip. We are our body, our feelings. Few things are more vulnerable, and we depend on them. We are inescapably passive before things; in fact passivity is our normal and typical material condition. Contingency, nature, givenness, passivity, finitude: we can name our condition as we like, but choosing a name for it seems the most we can do about it.

If all that is what we are, still it is not *all* that we are. We need to add a piece to this picture: there is something in us that transcends nature. Consider this.

John knew all along that unlike rubber (or air, as in the *Prolegomena*), porcelain is not elastic. He blames his clumsiness for breaking the cup because he knew all along that his cup is fragile in virtue of its being a porcelain object, of belonging to a kind he is familiar with. He also knew all along that falling on one's wrist while ice skating can hurt because he knew all along that he is subject to laws regarding impact and gravity in virtue of being a body like any other.

He knows that when he sees his friend he has a choice between patiently exercising self-restraint and letting out his justified anger. During their clarification he can wish to act—not react—according to justice, or dignity, or forgiveness, or love for his friend.

He gratefully recognizes that there is a pure enjoyment of beauty that puts out of play the concerns and preoccupations of daily life with its unshakable facts. His mind can shift from them to a world of play and art that is, in the words of the third *Critique*, indifferent to existence.

These are not things that happen to us but things *we do*. When what we do is at stake, it is not things that determine us; we are not subject to them. We do things on the basis of what happens to us, naturally: we gauge the range of possible action so as to negotiate and come to terms with what affects us. But however limited the results of our efforts may be, what we do and how we do it belong to an altogether different scope than our condition. If passivity is our material condition, what we do about it—how we live—is up to us. That is, we do live in nature but also in a symbolic world (in a non-Kantian word). Reason's world cannot be reduced to nature in any way. That is not because we delude ourselves we can disregard the importance of nature and loosen our dependence on it, but because we are addressing our activity and not a natural condition.

This may appear more plausible when it comes to the choices we make in our practical life but applies equally well to our cognitive activity regarding nature, which, as we have seen, has different layers. As an example consider how the cases of the cup and the wrist differ. In the first, the object is taken as belonging to a familiar kind with its own unique material or chemical composition. John has an empirical cognition that is in addition subsumed under a law. Here we presuppose the specific knowledge of the kind and also the general knowledge of gravity. This is comparable to Kant's example of a relative a priori in the Introduction to the first *Critique* (*KrV* B 2): I know a priori that if I undermine the foundations of my house it will fall. In the second, John does not subsume an empirical object under its particular kind, which he then brings back to a law, for unlike porcelain, 'body' is a fundamental and general concept of a science of nature. Here we presuppose an a priori knowledge of nature, in which no specific knowledge of a material or chemical composition is involved. In these two cases we bring objects back to an order ruled by laws.[1]

All of which is to say that we may be surrounded by objects, but even while cognizing them, reason is the origin of something that neither is reducible to nor derives from them in any sense. In other words, reason generates a cognition, and a cognition regarding nature is above nature. In a cognition reason transcends nature in one of two ways: by rising above our natural condition and making, for example, universal and necessary claims in theoretical and practical matters not determined by nature, or by assuming an impersonal objective perspective that remains irreducible to an individual I.

---

1. Both cases fall under my knowledge of objectivity. With respect to both the cup and the wrist I have universal cognitions regarding empirical objects, but the way they involve a priori knowledge differs. In the first case the empirical knowledge of a particular kind is a relative a priori, which Kant distinguishes from what is "entirely a priori" (*KrV* B 2). That is, we have learned empirically such kinds as porcelain objects and treat a cup as both the instance of the kind 'porcelain' and the manifestation of a universal law. By contrast, in the second case knowledge that ice-skating is risky is irrelevant because a body obeys the law of gravity irrespective of kinds and contexts (if John had fallen on his wrist while playing tennis it would have been the same).

This seems straightforward enough. You and I do not have a say on whether porcelain is fragile or free fall could one day take a different course. Reason is not my reason. Reason takes my experience as the *index* of a possible experience and what is given to me now as given in principle to any subject.

Reason is that in us which makes us transcend nature. Kant calls this power in us a faculty. But what is a faculty? In Nietzsche's *Beyond Good and Evil* we read the following aphorism.

> Kant "was proud of having *discovered* a new faculty in man, the faculty of synthetic judgment *a priori*. . . . But let us reflect for a moment—it is high time to do so. "How are synthetic judgments a priori *possible?*" Kant asks himself—and what is really his answer? *"By means of a faculty"*—but unfortunately not in five words, but so circumstantially, imposingly, and with such display of German profundity and verbal flourishes, that one altogether loses sight of the comical *niaiserie allemande* involved in such an answer. . . . Then came the honeymoon of German philosophy. All the young theologians of the Tübingen institution went immediately into the groves—all seeking for "faculties." . . . But is that—an answer? An explanation? Or is it rather a mere repetition of the question? How does opium induce sleep? "By means of a faculty," namely the *virtus dormitiva*, replies the doctor in Molière. . . . But such replies belong to the realm of comedy, and it is high time to replace the Kantian question, "How are synthetic judgments a priori possible?" by another question, "Why is belief in such judgments *necessary?*"—in effect, it is high time that we should understand that such judgments must be believed to be true, for the sake of the preservation of creatures like ourselves; though they still might naturally be *false* judgments![2]

I do not intend to criticize this passage or comment on it at length.[3] I want instead to address the only point worth calling a *thought* that Nietzsche, his sarcasms and rhetoric to one side, is also interested in and brilliantly

---

2. § 11, *Sämtliche Werke*, 5: 24–26.

3. I limit myself to pointing out the following. Nietzsche makes use of notions of truth and falsehood that seem hardly pertinent to Kant. Even more immaterial is the transformation of truth into useful belief—and yet, it is only because he assumes that all we have is useful belief that he can charge Kant with passing his invention of reason for a discovery. He might as well have spoken of judgments or concepts in general: the 'a priori' matters to him as little as the specific content of Kant's question. His reference to Hölderlin, Schelling, and Hegel, the Tübingen *Stiftler*, is amusing but quite gratuitous, as is the general portrayal of philosophers (at least most post-Kantians) as dupes.

formulates: How can a faculty not be the mere repetition of the problem it poses?

How are we supposed to understand a faculty? What can we learn from this notion of faculty that might help us to reach a verdict on Kant's reason and critical philosophy?

A faculty or power is, like *virtus* in Nietzsche's Molière but also *vis* in Baumgarten and the German scholastics, something elusive and evanescent, between being and nothing. If it is appealed to to explain a process, all it seems to do is give it a name. The Megarians put in question the fruitfulness of the notion of power. Why distinguish between something like fire and its possibility or power? Where would a power reside? Either you have fire or you don't, it seems. Something like 'combustibility' is, literally, neither here nor there.

If there is a distinction at all between power and actuality in the case of fire, it is an abstract one and the Megarians seem to have a point.[4] There is no potency unless it is actualized. Aristotle, who thought that the difference between potency and actuality must be safeguarded because all change is real as a transition from potency to actuality, distinguished between irrational and rational potentialities depending on whether they are bound to produce one effect only or can give rise to a plurality of effects spanning a range of contraries. His respective examples are fire's potentiality, which cannot be anything other than that of burning, and medical science, which is instead 'rational' insofar as it is the potentiality of contraries, health and illness (*Metaphysics* Θ 2). The way of being of a disposition, Aristotle adds, implies that it is not necessarily exercised; otherwise I would have to consider myself blind and deaf whenever I do not actually exercise sight and hearing (*Metaphysics* Θ 3, 1047a 8–10).

One last Aristotelian distinction pertinent in this context is that between movement and activity. In the former, the potential state is replaced by another state. Potentiality disappears once it has reached its end. Once I have lost five pounds, I have reached my standard weight; once I have finished my novel or my dinner, the process is complete and I am free to move on to something else. The result or product gives the movement its meaning and end. Other processes called activities, instead, are the strengthening or actualization of a power. Here the end is internal to the act and the exercise of the power has no end outside itself.[5]

4. See Rosen, "Much Ado about Nothing.".

5. For a discussion of these distinctions from *Metaphysics* Θ; *Physics* 3; *De anima* 2; and *Nicomachean Ethics* 1, 7, and 10; see my *Hegel and Aristotle*, 15–27.

We have seen in the discussion of essential ends in chapter 1 that Kant's reason exemplifies Aristotelian activity, not movement. The end of reason is the exercise of its activity, and this is a system of ends. Through its ideas, reason directs its activities according to an organic plan. If reason is a faculty, however, the question is: What is its mode of being? What does it mean for it to actualize itself? Is it comparable to fire? If it is, then it seems it undergoes its nature or destiny, which is to think. It is necessitated and definitely not free to choose to be what it is (or be different). If we look closer, we find once again that comparing reason's architectonic idea to a seed was as little an occasional incidental remark on Kant's part as is the remark in the *Metaphysics of Morals* that reason's will is not free.[6] The organic model—that is, life irrespective of individual inclinations or goals, an impersonal force we do not own or make—had to impose itself upon Kant's conception of reason.

But we know that reason is also an architect. Reason, which is nothing but autonomy, is a project. Ideas, its medium and element, define the goal of reason's inquiry and the plan and method for all its activities. Reason has no antecedently given standards; it is the government of itself. The *Critique of Pure Reason* shows that reason recognizes no authority higher than its own tribunal.

We can therefore reiterate that reason has the mode of being of an *activity*—a synthetic, productive one. As we have seen throughout this book, transcendental philosophy is not an analytical regress to a first ground. The form of intuition is not one such ground. It is not an inert form we are endowed with, separate from its application, for it comes only in the form of an activity: the synthetic activity that collects, runs through, and relates the sensible manifold. Likewise, both pure and empirical concepts are the result of a formation. In particular, a priori concepts are not innate abstractions because they are a form of activity. They are the result of a pure synthesis and consist in their use. A condition of possibility consists entirely (indeed, has no reality independently) of what it conditions and makes possible. Ideas are also a product of reason's totalization and a guide for every use we make of reason.

More specifically, then, we can say that reason's activity has the mode of being of a *source*. As such, reason has a functional-operative meaning. But it is a source of laws and rules. Its principles cannot be formal norms that act

---

6. In man choice is free, but the will "cannot be called either free or unfree, since it is not directed to actions but immediately to giving laws" (*Ak* 6: 226, ENG 380).

upon reason or that reason *discovers* behind its back. Reason has no foundation outside itself. Its principles cannot transcend it or be separate from what they govern. They generate their objects. We have seen the interrelation between objective reality and a priori synthesis: reason produces a world in the idea with all its concepts.

If reason cannot be something apart from what it is the faculty for, and if activity means the exercise of a faculty, it might seem that a transcendental condition is both necessary and sufficient for an activity and its exercise. Obviously it cannot be so, for a faculty is not always exercised (however elusive the distinction between essence and use of reason we saw in chapter 1 may be). The difference between reason and an irrational potency is that if reason is about which rules govern which of its activities, it is more comparable to medicine than to fire, for its causality has a plurality of possible effects. By contrast, we can now see that the relation between power and actuality in fire (or in Molière's *virtus*) is *analytic*.

An additional reason for denying reason the mode of activity of fire is that reason, even more fundamentally than a source, is first of all *reflection* on itself. Not only does logical reflection, as we have seen when speaking of the formation of concepts, play an indispensable role, but we also have a transcendental reflection that is no less central. If we cannot bring representations back to their source, if, that is, in the task of transcendental reflection reason fails, so do, for example, our views of causality (which Hume took as a product of imagination instead of a pure concept) and of the couple matter-form (which both Locke and Leibniz inverted). More fundamentally, as we have seen (chapter 3, § 2), transcendental philosophy has its own synthesis and criterion of truth, for reason is self-examination: knowledge of its principles, its inner constitution, and thus of the experience it makes possible. There is nothing mechanical or predetermined in this self-knowledge.

The redundancy that Nietzsche denounced can be avoided, if unlike fire reason is not another simple name for our question. But is it perhaps only—a *complex* name?

We have seen that reason is the source of laws. When it comes to nature, reason is the origin of a mechanism and of the transcendental affinity (nature as the lawful totality of all appearances). As a result, it cannot be subject to the same mechanistic laws it issues. Determinism does not apply to reason. To paraphrase Sartre, there can be a source and a consciousness of laws, but no law of sources or consciousness.

But if reason is groundless, i.e., not grounded from without, can we say it grounds itself? Can we say that reason is a *causa sui*, i.e., a substance that is its own foundation and the cause of its own exercise? Or, despite the impossibility of a determinism of reason and for all its difference from fire, must we speak of a *facticity of reason*?

Here is another qualification to the notion of the powers of reason. Reason cannot have absolute power over itself. Even if I have emphasized the positive role of ideas and of the Transcendental Dialectic for the sake of a more comprehensive account calling into question the assumptions of the standard reading of Kant, there is no denying that reason's authority over itself is relative. Reason is the production of laws, but not of itself. In fact, as we know, it can control itself to a degree but not redeem itself from its tendency to misunderstand, deceive, or illude itself. No process of habituation can give reason the shape of a second nature that at some point becomes effortlessly and instinctively purposive. That is, reason cannot become spontaneously virtuous—inherently good, or whole. Reason must discipline itself because it is divided against itself. If reason is spontaneously dialectical, it cannot trust itself fully.

Even its unity is not to be taken for granted. We must, writes Kant in the Dialectic (*KrV* A 650–51/B 678–79), seek a unity for reason's rules. The logical principle of this unity rests on a transcendental principle that assumes as necessary a systematic unity. As we see, unity is necessary, even beneficial in the understanding's search for regularities, but it is not an objective matter of fact. It is *an idea*. It is necessary, but because it is inevitable for our reason to give itself this direction. As a result, reason cannot choose to be different or change its course at will.

Finally, recall the end of chapter 1. Reason's teleology, I argued, is a genitive in both senses: reason aims at ends, and reason (the practice of rational activity) is the end of its own strivings. And yet, if the unity and hierarchy of ends are established by philosophy, reason's activity is not an absolute or *final* end. Reason is subordinated to the question of our ultimate destination. It is addressed to the highest good. It aims beyond itself.

On the basis of the above considerations I can now answer the question I have raised: reason cannot choose what it wants to be, but *we as individuals* are free to choose whether or not to *endorse reason*: to care about it, to make it actual. We exercise choice all the time, even when we fail to choose, and we fail to choose reason when we choose to eschew responsibility instead. We are fundamentally free to dodge enlightenment and live in a state of minority.

Recall that reason is an internally articulated faculty. Its different subfaculties and powers, which for all we know do not stem from one original source or common root, are different names for modalities of reason's unitary activity.[7] In the Dohna Metaphysics Kant criticizes Baumgarten for confusing power and substance. The definition of the soul as *vis repraesentativa universi*, the 'power to represent the world,' does not satisfy Kant. Kant does not object (as would Husserl in the *Cartesian Meditations*) that the soul is not separated neatly enough from the world of which it is the source. His problem is a different one. He believes that Baumgarten's definition fails to identify a substance and describes instead a power, which can be considered "the relation of the substance to the accident" (*Ak* 28: 671, ENG 373).

If Kant has shown that reason's mode of being is activity, however, this criticism does not stand—other than as an ad hominem argument. For *reason is a power without a substance*. When Kant speaks of the substantiality of reason, his argument is devised, it seems to me, to compel Baumgarten to gauge the distance between his wish to substantialize the soul and his actual definition, which cannot sustain his ambition. For Baumgarten the mind is still "a piece of the world" (*Ak* 28: 671, ENG 373), and in this world there are substances that have powers. Yet, as we know from both the pages on self-consciousness and the Paralogisms, neither reason nor the I is a substance or belongs in the world. Regarding reason we can say that *esse sequitur operari*—being follows from the activity, not vice versa.

In different ways Heidegger and Sartre contrast essence and existence. Things are necessitated by what is inscribed in and dictated by their essences, but human beings are not similarly necessitated, for they have no given essence. Whatever nature they have comes after existence, which must be seen as a free projection of possibilities. I think that in spite of its constructivist side, Kant's reason is not likewise free. It is as individuals that we are free to make reason our guide or not. Simply put, the constructivist side must coexist with the organic side.

---

7. Recall also that a faculty generally can be distinguished from a power. Still, Kant's use is not consistent: we have faculties of the soul and cognitive faculties, but among powers (*Kräfte*) we have *Einbildungskraft* and *Urteilskraft*, which are sometimes functions of other faculties (and substantial problems arise when we must determine if, for example, imagination is a function of sensibility or the understanding), sometimes independent faculties with their own a priori principle (like the power of judgment in the third *Critique*). This bare fact contradicts the distinction in the Metaphysics Volckmann (*Ak* 28: 434) between a faculty, which represents the possibility of an action, and a power, which is its sufficient reason and moves to action. On the number of faculties, Kant is relatively parsimonious except when he relies on Baumgarten (see how the imagination belonging in the sensitive faculty is divided into several *facultates* in the Metaphysics L1, *Ak* 28: 230–31, ENG 49–50).

2. In Closing

Key to my interpretation of Kant's new conception of reason is its teleology. Philosophy consists more in the promotion of reason's ends than in logical self-consistency or in being the instrument of mankind's progress. This is why I have taken my bearings from the architectonic description of reason in the Doctrine of Method and from the description of the ideas as the result of reason's totalizing drive in the Transcendental Dialectic and brought this conception to bear on the second and third *Critiques*.

Reason is a legislative, end-setting, self-organizing, architectonic, unifying, and autonomous power. The problem that moves Kant in his conception of reason is a metaphysical one, and critical inquiries serve the ultimate metaphysical need of reason. This is why I think we must challenge the widespread tendency to ascribe mentalistic premises to Kant and to treat the problem of skepticism (the response to Hume) as the issue that animates critical arguments. In this book I have tried to show the limits of what I have called the standard reading of Kant. This widespread form of interpretation has failed to do justice to Kant's philosophy primarily because it is infected with several uncritical and unjustified reductionist assumptions. Two are particularly egregious: a compartmentalization of the first *Critique*, and an isolation of each *Critique* from the others.

Five reasons why the standard reading falls short, all of which result from these assumptions, are the following. First, it misunderstands pure reason's finitude by construing it as the situatedness of human nature. Second, it assumes an implicit positivism, which in turn legitimates its dismissal of ideas and noumena through the reduction of the Transcendental Dialectic to the thesis that we cannot know things in themselves. Third, it ascribes inert and given forms to reason, akin to natural or innate faculties we are endowed with, and cannot grasp that reason is activity and a priori synthesis. Fourth, it operates with an impoverished notion of philosophy as conceptual analysis that prudently stays away from all concerns with ends and worth, and it cannot recognize the pervasive importance of cosmic philosophy or the subordination of scientific cognitions to it. Fifth, it conflates concepts and ideas. The formation, function, identity, and goals of concepts and ideas differ sharply. The standard reading does not respect this crucial difference. Nor does it recognize the even more fundamental fact that the different functions are adopted by pure reason according to its different needs and ends, because it portrays reason all too often in the terms of the understanding: adopting a method from without, functioning as a tool for ends it has not determined, being subjected to criteria of truth and effectiveness it finds readymade.

At the same time, it must be acknowledged that the standard reading is substantially justified on textual grounds. Scholars can always appeal to statements made by Kant himself supporting their simplifications. For, unfortunately, it is Kant himself who all too often frames questions concerning reason in terms of understanding. It is Kant who proves indecisive and ambivalent on the role of ideas and the status of cognition. As this book has demonstrated, when he retrospectively summarizes what he has accomplished in a certain text, Kant can be incredibly misleading. Furthermore, Kant's fine distinctions hide numerous ambiguities, oscillations, and occasional contradictions.

This book argues that these apparent flaws, while posing serious problems, are not fatal to Kant's articulation of the powers of reason. Kant's conception of the unity of reason is hard to recognize because critical philosophy is a work in progress that subtly changed countless times. The interpreter must approach Kant's thought architectonically and systematically and attempt to accomplish two tasks at once: reconstruct its development (noting, for example, Kant's frequent shifts on issues such as the propaedeutic role of a critique of reason and the understanding of metaphysics) and be alert for the possibility of problems and ambiguities.

This book therefore adopts methodically an internal critique. It highlights problems inherent in Kant's philosophy not in order to dismiss it, but to bring it to its implicit results. Rather than forcing artificial solutions and enclosing Kant's thinking in yet another tidy packaging, I have done my best to keep Kant's ambiguities and even inconsistencies alive. The outcome is the image of a thinker who relentlessly returns to his points to delve deeper into them. The fact that it is also the image of an often incoherent philosopher is no ground to reject his philosophy: my mention of gratitude in the Introduction was no lip service. Whatever inconsistencies I have pointed out, they do not mar the whole. They make it more complex and intricate.

In other cases, the whole is not just more involved, but also more instructive as a result. For if certain problems admit of a reconstruction (requiring us painstakingly to follow their genesis), others are deep-seated and radical. They seem to leave us in an impasse. Far from being different or additional reasons to dismiss Kant, these are in my judgment even more important, for they bring to light an underlying, surd, possibly insoluble core that forms human reason's lot and therefore returns at decisive moments in the history of philosophy. The resilient tension between organic and constructive metaphors for reason is the most obvious example. In one respect reason is subject to a force it does not make, and in the other it is self-making. This cannot be taken as a mere inconsistency on Kant's part. It is a decisive tension that keeps Kant's reason alive. It is also—I suggest, going beyond Kant's intentions—the recognition that certain problems outlast whatever solutions pretend to exhaust them.

I suggest we can consider this tension the way Kant stumbles upon the problem of the nonidentity of reason and subjectivity. We have seen that reason is not my reason; it is not reducible to an I. At the same time, reason works through an I. In chapter 3, § 4, we have seen that reason is not constituted; it is unconditional and acts on itself. My I instead is comparable to the finite result of reason's activity. We have seen how self-knowledge differs for reason, transcendental apperception, and consciousness. If we disregard this crucial difference and reduce reason to the unity of consciousness and to the I, we end up having to interpret Kant as does Hegel, for whom Kant's reason is a finite and subjective I as opposed to the world. Throughout this book I have tried to resist this oversimplification of Kant's thought that hastily and summarily dismisses it as subjectivism.

I think Kant is primarily the philosopher of reason, not of subjectivity, as the standard reading has it and as Hegel, who otherwise gives us the critical means to put it in question, is the first to claim resolutely. At the same time, I think that this nonidentity may well be the fundamental problem Kant bequeaths to post-Kantian philosophy.[8]

---

8. This very tension internal to ideas, which are both a seed and a design or plan, is mirrored in Hegel's logic. Hegel inherits Kant's tension in the duplicity of thought as a spontaneous force that at first moves unconsciously and as absolute self-consciousness. Thought is for Hegel reason's force and life, at once a logical instinct driven by the desire to be-at-home in the world and the knowledge of its self-realization in the world. Naturally Hegel's solution of the problem of the relation between thought and I differs from Kant's. See my "Spontaneity and Reification" and Il pensare.

On Schematized Categories: An Antinomy

"Instead of what is *likely*," said Socrates, "ask yourself
whether it is necessary that this be so."
—Plato, *Symposium* 200a 8–9

Seems, madam! nay, it is: I know not seems.
—W. Shakespeare, *Hamlet*, Act 1, Scene 2

Everybody, whether a philosopher or not, upon hearing the name of Kant, seems to have a definite acquaintance with well-known and obvious basic cognitions from which to start before things get too difficult and slip out of control: a few notions, often in the form of hollow and trite platitudes, to be easily repeated and memorized. Some clichés seem to be universally familiar to laymen and specialists alike, whether it is Kant's rigoristic, almost forbidding sense of morality or his transcendental idealism (minimally: we cannot know things in themselves), the starry heaven and the moral law, his role in the Enlightenment, his having been awakened by Hume, and the like. The fundamental ground of common knowledge, or, better, shared familiarity is so deeply ingrained that nobody ever even considers putting it in question.

As to the first *Critique*, nobody ignores the central thesis of the Transcendental Analytic: categories apply only to objects of possible experience. This thesis is so famous and recognizable that all attitudes with regard to Kant's thought take it for granted as a foundation, before students start delving deeper into their copy of the text, and before philosophers and scholars either critically address it and try to prove it wrong or one-sided, or try to defend it, usually through a close study of the Transcendental Deduction.

In this appendix I will do neither. I would like to show that things are not so simple and that it is worth asking questions about that thesis. I want to carry out this job by expounding what seems to me an antinomy, by which I mean a conflict with no apparent solution, but not one regarding cosmology. At stake is an interpretation of that thesis that asks where exactly it comes from, i.e., from what premises and by what means Kant supposes it should be clear to everybody. Retaining my doubts and perplexity, I cannot promise the solution of the antinomy in Kantian fashion by pointing to the different respects or scopes it refers to.

Let me start from this passage in the first chapter of the Analytic of Principles. Kant's disbelieving statement trying to contain the frustration and loss of residual patience is almost intimidating: "After what has been shown in the deduction of the categories, hopefully no one will be in doubt about how to decide the question, whether these pure concepts of the understanding are of merely empirical or also of transcendental use, i.e., whether . . . they relate a priori solely to appearances . . . or they can be extended to objects in themselves. For we have seen that these concepts are entirely impossible and cannot have any significance, where an object is not given" (*KrV* A 139/B 178).

I confess that this statement (its tone in particular) has always baffled me. The reason is plain: is the Dialectic not about the illusory extension of pure concepts to things in themselves? Does the fault of a dialectical reason not lie in its turning the canon of general logic into an organon (*KrV* A 61/B 85), and thus conflating thinking and knowing (*KrV* B 146)? Do I not in traditional dogmatic metaphysics make illegitimate statements on God as the cause of being or on the substantiality of the soul? Does that not show that categories are indeed possible, if without a meaning?

About meaning specifically,[1] should we not remind ourselves that a mere few pages later Kant says that pure concepts do "have a significance independent of all schemata and extending far beyond them" (*KrV* A 147/B 186), even if only a logical significance and not the meaning that pertains to concepts of objects? The ambiguity about meaning seems to underlie the text more than we would like it to. On the previous page Kant wrote

---

1. Meaning, reference, significance, like similar English expressions, all serve as translations of the German *Bedeutung* (in certain cases 'reference' is the concepts' *Beziehung*, 'relation,' to sensibility). It is possible to conjecture that Guyer and Wood adopt slightly different translations because they are uneasy about the contradictory use of *Bedeutung* (i.e., they tend to use 'significance' for the logical *Bedeutung* of concepts used beyond experience, and 'meaning' for the reference of concepts to possible experience). But even if my conjecture were to hold, they do not follow this practice consistently.

that because schemata give concepts a meaning, categories have no other use than the empirical (*KrV* A 146/B 185). That 'meaning' has two different senses is undeniable already here, because within the space of a few lines Kant says first that categories without reference to sensibility have significance (*KrV* A 147/B 186), and then that "significance comes to them from sensibility, which realizes the understanding at the same time as it restricts it" (*KrV* A 147/B 187).

We can either postulate two senses of significance or meaning (*Bedeutung*), or distinguish usefully between meaning, reference, use, object, and content. Let us go back to an earlier passage (*KrV* A 136/B 175): transcendental philosophy "deals with concepts that are to be related to their object a priori." This is clear. The Transcendental Deduction has proven (whether successfully or not I am not interested here in judging) the objective validity of pure concepts; "pure concepts without all content" "would be mere logical forms and not pure concepts of the understanding" (ibid.). Content and meaning are equivalent here (and the suggestion is that pure concepts have a content). But transcendent ideas do have a meaning (even if only a lexical and analytic one: I do not confuse 'God' and 'soul' in my dogmatic statements). What they do not have is an object. Indeed, in the chapter on phenomena and noumena, Kant will distinguish between logical and transcendental meaning—but not in the sense we would have anticipated: "the pure categories, without the formal conditions of sensibility, have merely transcendental significance, but are not of transcendental use" (*KrV* A 248/B 305). *Bedeutung* differs from *Gebrauch*, clearly.

But notice that here we have something different. It turns out that it was insufficient to distinguish between two senses of meaning and ascribe meaning only to schematized categories and logical meaning to unschematized categories, for what has transcendental meaning here are *unschematized* categories. Notice, however, that here 'transcendental' does not have its usual meaning; and that whatever it means, that meaning differs from the (merely) logical meaning usually ascribed to ideas. If the transcendent use is illegitimate, and concepts do have a transcendental significance according to Kant's words here, why should pure concepts applied to noumena be said to be impossible or without any significance? Why then the self-assured tone of the statement from which we started if it is so off (and was in part rephrased by Kant in a handwritten note on his own copy of the book)? And why all these ambiguities, if things should by now be settled once and for all?

On the one hand we face some alternatives that rest on a prior decision (which we can hardly be called upon to make in lieu of Kant) on the exact meaning of categories: Kant gives two different accounts of them (to which I will return presently), and clearly he has not thought that their coexistence raised a problem. On the other hand, depending on how we solve this dilemma, opposite consequences follow, each of which raises problems of compatibility with other passages and concepts and compels us to sacrifice something crucial as we push transcendental philosophy down inconsistent paths. The question is the meaning of pure concepts and the necessity of a schematism and a power of judgment as restricting conditions; but it depends on how the result of the Transcendental Deduction is interpreted.

Because pure concepts stem from the understanding in complete independence of experience, they are separate from intuition. Thinking and knowing are likewise separate; general logic is concerned with conceptual forms alone, while transcendental logic deals with pure concepts as they refer to intuition. These points indicate clearly that the general logic exceeds the transcendental logic in scope. If logic is wider than transcendental logic, and thought wider than cognition, it seems that transcendental logic and cognition arise out of a *restriction*. The restriction, however, may be in usage only or modify the very essence of what is said to be restricted: that is, either categories may be employed with or without a content (or object or meaning or reference), or they *are* only insofar as they are schematized (otherwise they are impossible, and if we think they play a role we are mistaken). That such a restriction occurs is well-known: the schematism at once realizes categories and restricts them to the conditions of sensibility (*KrV* A 146/B 186).

The question can be phrased thus: Are categories intrinsically and necessarily schematized? Or does the restriction intervene on originally unrestricted categories? It seems to me that Kant leans toward the former view, but that his arguments and his wording tend to support the latter perhaps more strongly.

Let me put the alternative in terms as simple and sharp as possible (and let me call the position of the originally schematized categories the THESIS, the schematization derived from the restriction out of a wider scope the ANTITHESIS).

The THESIS is expressed in the passage from which we started (recall *KrV* A 139/B 178: "pure concepts of the understanding are of merely empirical . . . use. For we have seen that these concepts are entirely impossible and cannot have any significance, where an object is not given"). In the THESIS, if categories are in themselves and necessarily schematized, i.e., restricted to the forms of sensibility, then they must be distinct from concepts as these are used in logical thinking unrelated to experience, in fact, not directed at cognition.

In that case, the ANTITHESIS asks, why does Kant not distinguish them sharply? And, more importantly, why would we need the power of judgment and the schematism as the bridge between two heterogeneous scopes, i.e., why would we need schemata in addition to elementary concepts if these have no independence and if the presumed heterogeneity has always already been bridged? Why is the schematization of categories the object of a distinct and later chapter that comes *after* the Transcendental Deduction? Either schematized categories are a subset of categories, a narrower group, or they are equivalent to them; but in that case, why two different presentations? Is this not a duplication?

In the THESIS, the schematism would be at most the explanation of the *how* of a process that is involved always and anyway:[2] the schematism would be a mechanical and automatic application. Admittedly, the power of judgment as the natural talent of telling whether or not an event is an instance of a rule applies only to general logic, not to transcendental logic; judge, physician, and politician are examples of *general* logic (*KrV* A 134/B 173), and it is here that intelligent application is key.

Still, in the THESIS of schematized categories we would not need an intelligent discrimination on the part of the power of judgment in that or *any* other way. Accordingly, we would not understand why we should deduce categories in any other form than as already schematized and why Kant concludes the introduction to the power of judgment (and prefaces the entrance of the Schematism) with these words: the Schematism deals "with the sensible condition under which alone pure concepts of the understanding *can* be employed" (*KrV* A 136/B 175, italics mine). Why would we need a power of judgment and not, for example, the simple action of a blind imagination that provides the concepts with their schemata, if judgment involved no thinking? The ANTITHESIS might want to argue that thinking must be involved if for no other reason than because a blind imagination may effect a synthesis, but cannot constitute the *rule or unity* of the synthesis.

In the ANTITHESIS, categories are used in many of our statements whether or not they have meaning, the determination of which is a subsequent and independent question. After all, categorical determinant judgments are not all there is to rational discourse (in fact, they are made possible

2. Kant at times distinguishes the results of the Transcendental Deduction and those of the Schematism by saying that the former show the *that (dass)*, the latter the *how (wie)*, of the relation of concepts to intuition (e.g., *KrV* B 167).

by a prior reflection). Besides, categorical determinant judgments often turn out not to be grounded at all to begin with (viz., in dogmatic metaphysics). In sum, thinking is irreducible, and prior, to talking about experience with a guaranteed reference (or content or object). This is why Kant distinguishes between reason and its several uses or applications, which are not implicitly or analytically contained in it. This is why in the case of experience application requires an intelligent power of judgment; and why we must keep concepts and their application distinct.[3] Here the schematism takes on a more dramatic role, almost that of a deus ex machina. The problem is that it must reconcile singlehandedly what has been declared as heterogeneous. But this *is* the role it is allotted, indeed burdened with, from the outset, and the one that Kant's retrospective look in the chapter on phenomena and noumena just recalled assigns it: "the Transcendental Analytic has this important result: that the understanding can never accomplish a priori anything more than to anticipate the form of a possible experience in general . . . [;] to the use of a concept there also belongs a function of the power of judgment, whereby an object is subsumed under it. . . . If this condition of the power of judgment (schema) is missing, then all subsumption disappears."[4] Not only are concepts and their use distinct; according to this passage, the condition of judgment may be missing, so that after the Transcendental Deduction we still need the additional chapter on schematism.

Many key passages and chapters in the first *Critique*, however, seem to contradict the ANTITHESIS. In particular, as the THESIS no doubt would rush to add, if categories are described in 1787 as "a priori cognitions of objects of an intuition in general" (*KrV* B 159), it seems that a transcendent use of categories must be either out of the question or based on an equivocation. Categories are concepts of an object in general. The problem, however, is that we have proven that pure concepts anticipate experience, not that they must, i.e., that that is all they can do. The Transcendental Deduction shows that categories *are* related to objects, but it does not show that they *must be* related to objects, i.e., that it is impossible for them to do otherwise.[5]

And the other problem—the ANTITHESIS might reply—is that this description in B used by the THESIS is not the only one we have of the

3. See B 169: after presenting elementary concepts, "now we will represent their use." A rule or concept is always in view of application, but the THESIS, so would ring the objection of the ANTITHESIS, cannot even allow for a difference between a rule and its application. This is the beginning of a response to the Wittgensteinian spirit of Warnock's objection ("Concepts and Schematism"). Here I am not going to comment on the schematism; see my *Kant on Imagination*.

4. A 247/B 304. See also the conclusion of *ÜGTP* (Ak 8: 184, ENG 218).

5. See also Carl, *Der schweigende Kant*, 165–71.

categories. If categories may equally be logical functions of the understanding for the synthesis of concepts (as in the Metaphysical Deduction), then they receive their reference to objects only from schemata (i.e., categories are one thing, schematized categories another).

It is obviously not up to us to decide. Also, it is impossible to decide, because for each text there seems to be another that contradicts it. Moreover, the premise regarding the exact identity of categories admits of different interpretations.[6] True, we can look at the opposite consequences of THESIS and ANTITHESIS, and what I can do is show that it is a very interesting look. But the premise is still not obvious. How are categories to be described: according to the Metaphysical Deduction or the Transcendental Deduction? And the difficulty of resolving this question is preparatory and integral to another one: how do we interpret the schematism, as original (necessary, even though simply a different version of the Transcendental Deduction: the THESIS), or derivative (supplementary, not dictated by the categories but only by our judgment's activity of subsuming the sensible manifold under them and applying them to objects: the ANTITHESIS)?

According to the THESIS, the manifold of intuition is in conformity with schematized categories from the outset (it is just a matter of discovering it); the ANTITHESIS takes the intuitive grasp of the sensible as independent of the schema of the pure concept. The THESIS, let me add, leans on the tight unity of the three syntheses in the A Deduction; the ANTITHESIS on the distinctness of the functions of apprehension, reproduction, recognition, and schematism, in order to safeguard the possibility that the appearance we apprehend be not yet subsumed under pure concepts.

The THESIS may want to lean on the key passage of the Metaphysical Deduction: a pure concept is the same function that "gives unity to the mere synthesis of different representations in a judgment" and "gives unity to the mere synthesis of different representations in an intuition" (*KrV* A 79/B 105). The ANTITHESIS may want to remind the THESIS of the independence of intuition and its heterogeneity from concepts, which prompted the Transcendental Deduction to begin with (pure concepts need to be deduced precisely because they originate in the understanding, which has no intrinsic relation to intuition).

The THESIS can appeal to many passages in its favor (besides the one from which we started), and especially can adduce the Transcendental Deduction in B as evidence for itself. The B Transcendental Deduction (in its

6. As shown by Seel, "Die Einleitung," 221–26, and Detel, "Zur Funktion des Schematismuskapitels," 40.

second part, §§ 21–26) shows that pure concepts refer not only to intuition but more specifically to our human intuition, space and time. Intuitions and concepts have an internal reference to one another ("all the manifold of intuition stand under conditions of the original synthetic unity of apperception," *KrV* B 136). The Transcendental Deduction is prefaced by these words: pure concepts "must be recognized as a priori conditions of the possibility of experience (whether of the intuition that is encountered in them, or of the thinking)" (*KrV* A 94/B 126).[7]

On the side of the ANTITHESIS we find no less relevant passages. In particular, the ANTITHESIS might want to reiterate the strong sense of restriction, as if it came from a space of thinking presupposed as wider. 'Restricted,' the ANTITHESIS might want to point out, is a past participle, i.e., a verb modified into a state, and thus the result of a preliminary act of restricting. At A 57/B 81 Kant writes that transcendental logic "has to do merely with the laws of the understanding and reason, but *solely insofar as* they are related to objects a priori, and not, as in the case of general logic, to empirical as well as pure cognitions of reason" (italics mine). This is unambiguously a limiting clause, a restriction. The same point in favor of the ANTITHESIS is scored in the footnote at B 166: "the categories are not restricted in *thinking* by the conditions of our sensible intuition, but have an unbounded field, and only the *cognition* of objects that we think, the determination of the object, requires intuition." It is curious that the THESIS, which finds in the B Deduction (and specifically in the internal reference of pure concepts to intuition presumably proven by it) its strongest ally, should now be undermined by the words with which the B Deduction closes.[8]

Let us pause for a moment and try to locate where the antinomy comes from by turning to the priorities and points of departure respectively affirmed by THESIS and ANTITHESIS. The dilemma of schematized categories turns out to be: does thinking come before the particular kind of thinking that aims at cognition and determines its object, or is knowledge the cognition of experience of which thinking is the unrestricted and indiscriminate use? Is logic prior to knowledge (i.e., is thinking, whether immanent or transcendent, prior to the constitutive use of the understanding in experience), or vice versa? Determining this will result in significantly and importantly different consequences, too.

---

7. Notice the wording: once again it describes the necessity for categories to make experience possible; it does not describe the necessity for categories to be or do only that.

8. Recall, also, that pure concepts "have a significance independent of all schemata and extending far beyond them" (*KrV* A 147/B 186).

The ANTITHESIS appears more reasonable but not necessarily a better option. It goes like this: Kant approaches his problems of foundation by first assuming a thinking that then acquires the restriction to certain conditions under which alone I can say I know appearances. Reason is not primarily directed to knowing. It is not a faculty of knowledge but *becomes* one when it is employed in experience and when its modes of thought (pure concepts in particular) apply to the conditions of sensibility. Transcendental logic explains under what conditions thinking becomes knowing. Thereby categories acquire meaning, and we can think about experience in a systematic way.

A 'systematic way' includes the distinction between what is necessary and what is not about experience (recall the judgments of perception and the distinction between objective and subjective unity of apperception, and between knowledge of objectivity and objective knowledge in chapter 2, § 7a). Thinking otherwise would surreptitiously assume that a nonnecessary judgment on experience is simply the subjective ignorance of what is writ large in the great book, not of nature, but of the mind. It would make experience a disguised and unself-conscious form of science. It would also reduce reason to an understanding that has inexplicably built into itself a reference to intuition, i.e. conveniently integrated in itself what it needs so as to be applied meaningfully. The ANTITHESIS thus starts from the givenness of reason that is a problem to itself; that, stated in words borrowed from Augustine, can say: 'quaestio mihi factus sum' (I have become a problem to myself).

There is hardly a more Kantian beginning.

By contrast, the THESIS claims that categories constitute experience, and every other mode of thinking is derivative, including the illicit extension of concepts in metaphysics. Thinking is originally meaningful and cognitive; it becomes empty and deceptive when it transgresses the conditions of sensibility. Constitution comes first, as does transcendental logic. General logic is derivative, as it "abstracts from all content of cognition" (*KrV* A 76/B 102). Recall that *categories are cognitions*, not mere conditions of possibility. That point, with its a priori origin grounding all other cognitions, acquires a new relevance now in light of the THESIS. The THESIS does not come up against the problem that categories seem to be presupposed inexplicably, as if they were inborn or a primary given, because what comes first is the manifold to synthesize (*"pure synthesis, generally represented,* yields the pure concept of the understanding," *KrV* A 78/B 104). Synthesis precedes analysis; without givenness we would know nothing.

There is hardly a more Kantian beginning.

The THESIS starts from the givenness of a manifold. Notice that, surprisingly enough, the THESIS is forced to retrieve the indispensability, even primacy, of the imagination it threw out the door when it read the schematism chapter as virtually redundant, because on this same page we find the famous dictum that synthesis is "the mere effect of the imagination" (*KrV* A 78/B 104). Notice also that if the THESIS is favored, transcendental logic is prior to general logic. But that implies that the Transcendental Deduction actually grounds the Metaphysical Deduction that it nonetheless uses for the derivation of the logical forms. This must not be our conclusion if the ANTITHESIS is favored.

In keeping with the theme recurrent in this book, which is to highlight the relevance of the connection between concepts and ideas, we can resume our discussion and try a fresh perspective to see if we find any help. Before we do, let me also mention the possibility of doing away with all scruples and hesitation and taking an easy way out: we could say that pure concepts are categories if they refer a priori to their object, and otherwise they are simple logical forms. This is the shortcut of A 136/B 175.[9] The different perspective I am introducing now lies in approaching the problem from the vantage point of ideas. For it is inevitable that ideas change their role and status as do concepts in THESIS and ANTITHESIS.

Here, however, we find passages that do not allow us to settle the dispute one way or the other (not to mention the problem that Kant's shifting position on the ideas' negative and positive import makes it difficult to do so). Consider the passage at A 146/B 186: "If we leave aside a restricting condition, it may seem as if we amplify the previously limited concept."[10] Is the concept originally limited, so that the idea liberates it from its restriction? Or is the concept in itself indeterminate until we limit and restrict it for its use in experience, so that the idea then frees it? At A 409/B 435 we find the same point: "reason really cannot generate any concept at all, but can at most *free a concept of the understanding* from the unavoidable limitations of a possible experience." In the end, the Dialectic too, then, takes the easy shortcut. In the Paralogisms Kant writes that the modes of self-consciousness "are therefore not yet themselves concepts of the understanding of objects

9. "[F]or otherwise they would be without content, and thus would be mere logical forms and not pure concepts of the understanding."

10. "Wenn wir nun eine restringierende Bedingung weglassen: so amplifizieren wir, wie es scheint, den vorher eingeschränkten Begriff." As we see, Kant uses indifferently words with Latin and German roots for 'restriction' and 'limitation' (*restringieren, einschränken*). See also the note in the margin of Kant's copy of the first *Critique* (*Ak* 23: 20: "Die Aufhebung der restriction scheint eine Amplification zu seyn"), and the analogous passage at *KrV* A 252.

(categories), but mere functions, which provide thought with no object at all" (*KrV* B 407). It would not be true, then, that when Descartes substantializes the cogito he illegitimately recurs to the category of substance when all he has is an I-think: the category of substance is only a logical function, not a category strictly speaking.

All of that does not settle the issue from which we started: when the pure concept is used outside experience it has no content (or object or meaning), but it does have a significance. And we have known all along that concepts pretending to refer to supersensible objects have neither objective reality nor validity.[11]

And yet it shows that thought is independent of the objects of experience; its significance (transcendental *or* logical) transcends its use (in experience or beyond it, i.e., legitimate or illegitimate). The transcendental significance has no object. But precisely because it misses (it must not concern itself with) an objective reference, it can make the unconditional totality, the maximum to which it strives, appear in the form of a soul or of a God as *omnitudo realitatis*. Transcending experience gives an idea its life and necessity, not just its usefulness and guidance for empirical sciences. We may want to obliterate progressively this character of ideas, as does Kant, or deplore that he leaves the notions of the transcendental significance and the objective validity of ideas not further explored and dangling in the air.

There is, however, another way in which bringing in ideas might be of interest to our present discussion. If the THESIS wins, then ideas are indeed belittled: they are simply the negative extension of what is originally meaningful to what cannot be talked about sensibly at all. As we know, this is what Kant is often tempted to say and what most of the literature claims.

We cannot, however, say that the illegitimate extension to ideas regards logical functions but not categories: noumena have a definite *reality*. Besides, it is true that ideas are based on concepts, but this is not all. Were it so, reason would be no more than a product of the understanding, against what the Architectonic claims about the inner articulation of reason (of which the understanding is but one function) and against Kant's countless conceptual positions we have seen in this book. No *metaphysics* would be possible other than as *ontology*; and we have seen that this is not Kant's considered judgment.

---

11. A certain "objective validity" (*KrV* A 670/B 698) is granted ideas, raising further problems about the consistency of even 'objective validity': at A 663/B 691 Kant writes that a transcendental deduction for ideas is impossible, and at A 670/B 698 he undertakes one, and even writes that "that deduction is the completion of the critical business of pure reason."

At A 558/B 586 Kant writes that he is not about to establish the reality of freedom: that

> could not have succeeded, since from experience we can never infer something that does not have to be thought in accord with the laws of experience. Further, we have not even tried to prove the *possibility* of freedom; for this could not have succeeded either, because from mere concepts a priori we cannot cognize anything about the possibility of any real ground or any causality. Freedom is here treated as a transcendental idea.

In the third antinomy of the Dialectic, freedom is understood as possible only insofar as it stems from a noumenal world. Thereby no conflict with the mechanism of nature or the sum total of appearances arises. But if ideas are merely the negative extension beyond sense, the liberation from meaning, then they are possible only insofar as they are harmless. They can stake no claim whatever. But if this is so, how can Kant then go on to write works not only in metaphysics, but, no less importantly, in moral philosophy? For they are based not on a fiction or a merely logical and noncontradictory meaning, but on the assumption that freedom does have a positive *reality*; that it is a *causality* (of effects in the phenomenal world, even if it does not find itself among appearances). These are not logical functions, but categories. Indeed, if the THESIS wins, what happens to noumena and to reason's *Kausalität durch Freiheit*? What happens to the use and application of categories to noumena without which the *Groundwork* and the second *Critique* would not be possible (indeed, which they introduced as they discovered how necessary that move was to address the problem of freedom and autonomy)?[12]

If, on this evidence, we consider the THESIS simply wrong, must we say that it holds as long as we stay within the limits of the first *Critique*?[13] This would seem inevitable, and yet it is not a viable option. For (1) we would have to attribute the THESIS to the 1781 edition, and (2) conclude that Kant's later practical philosophy undermines it; (3) we must perhaps add that Kant should have revised his position after he wrote his practical

---

12. The *Critique of Practical Reason* removes all doubts about this application of pure concepts to noumena: pure concepts, "applied to an object given by pure practical reason, also serve for *a determined thought of the supersensible*" (*Ak* 5: 141, ENG 253). This passage lends further support to the ANTITHESIS as it claims, almost in passing and as if it went without saying, that categories "are referred *to objects in general* independently of intuition of these objects" (ibid.).

13. Recall that in the second *Critique* Kant presents the problem of pure reason as if it originated in the reality of freedom.

philosophy (but unfortunately did not as he published the B edition); but (4) we *cannot* conclude thus, because it is on the basis of the Transcendental Deduction of the second edition (1787) that the THESIS is claimed.

The THESIS will want to distinguish between the practical and the speculative import of ideas. While qua speculative, i.e., aimed at cognition, ideas have no constitutive role to play for the employment of the understanding, the practical understanding of ideas admits a wider scope of use for them. But a wider scope does not mean their reality—and an idea is real insofar as it is a whole prior to its parts, not the result of their aggregation. Now even if we assume, with the THESIS, that practical ideas arise out of speculative ideas precisely as a result of an extension of our concepts and thereby obtain reality, the THESIS seems compelled to conclude that the practical reality of ideas contravenes its prescriptions.

Pure reason is guilty of a (theoretical) felony.

The conclusion is of an extreme irony: morality rests on the transgression of a rule.

Here the THESIS really has too dear a price to pay.

Since chapter 1 is more exploratory than the other two and its topics and issues are much less analyzed in the literature, for the benefit of the reader I have indicated all titles I have collected regarding it as comprehensively as I could. As to the other two chapters and the appendix, in this bibliography I list only works I actually quote or discuss there.

Abbagnano, N. *Dizionario di filosofia*. Turin, 1971.

Adickes, E. *Kants Systematik als systembildender Faktor*. Berlin, 1887.

Allison, H. E. "Transcendental Schematism and the Problem of the Synthetic a priori." *Dialectica* 35, 1981, 57–83.

———. *Idealism and Freedom: Essays on Kant's Theoretical and Practical Philosophy*. Cambridge, UK, 1996.

———. *Kant's Theory of Taste: A Reading of the Critique of Aesthetic Judgment*. Cambridge, UK, 2001.

———. *Kant's Transcendental Idealism: An Interpretation and a Defense*. New Haven, 1983; revised and enlarged edition, 2004.

———. "Teleology and History in Kant: The Critical Foundations of Kant's Philosophy of History." In *Kant's Idea for a Universal History with a Cosmopolitan Aim*, ed. A. O. Rorty and J. Schmidt. Cambridge, UK, 2009, 24–45.

Amoroso, L. *Senso e consenso. Uno studio kantiano*. Naples, 1984.

Arnauld, A. *La Logique, ou l'art de penser*. Paris, 1662; Amsterdam, 1685. Eng. trans., *The Art of Thinking*, trans. J. Dichoff and P. James. Indianapolis, IN, 1964.

Baeumler, A. *Kants Kritik der Urteilskraft. Ihre Geschichte und Systematik*. Halle, 1923.

Barale, M. *Kant e il metodo della filosofia*. Pisa, 1988.

———. "Rileggere Kant." In *Congedarsi da Kant? Interventi sul Goodbye Kant di Ferraris*, ed. A. Ferrarin. Pisa, 2006, 101–39.

———. "Forme di soggettività e modelli di razionalità." In *Dimensioni della soggettività*, ed. Barale. Pisa, 2008, 213–99.

Beck, J. S. *Einzig möglicher Standpunkt, aus welchem die kritische Philosophie beurteilt werden muss*. Riga, 1796.

Beck, L. W. *A Commentary on Kant's Critique of Practical Reason*. Chicago, 1960.

Beiser, F. *The Fate of Reason: German Philosophy from Kant to Fichte*. Cambridge, MA, 1987.

Bencivenga, E. *Kant's Copernican Revolution*. Oxford, 1987.

Benjamin, W. *Gesammelte Schriften*. Ed. R. Tiedemann and H. Schweppenhäuser. Frankfurt a. M., 1985.

Bianco, B. "Schulbegriff und Weltbegriff der Philosophie in der Wiener Logik." In *Vernunftkritik und Aufklärung*, ed. M. Oberhausen, H. Delfosse, and R. Pozzo. Stuttgart, 2001, 41–57.

Bianco, L. *Analogia e storia in Kant*. Naples, 2003.

Blumenberg, H. *The Legitimacy of the Modern* Age. Trans. R. M. Wallace. Cambridge, MA, 1985. Orig. *Die Legitimität der Neuzeit*; new ed., Frankfurt a. M., 1976; first edition, 1966.

———. *Die Genesis der kopernikanischen Welt*. Frankfurt am Main, 1975. Eng. trans., *The Genesis of the Copernican World*, trans. R. M. Wallace. Cambridge, MA, 1987.

Böhr, C. *Philosophie für die Welt. Die Popularphilosophie der deutschen Spätaufklärung im Zeitalter Kants*. Stuttgart, 2003.

Bonevac, D. "Kant's Copernican Revolution." In *Routledge History of Philosophy*, ed. R. C. Solomon and K. M. Higgins. London, 1993, 6: 40–68.

Brague, R. *La sagesse du monde*. Paris, 1999.

Brandt, R. "The Deductions in the *Critique of Judgment*: Comments on Hampshire and Horstmann." In E. *Kant's Transcendental Deductions*, ed. E. Förster. Stanford, 1989, 177–90.

———. *Die Bestimmung des Menschen bei Kant*. Hamburg, 2007.

Caimi, M. "Gedanken ohne Inhalt sind leer." *Kant-Studien* 96: 2, 2005, 135–46.

———. *Leçons sur Kant*. Paris, 2007.

Callanan, J. "Kant on Analogy." *British Journal for the History of Philosophy* 16, 2008, 747–72.

Capozzi, M. *Kant e la logica*. Naples, 2003.

———. "Kant on Heuristics as a desirable Addition to Logic." In *Demonstrative and Non-demonstrative Reasoning in Mathematics and Natural Science*, ed. C. Cellucci and P. Pecere. Cassino, 2006, 123–81.

———. "La teoria kantiana dei concetti e dei nomi propri." *Dianoia* 14, 2009, 119–46.

Carl, W. *Der schweigende Kant. Die Entwürfe zu einer Deduktion der Kategorien vor 1781*. Göttingen, 1989.

———. *Die transzendentale Deduktion der Kategorien in der ersten Auflage der Kritik der reinen Vernunft. Ein Kommentar*. Frankfurt a. M., 1992.

———. "Kants kopernikanische Wende." In *Kant und die Philosophie in weltbürgerlichen Absicht. Akten des XI. Kant-Kongresses 2010/Kant and Philosophy in a Cosmopolitan Sense: Proceedings of the Eleventh International Kant Congress*, ed. S. Bacin, A. Ferrarin, C. La Rocca, M. Ruffing. 5 vols. Berlin, 2013, 1: 163–77.

Cassirer, E. *Essay on Man*. New Haven, 1944.

Centi, B. *Coscienza, etica, architettonica in Kant*. Pisa, 2002.

Chiereghin, F. "Die Metaphysik als Wissenschaft und Erfahrung der Grenze. Symbolisches Verhältnis und praktische Selbstbestimmung nach Kant." In *Metaphysik nach Kant?*, ed. D. Henrich and R. P. Horstmann. Stuttgart, 1988, 469–93.

———. "Il concetto di totalità sistematica in Kant e in Hegel." In *Metafisica e modernità. Studi in onore di Pietro Faggiotto*, ed. F. Chiereghin and F. L. Marcolungo. Padua, 1993, 167–92.

Ciafardone, R. Introduzione. In J. N. Tetens, *Saggi filosofici sulla natura umana e il suo sviluppo*. Milan, 2008, 7–51.

de Boer, K. "Transformations of Transcendental Philosophy: Wolff, Kant, and Hegel." *Bulletin of the Hegel Society of Great Britain*, 2011, 50–79.

de Jong, W. R. "How Is Metaphysics as a Science Possible? Kant on the Distinction between Philosophical and Mathematical Method." *Review of Metaphysics* 49: 2, 1995, 235–74.

Descartes, R. *Oeuvres de Descartes.* Ed. C. Adam and P. Tannery. 11 vols. 1896, repr. Paris, 1996.

Detel, W. "Zur Funktion des Schematismuskapitels in Kants *Kritik der reinen Vernunft.*" *Kant-Studien* 69: 1, 1978, 17–45.

De Vleeschauwer, H. J. *La déduction transcendentale dans l'oeuvre de Kant.* 3 vols. Antwerp, 1934–37, repr. New York, 1976.

Dictionnaire de spiritualité ascétique et mystique. Doctrine et histoire. Founded by M. Viller. Paris, 1937–95.

Dörflinger, B. "The Underlying Teleology of the First Critique." In *Proceedings of the Eighth International Kant Congress*, ed. H. Robinson. Milwaukee, 1995, 1: 2, 813–26.

———. *Das Leben theoretischer Vernunft.* Berlin, 2000.

Eco, U. *Kant e l'ornitorinco.* Milan, 1997. Eng. trans., *Kant and the Platypus*, trans. A. McEwen. London, 2000.

Engel, S. M. "Kant's Copernican Analogy: A Re-examination." *Kant-Studien* 54, 1963, 243–51.

Ewing, A. C. *A Short Commentary to Kant's "Critique of Pure Reason."* Chicago, 1938.

Fabbri Bertoletti, S. *Impulso formazione organismo. Per una storia del concetto di Bildungstrieb nella cultura tedesca.* Florence, 1990.

Fabbrizi, C. *Mente e corpo in Kant.* Rome, 2008.

Faggiotto, P. *Introduzione alla metafisica kantiana dell'analogia.* Milan, 1989.

Failla, M. *Verità e saggezza in Kant.* Milan, 2000.

Ferrarin, A. "Mathesis e costruzione tra geometria antica e moderna." *Teoria* 11: 2, 1991, 87–104.

———. "Autocoscienza, riferimento dell'io e conoscenza di sé. Introduzione ad un dibattito contemporaneo." *Teoria* 12: 1, 1992, 111–52.

———. "Kant's Productive Imagination and Its Alleged Antecedents." *Graduate Faculty Philosophy Journal* 18: 1, 1995, 65–92.

———. "Construction and Mathematical Schematism: Kant on the Exhibition of a Concept in Intuition." *Kant-Studien* 86: 2, 1995, 131–74.

———. M. Heidegger, *La questione della cosa (Die Frage nach dem Ding). Man and World* 1996, 94–102.

———. "Homo Faber, Homo Sapiens or Homo Politicus? The Myth of Prometheus in Plato's *Protagoras.*" *Review of Metaphysics* 54: 2, Dec. 2000, 500–531.

———. *Hegel and Aristotle.* Cambridge, UK, 2001.

———. *Artificio, desiderio, considerazione di sé. Hobbes e i fondamenti antropologici della politica.* Pisa, 2001.

———. "Esistenza e giudizio." *Studi kantiani* 15, 2002, 237–47.

———. *Saggezza, immaginazione e giudizio pratico. Studio su Aristotele e Kant.* Pisa, 2004.

———. "Aristotle on *Phantasia.*" In *Proceedings of the Boston Area Colloquium in Ancient Philosophy*, vol. 21, ed. J. J. Cleary and G. M. Gurtler. Leiden: Brill, 2006, 89–123.

———. "'Goodbye is too good a word': Sulle difficoltà del congedo di Ferraris." In *Congedarsi da Kant? Interventi sul Good-bye Kant di Ferraris*, ed. A. Ferrarin. Pisa, 2006, 17–35.

———. "Lived Space, Geometric Space in Kant." *Studi kantiani* 19, 2006, 11–30.

———. "Immaginazione e memoria in Hobbes e Cartesio." In *Tracce nella mente. Teorie della memoria da Platone ai moderni*, ed. M. M. Sassi. Pisa, 2007, 159–89.

————. "Imagination and Judgment in Kant's Practical Philosophy." In "The Uses of Judgment," special issue of *Philosophy and Social Criticism*, ed. A. Ferrara, 34: 1–2, 2008, 101–21.

————. "Kant and Imagination." *Fenomenologia e società* 32, 2009, 7–19.

————. "Com'è possibile comprendere i giudizi sintetici a priori?" In *Critica della ragione e forme dell'esperienza*, ed. L. Amoroso, C. La Rocca, and A. Ferrarin. Pisa, 2011, 75–94.

————. "Pure Intuition in Mathematics: Historical Origins of a Misunderstanding." *Studi kantiani* 25, 2012, 31–44.

————. "The Unity of Reason: On Cyclopes, Architects, and the Cosmic Philosopher's Vision." In *Kant und die Philosophie in weltbürgerlichen Absicht. Akten des XI. Kant-Kongresses 2010/Kant and Philosophy in a Cosmopolitan Sense: Proceedings of the Eleventh International Kant Congress*, ed. S. Bacin, A. Ferrarin, C. La Rocca, M. Ruffing. 5 vols. Berlin, 2013, 1: 213–28.

————. "From the World to Philosophy, and Back: Husserl, Aristotle and Kant before the World." In *Phenomenology in a New Key: Essays in Honor of Richard Cobb-Stevens*, ed. Jeffrey Bloechl and Nicolas de Warren. Dordrecht, 2015, 63–92.

————. *Galilei e la matematica della natura.* Pisa, 2014.

————. "Spontaneity and Reification: What Does Hegel Mean by Thinking?" In *System und Logik bei Hegel. 200 Jahre nach der Wissenschaft der Logik*, ed. L. Fonnesu. Hildesheim, 2015.

————. *Il pensare e l'Io. Hegel e la critica a Kant.* Forthcoming, 2015.

————. *Kant on Imagination.* Forthcoming.

Ferraris, M. *Good-bye Kant!* Milan, 2004.

————. *Documentalità. Perché è necessario lasciar tracce.* Bari, 2009.

Fichte, J. G. *Werke. Auswahl in sechs Bänden.* Ed. F. Medicus. Leipzig, 1908–1912; repr. Darmstadt, 1962.

————. *Gesamtausgabe.* Ed. R. Lauth and H. Gliwitzky. Stuttgart, 1962–.

————. *Sämmtliche Werke.* Ed. I. H. Fichte. Berlin 1945–46; repr. Berlin, 1965.

Förster, E. "Kant's Notion of Philosophy." *Monist* 72, 1989, 285–304.

————. "Die Vorreden." In *Immanuel Kant. Kritik der reinen Vernunft*, ed. G. Mohr and M. Willaschek. Berlin, 1998, 37–55.

————. "The Hidden Plan of Nature." In *Kant's Idea for a Universal History with a Cosmopolitan Aim*, ed. A. O. Rorty and J. Schmidt. Cambridge, UK, 2009, 187–99.

Frankfurt, H. G. *The Importance of What We Care About.* Cambridge, UK, 1998.

Friedman, M. *Kant and the Exact Sciences.* Cambridge, MA, 1992.

Fulda, H. F., and J. Stolzenberg, eds. *Architektonik und System in der Philosophie Kants.* Hamburg, 2001.

Garelli, G. *La teleologia secondo Kant. Architettonica, finalità, sistema.* Bologna, 1999.

Gerhardt, V. "Kants kopernikanische Wende. Friedrich Kaulbach zum 75. Geburtstag." *Kant-Studien* 78: 2, 1987, 133–52.

Ginsborg, H. "Was Kant a Nonconceptualist?" *Philosophical Studies* 137, 2008, 65–77.

Givone, S. *La storia della filosofia secondo Kant.* Turin, 1972.

Goethe, J. W. *Werke in zwölf Bänden.* Berlin, 1981.

Graubner, H. *Form und Wesen. Ein Beitrag zur Deutung der Formbegriffe in Kants Kritik der reinen Vernunft.* Bonn, 1972.

Grier, M. *Kant's Doctrine of Transcendental Illusion.* Cambridge, UK, 2001.

Guyer, P. "The Unity of Reason: Pure Reason as Practical Reason in Kant's Early Conception of the Transcendental Dialectic." *Monist* 72, 1989, 139–67.

Hadot, P. *Qu'est-ce que la philosophie antique?* Paris, 1995.

Hanna, R. "Kant and Nonconceptual Content." *European Journal of Philosophy* 13, 2005, 247–90.

Hanson, N. R. "Copernicus' Role in Kant's Revolution." *Journal of the History of Ideas* 20: 2, 1959, 274–81.

Hegel, G. W. F. *Gesammelte Werke.* Ed. Deutsche Forschungsgemeinschaft and Rheinisch-Westphälische Akademie der Wissenschaften. Hamburg, 1968–.

———. *Hegel's Science of Logic.* Trans. A. V. Miller, with foreword by J. N. Findlay. London, 1969.

———. *Werke in zwanzig Bänden.* Ed. E. Moldenhauer and K. M. Michel. Frankfurt a. M., 1969–71.

Heidegger, M. *Zur Bestimmung der Philosophie.* Lecture course of 1919. Ed. B. Heimbüchel. Frankfurt a. M., 1987.

———. *Phänomenologische Interpretation von Kants Kritik der reinen Vernunft.* Lecture course of 1927–28. Frankfurt a. M., 1977. Eng. trans., *Phenomenological Interpretation of Kant's Critique of Pure Reason*, trans. P. Emad and K. Maly. Bloomington, IN, 1997.

———. *Kant und das Problem der Metaphysik.* Orig. 1929; Frankfurt a. M., 1973. Eng. trans., *Kant and the Problem of Metaphysics*, trans. R. Taft. Bloomington, IN, 1997.

———. "Vom Wesen des Grundes." Orig. 1929; Frankfurt a. M., 1983.

———. *Die Frage nach dem Ding.* Lecture course of 1935–36. Frankfurt a. M., 1962. Eng. trans., *What Is a Thing?*, trans. W. B. Barton and V. Deutsch. South Bend, IN, 1967.

Heidemann, D. "Vom Empfinden zum Begreifen. Kant im Kontext der gegenwärtigen Erkenntnistheorie." In *Warum Kant heute?*, ed. D. Heidemann and Kristina Engelhardt. Berlin, 2003, 14–43.

Heimsoeth, H. *Transzendentale Dialektik. Ein Kommentar zu Kants Kritik der reinen Vernunft*, part 4: Die Methodenlehre. Berlin, 1971.

Henrich, D. "Fichtes ursprüngliche Einsicht." In *Subjektivität und Metaphysik. Festschrift für W. Cramer*, ed. D. Henrich and H. Wagner. Frankfurt a. M., 1966, 188–232.

———. *The Unity of Reason: Essays on Kant's Philosophy.* Ed. R. L. Velkley. Cambridge, MA, 1994.

Hinske, N. *Zwischen Aufklärung und Vernunftkritik. Studien zum Kantschen Logikcorpus.* Stuttgart, 1998.

Hobbes, T. *Thomae Hobbes Malmesburiensis Opera Philosophica quae latine scripsit Omnia . . . studio et labore Guglielmi Molesworth.* 5 vols. London, 1839–45.

Höffe, O. "Architektonik und Geschichte der reinen Vernunft." In *Immanuel Kant. Kritik der reinen Vernunft*, ed. G. Mohr and M. Willaschek. Berlin, 1998, 618–45.

Hohenegger, H. "Der Weg der Wissenschaft und die Arbeitsteilung der Philosophie." In *Vernunftkritik und Aufklärung*, ed. M. Oberhausen, H. Delfosse, and R. Pozzo. Stuttgart, 2001, 161–85.

———. *Kant, filosofo dell'architettonica.* Macerata, 2004.

Holzhey, H. "Der Philosoph für die Welt—eine Chimäre der deutschen Aufklärung?" In *Esoterik und Exoterik in der Philosophie*, ed. H. Holzhey and W. C. Zimmerli. Basel, 1977, 117–38.

Hoppe, H. G. *Synthesis bei Kant.* Berlin, 1983.

Hume, D. *A Treatise of Human Nature.* Orig. 1739–40; 2nd ed., ed. P. H. Nidditch. Oxford, 1978.

Husserl, E. *Gesammelte Werke.* The Hague–Dordrecht, 1950–86.

Illetterati, L. *Figure del limite.* Trento, 1996.

———. "Tra scienza e saggezza. Intorno allo statuto della filosofia in Kant." *Verifiche* 35: 3–4, 2006, 103–32.

Jacobi, F. H. *Über das Unternehmen des Kriticismus die Vernunft zu Verstande zu bringen.* In *Werke*, ed. F. Roth and F. Köppen. 6 vols. Darmstadt, 1968–80, 3: 61–195.

Kaulbach, F. "Die Copernicanische Denkfigur bei Kant." *Kant-Studien* 64: 1, 1973, 30–48.

Kemp Smith, N. "The Meaning of Kant's Copernican Analogy." *Mind* 22: 88, 1913, 549–51.

———. *Commentary to Kant's "Critique of Pure Reason."* London, 1923.

Kern, I. *Husserl und Kant.* The Hague, 1964.

Kerszberg, P. "Two Senses of Kant's Copernican Revolution." *Kant-Studien* 80: 1, 1989, 63–80.

———. *Critique and Totality.* Albany, NY, 1997.

———. "La mathématique à l'épreuve de l'histoire. Perspective critique." *Les cahiers philosophiques de Strasbourg* 27: 1, 2010, 251–73.

Kitcher, P. *Kant's Transcendental Psychology.* Oxford, 1990.

Kleingeld, P. "The Conative Character of Reason in Kant's Philosophy." *Journal of the History of Philosophy* 36: 1, 1998, 77–97.

Kojève, A. *Kant.* Paris, 1973.

Kotzin, R. H., and J. Baumgärten. "Sensations and Judgments of Perceptions: Diagnosis and Rehabilitation of Some of Kant's Misleading Examples." *Kant-Studien* 81, 1990, 401–12.

Lachterman, D. *The Ethics of Geometry: A Genealogy of Modernity.* New York, 1989.

———. "Kant: The Faculty of Desire." *Graduate Faculty Philosophy Journal* 13: 2, 1990, 181–211.

Langston, R. F., et al. "Development of the Spatial Representation System in the Rat." *Science* 328, 2010, 1576–80.

La Rocca, C. *Esistenza e giudizio. Linguaggio e ontologia in Kant.* Pisa, 1999.

———. "Chi è lo Zarathustra di Kant? Filosofia trascendentale e saggezza tra la *Critica della ragion pura* e l'*Opus postumum*." In *Kant e l'Opus postumum*, ed. S Marcucci. Pisa, 2001, 35–62.

———. *Soggetto e mondo. Studi su Kant.* Venice, 2003.

———. "How Are Synthetic A Priori Judgments Possible?" *Quaestio*, 2004, 265–93.

———. "L'intelletto oscuro. Inconscio e autocoscienza in Kant." In *Leggere Kant. Dimensioni della filosofia critica*, ed. La Rocca. Pisa, 2007, 63–116.

Lehmann, G. "System und Geschichte in Kants Philosophie." *Il pensiero* 3: 1, 1958, 14–34.

Leibniz, G. W. *Die philosophischen Schriften von Gottfried Wilhelm Leibniz.* Ed. C. I. Gerhardt. 7 vols. Berlin, 1875–90.

———. *Philosophical Papers and Letters.* Chicago, 1956.

Lenoir, T. "Kant, Blumenbach, and Vital Materialism in German Biology." *Isis* 72, 1980, 77–108.

Lindgren, B. "Kant's conceptus cosmicus." *Dialogue* 2: 3, 1963, 280–300.

Locke, J. *An Essay concerning Human Understanding.* Ed. A. C. Fraser. New York, 1959.

Longuenesse, B. "Kant et les jugements empiriques." *Kant-Studien* 86, 1995, 278–307.

———. *Kant and the Capacity to Judge: Sensibility and Discursivity in the Transcendental Analytic of the Critique of Pure Reason.* Trans. from the French by C. T. Wolfe. Princeton, 1998.

———. *Kant on the Human Standpoint.* Cambridge, UK, 2005.

Lorenz, K. "Kants Lehre vom apriorischen im Lichte gegenwärtigen Biologie." *Blätter für deutsche Philosophie* 15: 1–2, 1941–42.

Manchester, P. "What Kant Means by Architectonic." In *Kant und die Berliner Aufklärung. Akten des IX. Internationalen Kant-Kongresses*, ed. V. Gerhardt, R.-P. Horstmann, R. Schumacher. Berlin, 2001, 2: 622–30.

————. "Kant's Conception of Architectonic in Its Philosophical Context." *Kant-Studien* 99: 2, 2008, 133–51.

Marcucci, S. *Aspetti epistemologici della finalità in Kant.* Florence, 1972.

————. "L'idea di mondo in Kant." In Marcucci, *Scritti su Kant*, ed. C. La Rocca. Pisa, 2010; orig. 2004.

Marini, G. *La filosofia cosmopolitica di Kant.* Bari, 2007.

Martin, G. *Immanuel Kant. Ontologie und Wissenschaftstheorie.* Berlin, 1969.

Marty, F. *La naissance de la métaphysique chez Kant. Une étude sur la notion kantienne d'analogie.* Paris, 1980.

McDowell, J. *Mind and World.* Cambridge, MA, 1996.

————. *Having the World in View: Essays on Kant, Hegel and Sellars.* Cambridge, MA, 2009.

Meier, G. F. *Auszug aus der Vernunftlehre.* Halle, 1752; repr. in *Ak* 16.

Melchiorre, V. *Analogia e analisi trascendentale. Linee per una nuova lettura di Kant.* Milan, 1991.

Micheli, G. *Matematica e metafisica in Kant.* Padua, 1998.

————. "L'insegnamento della filosofia secondo Kant." In *Insegnare filosofia*, ed. L. Illetterati. Turin, 2007, 136–59.

Miles, M. "Kant's 'Copernican Revolution': Toward Rehabilitation of a Concept and Provision for the Interpretation of the *Critique of Pure Reason*." *Kant-Studien* 97: 1, 2006, 1–32.

Munzel, F. "'The Beautiful Is the Symbol of the Morally-Good': Kant's Philosophical Basis of Proof for the Idea of the Morally-Good." *Journal of the History of Philosophy* 33, 1995, 301–30.

Natorp, P. "Die kosmologische Reform des Kopernikus in ihrer Bedeutung für die Philosophie." *Preussische Jahrbücher* 49, 1882.

Neiman, S. *The Unity of Reason: Rereading Kant.* Oxford, 1994.

Nietzsche, F. *Friedrich Nietzsche. Sämtliche Werke.* Kritische Studienausgabe in 15 vols. Ed. G. Colli and M. Montinari. Berlin, 1988.

Nuzzo, A. "'Idee' bei Kant und Hegel." In *Das Recht der Vernunft*, ed. C. Fricke, P. König, T. Petersen. Stuttgart, 1995, 81–120.

————. *Ideal Embodiment.* Bloomington, IN, 2008.

Oberhausen, M. *Das neue Apriori. Kants Lehre von einer 'ursprünglichen Erwerbung' apriorischer Vorstellungen.* Stuttgart, 1997.

O'Neill, O. *Constructions of Reason: Explorations of Kant's Practical Philosophy.* Cambridge, UK, 1989.

————. "Vindicating Reason." In *The Cambridge Companion to Kant*, ed. P. Guyer. Cambridge, UK, 1992, 280–308.

Orsini, F. "*Il metodo della critica di Hegel alla filosofia pratica di Kant.*" PhD diss., Pisa, 2009.

Ottaviani, O. "*Possibilità ed esistenza in Kant. Il problema della modalità.*" PhD diss., Pisa, 2011.

Palmer, L., and G. Lynch. "A Kantian View of Space." *Science* 328: 5985, 2010, 1487–88.

Paton, H. J. *Kant's Metaphysic of Experience: A Commentary on the First Half of the Kritik der reinen Vernunft.* 2 vols. New York, 1936.

Petrone, T. "Kant on Reason and the Synthesis of Ideas." In *Recht und Frieden in der Philosophie Kants. Akten des X. Internationalen Kant-Kongresses*, ed. V. Rohden, R. Terra, G. de Almeida, and M. Ruffing. 5 vols. Berlin, 2008, 2: 561–71.

Philonenko, A. *Qu'est-ce que la philosophie? Kant et Fichte.* Paris, 1991.

Pierobon, F. *Kant et la fondation architectonique de la métaphysique.* Grenoble, 1990.

Pippin, R. *Kant's Theory of Form.* New Haven, 1982.

Popper, K. R. *Conjectures and Refutations*. London, 1963.

Prauss, G. *Erscheinung bei Kant. Ein Problem der Kritik der reinen Vernunft*. Berlin, 1971.

Rauscher, F. "The Appendix to the Dialectic and the Canon of Pure Reason: The Positive Role of Reason." In *The Cambridge Companion to Kant's* Critique of Pure Reason, ed. P. Guyer. Cambridge, UK, 2010, 290–309.

Reinhold, K. L. *Briefe über die kantische Philosophie*. 2 vols. Leipzig, 1790–92.

———. *Über das Fundament des philosophischen Wissens*. Jena, 1791.

Ricoeur, P. *La métaphore vive*. Paris, 1975. Eng. trans., *The Rule of Metaphor*, trans R. Czerny. Toronto, 1977.

Roe, S. A. *Matter, Life and Generation: Eighteenth Century Embryology and the Haller-Wolf Debate*. Cambridge, UK, 1981.

Rosen, S. H. "Much Ado about Nothing: Aristotle contra Eleaticism." In Rosen, *The Quarrel between Philosophy and Poetry*. New York, 1988, 148–82.

Rumore, P. *L'ordine delle idee. La genesi del concetto di 'rappresentazione' in Kant attraverso le sue fonti Wolffiane (1747–87)*. Florence, 2007.

Russell, B. *Human Knowledge, Its Scope and Limits*. London, 1948.

Schiller, F. *Sämtliche Werke*. Berliner Ausgabe, ed. H. G. Thalheim. 5 vols. Berlin, 1980.

Schlegel, F. *Dichtungen und Aufsätze*. Ed. W. Rasch. Munich, 1984.

Schneiders, W. "Zwischen Welt und Weisheit. Zur Verweltlichung der Philosophie in der frühen Moderne." *Studia leibnitiana* 15, 1983, 2–18.

———. *Aufklärung und Vorurteilstheorie. Studien zur Geschichte der Vorurteilstheorie*. Stuttgart, 1983.

Schönecker, D., D. Schulting, N. Strobach. "Kants kopernikanisch-newtonische Analogie." *Deutsche Zeitschrift für Philosophie* 59: 4, 2011, 497–518.

Schulting, D. *Aufklärung und Vorurteilstheorie*. Stuttgart, 1983.

———. "Kant's Copernican Analogy: Beyond the Non-specific Reading." *Studi kantiani* 22, 2009, 39–65.

Scribano, E. *Angeli e beati. Modelli di conoscenza da Tommaso a Spinoza*. Bari, 2006.

Seel, G. "Die Einleitung in die Analytik der Grundsätze, der Schematismus und die obersten Grundsätze." In *Immanuel Kant. Kritik der reinen Vernunft*, ed. G. Mohr and M. Willaschek. Berlin, 1998, 217–46.

Strawson, P. F. *The Bounds of Sense: An Essay on Kant's Critique of Pure Reason*. London, 1966.

Tetens, J. N. *Philosophische Versuche über die menschliche Natur und ihre Entwicklung*. 2 vols. Leipzig, 1777; repr. Hildesheim, 1979.

Thöle, B. *Kant und das Problem der Gesetzmässigkeit der Natur*. Berlin, 1991.

Tonelli, G. *Kant, dall'estetica metafisica all'estetica psicoempirica. Studi sulla genesi del criticismo (1754–1771) e sulle sue fonti*. Turin, 1955.

———. "Kant's Early Theory of Genius." *Journal of the History of Philosophy* 4, 1966, 109–31 and 209–24.

———. "Kant's Ethics as a Part of Metaphysics: A Possible Newtonian Suggestion? With Some Comments on Kant's 'Dreams of a Seer.'" In *Philosophy and the Civilizing Arts*, ed. C. Walton and J. P. Anton. Athens, OH, 1974, 236–63.

———. *Kant's Critique of Pure Reason within the Tradition of Modern Logic*. Berlin, 1994.

Trendelenburg, A. *Logische Untersuchungen*. 2nd ed. 2 vols. Berlin, 1840.

Vaihinger, H. *Commentar zu Kants Kritik der reinen Vernunft*. 2 vols. Stuttgart, 1881.

Vanzo, A. "Kant on the Nominal Definition of Truth." *Kant-Studien* 101, 2010, 147–66.

Velkley, R. *Freedom and the End of Reason: On the Moral Foundation of Kant's Critical Philosophy*. Chicago, 1989.

Warnock, G. J. "Concepts and Schematism." *Analysis* 9: 5, 1949, 77–82.

Waxman, W. *Kant's Model of the Mind*. Oxford, 1991.

Weil, E. *Logique de la philosophie*. Paris, 1985.

Wills, T. J., et al. "Development of the Hippocampal Cognitive Map in Preweanling Rats." *Science* 328, 2010, 1573–76.

Wolff, C. *Vernünftige Gedanken von Gott, der Welt und der Seele des Menschen*. Halle, 1720; 2nd ed., 1751. In *Gesammelte Werke*, ed. J. École et al. Hildesheim, 1962–.

———. *Philosophia prima sive Ontologia*. Halle, 1736. In *Gesammelte Werke*, ed. J. École et al. Hildesheim, 1962–.

———. *Psychologia empirica methodo scientifico pertractata*. Halle, 1745. In *Gesammelte Werke*, ed. J. École. Hildesheim, 1962–.

Wolfson, H. A. *The Philosophy of the Church Fathers*, vol. 1: *Faith, Trinity, Incarnation*. Cambridge, MA, 1956.

Yovel, Y. *Kant and the Philosophy of History*. Princeton, 1982.

Zöller, G. "From Innate to A priori: Kant's Radical Transformation of a Cartesian-Leibnizian Legacy." *Monist* 72, 1989, 222–35.

Made in the USA
Lexington, KY
03 February 2017